PLAYFAIR
CRICK

E

Statistics by
Michael Fordham, Barry McCaully and Brian Heald

Front cover: Allan Lamb. Photo: Adrian Murrell/All Sport Photographic

PICK THE BEST
NATWEST BANK TROPHY TEAM
AFTER THE FIRST GREAT YEAR

£1000 TO BE WON

Prizes 1st: £300 2nd: £200 3rd: £150 4th: £100
Plus twenty-five prizes of £10 each

How to enter: Pick the best NatWest Bank Trophy team from the 40 cricketers shown below who played in the competition last season. Then write in 20 words what you think is the greatest virtue of 60-overs cricket.

Write the names on the entry form on the opposite page with your name and address and post to the address shown.

Your Choice

Paul Allott, David Bairstow, Ian Botham, Geoff Boycott, Mike Brearley, Geoff Cook, Wayne Daniel, Brian Davison, Graham Dilley, John Emburey, Keith Fletcher, Joel Garner, Mike Gatting, Imran Khan, Graham Gooch, David Gower, Gordon Greenidge, Ian Greig, Richard Hadlee, Mike Hendrick, Robin Jackman, Javed Miandad, Peter Kirsten, Alan Knott, Allan Lamb, Wayne Larkins, John Lever, Clive Lloyd, Chris Old, Paul Parker, Clive Rice, Viv Richards, Chris Tavaré, Bob Taylor, Glenn Turner, Derek Underwood, Peter Willey, Bob Willis, Barry Wood and Zaheer Abbas.

Rules

Judging: Each entry will be considered by a panel of cricket experts and the entry which, in the opinion of the judges, constitutes the best NatWest Trophy team will be adjudged the winner. The decision of the judges is final and binding; no correspondence will be entered into. Employees of Macdonald & Co (Publishers) Ltd and their families are not eligible to compete.
Proof of entry: All entries must be on the entry form provided. Proof of posting is not proof of entry.

SLOW OVER-RATES AND BAD TEMPERS
The Ills of Test Cricket
by Gordon Ross

The winter's series in India, and Australia, has served to highlight – if, indeed, highlighting was necessary, we knew already – the cancer of modern Test matches. The slow over-rate has developed into brinkmanship and gamesmanship of the very worst order, depriving the spectator (who pays quite expensively for his cricket, these days) of his proper ration of entertainment. It is no use criticising a batsman for slow scoring without first looking at the number of overs bowled per hour during the day. The administrators of the game, world-wide, would do well to take the Fourth Test match at Madras as their guide-line in determining the medicine which must soon be applied as a cure. It has already been suggested in various quarters that there are too many Test matches these days, so in a sense, what used to be a great cricketing event, has now tended to be devalued by over-exposure. Be that as it may, if over-rates are not lifted, then a day's Test cricket will become a bore to the paying customer, and cricket will find that its principal source of revenue is on the rapid decline. Great haste has not been a determining factor in the past when problems affect all Test-playing countries, nor, indeed, has unanimity been easily achieved on such occasions, but in grasping this nettle speed must be the essence.

The general behaviour of players in Test matches leaves a very great deal to be desired, although it does seem that leading performers in sport, who are good television value, can expect only minor admonishings from their governing body. We have seen this all too clearly in tennis, for instance. The Australian Board of Control, with this situation looking over its shoulder, was surprisingly kind to Dennis Lillee after a disgraceful incident in the First Test between Australia and Pakistan. Provocation is not the prime factor to be considered except by the defence. When an umpire has to step between two warring cricketers on the field, suspension from a couple of one-day games hardly seems to be the appropriate punishment to fit the crime.

The old chestnuts of pitches is thrown up again as it always has been since the first ball was bowled back in the mists of antiquity. Indian pitches are well enough known to cricketers of all generations and are unlikely to change, but certainly they are not conducive to an even contest between bat and ball. To even finish a match in India is quite an event. Of course drawn games can be exciting – there rarely has ever been a more gripping finish to a Test match than when Colin Cowdrey with a broken arm in plaster, walked to the wicket at Lord's to save a match against West Indies – but repetitive draws as games fade away into the inevitable can be tedious. As the stark contrast, take last summer's Test series against Australia, and the winter series against India; circumstances were different – of course they were – but it does show the glamour and the tedium of a series in complete contrast to one another.

As we talk of English Test cricket we talk of the amazing Ian Botham and his performances last summer in the Test arena which put him among the elite of all-rounders. Could he one day be the greatest of them all? We think, too, of Geoffrey Boycott, and meditate at the time of writing on whether or not he will ever play for England again. We think of the England team as a whole. Are there still a few question marks after some of the names. Will Keith Fletcher captain this summer – a decision obviously not taken at the time of writing. Who else? India and Pakistan are likely to provide quite considerable opposition. If Bob Willis is coming to the end of a marvellous career during which he has shown great courage and determination, are Allott or Dilley, or anyone else for that matter, made of the same sort of stuff? There must be lingering doubts in some people's minds. If you take Botham and Boycott away from England are we strong enough to match all opposition? All this is certainly food for thought as spring heralds another cricket season in England.

Looking back to 1981 is a happy piece of nostalgia, for there was so much wonderful cricket in every branch of the game – five-day, three-day, one-day. The series against Australia will become a legend – a Botham legend. There was elation at Trent Bridge as Nottinghamshire won the County Championship for the first time since 1929 (shades of Voce and Larwood); and two semi-finals and a Final in the NatWest Trophy (replacing The Gillette Cup) which surely can never again be matched between now and eternity. All three games were won off the last ball; all three games, at one stage, showed three likely winners, who all turned out to be losers! Breathtaking it was, if you were lucky enough to be there, or watching on television. Derbyshire were the winners, yet in neither the semi-final nor the Final did they score more runs than the vanquished, almost an anomaly, but it just happens to be true. Few cricketers can ever have been more physically and mentally shattered than were the players of Northants after the presentation to the teams at Lord's on this memorable first NatWest Bank Final day.

The drama of all this was in contrast to the Benson and Hedges Final which had been won overwhelmingly by Somerset, but the spectators had ample compensation for a rather one-sided game by watching Viv Richards in full flow, a piece of cricket for the treasure-box; his 132 not out will long be remembered by all who saw it, as Somerset beat Surrey by seven wickets. Essex completed the season's honours winners, by taking the John Player League, so it was an invigorating season with the honours nicely shared, and some of the winners long overdue. Derbyshire's first success since 1936; Notts' first since 1929; Essex won the John Player for the first time – and Somerset had never before won the Benson and Hedges. Competition these days is so keen that you could almost wager that none of these four will win the same competition again in 1982. In fact you could wager it, and it would make fascinating speculation, and possibly a good investment, too!

With the start of the new season imminent it is prudent to list the various decisions taken at The Test and County Cricket Board's Winter meeting. They are as follows:

1. Undertaking given by counties not to prepare pitches for own benefit.

2. Schweppes Championship matches increased from 22 to 24 in 1983.

3. New ball after 100 overs in 1982.

4. Hours of play standardised: 11-6.30.

5. Fines for slow over-rate substantially increased.

6. Circles to be used in all limited-over matches.

7. Penalties for slow over-rate in John Player League imposed.

8. Lambert and Butler floodlit competition discontinued.

9. Substitute will be allowed only if player leaving field convinces umpires he is injured or ill.

New Zealand v India 1980 – 81

FIRST TEST MATCH

PLAYED AT WELLINGTON, 21, 22, 23, 25 FEBRUARY
NEW ZEALAND WON BY 62 RUNS

NEW ZEALAND

J.G. Wright c Binny b Yograj	32	c Viswanath b Kapil Dev	8
B.A. Edgar c Kirmani b Patil	39	c Patil b Binny	28
J.F. Reid c Kirmani b Patil	46	lbw b Kapil Dev	7
*G.P. Howarth not out	137	c Kirmani b Patil	7
J.V. Coney c & b Shastri	4	c sub b Kapil Dev	8
G.N. Edwards c Kirmani b Kapil Dev	23	c sub b Kapil Dev	6
†I.D.S. Smith c Vengsarkar b Kapil Dev	20	not out	15
R.J. Hadlee c Kirmani b Binny	20	c Kirmani b Binny	7
B.L. Cairns c Gavaskar b Kapil Dev	13	c Vengsarkar b Shastri	0
M.C. Snedden b Shastri	2	c Vengsarkar b Shastri	0
G.B. Troup c Gavaskar b Shastri	0	c Vensarkar b Shastri	0
Extras (B4, LB17, NB17, W1)	39	(LB9, NB3, W2)	14
Total	**375**		**100**

INDIA

*S.M. Gavaskar b Cairns	23	b Snedden	12
C.P.S. Chauhan c Coney b Troup	17	b Hadlee	1
D.B. Vengsarkar lbw b Cairns	39	c Smith b Hadlee	26
G.R. Viswanath b Cairns	0	b Troup	9
S.M. Patil c Smith b Troup	64	c Smith b Cairns	42
Kirti Azad b Cairns	20	b Hadlee	16
Kapil Dev c Smith b Troup	0	c Hadlee b Troup	9
†S.M.H. Kirmani run out	13	b Cairns	11
R.M.H. Binny b Snedden	11	not out	26
R. Shastri not out	3	c Smith b Snedden	19
Yograj Singh c Smith b Cairns	4	c Smith b Hadlee	6
Extras (B10, LB13, NB6)	29	(B2, LB5, NB6)	13
Total	**223**		**190**

BOWLING

INDIA	O	M	R	W	O	M	R	W	FALL OF WICKETS			
										NZ	I	NZ	I
Kapil Dev	39	9	112	3	—	16	4	34	4				
Yograj Singh	15	3	63	1	—	—	—	—	—		1st	1st	2nd	2nd
Binny	22	4	67	1	—	12	4	26	2	1st	60	32	17	10
Shastri	28	9	54	3	—	3	0	9	3	2nd	101	70	35	30
Patil	16	4	40	2	—	17	10	12	1	3rd	200	70	57	50
Kirti Azad	—	—	—	—	—	1	0	5	0	4th	215	116	58	74
N. ZEALAND										5th	245	183	73	111
Hadlee	16	4	62	0	—	22.3	6	65	4	6th	292	183	73	117
Cairns	19.4	8	33	5	—	19	8	30	2	7th	331	198	99	136
Snedden	20	7	56	1	—	17	4	39	2	8th	364	213	100	136
Troup	17	5	43	3	—	13	4	34	2	9th	375	218	100	170
Coney					—	4	1	9	0	10th	375	223	100	190

SECOND TEST MATCH

PLAYED AT CHRISTCHURCH, 6, 7, 9, 10, 11 MARCH
MATCH DRAWN

INDIA

*S.M. Gavaskar c Smith b Hadlee		53
C.P.S. Chauhan c Smith b Hadlee		78
D.B. Vengsarkar b Snedden		61
G.R. Viswanath b Hadlee		7
S.M. Patil c Reid b Hadlee		4
Yashpal Sharma c Howarth b Hadlee		0
Kapil Dev c & b Snedden		0
†S.M.H. Kirmani retired hurt		9
K.D. Ghavri c Reid b Coney		17
R. Shastri not out		12
D.R. Doshi b Coney		0
Extras (B4, LB5, NB5)		14
		—
Total		**255**

NEW ZEALAND

J.G. Wright c Vengsarkar b Ghavri		18
B.A. Edgar lbw b Shastri		49
*G.P. Howarth c sub b Doshi		26
J.V. Coney c Chauhan b Patil		15
G.N. Edwards b Shastri		23
J.F. Reid not out		123
†I.D.S. Smith not out		11
R.J. Hadlee		
B.L. Cairns		
G.B. Troup		
M.C. Snedden		
Extras (B6, LB8, NB7)		21
		—
Total (5 wkts)		**286**

BOWLING

N. ZEALAND	O	M	R	W			FALL OF WICKETS	
							I	*NZ*
Hadlee	33	12	47	5	—		*1st*	*1st*
Troup	26	6	60	0	—			
Cairns	33	16	57	0	—	1st	114	27
Snedden	23	6	63	2	—	2nd	168	152
Coney	9	4	12	2	—	3rd	200	201
Howarth	3	2	2	0	—	4th	210	235
INDIA						5th	210	265
Kapil Dev	22	2	60	0	—	6th	224	—
Ghavri	10	4	33	1	—	7th	224	—
Patil	12	4	14	1	—	8th	255	—
Doshi	49	23	67	1	—	9th	255	—
Shastri	42	21	65	2	—	10th	—	—
Chauhan	5	1	12	0	—			
Gavaskar	3	1	11	0	—			
Vengsarkar	2	1	3	0	—			

9

THIRD TEST MATCH

INDIA

*S.M. Gavaskar	c Smith b Snedden	5	c Wright b Bracewell	33
C.P.S. Chauhan	c Cairns b Bracewell	36	c Cairns b Bracewell	7
D.B. Vengsarkar	c Howarth b Snedden	0	not out	52
S.M. Patil	c Smith b Cairns	19	b Bracewell	57
G.R. Viswanath	lbw b Hadlee	2	run out	46
T.E. Srinivasan	c Smith b Bracewell	29	c Wright b Cairns	19
R. Shastri	c & b Cairns	5	run out	9
†S.M.H. Kirmani	b Bracewell	78	b Bracewell	1
Kapil Dev	b Cairns	4	c Edgar b Cairns	14
N.S. Yadav	c Hadlee b Bracewell	43	c Smith b Bracewell	1
D.R. Doshi	not out	3	b Cairns	2
Extras	(B5, LB3, NB6)	14	(B23, LB7, NB13)	43
Total		**238**		**284**

NEW ZEALAND

J.G. Wright	c Kirmani b Chauhan	110	not out	33
B.A. Edgar	c Shastri b Patil	0	c Kirmani b Kapil Dev	1
J.F. Reid	c Viswanath b Shastri	74	lbw b Doshi	0
*G.P. Howarth	c sub b Shastri	0	c Chauhan b Doshi	2
J.V. Coney	c & b Doshi	65	not out	0
G.N. Edwards	c & b Doshi	34	c & b Shastri	47
R.J. Hadlee	c Chauhan b Yadav	0	b Shastri	2
B.L. Cairns	c Gavaskar b Shastri	41		
†I.D.S Smith	b Shastri	10		
J.G. Bracewell	lbw b Shastri	1		
M.C. Snedden	not out	0		
Extras	(B14, LB10, NB7)	31	(B3, LB4, NB3)	10
Total		**366**	(5wkts)	**95**

BOWLING

N. ZEALAND	O	M	R	W	O	M	R	W	FALL OF WICKETS			
										I	*NZ*	*I*	*NZ*
Hadlee	26	10	49	1	—	21	3	65	0		*1st*	*1st*	*2nd*	*2nd*
Snedden	22	5	52	2	—	13	4	40	0	*1st*	9	0	43	1
Cairns	27	13	37	3	—	35.5	16	47	3	1st	9	0	43	1
Coney	9	1	14	0	—	4	1	3	0	2nd	10	148	50	83
Bracewell	42.3	17	61	4	—	41	19	75	5	3rd	43	152	93	87
Howarth	3	0	11	0	—	6	3	11	0	4th	50	251	143	94
INDIA										5th	97	301	236	95
Kapil Dev	20	6	34	0	—	10	6	15	1	6th	100	302	260	—
Patil	6	4	2	1	—	4	0	8	0	7th	114	332	261	—
Yadav	33	8	91	1	—	11	4	20	0	8th	124	354	277	—
Doshi	69	35	79	2	—	19	9	18	2	9th	229	365	279	—
Shastri	56	13	125	5	—	18	8	24	2	10th	238	366	284	—
Chauhan	2	0	4	1	—	—	—	—	—				

West Indies v England 1980 – 81

FIRST TEST MATCH

PLAYED AT PORT-OF-SPAIN, 13, 14, 16, 17, 18 FEBRUARY

WEST INDIES WON BY AN INNINGS AND 79 RUNS

WEST INDIES

C.G. Greenidge c Botham b Emburey	84
D.L. Haynes c & b Emburey	96
I.V.A. Richards c Gower b Miller	29
E. Mattis c Miller b Emburey	0
H.A. Gomes c Downton b Old	5
*C.H. Lloyd b Emburey	64
†D.A. Murray c Botham b Emburey	46
A.M.E. Roberts not out	50
M.E. Holding lbw b Botham	26
J. Garner lbw b Botham	4
C.E.H. Croft not out	4
Extras (LB15, NB3)	18
Total (9 wkts dec)	**426**

ENGLAND

G.A. Gooch b Roberts	41	lbw b Holding	5
G. Boycott c Richards b Croft	30	c Haynes b Holding	70
B.C. Rose c Haynes b Garner	10	c Murray b Holding	5
D.I. Gower lbw b Croft	48	c Murray b Roberts	27
G. Miller c Murray b Croft	3	c Greenidge b Croft	8
*I.T. Botham lbw b Croft	0	c Holding b Richards	16
P. Willey lbw b Garner	13	c Lloyd b Garner	21
†P.R. Downton b Gomes	4	c Lloyd b Roberts	5
J.E. Emburey not out	17	b Roberts	1
G.R Dilley b Croft	0	not out	1
C.M. Old b Roberts	1	c sub b Garner	0
Extras (B4, LB4, NB3)	11	(B1, LB3, NB6)	10
Total	**178**		**169**

BOWLING

ENGLAND	O	M	R	W	O	M	R	W	FALL OF WICKETS			
										WI	E	E
Dilley	28	4	73	0	—	—	—	—		1st	1st	2nd
Botham	28	6	113	2	—	—	—	—	1st	168	45	19
Old	16	4	49	1	—	—	—	—	2nd	203	63	25
Emburey	52	16	124	5	—	—	—	—	3rd	203	110	86
Miller	18	4	42	1	—	—	—	—	4th	215	121	103
Gooch	2	0	3	0	—	—	—	—	5th	257	127	134
Willey	3	1	4	0	—	—	—	—	6th	332	143	142
W. INDIES									7th	342	151	163
Roberts	13	3	41	2	21	7	41	3	8th	383	163	167
Holding	11	3	29	0	18	6	38	3	9th	393	167	169
Croft	22	6	40	5	16	5	26	1	10th	—	178	169
Garner	23	8	37	2	25	10	31	2				
Richards	7	2	16	0	10	6	9	1				
Gomes	2	1	4	1	9	4	14	0				

SECOND TEST MATCH

WEST INDIES

C.G. Greenidge c Gooch b Jackman	14	lbw b Dilley	0
D.L. Haynes c Bairstow b Jackman	25	lbw b Botham	25
I.V.A. Richards c Botham b Dilley	0	not out	182
E.H. Mattis lbw b Botham	16	c Butcher b Jackman	24
*C.H. Lloyd c Gooch b Jackman	100	lbw b Botham	66
H.A. Gomes c Botham b Dilley	58	run out	34
†D.A. Murray c Bairstow b Dilley	9	not out	5
A.M.E. Roberts c Bairstow b Botham	14	c Bairstow b Botham	0
J. Garner c Bairstow b Botham	15		
M.A. Holding c Gatting b Botham	0		
C.E.H. Croft not out	0	c Boycott b Jackman	33
Extras (B4, LB6, NB2, W2)	14	(B3, LB7)	10
Total	**265**	(7 wkts dec)	**379**

ENGLAND

G.A. Gooch b Garner	26	c Garner b Croft	116
G. Boycott b Holding	0	c Garner b Holding	1
M.W. Gatting c Greenidge b Roberts	2	b Holding	0
D.I. Gower c Mattis b Croft	17	b Richards	54
R.O. Butcher c Richards b Croft	17	lbw b Richards	2
*I.T. Botham c Murray b Holding	26	c Lloyd b Roberts	2
P. Willey not out	19	lbw b Croft	17
† D.L. Bairstow c Mattis b Holding	0	c Murray b Croft	2
J.E. Emburey c Lloyd b Roberts	0	b Garner	9
R.D. Jackman c Roberts b Croft	7	b Garner	7
G.R. Dilley c Gomes b Croft	0	not out	7
Extras (B1, LB1, NB6)	8	(B1, LB3, NB4)	8
Total	**122**		**224**

BOWLING

ENGLAND	O	M	R	W		O	M	R	W	FALL OF WICKETS				
											WI	E	WI	E
Dilley	23	7	51	3	—	25	3	111	1		1st	1st	2nd	2nd
Botham	25.1	5	77	4	—	29	5	102	3	1st	24	6	10	2
Jackman	22	4	65	3	—	25	5	76	2	2nd	25	11	57	2
Emburey	18	4	45	0	—	24	7	57	0	3rd	47	40	71	122
Gooch	2	0	13	0	—	—	—	—	—	4th	65	55	130	134
Willey	—	—	—	—	—	6	0	23	0	5th	219	72	212	139
W. INDIES										6th	224	94	365	196
Roberts	11	3	29	2	—	20	6	42	1	7th	236	94	365	198
Holding	11	7	16	3	—	19	6	46	2	8th	258	97	—	201
Croft	13.5	2	39	4	—	19	1	65	3	9th	258	122	—	213
Garner	12	5	30	1	—	16.2	6	39	2	10th	265	122	—	224
Richards	—	—	—	—	—	17	6	24	2					

THIRD TEST MATCH

PLAYED AT ST. JOHNS, ANTIGUA, 27, 28, 29, 31 MARCH, 1 APRIL

MATCH DRAWN

ENGLAND

G.A. Gooch run out		33	c Greenidge b Richards		83
G. Boycott c Murray b Croft		38	not out		104
C.W.J. Athey c Lloyd b Croft		2	c Richards b Croft		1
D.I. Gower c Mattis b Holding		32	c Murray b Croft		22
R.C. Butcher c Greenidge b Croft		20			
*I.T. Botham c Lloyd b Croft		1			
P. Willey not out		102	not out		1
†P.R. Downton c Murray b Garner		13			
J.E. Emburey b Croft		10			
G.B. Stevenson b Croft		1			
G.R. Dilley c Murray b Holding		2			
Extras (B6, LB7, NB3, W1)		17	(B11, LB3, NB9)		23
Total		**271**	(3 wkts)		**234**

WEST INDIES

C.G. Greenidge c Athey b Stevenson	63
D.L. Haynes c Downton b Botham	4
I.V.A. Richards c Emburey b Dilley	114
E.H. Mattis c Butcher b Botham	71
H.A. Gomes c Gower b Botham	12
*C.H. Lloyd c Downton b Stevenson	58
†D.A. Murray c Boycott b Botham	1
A.M.E. Roberts b Stevenson	13
J. Garner c Butcher b Dilley	46
M.A. Holding not out	58
C.E.H. Croft not out	17
Extras (B1, LB7, NB2, W1)	11
Total (9 wkts dec)	**468**

BOWLING

W. INDIES	O	M	R	W		O	M	R	W	FALL OF WICKETS			
Roberts	22	4	59	0	—	17	5	39	0		*E*	*WI*	*E*
Holding	18.2	4	51	2	—	9	2	21	0		*1st*	*1st*	*2nd*
Garner	16	5	44	1	—	15	3	33	0	1st	60	12	144
Croft	25	5	74	6	—	16	4	39	2	2nd	70	133	146
Richards	9	4	26	0	—	22	7	54	1	3rd	95	241	217
Gomes	—	—	—	—	—	13	5	21	0	4th	135	268	—
Mattis	—	—	—	—	—	1	0	4	0	5th	138	269	—
ENGLAND									*	6th	138	271	—
Dilley	25	5	99	2	—	—	—	—	—	7th	176	296	—
Botham	37	6	127	4	—	—	—	—	—	8th	233	379	—
Stevenson	33	5	111	3	—	—	—	—	—	9th	235	401	—
Emburey	35	12	85	0	—	—	—	—	—	10th	271	—	—
Willey	20	8	30	0									
Gooch	2	2	0	0									
Boycott	3	2	5	0									

13

FOURTH TEST MATCH

ENGLAND

G.A. Gooch c Murray b Holding	153	c Lloyd b Marshall	3
G. Boycott c Murray b Garner	40	c Garner b Croft	12
C.W.J. Athey b Holding	3	c Murray b Holding	1
D.I. Gower b Croft	22	not out	154
P. Willey c Murray b Marshall	4	c Greenidge b Richards	67
R.O. Butcher b Garner	32	lbw b Croft	0
*I.T. Botham c Greenidge b Marshall	13	c Garner b Holding	16
†P.R. Downton c Croft b Holding	0	not out	26
J.E. Emburey b Holding	1		
R.D. Jackman c Haynes b Holding	0		
G.R. Dilley not out	1		
Extras (B8, NB8)	16	(B6, LB13, NB4)	23
Total	**285**	**(6 wkts dec)**	**302**

WEST INDIES

C.G. Greenidge c Botham b Dilley	62
D.L. Haynes b Willey	84
I.V.A. Richards c Downton b Dilley	15
E.H. Mattis c sub b Dilley	34
*C.H. Lloyd c Downton b Jackman	95
H.A. Gomes not out	90
†D.A. Murray c Gooch b Emburey	14
M.D. Marshall b Emburey	15
J. Garner c sub b Dilley	19
M.A. Holding c Downton b Botham	0
C.E.H. Croft c sub b Botham	0
Extras (LB8, NB5, W1)	14
Total	**442**

BOWLING

W. INDIES	O	M	R	W		O	M	R	W	FALL OF WICKETS			
											E	WI	E
Holding	18	3	56	5	—	28	7	58	2		1st	1st	2nd
Marshall	16	2	49	2	—	5	0	15	1	1st	93	116	5
Croft	17	4	92	1	—	29	7	80	2	2nd	148	136	10
Garner	20	4	43	2	—	24	7	46	0	3rd	196	179	32
Richards	12	2	29	0	—	23	8	48	1	4th	210	227	168
Gomes	—	—	—	—	—	13	3	18	0	5th	249	345	168
Mattis	—	—	—	—	—	5	1	10	0	6th	275	372	215
Haynes	—	—	—	—	—	1	0	4	0	7th	283	415	—
ENGLAND										8th	283	441	—
Dilley	28.4	6	116	4	—					9th	284	442	—
Botham	26.1	9	73	2	—					10th	285	442	—
Jackman	26.2	6	57	1	—								
Gooch	8	3	20	0									
Emburey	56	23	108	2									
Willey	18	3	54	1									

TEST MATCH AVERAGES

WEST INDIES

	M	I	NO	Runs	HS	Avge	100	50	Ct	St
I.V.A. Richards	4	5	1	340	182*	85.00	2	—	3	—
C.H. Lloyd	4	5	0	383	100	76.60	1	4	7	—
H.A. Gomes	4	5	1	199	90*	49.75	—	2	1	—
D.L. Haynes	4	5	0	234	96	46.80	—	2	3	—
C.G. Greenidge	4	5	0	223	84	44.60	—	3	6	—
E.H. Mattis	4	5	0	145	71	29.00	—	1	3	—
M.A. Holding	4	4	1	84	58*	28.00	—	1	1	—
C.E.H. Croft	4	5	3	54	33	27.00	—	—	1	—
A.M.E. Roberts	3	4	1	77	50*	25.66	—	1	1	—
J. Garner	4	4	0	84	46	21.00	—	—	4	—
D.A. Murray	4	5	1	75	46	18.75	—	—	13	—

Played in one Test: M.D. Marshall 15 (1 ct).

	Overs	Mdns	Runs	Wkts	Avge	Best	5 wI	10 wM
M.A. Holding	132.2	38	315	17	18.52	5/56	1	—
C.E.H. Croft	157.5	34	455	24	18.95	6/74	2	—
J. Garner	151.2	48	303	10	30.30	2/31	—	—
A.M.E. Roberts	104	27	251	8	31.37	3/41	—	—
I.V.A. Richards	104	35	206	5	41.20	2/24	—	—

Also bowled: H.A. Gomes 37-13-57-1; D.L. Haynes 1-0-4-0; M.D. Marshall 21-2-64-3; E.H. Mattis 6-1-14-0.

ENGLAND

	M	I	NO	Runs	HS	Avge	100	50	Ct	St
G.A. Gooch	4	8	0	460	153	57.50	2	1	3	—
D.I. Gower	4	8	1	376	154*	53.71	1	1	2	—
P. Willey	4	8	3	244	102*	48.80	1	1	—	—
G. Boycott	4	8	1	295	104*	42.14	1	1	2	—
R.O. Butcher	3	5	0	71	32	14.20	—	—	3	—
P.R. Downton	3	5	1	48	26*	12.00	—	—	6	—
I.T. Botham	4	7	0	73	26	10.42	—	—	5	—
J.E. Emburey	4	6	1	38	17*	7.60	—	—	2	—
R.D. Jackman	2	3	0	14	7	4.66	—	—	—	—
G.R. Dilley	4	6	3	11	7*	3.66	—	—	—	—
C.W.J. Athey	2	4	0	7	3	1.75	—	—	1	—
G.B. Stevenson	1	1	0	1	1	1.00	—	—	—	—

Played in one Test: D.L. Bairstow, 0, 2 (5 ct); M.W. Gatting 2, 0 (1 ct); G. Miller 3, 8 (1); C.M. Old 1, 0; B.C. Rose 10, 5; G.B. Stevenson 1.

	Overs	Mdns	Runs	Wkts	Avge	Best	5 wI	10 wM
I.T. Botham	145.2	31	492	15	32.80	4/77	—	—
R.D. Jackman	73.2	15	198	6	33.00	3/65	—	—
G.B. Stevenson	33	5	111	3	37.00	3/111	—	—
G.R. Dilley	129.4	25	450	10	45.00	4/116	—	—
J.E. Emburey	185	62	419	7	59.85	5/124	1	—
P. Willey	47	12	111	1	111.00	1/54	—	—

Also bowled: G. Boycott 3-2-5-0; G.A. Gooch 14-5-36-0; G. Miller 18-4-42-1; C.M. Old 16-4-49-1.

England v Australia 1981

FIRST CORNHILL TEST MATCH

PLAYED AT TRENT BRIDGE, 18, 19, 20, 21 JUNE

AUSTRALIA WON BY 4 WICKETS

ENGLAND

G.A. Gooch c Wood b Lillee	10	c Yallop b Lillee	6
G. Boycott c Border b Alderman	27	c Marsh b Alderman	4
R.A. Woolmer c Wood b Lillee	0	c Marsh b Alderman	0
D.I. Gower c Yallop b Lillee	26	c sub b Lillee	28
M.W. Gatting lbw b Hogg	52	lbw b Alderman	15
P. Willey c Border b Alderman	10	lbw b Lillee	13
*I.T. Botham b Alderman	1	c Border b Lillee	33
†P.R. Downton c Yallop b Alderman	8	lbw b Alderman	3
G.R. Dilley b Hogg	34	c Marsh b Alderman	13
R.G.D. Willis c Marsh b Hogg	0	c Chappell b Lillee	1
M. Hendrick not out	6	not out	0
Extras (LB6, NB4, W1)	11	(LB8, NB1)	9
Total	**185**		**125**

AUSTRALIA

G.M. Wood lbw b Dilley	0	c Woolmer b Willis	8
J. Dyson c Woolmer b Willis	5	c Downton b Dilley	38
G.N. Yallop b Hendrick	13	c Gatting b Botham	6
*K.J. Hughes lbw b Willis	7	lbw b Dilley	22
T.M. Chappell b Hendrick	17	not out	20
A.R. Border c & b Botham	63	b Dilley	20
†R.W. Marsh c Boycott b Willis	19	lbw b Dilley	0
G.F. Lawson c Gower b Botham	14	not out	5
D.K. Lillee c Downton b Dilley	12		
R.M. Hogg c Boycott b Dilley	0		
T.M. Alderman not out	12		
Extras (B4, LB8, NB4, W1)	17	(B1, LB6, NB6)	13
Total	**179**	**(6 wkts)**	**132**

Man of the Match: D.K. Lillee

BOWLING

AUSTRALIA	O	M	R	W		O	M	R	W
Lillee	13	3	34	3	—	16.4	2	46	5
Alderman	24	7	68	4	—	19	3	62	5
Hogg	11.4	1	47	3	—	3	1	8	0
Lawson	8	3	25	0	—	—	—	—	—
ENGLAND									
Dilley	20	7	38	3	—	11.1	4	24	4
Willis	30	14	47	3	—	13	2	28	1
Hendrick	20	7	43	2	—	20	7	33	0
Botham	16.5	6	34	2	—	10	1	34	1

FALL OF WICKETS

	E	A	E	A
	1st	1st	2nd	2nd
1st	13	0	12	20
2nd	13	21	12	40
3rd	57	21	13	77
4th	67	33	39	80
5th	92	64	61	122
6th	96	89	94	122
7th	116	110	109	—
8th	159	147	113	—
9th	159	153	125	—
10th	185	179	125	—

SECOND CORNHILL TEST MATCH
PLAYED AT LORD'S, 2, 3, 4, 6, 7 JULY
MATCH DRAWN

ENGLAND

G.A. Gooch c Yallop b Lawson	44	lbw b Lawson	20
G. Boycott c Alderman b Lawson	17	c Marsh b Lillee	60
R.A. Woolmer c Marsh b Lawson	21	lbw b Alderman	9
D.I. Gower c Marsh b Lawson	27	c Alderman b Lillee	89
M.W. Gatting lbw b Bright	59	c Wood b Bright	16
P. Willey c Border b Alderman	82	c Chappell b Bright	12
J.E. Emburey run out	31		
*I.T. Botham lbw b Lawson	0	b Bright	0
†R.W. Taylor c Hughes b Lawson	0	b Lillee	9
G.R. Dilley not out	7	not out	27
R.G.D. Willis c Wood b Lawson	5		
Extras (B2, LB3, NB10, W3)	18	(B2, LB8, NB13)	23
Total	**311**	**(8 wkts dec)**	**265**

AUSTRALIA

G.M. Wood c Taylor b Willis	44	not out	62
J. Dyson c Gower b Botham	7	lbw b Dilley	1
G.N. Yallop b Dilley	1	c Botham b Willis	3
*K.J. Hughes c Willis b Emburey	42	lbw b Dilley	4
T.M. Chappell c Taylor b Dilley	2	c Taylor b Botham	5
A.R. Border c Gatting b Botham	64	not out	12
†R.W. Marsh lbw b Dilley	47		
R.J. Bright lbw b Emburey	33		
G.F. Lawson lbw b Willis	5		
D.K. Lillee not out	40		
T.M. Alderman c Taylor b Willis	5		
Extras (B6, LB11, NB32, W6)	55	(NB2, W1)	3
Total	**345**	**(4 wkts)**	**90**

Man of the Match: G.F. Lawson

BOWLING

AUSTRALIA	O	M	R	W		O	M	R	W
Lillee	35.4	7	102	0	—	26.4	8	82	3
Alderman	30.2	7	79	1	—	17	2	42	1
Lawson	43.1	14	81	7	—	19	6	51	1
Bright	15	7	31	1	—	36	18	67	3
ENGLAND									
Willis	27.4	9	50	3	—	12	3	35	1
Dilley	30	8	106	3	—	7.5	1	18	2
Botham	26	8	71	2	—	8	3	10	1
Gooch	10	4	28	0	—	—	—	—	—
Emburey	25	12	35	2	—	21	10	24	0

FALL OF WICKETS	E	A	E	A
	1st	1st	2nd	2nd
1st	60	62	31	2
2nd	65	62	55	11
3rd	134	69	178	17
4th	187	81	217	62
5th	204	107	217	—
6th	293	244	217	—
7th	293	257	242	—
8th	293	268	265	—
9th	298	314	—	—
10th	31	345	—	—

THIRD CORNHILL TEST MATCH

PLAYED AT HEADINGLEY, 16, 17, 18, 20, 21 JULY
ENGLAND WON BY 18 RUNS

AUSTRALIA

J. Dyson b Dilley	102	c Taylor b Willis		34
G.M. Wood lbw b Botham	34	c Taylor b Botham		10
T.M. Chappell c Taylor b Willey	27	c Taylor b Willis		8
*K.J. Hughes c & b Botham	89	c Botham b Willis		0
R.J. Bright b Dilley	7	b Willis		19
G.N. Yallop c Taylor b Botham	58	c Gatting b Willis		0
A.R. Border lbw b Botham	8	b Old		0
†R.W. Marsh b Botham	28	c Dilley b Willis		4
G.F. Lawson c Taylor b Botham	13	c Taylor b Willis		1
D.K. Lillee not out	3	c Gatting b Willis		17
T.M. Alderman not out	0	not out		0
Extras (B4, LB13, NB12, W3)	32	(LB3, NB14, W1)		18
Total (9 wkts dec)	**401**			**111**

ENGLAND

G.A. Gooch lbw b Alderman	2	c Alderman b Lillee		0
G. Boycott b Lawson	12	lbw b Alderman		46
*J.M. Brearley c Marsh b Alderman	10	c Alderman b Lillee		14
D.I. Gower c Marsh b Lawson	24	c Border b Alderman		9
M.W. Gatting lbw b Lillee	15	lbw b Alderman		1
P. Willey b Lawson	8	c Dyson b Lillee		33
I.T. Botham c Marsh b Lillee	50	not out		149
†R.W. Taylor c Marsh b Lillee	5	c Bright b Alderman		1
G.R. Dilley c & b Lillee	13	b Alderman		56
C.M. Old c Border b Alderman	0	b Lawson		29
R.G.D. Willis not out	1	c Border b Alderman		2
Extras (B6, LB11, NB11, W6)	34	(B5, LB3, NB5, W3)		16
Total	**174**			**356**

Man of the Match: I.T. Botham

BOWLING

ENGLAND	O	M	R	W		O	M	R	W
Willis	30	8	72	0	—	15.1	3	43	8
Old	43	14	91	0	—	9	1	21	1
Dilley	27	4	78	2	—	2	0	11	0
Botham	39	11	95	6	—	7	3	14	1
Willey	13	2	31	1	—	3	1	4	0
Boycott	3	2	2	0	—				
AUSTRALIA									
Lillee	18.5	7	49	4	—	25	6	94	3
Alderman	19	4	59	3	—	35.3	6	135	6
Lawson	13	3	32	3	—	23	4	96	1
Bright					—	4	0	15	0

FALL OF WICKETS

	A	E	E	A
	1st	1st	2nd	2nd
1st	55	12	0	13
2nd	149	40	18	56
3rd	196	42	37	58
4th	220	84	41	58
5th	332	87	105	65
6th	354	112	133	68
7th	357	148	135	74
8th	396	166	252	75
9th	401	167	319	110
10th	—	174	356	111

FOURTH CORNHILL TEST MATCH

PLAYED AT EDGBASTON, 30, 31 JULY, 1, 2 AUGUST
ENGLAND WON BY 29 RUNS

ENGLAND

G. Boycott	c Marsh b Alderman	13	c Marsh b Bright	29
*J.M. Brearley	c Border b Lillee	48	lbw b Lillee	13
D.I. Gower	c Hogg b Alderman	0	c Border b Bright	23
G.A. Gooch	c Marsh b Bright	21	b Bright	21
M.W. Gatting	c Alderman b Lillee	21	b Bright	39
P. Willey	b Bright	16	b Bright	5
I.T. Botham	b Alderman	26	c Marsh b Lillee	3
J.E. Emburey	b Hogg	3	not out	37
†R.W. Taylor	b Alderman	0	lbw b Alderman	8
C.M. Old	not out	11	c Marsh b Alderman	23
R.G.D. Willis	c Marsh b Alderman	13	c Marsh b Alderman	2
Extras	(B1, LB5, NB10, W1)	17	(LB6, NB9, W1)	16
Total		**189**		**219**

AUSTRALIA

G.M. Wood	run out	38	lbw b Old	2
J. Dyson	b Old	1	lbw b Willis	13
A.R. Border	c Taylor b Old	2	c Gatting b Emburey	40
R.J. Bright	lbw b Botham	27	lbw b Botham	0
*K.J. Hughes	lbw b Old	47	c Emburey b Willis	5
G.N. Yallop	b Emburey	30	c Botham b Emburey	30
M.F. Kent	c Willis b Emburey	46	b Botham	10
†R.W. Marsh	b Emburey	2	b Botham	4
D.K. Lillee	b Emburey	18	c Taylor b Botham	3
R.M. Hogg	run out	0	not out	0
T.M. Alderman	not out	3	b Botham	0
Extras	(B4, LB19, NB21)	44	(B1, LB2, NB11)	14
Total		**258**		**121**

Man of the Match: I.T. Botham

BOWLING

AUSTRALIA	O	M	R	W		O	M	R	W
Lillee	18	4	61	2	—	26	9	51	2
Alderman	23.1	8	42	5	—	22	5	65	3
Hogg	16	3	49	1	—	10	3	19	0
Bright	12	4	20	2	—	34	17	68	5
ENGLAND									
Willis	19	3	63	0	—	20	6	37	2
Old	21	8	44	3	—	11	4	19	1
Emburey	26.5	12	43	4	—	22	10	40	2
Botham	20	1	64	1	—	14	9	11	5

FALL OF WICKETS

	E	A	E	A
	1st	1st	2nd	2nd
1st	29	5	18	2
2nd	29	14	52	19
3rd	60	62	89	69
4th	101	115	98	87
5th	176	166	115	103
6th	145	203	116	114
7th	161	220	154	114
8th	161	253	167	120
9th	165	253	217	121
10th	189	258	219	121

FIFTH CORNHILL TEST MATCH

PLAYED AT OLD TRAFFORD, 13, 14, 15, 16, 17 AUGUST
ENGLAND WON BY 103 RUNS

ENGLAND

G.A. Gooch	lbw b Lillee	10	b Alderman	5
G. Boycott	c Marsh b Alderman	10	lbw b Alderman	37
C.J. Tavaré	c Alderman b Whitney	69	c Kent b Alderman	78
D.I. Gower	c Yallop b Whitney	23	c Bright b Lillee	1
*J.M. Brearley	lbw b Alderman	2	c Marsh b Alderman	3
M.W. Gatting	c Border b Lillee	32	lbw b Alderman	11
I.T. Botham	c Bright b Lillee	0	c Marsh b Whitney	118
†A.P.E. Knott	c Border b Alderman	13	c Dyson b Lillee	59
J.E. Emburey	c Border b Alderman	1	c Kent b Whitney	57
P.J.W. Allott	not out	52	c Hughes b Bright	14
R.G.D. Willis	b Hughes b Lillee	11	not out	5
Extras	(LB6, W2)	8	(B1, LB12, NB3)	16
Total		**231**		**404**

AUSTRALIA

G.M. Wood	lbw b Allott	19	c Knott b Allott	6
J. Dyson	c Botham b Willis	0	run out	5
*K.J. Hughes	lbw b Willis	4	lbw b Botham	43
G.N. Yallop	c Botham b Willis	0	b Emburey	114
M.F. Kent	c Knott b Emburey	52	c Brearley b Emburey	2
A.R. Border	c Gower b Botham	11	not out	123
†R.W. Marsh	c Botham b Willis	1	c Knott b Willis	47
R.J. Bright	c Knott b Botham	22	c Knott b Willis	5
D.K. Lillee	c Gooch b Botham	13	c Botham b Allott	28
M.R. Whitney	b Allott	0	c Gatting b Willis	0
T.M. Alderman	not out	2	lbw b Botham	0
Extras	(NB6)	6	(LB9, NB18, W2)	29
Total		**130**		**402**

Man of the Match: I.T. Botham

BOWLING

AUSTRALIA	O	M	R	W	—	O	M	R	W
Lillee	24.1	8	55	4	—	46	13	137	2
Alderman	29	5	88	4	—	52	19	109	5
Whitney	17	3	50	2	—	27	6	74	2
Bright	16	6	30	0	—	26.4	12	68	1
ENGLAND									
Willis	14	0	63	4	—	30.5	2	96	3
Allott	6	1	17	2	—	17	3	71	2
Botham	6.2	1	28	3	—	36	16	86	2
Emburey	4	0	16	1	—	49	9	107	2
Gatting					—	3	1	13	0

FALL OF WICKETS

	E	A	E	A
	1st	1st	2nd	2nd
1st	19	20	7	7
2nd	25	24	79	24
3rd	57	24	80	119
4th	62	24	98	198
5th	109	58	104	206
6th	109	59	253	296
7th	131	104	282	322
8th	137	125	356	373
9th	175	126	396	378
10th	231	130	404	402

SIXTH CORNHILL TEST MATCH

PLAYED AT THE OVAL, 27, 28, 29, 31 AUGUST
MATCH DRAWN

AUSTRALIA

G.M. Wood c Brearley b Botham	66	c Knott b Hendrick	21
M.F. Kent c Gatting b Botham	54	c Brearley b Botham	7
*K.J. Hughes hit wkt b Botham	31	lbw b Hendrick	6
G.N. Yallop c Botham b Willis	26	b Hendrick	35
A.R. Border not out	106	c Tavare b Emburey	84
D.M. Wellham b Willis	24	lbw b Botham	103
†R.W. Marsh c Botham b Willis	12	c Gatting b Botham	52
R.J. Bright c Brearley b Botham	3	b Botham	11
D.K. Lillee b Willis	11	not out	8
T.M. Alderman b Botham	0		
M.R. Whitney b Botham	4	c Botham b Hendrick	0
Extras (B4, LB6, NB4, W1)	15	(B1, LB8, NB7, W1)	17
Total	**352**	**(9 wkts dec)**	**344**

ENGLAND

G. Boycott c Yallop b Lillee	137	lbw b Lillee	0
W. Larkins c Alderman b Lillee	34	c Alderman b Lillee	24
C.J. Tavaré c Marsh b Lillee	24	c Kent b Whitney	8
M.W. Gatting b Lillee	53	c Kent b Lillee	56
*J.M. Brearley c Bright b Alderman	0	c Marsh b Lillee	51
P.W.G. Parker c Kent b Alderman	0	c Kent b Alderman	13
I.T. Botham c Yallop b Lillee	3	lbw b Alderman	16
†A.P.E. Knott b Lillee	36	not out	70
J.E. Emburey lbw b Lillee	0	not out	5
R.G.D. Willis b Alderman	3		
M. Hendrick not out	0		
Extras (LB9, NB12, W3)	24	(B2, LB5, NB9, W2)	18
Total	**314**	**(7 wkts)**	**261**

Man of the Match: D.K. Lillee

Man of the Series: I.T. Botham

BOWLING

ENGLAND	O	M	R	W		O	M	R	W
Willis	31	6	91	4	—	10	0	41	0
Hendrick	31	8	63	0	—	29.2	6	82	4
Botham	47	13	125	6	—	42	9	128	4
Emburey	23	2	58	0	—	23	3	76	1
AUSTRALIA									
Lillee	31.4	4	89	7	—	30	10	70	4
Alderman	35	4	84	3	—	19	6	60	2
Whitney	23	3	76	0	—	11	4	46	1
Bright	21	6	41	0	—	27	12	50	0
Yallop	—	—	—	—	—	8	2	17	0

FALL OF WICKETS

	A 1st	E 1st	A 2nd	E 2nd
1st	120	61	26	0
2nd	125	131	36	18
3rd	169	246	41	88
4th	199	248	104	101
5th	260	248	205	127
6th	280	256	291	144
7th	303	293	332	237
8th	319	293	343	—
9th	320	302	344	—
10th	352	314	—	—

TEST MATCH AVERAGES
ENGLAND

	M	I	NO	Runs	HS	Avge	100	50	Ct	St
A.P.E. Knott	2	4	1	178	70*	59.33	—	2	6	—
C.J. Tavaré	2	4	0	179	78	44.75	—	2	1	—
G.R. Dilley	3	6	2	150	56	37.50	—	1	1	—
I.T. Botham	6	12	1	399	149*	36.27	2	1	12	—
G. Boycott	6	12	0	392	137	32.66	1	1	2	—
M.W. Gatting	6	12	0	370	59	30.83	—	4	8	—
J.E. Emburey	4	7	2	134	57	26.80	—	1	1	—
D.I. Gower	5	10	0	250	89	25.00	—	1	3	—
P. Willey	4	8	0	179	82	22.37	—	1	—	—
C.M. Old	2	4	1	63	29	21.00	—	—	—	—
J.M. Brearley	4	8	0	141	51	17.62	—	1	4	—
G.A. Gooch	5	10	0	139	44	13.90	—	1	—	—
R.G.D. Willis	6	10	2	43	13	5.37	—	—	2	—
R.W. Taylor	3	6	0	23	9	3.83	—	—	13	—

Played in two Tests: M. Hendrick 6*, 0* & 0*; R.A. Woolmer 0, 0, & 21, 9 (2 ct).
Played in one Test: P.J.W. Allott 52*, 14; P.R. Downton 8, 3 (2 ct); W. Larkins 34, 24; P.W.G. Parker 0, 13.

	Overs	Mdns	Runs	Wkts	Avge	Best	5 wI	10 wM
G.R. Dilley	98	24	275	14	19.64	4-24	—	—
I.T. Botham	272.3	81	700	34	20.58	6-95	3	1
R.G.D. Willis	252.4	56	666	29	22.96	8-43	1	—
J.E. Emburey	193.5	58	399	12	33.25	4-43	—	—
C.M. Old	84	27	175	5	35.00	3-44	—	—
M. Hendrick	100.2	28	221	6	36.83	4-82	—	—

Also bowled: P.J.W. Allott 23-4-88-4; P. Willey 16-3-35-1; G. Boycott 3-2-2-0; M.W. Gatting 3-1-13-0; G.A. Gooch 10-4-28-0.

AUSTRALIA

	M	I	NO	Runs	HS	Avge	100	50	Ct	St
A.R. Border	6	12	3	533	123*	59.22	2	3	12	—
M.F. Kent	3	6	0	171	54	28.50	—	2	6	—
G.M. Wood	6	12	1	310	66	28.18	—	2	4	—
G.N. Yallop	6	12	0	316	114	26.33	1	1	7	—
K.J. Hughes	6	12	0	300	89	25.00	—	1	3	—
D.K. Lillee	6	10	3	153	40*	21.85	—	—	1	—
J. Dyson	5	10	0	206	102	20.60	1	—	2	—
R.W. Marsh	6	11	0	216	52	19.63	—	1	23	—
T.M. Chappell	3	6	1	79	27	15.80	—	—	2	—
R.J. Bright	5	9	0	127	33	14.11	—	—	4	—
G.F. Lawson	3	5	1	38	14	9.50	—	—	—	—
T.M. Alderman	6	9	5	22	12*	5.50	—	—	8	—

Played in two Tests: R.M. Hogg 0 & 0, 0* (1 ct); M.R. Whitney 0, 0 & 4, 0.
Played in one Test: D.M. Welham 24, 103.

	Overs	Mdns	Runs	Wkts	Avge	Best	5 wI	10 wM
T.M. Alderman	325	76	893	42	21.26	6-135	4	—
D.K. Lillee	311.4	81	870	39	22.30	7-89	2	1
G.F. Lawson	106.1	30	285	12	23.75	7-81	1	—
R.J. Bright	191.4	82	390	12	32.50	5-68	1	—

Also bowled: R.M. Hogg 40-4-8-123-4; M.R. Whitney 78-16-246-5; G.N. Yallop 8-2-17-0.

Australia v Pakistan 1981-82

FIRST TEST MATCH

PLAYED AT PERTH, 13, 14, 15, 16, 17, NOVEMBER 1981

AUSTRALIA WON BY 286 RUNS

AUSTRALIA

B.M. Laird	c Bari b Imran	27	c Bari b Imran	85
G.M. Wood	lbw b Sikander	33	b Qasim	49
*G.S. Chappell	lbw b Imran	22	b Imran	6
K.J. Hughes	b Sarfraz	14	c Majid b Imran	106
G.N. Yallop	c & b Qasim	20	c Imran b Sikander	38
A.R. Border	c Bari b Sarfraz	3	c Mudassar b Sikander	37
†R.W. Marsh	c Qasim b Sikander	16	c Mansoor b Raja	47
B. Yardley	c Bari b Imran	9	st Bari b Qasim	22
D.K. Lillee	c Bari b Raja	16	not out	4
J.R. Thomson	b Imran	2	not out	5
T.M. Alderman	not out	0		
	Extras (LB5, NB12, W1)	18	(B1, LB9, NB14, W1)	25
	Total	**180**	**(8 wkts dec)**	**424**

PAKISTAN

Mudassar Nazar	c Marsh b Lillee	0	lbw b Alderman	5
Rizwan-Uz-Zaman	lbw b Alderman	0	c Marsh b Alderman	8
Mansoor Akhtar	c Marsh b Alderman	6	c Hughes b Thomson	36
*Javed Miandad	c Hughes b Alderman	6	b Yardley	79
Majid Khan	c Marsh b Lillee	3	c Marsh b Yardley	0
Wasim Raja	c Thomson b Lillee	4	c Hughes b Yardley	48
Imran Khan	c Yardley b Lillee	4	c Alderman b Yardley	31
Sarfraz Nawaz	c Marsh b Alderman	26	c & b Yardley	9
†Wasim Bari	c Marsh b Lillee	1	c Border b Yardley	20
Iqbal Qasim	c Alderman b Thomson	5	c Alderman b Lillee	4
Sikander Bakht	not out	3	not out	0
	Extras (NB4)	4	(LB1, NB15)	16
	Total	**62**		**256**

BOWLING

PAKISTAN	O	M	R	W		O	M	R	W	FALL OF WICKETS				
											A	*P*	*A*	*P*
Imran	31.4	8	66	4	—	39	12	90	3		*1st*	*1st*	*2nd*	*2nd*
Sarfraz	27	10	43	2	—	27	5	88	0	1st	45	1	92	8
Sikander	21	4	47	2	—	23	3	79	2	2nd	81	1	105	27
Qasim	3	1	6	1	—	26	4	81	2	3rd	89	14	192	96
Raja	1	1	0	1	—	20	3	58	0	4th	113	17	262	99
Miandad	—	—	—	—	—	1	0	2	0	5th	119	21	327	174
Mudassar	—	—	—	—	—	2	1	0	0	6th	136	25	360	198
AUSTRALIA										7th	154	25	412	229
Lillee	9	3	18	5	—	20	3	78	1	8th	165	26	416	236
Alderman	10.2	2	36	4	—	16	4	43	2	9th	180	57	—	254
Thomson	2	1	4	1	—	12	4	35	1	10th	180	62	—	256
Yardley	—	—	—	—	—	25.5	5	84	6					

SECOND TEST MATCH

PLAYED AT BRISBANE, 27, 28, 29, 30 NOVEMBER, 1 DECEMBER 1981

AUSTRALIA WON BY 10 WICKETS

PAKISTAN

Mudassar Nazar c Marsh b Lillee	36	c Laird b Lillee	33
Mohsin Khan c Border b Chappell	11	c Marsh b Lillee	43
Majid Khan c Chappell b Lillee	29	c Chappell b Yardley	15
*Javed Miandad b Lillee	20	lbw b Lillee	38
Zaheer Abbas b Lillee	80	lbw b Yardley	0
Wasim Raja c Laird b Lillee	43	b Lillee	36
Imran Khan c Marsh b Alderman	0	c Wellham b Yardley	3
Ejaz Faqih b Yardley	34	c Chappell b Thomson	21
Sarfraz Nawaz c Border b Alderman	4	c Alderman b Yardley	13
†Wasim Bari c Marsh b Thomson	7	not out	4
Sikander Bakht not out	1	b Thomson	2
Extras (B12, LB1, NB12, W1)	26	(B2, LB3, NB9, W1)	15
Total	**291**		**223**

AUSTRALIA

B.M. Laird c Zaheer b Ejaz	44	not out	3
G.M. Wood c Mudassar b Raja	72	not out	0
*G.S. Chappell c Zaheer b Sikander	201		
A.R. Border b Imran	36		
K.J. Hughes b Imran	28		
D.M. Wellham b Imran	36		
†R.W. Marsh c Zaheer b Imran	27		
B Yardley b Sarfraz	2		
D.K. Lillee b Sarfraz	14		
J.R. Thomson not out	22		
T.M. Alderman not out	5		
Extras (B1, LB5, NB17, W2)	25		
Total (9 wkts dec)	**512**	(0 wkt)	**3**

BOWLING

AUSTRALIA	O	M	R	W		O	M	R	W	FALL OF WICKETS			
											P	A	P
Lillee	20	3	81	5	—	19	4	51	4		*1st*	*1st*	*2nd*
Alderman	25	6	74	2	—	15	3	37	0	1st	40	109	72
Thomson	15	2	52	1	—	15	3	43	2	2nd	60	149	90
Chappell	3	1	6	1	—					3rd	105	219	115
Yardley	15	1	51	1	—	24	4	77	4	4th	111	298	115
Border	1	0	1	0	—					5th	236	429	177
PAKISTAN										6th	237	448	178
Imran	40	6	92	4	—	1.2	1	2	0	7th	245	469	189
Sarfraz	35	4	121	2	—	—	—	—	—	8th	263	470	216
Sikander	24	2	81	1	—	1	0	1	0	9th	285	492	219
Ejaz	22	1	76	1	—	—	—	—	—	10th	291	—	223
Raja	17	0	68	1	—	—	—	—	—				
Mudassar	2	0	10	0	—	—	—	—	—				
Miandad	3	0	18	0	—	—	—	—	—				
Majid	9	1	21	0	—	—	—	—	—				

THIRD TEST MATCH

PLAYED AT MELBOURNE, 11, 12, 13, 14, 15 DECEMBER
PAKISTAN WON BY AN INNINGS AND 82 RUNS

PAKISTAN

Mudassar Nazar c Lillee b Yardley	95
Mohsin Khan c Thomson b Yardley	17
Majid Khan c Wood b Yardley	74
*Javed Miandad lbw b Yardley	62
Zaheer Abbas c & b Yardley	90
Wasim Raja c Laird b Yardley	50
Imran Khan not out	70
Sarfraz Nawaz c Yardley b Chappell	0
†Wasim Bari b Yardley	8
Iqbal Qasim not out	16
Sikander Bakht did not bat	
Extras (B1, LB5, NB12)	18
Total (8 wkts dec)	500

AUSTRALIA

B.M. Laird lbw b Qasim	35	c Sarfraz b Qasim	52
G.M. Wood c Mohsin b Sarfraz	100	c Bari b Sarfraz	1
*G.S. Chappell c Bari b Raja	22	c Miandad b Sarfraz	0
A.R. Border run out	7	run out	1
K.J. Hughes c & b Qasim	34	c Majid b Qasim	11
D.M. Wellham c Mudassar b Sarfraz	26	b Sarfraz	13
†R.W. Marsh c Mudassar b Imran	31	c Mohsin b Qasim	21
B. Yardley b Qasim	20	b Imran	0
D.K. Lillee lbw b Imran	1	c Bari b Qasim	4
J.R. Thomson not out	3	b Imran	17
T.M. Alderman lbw b Imran	1	not out	4
Extras (B4, LB6, NB3)	13	(B1)	1
Total	293		125

BOWLING

AUSTRALIA	O	M	R	W	O	M	R	W	FALL OF WICKETS		
										P	A	A
Lillee	36.3	9	104	0	—	—	—	—		1st	1st	2nd
Alderman	27	8	62	0	—	—	—	—	1st	40	75	1
Chappell	9	2	17	1	—	—	—	—	2nd	181	118	9
Thomson	25	2	85	0	—	—	—	—	3rd	201	127	13
Yardley	66	16	187	7	—	—	—	—	4th	329	173	29
Border	4	1	16	0	—	—	—	—	5th	363	232	77
Hughes	3	1	2	0	—	—	—	—	6th	443	235	78
Laird	1	0	9	0	—	—	—	—	7th	444	286	79
PAKISTAN									8th	457	288	92
Imran	24.1	7	41	3	14.1	5	21	2	9th	—	288	121
Sarfraz	14	3	43	2	15	10	11	3	10th		293	125
Raja	37	7	73	1	13	2	34	0				
Qasim	55	17	104	3	24	11	44	4				
Sikander	2	0	9	0	—	—	—	—				
Majid	2	0	10	0	4	1	5	0				
Miandad	—	—	—	—	2	0	9	0				

AUSTRALIA v WEST INDIES 1981–82

FIRST TEST MATCH

PLAYED AT MELBOURNE, 26, 27, 28, 29, 30 DECEMBER 1981

AUSTRALIA WON BY 58 RUNS

AUSTRALIA

B.M. Laird c Murray b Holding	4	(2) lbw b Croft	64
G.M. Wood c Murray b Roberts	3	(1) c Murray b Garner	46
*G.S. Chappell c Murray b Holding	0	c Murray b Garner	6
A.R. Border c Murray b Holding	4	b Holding	66
K.J. Hughes not out	100	b Holding	8
D.M. Wellham c sub (Logie) b Croft	17	b Holding	2
†R.W. Marsh c Richards b Garner	21	c Murray b Holding	2
B. Yardley b Garner	21	b Garner	13
D.K. Lillie c Gomes b Holding	1	c Murray b Holding	0
G.F. Lawson b Holding	2	not out	0
T.M. Alderman c Murray b Croft	10	b Holding	1
Extras (B1, LB6, NB8)	15	(B5, LB4, NB4, W1)	14
Total	**198**		**222**

WEST INDIES

D.L. Haynes c Border b Lillee	1	c Lillee b Yardley	28
S.F.A. Bacchus c Wood b Alderman	1	lbw b Alderman	0
C.E.H. Croft lbw b Lillee	0	(11) not out	0
I.V.A. Richards b Lillee	2	(3) b Alderman	0
*C.H. Lloyd c Alderman b Yardley	29	(4) c Border b Lawson	19
H.A. Gomes c Chappell b Yardley	55	(5) b Yardley	24
P.J. Dujon c Hughes b Lillee	41	(6) c Marsh b Yardley	43
†D.A. Murray not out	32	(7) c Marsh b Yardley	10
A.M.E. Roberts c Marsh b Lillee	18	(8) lbw b Lillee	10
M.A. Holding c & b Alderman	2	(9) lbw b Lillee	7
J. Garner c Laird b Lillee	7	(10) lbw b Lillee	0
Extras (B1, LB3, NB9)	13	(B1, LB10, NB9)	20
Total	**201**		**161**

BOWLING

WEST INDIES	O	M	R	W	O	M	R	W	FALL OF WICKETS				
										A	WI	A	WI
Holding	17	3	45	5	— 21.3	5	62	6		1st	1st	2nd	2nd
Roberts	15	6	40	1	— 18	4	31	0	1st	4	3	82	4
Garner	20	4	59	2	— 18	5	37	3	2nd	4	5	106	4
Croft	16.1	3	39	2	— 20	2	61	1	3rd	8	6	139	38
Richards					— 5	0	17	0	4th	26	10	184	80
AUSTRALIA									5th	59	62	190	88
Lillee	26.3	3	83	7	— 27.1	8	44	3	6th	82	134	199	116
Alderman	18	3	54	2	— 9	3	23	2	7th	106	147	215	150
Lawson	9	2	28	0	— 17	3	36	1	8th	139	174	218	154
Chappell	2	2	0	0	—				9th	184	183	220	154
Yardley	7	2	23	1	— 21	7	38	4	10th	190	201	220	161

SECOND TEST MATCH

PLAYED AT SYDNEY, 2, 3, 4, 5, 6 JANUARY 1982
MATCH DRAWN

WEST INDIES

C. G. Greenidge c Laird b Lillee	66	c Yardley b Lillee	8
D.L. Haynes lbw b Thomson	15	lbw b Lillee	51
I.V.A. Richards c Marsh b Lillee	44	c Border b Alderman	22
H.A. Gomes c Chappell b Yardley	126	c Border b Yardley	43
*C.H. Lloyd c Marsh b Thomson	40	c Hughes b Yardley	57
P.J. Dujon c & b Thomson	44	c & b Yardley	48
†D.A. Murray b Yardley	13	c Laird b Yardley	1
M.A. Holding lbw b Lillee	9	c Dyson b Yardley	5
S.T. Clarke b Yardley	14	c Dyson b Yardley	5
J. Garner c Marsh b Lillee	1	(11) b Yardley	0
C.E.H. Croft not out	0	(10) not out	4
Extras (LB3, NB9)	12	(LB1, NB5, W5)	11
Total	**384**		**255**

AUSTRALIA

B.M. Laird c Dujon b Garner	14	c Murray b Croft	38
G.M. Wood c Murray b Holding	63	(6) not out	7
J. Dyson lbw b Holding	28	(2) not out	127
*G.S. Chappell c Dujon b Holding	12	(3) c Murray b Croft	0
T.M. Alderman b Clarke	0		
K.J. Hughes b Garner	16	(4) lbw b Gomes	13
A.R. Border not out	53	(5) b Gomes	9
†R.W. Marsh c Holding b Gomes	17		
B. Yardley b Holding	45		
D.K. Lillee c Garner b Holding	4		
J.R. Thomson run out	8		
Extras (B1, LB2, NB2, W2)	7	(B2, LB1, NB3)	6
Total	**267**	**(4 wkts)**	**200**

BOWLING

AUSTRALIA	O	M	R	W		O	M	R	W	FALL OF WICKETS				
											WI	A	WI	A
Lillee	39	6	119	4	—	20	6	50	2		1st	1st	2nd	2nd
Alderman	30	9	73	0	—	12	2	46	1	1st	37	38	29	104
Thomson	20	1	93	3	—	15	3	50	0	2nd	128	108	52	104
Yardley	26.2	3	87	3	—	31.4	6	98	7	3rd	133	111	112	149
Border	1	1	0	0	—	—	—	—	—	4th	229	112	179	169
WEST INDIES										5th	375	128	201	
Holding	29	9	64	5	—	19	6	31	0	6th	345	141	225	—
Clarke	16	4	51	1		16	5	25	0	7th	363	172	231	—
Garner	20	4	52	2	—	12	3	27	0	8th	379	242	246	—
Croft	20	7	53	0	—	27	5	58	2	9th	380	246	255	—
Richards	13	7	21	0	—	13	3	33	0	10th	384	267	255	—
Gomes	9	1	19	1	—	15	7	20	2					

27

THIRD TEST MATCH

PLAYED AT ADELAIDE, 30, 31 JANUARY, 1, 2, 3 FEBRUARY 1982
WEST INDIES WON BY 5 WICKETS

AUSTRALIA

B.M. Laird c Dujon b Roberts	2	c Dujon b Croft	78
G.M. Wood c Garner b Roberts	5	c & b Holding	6
J. Dyson c Dujon b Holding	1	c Lloyd b Garner	10
K.J. Hughes c Greenidge b Holding	5	c Bacchus b Garner	84
*G.S. Chappell c Garner b Holding	61	lbw b Holding	7
A.R. Border c Dujon b Holding	78	c Dujon b Roberts	126
†R.W. Marsh c Dujon b Holding	39	c Haynes b Holding	38
B. Yardley b Croft	8	b Garner	6
D.K. Lillee b Roberts	2	c Dujon b Garner	1
J.R. Thomson not out	18	c Bacchus b Garner	0
L.S. Pascoe b Holding	10	not out	0
Extras (B1, LB2, W1, NB5)	9	(B7, LB10, NB13)	30
Total	**238**		**386**

WEST INDIES

C.G. Greenidge c Border b Thomson	8	c Marsh b Thomson	52
D.I. Haynes c Marsh b Thomson	26	c Marsh b Thomson	4
I.V.A. Richards c Laird b Yardley	42	b Pascoe	50
H.A. Gomes not out	124	b Pascoe	21
S.F.A. Bacchus c Laird b Pascoe	0	c Lillee b Pascoe	27
*C.H. Lloyd c Marsh b Thomson	53	not out	77
C.E.H. Croft b Thomson	0		
†P.J. Dujon c Thomson b Yardley	51	not out	0
A.M.E. Roberts c sub (Hookes) b Yardley	42		
M.A. Holding b Yardley	3		
J. Garner c Wood b Yardley	12		
Extras (B4, LB7, W3, NB14)	28	(LB2, W1, NB5)	8
Total	**389**	**(5 wkts)**	**239**

BOWLING

WEST INDIES	O	M	R	W		O	M	R	W	FALL OF WICKETS				
											A	WI	A	WI
Holding	25	5	72	5	—	29	9	70	3		1st	1st	2nd	2nd
Roberts	19	7	43	4	—	24	7	64	1	1st	3	12	10	7
Croft	23	4	60	1	—	32	4	90	1	2nd	8	85	35	107
Garner	17	4	44	0	—	35	15	56	5	3rd	8	92	201	114
Gomes	7	3	10	0	—	14	1	38	0	4th	17	194	267	176
Richards	—	—	—	—	—	18	3	38	0	5th	122	194	362	235
AUSTRALIA					—					6th	193	283	373	—
Lillee	4.5	3	4	0	—	4	0	17	0	7th	206	365	383	—
Thomson	29	1	112	4	—	19.1	4	62	2	8th	209	369	383	—
Yardley	40.5	10	132	5	—	16	0	68	0	9th	210	389	383	—
Pascoe	30	3	94	1	—	22	3	84	2	10th	238	389	386	—
Border	5	0	19	0	—	—	—	—	—					

India v England 1981-82

FIRST TEST MATCH

PLAYED AT BOMBAY 27, 28, 29 NOVEMBER, 1 DECEMBER

INDIA WON BY 138 RUNS

INDIA

*S.M. Gavaskar c Taylor b Botham	55	c Taylor b Botham	14
K. Srikkanth c Fletcher b Willis	0	run out	13
D.B. Vengsarkar c Tavare b Dilley	17	c Tavare b Botham	5
G.R. Viswanath c Boycott b Botham	8	c Taylor b Botham	37
S.M. Patil lbw b Botham	17	lbw b Botham	13
Kirti Azad c sub (Gatting) b Underwood	14	lbw b Emburey	17
Kapil Dev c Taylor b Botham	38	lbw b Willis	46
†S.M.H. Kirmani lbw b Dilley	12	c Taylor b Emburey	0
S. Madan Lal c Taylor b Dilley	0	not out	17
R.J. Shastri not out	3	lbw b Dilley	33
D.R. Doshi c Taylor b Dilley	7	b Botham	7
Extras (LB5, NB10)	15	(B8, LB8, NB9)	25
Total	**179**		**227**

ENGLAND

G.A. Gooch b Madan Lal	2	c Kirmani b Kapil Dev	1
G. Boycott c Srikkanth b Kirti Azad	60	lbw b Madan Lal	3
C.J. Tavare c Shastri b Doshi	56	c Gavaskar b Kapil Dev	0
D.I. Gower run out	5	lbw b Kapil Dev	20
*K.W.R. Fletcher lbw b Doshi	15	lbw b Madan Lal	3
I.T. Botham c Gavaskar b Doshi	7	c Kirti Azad b Kapil Dev	29
J.E. Emburey lbw b Doshi	0	c Gavaskar b Madan Lal	1
G.R. Dilley b Shastri	0	b Madan Lal	9
†R.W. Taylor not out	9	b Madan Lal	1
D.L. Underwood c Kirmani b Kapil Dev	8	not out	13
R.G.D. Willis c Gavaskar b Doshi	1	c Kirmani b Kapil Dev	13
Extras (B1, LB2)	3	(B4, LB3, NB2)	9
Total	**166**		**102**

BOWLING

ENGLAND	O	M	R	W		O	M	R	W
Willis	12	5	33	1	—	13	4	31	1
Botham	28	6	72	4	—	22.3	3	61	5
Dilley	13	1	47	4	—	18	5	61	1
Underwood	4	2	12	1	—	11	4	14	0
Emburey	—	—	—	—	—	13	2	35	2
INDIA									
Kapil Dev	22	10	29	1	—	13.2	0	70	5
Madan Lal	12	2	24	1	—	12	6	23	5
Doshi	29.1	17	39	5	—	1	1	0	0
Shastri	19	6	27	1	—				
Patil	3	0	9	0	—				
Kirti Azad	15	4	35	1	—				

FALL OF WICKETS

	I	E	I	E
	1st	1st	2nd	2nd
1st	1	3	19	2
2nd	40	95	24	4
3rd	70	105	43	28
4th	104	131	72	29
5th	112	143	90	42
6th	164	146	138	50
7th	164	147	154	73
8th	168	157		74
9th	179	163	203	75
10th	179	166	227	102

SECOND TEST MATCH

PLAYED AT BANGALORE, ON 9, 10, 12, 13, 14 DECEMBER 1981
MATCH DRAWN

ENGLAND

G.A. Gooch c Gavaskar b Shastri	58	lbw b Kapil Dev		40
G. Boycott c Gavaskar b Kapil Dev	36	b Doshi		50
C.J. Tavaré lbw b Madan Lal	22	c Patil b Shastri		31
D.I. Gower lbw b Shastri	82	not out		34
J.K. Lever lbw b Kapil Dev	1			
*K.W.R. Fletcher c Kirmani b Shastri	25	not out		12
I.T. Botham c Madan Lal b Doshi	55			
M.W. Gatting lbw b Kapil Dev	29			
G.R. Dilley c Gavaskah b Shastri	52			
†R.W. Taylor c Kapil Dev b Doshi	33			
D.L. Underwood not out	2			
Extras (LB2, NB3)	5	(LB6, NB1)		7
Total	**400**	**(3 wkts)**		**174**

INDIA

*S.M. Gavaskar c & b Underwood	172
K. Srikkanth c Gooch b Botham	65
D.B. Vengsarkar c Taylor b Lever	43
G.R. Viswanath lbw b Lever	3
R.J. Shastri lbw b Lever	1
S.M. Patil lbw b Lever	17
Kirti Azad c Fletcher b Underwood	24
Kapil Dev c Taylor b Lever	59
†S.M.H. Kirmani lbw b Botham	9
S. Madan Lal not out	7
D.R. Doshi c Boycott b Underwood	0
Extras (B2, LB14, NB9, W3)	28
Total	**428**

BOWLING

INDIA	O	M	R	W		O	M	R	W	FALL OF WICKETS			
											E	*I*	*E*
Kapil Dev	40	3	136	3	—	12	2	49	1		1st	1st	2nd
Madan Lal	26	7	46	1	—	4	2	14	0	1st	88	102	59
Doshi	39	15	83	2	—	21	8	37	1	2nd	96	195	105
Kirti Azad	12	1	47	0	—	12	3	36	0	3rd	180	208	152
Shastri	43	14	83	4	—	29	7	31	1	4th	181	214	—
ENGLAND										5th	223	242	—
Botham	47	9	137	2	—	—	—	—	—	6th	230	284	—
Dilley	24	4	75	0	—	—	—	—	—	7th	272	376	—
Lever	36	9	100	5	—	—	—	—	—	8th	324	412	—
Underwood	43	21	88	3	—	—	—	—	—	9th	393	428	—
										10th	400	428	—

THIRD TEST MATCH

PLAYED AT DELHI, 23, 24, 26, 27, 28 DECEMBER 1981

MATCH DRAWN

ENGLAND

G.A. Gooch c Kapil Dev b Doshi	71	not out	20
G. Boycott c Madan Lal b Doshi	105	not out	34
C.J. Tavaré b Madan Lal	149		
D.I. Gower lbw b Madan Lal	0		
*K.W.R. Fletcher b Patil	51		
I.T. Botham c Kirti Azad b Madan Lal	66		
M.W. Gatting b Madan Lal	5		
†R.W. Taylor lbw b Madan Lal	0		
J.K. Lever b Kapil Dev	2		
D.L. Underwood not out	2		
R.G.D. Willis did not bat			
Extras (LB15, NB10)	25	(B9, NB5)	14
	—		—
Total (9 wkts, dec)	476	(0 wkt)	68

INDIA

*S.M. Gavaskar c Taylor b Lever	46
K. Srikkanth b Willis	6
D.B. Vengsarkar c Fletcher b Underwood	8
G.R. Viswanath b Botham	107
S.M. Patil b Willis	31
Kirti Azad st Taylor b Underwood	16
Kapil Dev c Gooch b Botham	16
R.J. Shastri lbw b Gooch	93
†S.M.H. Kirmani lbw b Lever	67
S. Madan Lal b Gooch	44
D.R. Doshi not out	0
Extras (B20, LB8, NB21, W4)	53
	—
Total	487

BOWLING

INDIA	O	M	R	W		O	M	R	W	FALL OF WICKETS		
Kapil Dev	40.4	5	126	1	—	4	1	18	0		E	I
Madan Lal	32	4	85	5	—	3	1	4	0		1st	1st
Doshi	40	15	68	2	—					1st	132	11
Shastri	27	3	109	0	—					2nd	248	41
Kirti Azad	9	2	35	0	—					3rd	248	89
Patil	8	1	28	1	—	3	1	10	0	4th	368	174
Srikkanth	—				—	6	1	10	0	5th	459	213
Gavaskar	—				—	3	0	12	0	6th	465	237
ENGLAND										7th	465	254
Willis	26	3	99	2	—					8th	474	382
Lever	37	7	104	2	—					9th	476	486
Underwood	48	18	97	2	—					10th	—	487
Botham	41	6	122	2	—							
Gooch	8.1	1	12	2	—							

FOURTH TEST MATCH

PLAYED AT CALCUTTA, 1, 2, 3, 5, 6 JANUARY 1982

MATCH DRAWN

ENGLAND

G.A. Gooch c Viswanath b Doshi		47	b Doshi	63
G. Boycott c Kirmani b Kapil Dev		18	lbw b Madan Lal	6
C.J. Tavaré c Kirmani b Kapil Dev		7	run out	25
D.I. Gower c Kirmani b Shastri		11	run out	74
*K.W.R. Fletcher lbw b Madan Lal		69	not out	60
I.T. Botham c Gavaskar b Kapil Dev		58	c Yadav b Doshi	31
D.L. Underwood c Patil b Kapil Dev		13		
M.W. Gatting c Kirmani b Kapil Dev		0	not out	2
J.E. Emburey lbw b Kapil Dev		1		
†R.W. Taylor c Vengsarkar b Doshi		6		
R.G.D. Willis not out		11		
Extras (LB3, NB4)		7	(LB4)	4
Total		**248**	(5 wkts, dec)	**265**

INDIA

*S.M. Gavaskar b Underwood		42	not out	83
K. Srikkanth b Underwood		10	c Botham b Emburey	25
D.B. Vengsarkar c Taylor b Botham		70	c Tavaré b Fletcher	32
G.R. Viswanath c & b Emburey		15	c Gooch b Emburey	0
S.M. Patil c Fletcher b Emburey		0	not out	17
Kapil Dev c Tavaré b Underwood		22		
R.J. Shastri run out		8		
†S.M.H. Kirmani b Botham		10		
S. Madan Lal c Gooch b Willis		1		
Shivlal Yadav c Taylor b Willis		5		
D.R. Doshi not out		7		
Extras (B2, LB4, NB11, W1)		18	(LB2, NB11)	13
Total		**208**	(3 wkts)	**170**

BOWLING

INDIA	O	M	R	W		O	M	R	W	FALL OF WICKETS				
											E	*I*	*E*	*I*
Kapil Dev	31	6	91	6	—	21	3	81	0		*1st*	*1st*	*2nd*	*2nd*
Madan Lal	20	4	58	1	—	19	3	58	1	1st	25	33	24	48
Doshi	19.2	8	28	2	—	27	5	63	2	2nd	39	83	88	117
Yadav	17	7	42	0	—	3	0	11	0	3rd	88	117	107	120
Shastri	21	10	22	1	—	17	4	35	0	4th	93	117	154	—
Patil	—	—	—	—	—	3	0	13	0	5th	188	143	259	—
ENGLAND										6th	216	180	—	—
Willis	14	3	28	2	—	6	0	21	0	7th	218	184	—	—
Botham	27	8	63	2	—	11	3	26	0	8th	224	187	—	—
Underwood	29	13	45	3	—	31	18	38	0	9th	230	196	—	—
Emburey	24	11	44	2	—	30	11	62	2	10th	248	208	—	—
Gooch	6	1	10	0	—	2	0	4	0					
Fletcher	—	—	—	—	—	3	1	6	1					

FIFTH TEST MATCH

PLAYED AT MADRAS, 13, 14, 15, 17, 18 JANUARY 1982

MATCH DRAWN

INDIA

*S.M. Gavaskar c Taylor b Willis	25	c Botham b Willis	11
P. Roy c Taylor b Dilley	6	not out	60
D.B. Vengsarkar retired hurt	71		
G.R. Viswanath b Willis	222		
Yashpal Sharma c Tavare b Botham	140	(4) c Botham b Underwood	25
Kapil Dev not out	6	(5) not out	15
A. Malhotra did not bat		(3) run out	31
R.J. Shastri did not bat			
†S.M.H. Kirmani did not bat			
S. Madan Lal did not bat			
D.R. Doshi did not bat			
Extras (LB1, NB9, W1)	11	(B12, LB1, NB5)	18
Total (4 wkts, dec)	481	(3 wkts, dec)	160

ENGLAND

G.A. Gooch c & b Shastri	127
C.J. Tavare c Gavaskar b Doshi	35
*K.W.R. Fletcher b Doshi	3
D.I. Gower lbw b Shastri	64
I.T. Botham c Kirmani b Shastri	52
M.W. Gatting c Vishwanath b Doshi	0
G.R. Dilley c & b Kapil Dev	8
†R.W. Taylor b Doshi	8
D.L. Underwood c Kirmani b Kapil Dev	0
P.J.W. Allott c Roy b Kapil Dev	6
R.G.D. Willis not out	1
Extras (B1, LB9, NB14)	24
Total	328

BOWLING

ENGLAND	O	M	R	W		O	M	R	W	FALL OF WICKETS			
											I	*E*	*I*
Willis	28.1	7	79	2	—	7	2	15	1		*Ist*	*Ist*	*2nd*
Botham	31	10	83	1	—	8	1	29	0	1st	19	155	19
Dilley	31	4	87	1	—	5	1	13	0	2nd	51	164	69
Allott	33	4	135	0	—	—	—	—	—	3rd	466	195	122
Underwood	22	7	59	0	—	15	8	30	1	4th	481	279	—
Gooch	9	2	27	0	—	8	2	24	0	5th	—	283	—
Fletcher	—	—	—	—	—	1	0	9	0	6th	—	307	—
Taylor	—	—	—	—	—	2	0	6	0	7th	—	307	—
Tavare	—	—	—	—	—	2	0	11	0	8th	—	311	—
Gower	—	—	—	—	—	1	0	1	0	9th	—	320	—
Gatting	—	—	—	—	—	1	0	4	0	10th	—	328	—
INDIA													
Kapil Dev	25.5	7	88	3	—	—	—	—	—				
Madan Lal	9	1	41	0	—	—	—	—	—				
Shastri	63	23	104	3	—	—	—	—	—				
Doshi	57	31	69	4	—	—	—	—	—				
Gavaskar	1	0	2	0	—	—	—	—	—				

SIXTH TEST MATCH

PLAYED AT KANPUR ON 30, 31 JANUARY, 1, 3, 4 FEBRUARY 1982

MATCH DRAWN

ENGLAND

G.A. Gooch b Doshi	58
C.J. Tavaré b Doshi	24
*K.W.R. Fletcher b Kapil Dev	14
D.I. Gower lbw b Kapil Dev	85
I.T. Botham st Kirmani b Doshi	142
M.W. Gatting c Madan Lal b Doshi	32
G.R. Dilley lbw b Shastri	1
†R.W. Taylor b Shastri	0
J.E. Emburey run out	2
D.L. Underwood not out	0
R.G.D. Willis did not bat	
Extras (B2, LB5, W6, NB7)	20
Total (9 wkts, dec)	**378**

INDIA

*S.M. Gavaskar run out	52
P. Roy b Botham	5
D.B. Vengsarker c Fletcher b Dilley	46
G.R. Viswanath c Gower b Willis	74
Y. Sharma not out	55
A. Malhotra lbw b Willis	0
Kapil Dev c Dilley b Gower	116
R.J. Shastri c Taylor b Willis	2
†S.M.H. Kirmani not out	1
S. Madan Lal did not bat	
D.R. Doshi did not bat	
Extras (B1, LB7, NB16, W2)	26
Total (7 wkts)	**377**

BOWLING

INDIA	O	M	R	W
Kapil Dev	34	3	147	2
Madan Lal	24	4	79	0
Doshi	34.2	8	81	4
Shastri	23	6	51	2
ENGLAND				
Willis	23	5	75	3
Botham	25	6	67	1
Dilley	14	2	67	1
Underwood	25	8	55	0
Emburey	32	7	81	0
Fletcher	2	1	5	0
Gower	1	0	1	1

FALL OF WICKETS

	E	I
	1st	1st
1st	82	12
2nd	89	79
3rd	121	166
4th	248	197
5th	349	197
6th	354	207
7th	354	376
8th	360	
9th	378	
10th		

TEST MATCH AVERAGES

ENGLAND

	M	I	NO	Runs	HS	Avge	100	50	Ct	St
I.T. Botham	6	8	0	440	142	55.00	1	4	3	—
G.A. Gooch	6	10	1	487	127	54.11	1	4	4	—
D.I. Gower	6	9	1	375	85	46.87	—	4	1	—
G. Boycott	4	8	1	312	105	44.57	1	2	2	—
C.J. Tavaré	6	9	0	349	149	38.77	1	1	5	—
K.W.R. Fletcher	6	9	2	252	69	36.00	—	3	5	—
G.R. Dilley	4	5	0	70	52	14.00	—	1	1	—
M.W. Gatting	5	6	1	68	32	13.60	—	—	—	—
R.G.D. Willis	5	4	2	26	13	13.00	—	—	—	—
D.L. Underwood	6	7	4	38	13*	12.66	—	—	1	—
R.W. Taylor	6	7	1	57	33	9.50	—	—	15	1
J.E. Emburey	3	4	0	4	2	1.00	—	—	1	—

Played in two Tests: J.K. Lever 1 & 2.
Played in one Test: P.J.W. Allott 6.

	Overs	Mdns	Runs	Wkts	Avge	Best	5 wI	10 wM
J.K. Lever	73	16	204	7	29.14	5-100	1	—
R.G.D. Willis	129.1	29	381	12	31.75	3-75	—	—
J.E. Emburey	99	31	222	6	37.00	2-35	—	—
I.T. Botham	240.3	52	660	17	38.82	5-61	1	—
D.L. Underwood	223	99	438	10	43.80	3-88	—	—
G.R. Dilley	105	17	350	7	50.00	4-47	—	—

Also bowled: P.J.W. Allott 33-4-135-0; K.W.R. Fletcher 6-2-20-1; M.W. Gatting 1-0-4-0; G.A. Gooch 33.1-6-77-2; D.I. Gower 2-0-2-1; J.K. Lever 73-16-204-7; C.J. Tavaré 2-0-11-0; R.W. Taylor 2-0-6-0.

INDIA

	M	I	NO	Runs	HS	Avge	100	50	Ct	St
Yashpal Sharma	2	3	1	220	140	110	1	1	—	—
S.M. Gavaskar	6	9	1	500	172	62.50	1	3	9	—
G.R. Viswanath	6	8	0	466	222	58.25	2	1	2	—
Kapil Dev	6	8	2	318	116	53.00	1	1	3	—
D.B. Vengsarkar	6	8	0	292	71	36.50	—	2	1	—
P. Roy	2	3	1	71	60*	35.50	—	1	1	—
R.J. Shastri	6	6	1	140	93	28.00	—	1	2	—
S. Madan Lal	6	5	2	69	44	23.00	—	—	3	—
K. Srikkanth	4	6	0	119	65	19.83	—	1	1	—
S.M.H. Kirmani	6	6	1	99	67	19.80	—	1	10	1
Kirti Azad	3	4	0	71	24	17.75	—	—	2	—
A. Malhotra	2	2	0	31	31	15.50	—	—	—	—
S.M. Patil	4	6	1	95	31	11.87	—	—	2	—
D.R. Doshi	6	5	2	14	7*	4.67	—	—	—	—

Played in one Test: Shirlad Yadar 5 (1 ct).

	Overs	Mdns	Runs	Wkts	Avge	Best	5 wI	10 wM
D.R. Doshi	267.5	103	468	22	21.27	5-39	1	—
S. Madan Lal	161	34	432	14	30.86	5-23	2	—
Kapil Dev	243.5	40	835	22	37.95	6-91	2	—
R.J. Shastri	242	73	462	12	38.50	·4-83	—	—

Also bowled: Kirti Azad 48-10-153-1; S.M. Gavaskar 4-0-14-0; S.M. Patil 17-2-60-1; K. Srikkanth 6-1-10-0; Shirlad Yadar 20-7-53-0.

One-Day Internationals

(England against West Indies, Australia
and India during 1980-81 to 1981-82)

WEST INDIES v ENGLAND AT ST VINCENT 4/2/81

West Indies 127 in 47.2 overs (Mattis 62)
England 125 in 48.2 overs (Botham 60, Croft 6-15)
Result: West Indies won by 2 runs

WEST INDIES v ENGLAND AT BERBICE 26/2/81

England 137 in 47.2 overs
West Indies 138-4 in 39.3 overs (Haynes 48)
Result: West Indies won by 6 wickets

ENGLAND v AUSTRALIA AT LORD'S 4/6/81

Australia 210-7 in 55 overs (Border 73*)
England 212-4 in 51.4 overs (Boycott 75, Gooch 53)
Result: England won by 6 wickets

ENGLAND v AUSTRALIA AT EDGBASTON 6/6/81

Australia 249-8 in 55 overs (Yallop 63, Wood 55)
England 247 in 54.5 overs (Gatting 96)
Result: Australia won by 2 runs

ENGLAND v AUSTRALIA AT HEADINGLEY 7/6/81

Australia 236-8 in 55 overs (Wood 108)
England 165 in 46.5 overs (Hogg 4-29)
Result: Australia won by 71 runs

INDIA v ENGLAND AT AHMEDABAD 25/11/81

India 156-7 in 46 overs
England 160-5 in 43.5 overs
Result: England won by 5 wickets

INDIA v ENGLAND AT JULLUNDUR 20/12/81

England 161-7 in 36 overs (Gatting 71*, Gower 53)
India 164-4 in 35.3 overs (Vengsarkar 88*)
Result: India won by 6 wickets

INDIA v ENGLAND AT CUTTACK 28/1/82

England 230-6 in 46 overs (Fletcher 69, Botham 52)
India 231-5 in 42 overs (Gavaskar 71, Patil 64)
Result: India won by 5 wickets

CRICKETERS IN THE MAKING

TREVOR BAILEY

A useful coaching book for all young cricketers, specially designed, illustrated and written with their requirements in mind.

Using schoolboys aged 10-13 to depict all aspects of batting, bowling, fielding and wicket-keeping, Trevor Bailey emphasises that young players should be coached according to their physical development rather than by imitation of established cricketers.

144pp   £6.95
Illustrated throughout with b/w photographs
Available from May

From good bookshops everywhere but in case of difficulty direct from Queen Anne Press Sales, 9 Partridge Drive, Orpington, Kent.
Cash with order + 80p p&p. Allow 28 days for delivery.

QUEEN ANNE PRESS
Macdonald & Company

World Series Cup 1981-82

WEST INDIES v PAKISTAN AT MELBOURNE 21/11/81

West Indies 245 (Greenidge 103, Haynes 84, Sarfaz 4-37)
Pakistan 227-6 in 50 overs (Majid 56, Miandad 74, Nazar 51)
Result: West Indies won by 18 runs

AUSTRALIA v PAKISTAN AT MELBOURNE 22/11/81

Australia 209-9 in 50 overs (Hughes 67, Sikander 4-34)
Pakistan 210-6 (Miandad 72)
Result: Pakistan won by 4 wickets

WEST INDIES v AUSTRALIA AT SYDNEY, 24/11/81

West Indies 236-8 in 49 overs (Lloyd 63)
Australia 237-3 (Laird 117, Hughes 62*)
Result: Australia won by 7 wickets

PAKISTAN v WEST INDIES AT ADELAIDE 5/12/81

Pakistan 140
West Indies 132 (Wasim 4-25)
Result: Pakistan won by 8 runs

AUSTRALIA v PAKISTAN AT ADELAIDE 6/12/81

Australia 208
Pakistan 170-8 in 50 overs
Result: Australia won by 38 runs

AUSTRALIA v PAKISTAN AT SYDNEY 17/12/81

Australia 222-6 in 50 overs (Darling 74)
Pakistan 223-4 (Zaheer 108, Mudassar 50)
Result: Pakistan won by 6 wickets

PAKISTAN v WEST INDIES AT PERTH 19/12/81

Pakistan 160
West Indies 161-3 (Haynes 82*)
Result: West Indies won by 7 wickets

AUSTRALIA v WEST INDIES AT PERTH 20/12/81

Australia 188-9 (Wood 54*)
West Indies 190-2 (Lloyd 80*, Richards 72*)
Result: West Indies won by 8 wickets

AUSTRALIA v PAKISTAN AT MELBOURNE 9/1/82

Pakistan 218-6 in 50 overs (Zaheer 84)
Australia 193 in 49 overs (Border 75*)
Result: Pakistan won by 25 runs

AUSTRALIA v WEST INDIES AT MELBOURNE 10/1/82

Australia 146 in 42.5 overs (Chappell 59, Holding 4-32)
West Indies 147-5 in 47.1 overs (Dujon 51*)
Result: West Indies won by 5 wickets

WEST INDIES v PAKISTAN AT SYDNEY 12/1/82

Pakistan 191-7 in 50 overs (Imran Khan 62*)
West Indies 192-3 in 42.1 overs (Greenidge 84)
Result: West Indies won by 7 wickets

AUSTRALIA v PAKISTAN AT SYDNEY 14/1/82

Australia 230-5 in 50 overs (Hughes 63*)
Pakistan 154 in 40.3 overs
Result: Australia won by 76 runs

WEST INDIES v PAKISTAN AT BRISBANE 16/1/82

Pakistan 177-9 in 50 overs
West Indies 107-9 in 28 overs
Result: West Indies won a rain-reduced match on scoring rates

AUSTRALIA v WEST INDIES AT BRISBANE 17/1/82

Australia 185-9 in 40 overs (Chappell 61)
West Indies 186-5 in 38.4 overs (Gomes 56*)
Result: West Indies won by 5 wickets

AUSTRALIA v WEST INDIES AT SYDNEY 19/1/82

West Indies 189 (Richards 64)
Australia 168-7 in 43.1 overs
Result: Australia won on run-rate in a rain-affected match

	P	W	L	Pts
West Indies	10	7	3	14
Australia	10	4	6	8
Pakistan	10	4	6	8

(Australia qualified for finals on overall run-rate)

THE FINALS
WEST INDIES v AUSTRALIA AT MELBOURNE 23/1/82

West Indies 216-8 in 49 overs (Richards 78, Greenidge 59)
Australia 130
Result: West Indies won by 86 runs

AUSTRALIA v WEST INDIES AT MELBOURNE 24/1/82

West Indies 235 (Richards 60, Haynes 52, Pascoe 4-39)
Australia 107 (Gomes 4-31)
Result: West Indies won by 128 runs

AUSTRALIA v WEST INDIES AT SYDNEY 26/1/82

Australia 214-8 in 50 overs (Border 69*)
West Indies 168 (Lloyd 63*)
Result: Australia won by 46 runs

WEST INDIES v AUSTRALIA AT SYDNEY 27/1/82

West Indies 234-6 in 50 overs (Richards 70, Greenidge 64)
Australia 216-9 in 50 overs (Wood 69)
Result: West Indies won by 18 runs

WEST INDIES WON THE SERIES

ENGLAND v INDIA
1932 TO 1981 – 82
SERIES BY SERIES

Season		Visiting Captain	P	E W	I W	D
1932	In England	C.K. Nayuda (I)	1	1	0	0
1933-34	In India	D.R. Jardine (E)	3	2	0	1
1936	In England	Maharaj of Vizianagram (I)	3	2	0	1
1946	In England	Nawab of Pataudi, Snr (I)	3	1	0	2
1951-52	In India	N.D. Howard (E)	5	1	1	3
1952	In England	V.S. Hazare (I)	4	3	0	1
1959	In England	D.K. Gaekwad (I)	5	5	0	0
1961-62	In India	E.R. Dexter (E)	5	0	2	3
1963-64	In India	M.J.K. Smith (E)	5	0	0	5
1967	In England	Nawab of Pataudi, Jnr (I)	3	3	0	0
1971	In England	A.L.Wadekar (I)	3	0	1	2
1972-73	In India	A.R. Lewis (E)	5	1	2	2
1974	In England	A.L. Wadekar (I)	3	3	0	0
1976-77	In India	A.W. Greig (E)	5	3	1	1
1979	In England	S. Venkataraghavan (I)	4	1	0	3
1979-80	In India	J.M. Brearley (E)	1	1	0	0
1981-82	In India	K.W.R. Fletcher (E)	6	0	1	5
At Lord's			9	7	0	2
At The Oval			6	2	1	3
At Leeds			4	3	0	1
At Manchester			6	3	0	3
At Nottingham			1	1	0	0
At Birmingham			3	3	0	0
At Bombay			8	2	1	5
At Calcutta			7	1	2	4
At Madras			7	2	3	2
At Delhi			6	2	0	4
At Kanpur			5	1	0	4
At Bangalore			2	0	1	1
In England			29	19	1	9
In India			35	8	7	20
Total			64	27	8	29

HIGHEST INNINGS TOTALS

England			India		
633-5d	Birmingham	1979	510	Leeds	1967
629	Lord's	1974	487	Delhi	1981-82
571-8d	Manchester	1936	485-9d	Bombay	1951-52
559-8d	Kanpur	1963-64	481-4d	Madras	1981-82
550-4d	Leeds	1963	467-8d	Kanpur	1961-62
537	Lord's	1952	466	Delhi	1961-62
500-8d	Bombay	1961-62	463-4	Delhi	1963-64
497-5	Kanpur	1961-62	457-9d	Madras	1951-52
490	Manchester	1959	457-7d	Madras	1963-64
483-8d	Leeds	1959			

LOWEST INNINGS TOTALS

England			India		
101	The Oval	1971	42	Lord's	1974
102	Bombay (2nd I)	1981-82	58	Manchester	1952
134	Lords	1936	82	Manchester	1957
159	Madras	1972-73	83	Madras	1976-77
163	Calcutta (2nd I)	1972-73	92	Birmingham	1967
166	Bombay (1st I)	1981-82	93	Lord's	1936
174	Calcutta (1st I)	1972-73	96	Lord's	1979
177	Bangalore	1976-77	98	The Oval	1952

HIGHEST INDIVIDUAL INNINGS FOR ENGLAND

246*	G. Boycott	at Leeds	1967
217	W.R. Hammond	at The Oval	1936
214*	D. Lloyd	at Birmingham	1974
205*	J. Hardstaff	at Lord's	1946
200*	D.I. Gower	at Birmingham	1979
188	D.L. Amiss	at Lord's	1974
179	D.L. Amiss	at Delhi	1976-77
175	T.W. Graveney	at Bombay	1951-52

A total of 51 centuries have been scored for England.

HIGHEST INDIVIDUAL INNINGS FOR INDIA

222	G.R. Viswanath	at Madras	1981-82
221	S.M. Gavaskar	at The Oval	1979
203*	Nawab of Pataudi, Junior	at Delhi	1963-64
192	B.K. Kunderan	at Madras	1963-64
189*	V.L. Manjrekar	at Delhi	1961-62
184	V.M.H. Mankad	at Lord's	1952
172	S.M. Gavaskar	at Bangalore	1981-82
164*	V.S. Hazare	at Delhi	1951-52
155	V.S. Hazare	at Bombay	1951-52
154	V.M. Merchant	at Delhi	1951-52

A total of 39 centuries have been scored for India.

A CENTURY IN EACH INNINGS OF A MATCH
No instance for either side.

A CENTURY ON DEBUT IN SERIES
FOR ENGLAND

246*	G. Boycott	at Leeds	1967
200*	D.I. Gower	at Birmingham	1979
175	T.W. Graveney	at Bombay	1951-52
137*	A.J. Watkins	at Delhi	1951-52
136	B.H. Valentine (on Test debut)	at Bombay	1933-34
109	B.L. D'Oliveira	at Leeds	1967
100	M.J.K. Smith	at Manchester	1959

FOR INDIA

118	L. Amarnath (on Test debut)	at Bombay	1933-34
112	A.A. Baig (on Test debut)	at Manchester	1959
105	Hanuman Singh (on Test debut)	at Delhi	1963-64

RECORD WICKET PARTNERSHIPS FOR ENGLAND

1st	159	P.E. Richardson & G. Pullar at Bombay	1961-62
2nd	221	D.L. Amiss & J.H. Edrich at Lords	1974

3rd	169	R. Subba Row & M.J.K. Smith at The Oval	1959
4th	266	W.R. Hammond & T.S. Worthington at The Oval	1936
5th	254	K.W.R. Fletcher & A.W. Greig at Bombay	1972-73
6th	171	I.T. Botham & R.W. Taylor at Bombay	1979-80
7th	103	A.P.E. Knott & R.A. Hutton at The Oval	1971
8th	168	R. Illingworth & P. Lever at Manchester	1971
9th	83	K.W.R. Fletcher & N. Gifford at Madras	1972-73
10th	57	J.T. Murray & R.N.S. Hobbs at Birmingham	1967

RECORD WICKET PARTNERSHIPS FOR INDIA

1st	213	S.M. Gavaskar & C.P.S. Chauhan at The Oval	1979
2nd	192	F.M. Engineer & A.L. Wadekar at Bombay	1972-73
3rd	316†	G.R. Viswanath & Yashpal Sharma at Madras	1981-82
4th	222	V.S. Hazare & V.L. Manjrekar at Leeds	1952
5th	190*	Nawab of Pataudi, Jnr. & C.G. Borde at Delhi	1963-64
6th	105	V.S. Hazare & D.G. Phadkar at Leeds	1952
7th	169	Yashpal Sharma & Kapil Dev at Kanpur	1981-82
8th	128	R.J. Shastri & S.M.H. Kirmani at Delhi	1981-82
9th	104	R.J. Shastri & S. Madan Lal at Delhi	1981-82
10th	51	R.G. Nadkarni & B.S. Chandrasekhar at Calcutta	1963-64

† 415 runs were added for this wicket in two separate partnerships. D.B. Vengsarkar
retired hurt and was replaced by Yashpal Sharma after 99 runs had been made.

HIGHEST RUN AGGREGATE IN A TEST RUBBER

England in England	399 (av. 79.80)	L. Hutton	1952
England in India	594 (Av. 99.00)	K.F. Barrington	1961-62
India in England	542 (Av. 77.42)	S.M. Gavaskar	1979
India in India	586 (Av. 83.71)	V.L. Manjrekar	1961-62

BEST INNINGS BOWLING FIGURES

England in England	8-31	F.S. Trueman at Manchester	1952
England in India	7-46	J.K. Lever at Delhi	1976-77
India in England	6-35	Amar Singh at Lord's	1936
India in India	8-55	V.M.H. Mankad at Madras	1951-52

TEN WICKETS OR MORE IN A MATCH FOR ENGLAND

13-106	I.T. Botham at Bombay	1979-80
11-93	A.V. Bedser at Manchester	1946
11-145	A.V. Bedser at Lord's	1946
11-153	H. Verity at Madras	1933-34
10-70	J.K. Lever at Delhi (Test debut)	1976-77
10-78	G.O. Allen at Lord's	1936

TEN WICKETS OR MORE IN A MATCH FOR INDIA

| 12-108 | V.M.H. Mankad at Madras | 1951-52 |
| 10-177 | S.A. Durani at Madras | 1961-62 |

HIGHEST WICKET AGGREGATE IN A TEST RUBBER

England in England	F.S. Trueman	29 (Av. 13.31)	1952
England in India	D.L. Underwood	29 (Av. 17.55)	1976-77
India in England	S.P. Gupte	17 (Av. 34.64)	1959
India in India	B.S. Chandrasekhar	35 (Av. 18.91)	1972-73

HIGHEST MATCH AGGREGATE   1,350-28 wkts at Leeds   1963

LOWEST MATCH AGGREGATE   482-31 wkts at Lord's   1936

ENGLAND v PAKISTAN
1954 TO 1978

SERIES BY SERIES

Season		Visiting Captain	P	E W	P W	D
1954	In England	A.H. Kardar (P)	4	1	1	2
1961-62	In Pakistan	E.R. Dexter (E)	3	1	0	2
1962	In England	Javed Burki (P)	5	4	0	1
1967	In England	Hanif Mohammad (P)	3	2	0	1
1968-69	In Pakistan	M.C. Cowdrey (E)	3	0	0	3
1971	In England	Intikhab Alam (P)	3	1	0	2
1972-73	In Pakistan	A.R. Lewis (E)	3	0	0	3
1974	In England	Intikab Alam (P)	3	0	0	3
1977-78	In Pakistan	J.M. Brearley (E)	3	0	0	3
1978	In England	Wasim Bari (P)	3	2	0	1
	At Lord's		6	2	0	4
	At The Oval		4	2	1	1
	At Leeds		4	2	0	2
	At Manchester		1	0	0	1
	At Nottingham		3	2	0	1
	At Birmingham		3	2	0	1
	At Karachi		4	0	0	4
	At Lahore		4	1	0	3
	At Dacca		2	0	0	2
	At Hyderabad		2	0	0	2
	In England		21	10	1	10
	In Pakistan		12	1	0	11
	Total		33	11	1	21

HIGHEST INNINGS TOTALS
England

558-6d	Nottingham	1954
545	The Oval	1974
544-5d	Birmingham	1962
507	Karachi	1961-62
502-7	Karachi	1968-69
487	Hyderabad	1972-73
480-5d	The Oval	1962
452-8d	Birmingham	1978

Pakistan

608-7d	Birmingham	1971
600-7d	The Oval	1974
569-9d	Hyderabad	1972-73
445-6d	Karachi	1972-73
422	Lahore	1972-73
407-9d	Lahore	1977-78

LOWEST INNINGS TOTALS
England

130	The Oval (1st inns.)	1954
143	The Oval (2nd inns.)	1954
183	Leeds	1974
191	Hyderabad	1977-78

Pakistan

87	Lords	1954
90	Manchester	1954
100	Lords	1962
105	Lord's	1978
114	Nottingham	1967
131	Leeds	1962

HIGHEST INDIVIDUAL INNINGS FOR ENGLAND

278	D.C.S. Compton	at Nottingham	1954
205	E.R. Dexter	at Karachi	1961-62
183	D.L. Amiss	at The Oval	1974
182	M.C. Cowdrey	at The Oval	1962
172	E.R. Dexter	at The Oval	1962
165	G. Pullar	at Dacca	1961-62
159	M.C. Cowdrey	at Birmingham	1962
158	D.L. Amiss	at Hyderabad	1972-73
153	T.W. Graveney	at Lord's	1962

A total of 33 centuries have been scored for England.

HIGHEST INDIVIDUAL INNINGS FOR PAKISTAN

274	Zaheer Abbas	at Birmingham	1971
240	Zaheer Abbas	at The Oval	1974
187*	Hanif Mohammad	at Lord's	1967
157	Mushtaq Mohammad	at Hyderabad	1972-73
146	Asif Iqbal	at The Oval	1967
140	Javed Burki	at Dacca	1961-62
138	Javed Burki	at Lahore	1961-62
138	Intikhab Alam	at Hyderabad	1972-73

A total of 21 centuries have been scored for Pakistan.

A CENTURY IN EACH INNINGS OF A MATCH
FOR ENGLAND
NIL

FOR PAKISTAN

111 & 104	Hanif Mohammad	at Dacca	1961-62

A CENTURY ON DEBUT IN SERIES
FOR ENGLAND

159	M.C. Cowdrey	at Birmingham	1962
139	K.F. Barrington	at Lahore	1961-62
108*	B.W. Luckhurst	at Birmingham	1971
106	C.T. Radley	at Birmingham	1978
100	I.T. Botham	at Birmingham	1978

FOR PAKISTAN

274	Zaheer Abbas	at Birmingham	1971
138	Javed Burki	at Lahore	1961-62
122	Haroon Rashid	at Lahore	1977-78
114	Mudassar Nazar	at Lahore	1977-78

RECORD WICKET PARTNERSHIPS FOR ENGLAND

1st	198	G. Pullar & R.W. Barber at Dacca	1961-62
2nd	248	M.C. Cowdrey & E.R. Dexter at The Oval	1962
3rd	201	K.F. Barrington & T.W. Graveney at Lord's	1967
4th	188	E.R. Dexter & P.H. Parfitt at Karachi	1961-62
5th	192	D.C.S. Compton & T.E. Bailey at Nottingham	1954
6th	153*	P.H. Parfitt & D.A. Allen at Birmingham	1962
7th	159	A.P.E. Knott & P. Lever at Birmingham	1971
8th	99	P.H. Parfitt & D.A. Allen at Leeds	1962
9th	76	T.W. Graveney & F.S. Trueman at Lord's	1962
10th	55	D.L. Underwood & P.L. Pocock at Hyderabad	1972-73

RECORD WICKET PARTNERSHIPS FOR PAKISTAN

1st	122	Hanif Mohammad & Alim-ud-Din at Dacca	1961-62
2nd	291	Zaheer Abbas & Mushtaq Mohammad at Birmingham	1971
3rd	180	Mudassar Nazar & Haroon Rashid at Lahore	1977-78
4th	153	Javed Burki & Mushtaq Mohammad at Lahore	1961-62
5th	197	Javed Burki & Nasim-ul-Ghani at Lord's	1962
6th	145	Mushtaq Mohammad & Intikhab Alam at Hyderabad	1972-73
7th	51	Saeed Ahmed & Nasim-ul-Ghani at Nottingham	1962
8th	130	Hanif Mohammad & Asif Iqbal at Lord's	1967
9th	190	Asif Iqbal & Intikhab Alam at The.Oval	1967
10th	62	Sarfraz Nawaz & Asif Masood at Leeds	1974

HIGHEST RUN AGGREGATE IN A TEST RUBBER

England in England	453 (Av. 90.60)	D.C.S. Compton	1954
England in Pakistan	406 (Av. 81.20)	D.L. Amiss	1972-73
Pakistan in England	401 (Av. 44.55)	Mushtaq Mohammad	1962
Pakistan in Pakistan	407 (Av. 67.83)	Hanif Mohammad	1961-62

BEST INNINGS BOWLING FIGURES

England in England	8-34	I.T. Botham at Lords	1978
England in Pakistan	7-66	P.H. Edmonds at Karachi	1977-78
Pakistan in England	6-46	Fazal Mahmood at The Oval	1954
Pakistan in Pakistan	6-44	Abdul Qadir at Hyderabad	1977-78

TEN WICKETS OR MORE IN A MATCH FOR ENGLAND

13-71	D.L. Underwood at Lord's	1974

TEN WICKETS OR MORE IN A MATCH FOR PAKISTAN

12-99	Fazal Mahmood at The Oval	1954

HIGHEST WICKET AGGREGATE IN A TEST RUBBER

England in England	F.S. Trueman	22 (Av. 19.95)	1962
England in Pakistan	D.A. Allen	13 (Av. 25.69)	1961-62
Pakistan in England	Fazal Mahmood	20 (Av. 20.40)	1954
Pakistan in Pakistan	Intikhab Alam	15 (Av. 28.55)	1972-73

HIGHEST MATCH AGGREGATE   1274-25 wkts at Hyderabad   1972-73

LOWEST MATCH AGGREGATE   509-28 wkts at Nottingham   1967

We are looking for small businesses looking for money.

In a time of recession, you may well be thinking the prospects of obtaining a business loan are wilting fast.

Nothing could be further from the truth.

Because we at NatWest are convinced that financial assistance for the many up-and-coming businesses in this country is exactly what our economy needs. That's why we pay out some £27 million in Business Development Loans each and every month to over 2,000 customers.

And why we're looking to talk to more small businesses in need of finance for sound and promising business ventures.

NatWest Business Development Loans range from £2,000 to £250,000 and can be granted for periods between 1 and 10 years.

The rates of interest are highly competitive.

Rates are fixed in advance, and repayments are worked out in equal monthly instalments.

So everything's planned in advance and cash flow's kept well under control.

Now we've made our position clear, all that may stand between you and a flourishing business is a phone call to the Manager at a NatWest branch near you.

Alternatively, if you want more time to think, fill in the coupon and we'll send you printed information on the subject.

Contact a NatWest branch near you or fill in this coupon for our leaflets "NatWest Business Development Loans" and "The Small Business Digest."

Send to: National Westminster Bank Ltd, FREEPOST, 41 Lothbury, London EC2P 2BP
(No postage stamp required)

Name _____

Company _____

Address _____

Fixed sum • Fixed interest • Fixed repayments • Fixed term ... for easier cash flow.

NatWest *Business Development Loans*

DERBYSHIRE WIN THE
FIRST NATWEST TROPHY

The NatWest Bank Trophy, a little slow in gathering momentum in the early stages when the principal round of eight matches was seriously impeded by bad weather, rose to unparalleled heights in the semi-finals and the final. Records are made to be broken, but it is likely that Derbyshire's exploits in winning their first competition since 1936 will never be equalled: they achieved their success without scoring any more runs than their opposition in both the semi-final and the final – and both victories came off the last ball of the match. The Gods could not have stage-managed it better. Northants were faced with a similar situation: in their semi-final they were batting, and won through, but in the final they were bowling and lost. Derbyshire were batting both times and their players will rarely, if ever, face such tensions again – nor indeed will many want to!

Derbyshire's quarter-final, too, had its moments when Notts were 75 for 1 seeking a modest total of 165 to win. So in three successive ties there was every possibility of Derbyshire going out – three times they survived heavily against the odds. It must have seemed a different world from the peace of their first round match in the Suffolk countryside at Bury St Edmunds when they won overwhelmingly by 171 runs. It is interesting that the first round produced the only century-makers of the whole competition, except for the final. There were three of them – Graham Gooch 101 against Hertfordshire, Chris Tavaré 118 not out against Yorkshire and Andrew Kennedy 102 not out against Durham – so Tavaré had the distinction of scoring the first century in the first year against a first-class county. His was also the highest score in this first summer of the competition, beating Cook's 111 in the final.

The draw for the semi-finals involving the grounds at Northampton and Derby, with the inevitable ticket problems which would not have existed on larger grounds, once again raised the old chestnut of semi-finals on a neutral ground, but it is really a question of swings and roundabouts. If the games are at Old Trafford and The Oval this year the question will die a natural death, as it has done many times before. It could be said that the people who packed the grounds at Northampton and Derby saw cricket of a lifetime. At Northampton, drizzle, appallingly bad light, and an intermission in the proceedings whilst the umpires threaded their way through the crowd to the score-box to enquire the relative scoring rates before the last over was bowled, was something of the bizarre, but how critically important. With the scores tied, if a wicket fell in that last over, Lancashire would win on less wickets lost. If it didn't, Northants were the winners. Tim Lamb and Jim Griffiths survived. Lancashire, masters of so many one-day games had been out-manoeuvred. At least, we said, there will never be another game like this one.

There wasn't – until the next day! Derbyshire's contest with Essex had been held up by the weather and was continued the next day with an almost identical grand finale. High jinks in the last over – bowled by a West Indian Test bowler – and a tie, if such a thing is possible in one-day cup cricket; it isn't, and Derbyshire went through on less wickets lost. Their heroes were the master-mind, Bob Taylor, and Paul Newman. Again, we said, there can be nothing like these two matches in the final – well, there couldn't be, in all honesty, except there was!

The setting for the Final was perfect. The day was fine, the pitch good, and the sides looked evenly balanced – but not quite as evenly balanced as subsequent events showed them to be. Derbyshire won the toss and put Northants in – that was the first piece of drama, and as Northants did not lose a wicket until 99 runs were on the board, this decision by Barry Wood looked a piece of folly. Yet despite Geoff Cook's magnificent century (111) and his opening partner, Wayne Larkins, scoring 52, the innings faded to a total of 235. When Derbyshire were 164 for 1 it looked to have become a rather one-sided contest. But when Neil Mallender prised out both Wright (76) and Kirsten (63) almost in the same breath, the way was wide open again for either side to take their pickings. Tension mounted. Derbyshire found two stout hearts in Geoff Miller and Colin Tunnicliffe; slowly they hauled Derbyshire back – and so to the last over. Every corner of this famous ground had come to life.

Seven runs were required for an outright win with six balls to go. Minutes before Northants were odds-on favourites but then 12 runs came from Sarfraz's last over, and sharply turned the tide of events. Seven precious runs then, or six would do to tie, and for Derbyshire to win on the basis of less wickets lost. Miller took two off the first ball and a single off the second; no score next ball – four off three needed; three off two and then to the last ball – and one would do. Whatever happened Derbyshire must run; everybody was in to stop the single. As soon as the ball was delivered, Miller, at the bowler's end, set off at a blistering pace. Tunnicliffe ran for dear life to the other end not knowing whether Miller was home or not. He was. Derbyshire had won a dramatic contest which will become as much an important part of cricket's folklore, as Jack Bond's catch or Boycott's century in the sawdust.

1981 RESULTS

FIRST ROUND

Hampshire v Cheshire at Southampton

Cheshire 137 (Malone 5-34)
Hampshire 138-4 (Greenidge 56)
Result: Hampshire won by 6 wickets
Man of the Match: C.G. Greenidge
Adjudicator: J.A. Jameson

Hertfordshire v Essex at Hitchin

Essex 306-8 in 60 overs (Gooch 101, Hardie 81, Fletcher 51*)
Hertfordshire 115
Result: Essex won by 191 runs
Man of the Match: G.A. Gooch
Adjudicator: J.M. Parks

Ireland v Gloucestershire at Clontarf, Dublin

Gloucestershire 246-8 in 60 overs (Sadiq Mohammad 50, Stovold 70, Bainbridge 61*)
Ireland 75 (Graveney 5-11)
Result: Gloucestershire won by 171 runs
Man of the Match: A.W. Stovold
Adjudicator: Sir Leonard Hutton

Lancashire v Durham at Old Trafford

Durham 187 (Atkinson 80)
Lancashire 190-2 (Kennedy 102*)
Result: Lancashire won by 8 wickets
Man of the Match: A. Kennedy
Adjudicator: D.B. Close

Kent v Yorkshire at Canterbury

Yorkshire 222-6 in 60 overs (Hampshire 63, Bairstow 52*, Cowdrey 4-41)
Kent 223-4 (Tavaré 118*, Benson 57)
Result: Kent won by 6 wickets
Man of the Match: C.J. Tavaré
Adjudicator: B.L. D'Oliveira

49

Oxfordshire v Glamorgan at Oxford
Oxfordshire 150 (Nurton 70, Nash 5-31)
Glamorgan 154-2 (Ontong 53*)
Result: Glamorgan won by 8 wickets
Man of the Match: M.D. Nurton
Adjudicator: R.E. Marshall

Suffolk v Derbyshire at Bury St Edmunds
Derbyshire 270-6 in 60 overs (Steele 89*, Miller 57)
Suffolk 99
Result: Derbyshire won by 171 runs
Man of the Match: D.S. Steele
Adjudicator: F.J. Titmus

SECOND ROUND
Glamorgan v Hampshire at Cardiff
Hampshire 176-7 in 60 overs (Jesty 67, Barwick 4-14)
Glamorgan 146 (Javed Miandad 64)
Result: Hampshire won by 30 runs
Man of the Match: T.E. Jesty
Adjudicator: J.A. Jameson

Northamptonshire v Somerset at Northampton
Somerset 202 (Popplewell 57)
Northamtonshire 204-3 (Larkins 59, Cook 50)
Result: Northamtonshire won by 7 wickets
Man of the Match: G. Cook
Adjudicator: D.B. Close

Warwickshire v Sussex at Edgbaston
Sussex 274-8 in 60 overs (Greig 82)
Warwickshire 150 (Greig 4-31)
Result: Sussex won by 124 runs
Man of the Match: I.A. Greig
Adjudicator: B.L. D'Oliveira

Kent v Nottinghamshire at Canterbury
Kent 154
Nottinghamshire 156-6
Result: Nottinghamshire won by 4 wickets
Man of the Match: R.J. Hadlee
Adjudicator: A.V. Bedser (first day only – then umpires)

Worcestershire v Derbyshire at Worcester
Worcestershire 228 (Turner 59, Tunnicliffe 5-50)
Derbyshire 229-6 (Kirsten 84*, Wright 50)
Result: Derbyshire won by 4 wickets
Man of the Match: P.N. Kirsten
Adjudicator: R.T. Simpson

Gloucestershire v Essex at Bristol
Essex 207
Gloucestershire 85
Result: Essex won by 122 runs
Man of the Match: D.E. East
Adjudicator: F.J. Titmus (first day only – then H. Blofeld)

Lancashire v Middlesex at Old Trafford
Lancashire 231-8 in 60 overs (D. Lloyd 81, Daniel 4-28)
Middlesex 189 (Slack 53)
Result: Lancashire won by 42 runs
Man of the Match: D. Lloyd
Adjudicator: P.J. Sharpe (first two days – then umpires)

Surrey v Leicestershire at The Oval
Leicestershire 104-5 in 10 overs
Surrey 88-2
Result: Leicestershire won by 16 runs
Man of the Match: B.F. Davison
Adjudicator: J.M. Parks (first two days – then G. Ross)

QUARTER-FINALS – 5 AUGUST
Hampshire v Lancashire at Southampton
Hampshire 167-9 in 60 overs
Lancashire 169-7 (C.H. Lloyd 82*)
Result: Lancashire won by 3 wickets
Man of the Match: C.H. Lloyd
Adjudicator: J.M. Parks

Derbyshire v Nottinghamshire at Derby
Derbyshire 164 in 59 overs
Nottinghamshire 141 (Todd 62)
Result: Derbyshire won by 23 runs
Man of the Match: P.A. Todd
Adjudicator: D.B. Close

Sussex v Essex at Hove
Essex 195-9 in 60 overs (le Roux 5-35)
Sussex 170
Result: Essex won by 25 runs
Man of the Match: J.K. Lever
Adjudicator: J.A. Jameson

Leicestershire v Northamptonshire at Leicester
Leicestershire 227 in 59.4 overs (Tolchard 70, Davison 67)
Northamptonshire 207-4 in 50.5 overs (Larkins 81*, Cook 63)
Result: Northamptonshire won by a faster scoring rate
Man of the Match: W. Larkins
Adjudicator: F.J. Titmus

SEMI-FINALS – 20–21 AUGUST
Derbyshire v Essex at Derby
Essex 149 in 60 overs
Derbyshire 149-8 in 60 overs (Barnett 59)
Result: Derbyshire won by losing fewer wickets
Man of the Match: K.J. Barnett
Adjudicator: R.T. Simpson

Northamptonshire v Lancashire at Northampton
Lancashire 186-9 in 60 overs (Fowler 57, D. Lloyd 52)
Northamptonshire 187-9 in 59.5 overs
Result: Northamptonshire won by 1 wicket
Man of the Match: T.M. Lamb
Adjudicator: J.M. Parks

NATWEST BANK TROPHY FINAL
PLAYED AT LORD'S 5 SEPTEMBER
DERBYSHIRE WON ON LESS WICKETS

NORTHAMPTONSHIRE

*G. Cook	lbw b Tunnicliffe	111
W. Larkins	c Miller b Wood	52
A.J. Lamb	run out	9
R.G. Williams	c Hill b Miller	14
P. Willey	run out	19
T.J. Yardley	run out	4
G. Sharp	c Kirsten b Tunnicliffe	5
Sarfraz Nawaz	not out	3
N.A. Mallender	c Taylor b Newman	0
T.M. Lamb	b Hendrick	4
B.J. Griffiths	did not bat	
Extras (B2, LB9, W1, NB2)		14
Total (60 overs) (9 wkts)		235

DERBYSHIRE

A. Hill	b Mallender	14
J.G. Wright	lbw b Mallender	76
P.N. Kirsten	lbw b Mallender	63
*B. Wood	b Sarfraz	10
K.J. Barnett	run out	19
D.S. Steele	b Griffiths	0
G. Miller	not out	22
C.J. Tunnicliffe	not out	15
*R.W. Taylor	did not bat	
P.G. Newman	did not bat	
M. Hendrick	did not bat	
Extras (B5, LB7, W3, NB1)		16
Total (60 overs) (6 wkts)		235

Man of the Match: G. Cook
Adjudicator: I.V.A. Richards

BOWLING

DERBYSHIRE	O	M	R	W		FALL OF WICKETS	
						N	D
Hendrick	12	3	50	1			
Tunnicliffe	12	1	42	2	1st	99	41
Wood	12	2	35	1	2nd	137	164
Newman	12	0	37	1	3rd	168	165
Steele	5	0	31	0	4th	204	189
Miller	7	0	26	1	5th	218	190
NORTHANTS					6th	225	213
Sarfraz	12	2	58	1	7th	227	—
Griffiths	12	2	40	1	8th	227	—
Mallender	10	1	35	3	9th	235	—
Willey	12	0	33	0	10th	—	—
Lamb	12	0	43	0			
Williams	2	0	10	0			

NATWEST BANK TROPHY
PRINCIPAL RECORDS 1981

Highest innings total: 306-8 off 60 overs, Essex v Hertfordshire (Hitchin).
Highest innings total by a Minor County: 187 off 55.4 overs, Durham v Lancashire (Manchester).
Highest innings total by a side batting second: 235-6 off 60 overs, Derbyshire v Northamptonshire (Lord's).
Highest innings total by a side batting first and losing: 235-9 off 60 overs, Northamptonshire v Derbyshire (Lord's)
Lowest innings total: 75 off 45.5 overs, Ireland v Gloucestershire (Clontarf, Dublin).
Lowest innings total by a first-class county: 85, Gloucestershire v Essex (Bristol).
Biggest victory: 191 runs, Essex beat Hertfordshire (Hitchin).
Highest individual innings: 118* C.J. Tavaré, Kent v Yorkshire (Canterbury).
Highest individual innings by a Minor County player: 80 S.R. Atkinson, Durham v Lancashire (Manchester).
Centuries: 4 centuries have been scored in the competition: C.J. Tavaré (118*), A. Kennedy (102*), G.A. Gooch (101), G. Cook (111).

Record Wicket Partnerships

1st	184	G.A. Gooch & B.R. Hardie, Essex v Hertfordshire (Hitchin).
2nd	138	J.G. Wright & P.N. Kirsten, Derbyshire v Northants (Lord's).
3rd	144	C.J. Tavaré & M.R. Benson, Kent v Yorkshire (Canterbury).
4th	139	D.S. Steele & G. Miller, Derbyshire v Suffolk (Bury St Edmunds).
5th	64	B.F. Davison & R.W. Tolchard, Leics v Northants (Leicester)
6th	73	A.W. Stovold & P. Bainbridge, Glos v Ireland (Clontarf, Dublin).
7th	77	B.N. French and R.J. Hadlee, Notts v Kent (Canterbury).
8th	32	N.F.M. Popplewell & J. Garner, Somerset v Northamptonshire (Northampton).
9th	46	N. Philip & D.E. East, Essex v Derbyshire (Derby).
10th	29	S.A. Westley & C. Rutterford, Suffolk v Derbyshire (Bury St Edmunds).

Best bowling: 5-11 D.A. Graveney, Gloucestershire v Ireland (Clontarf, Dublin).
5-31 M.A. Nash, Glamorgan v Oxfordshire (Oxford).
Hat-tricks: Nil.
Most wicket-keeping dismissals: 6 (5 ct 1 st) R.W. Taylor, Derbyshire v Essex (Derby).

GILLETTE CUP WINNERS

1963	Sussex	1972	Lancashire
1964	Sussex	1973	Gloucestershire
1965	Yorkshire	1974	Kent
1966	Warwickshire	1975	Lancashire
1967	Kent	1976	Northamptonshire
1968	Warwickshire	1977	Middlesex
1969	Yorkshire	1978	Sussex
1970	Lancashire	1979	Somerset
1971	Lancashire	1980	Middlesex

NATWEST BANK TROPHY WINNERS

1981 Derbyshire

NATWEST BANK TROPHY
PRINCIPAL RECORDS 1963-1981
(including those in the former Gillette Cup)

Highest innings total: 371-4 off 60 overs, Hampshire v Glamorgan (Southampton) 1975.

Highest innings total by a Minor County: 229-5 off 60 overs, Devon v Cornwall (Exeter) 1980.

Highest innings total by a side batting second: 297-4 off 57.1 overs, Somerset v Warwickshire (Taunton) 1978.

Highest innings total by a side batting first and losing: 292-5 off 60 overs, Warwickshire v Somerset (Taunton) 1978.

Lowest innings total: 41 off 20 overs, Cambridgeshire v Buckinghamshire (Cambridge) 1972; 41 off 19.4 overs, Middlesex v Essex (Westcliff) 1972; 41 off 36.1 overs, Shropshire v Essex (Wellington) 1974.

Lowest innings total by a side batting first and winning: 98 off 56.2 overs, Worcestershire v Durham (Chester-le-Street) 1968.

Highest individual innings: 177 C.G. Greenidge, Hampshire v Glamorgan (Southampton) 1975.

Highest individual innings by a Minor County player: 132 G. Robinson, Lincolnshire v Northumberland (Jesmond) 1971.

Centuries: 93 were scored in the Gillette Cup. 4 have been scored in the NatWest Bank Trophy.

Record Wicket Partnerships

1st	227	R.E. Marshall & B.L. Reed, Hampshire v Bedfordshire (Goldington)	1968
2nd	223	M.J. Smith & C.T. Radley, Middlesex v Hampshire (Lord's)	1977
3rd	160	B. Wood & F.C. Hayes, Lancashire v Warwickshire (Birmingham)	1976
4th	234	D. Lloyd & C.H. Lloyd, Lancashire v Gloucestershire (Manchester)	1978
5th	141	T.E. Jesty & N.E.J. Pocock, Hampshire v Derbyshire (Derby)	1980
6th	105	G.S. Sobers & R.A. White, Nottinghamshire v Worcestershire (Worcester)	1974
7th	107	D.R. Shepherd & D.A. Graveney, Gloucestershire v Surrey (Bristol)	1973
8th	69	S.J. Rouse & D.J. Brown, Warwickshire v Middlesex (Lord's)	1977
9th	87	M.A. Nash & A.E. Cordle, Glamorgan v Lincolnshire (Swansea)	1974
10th	45	A.T. Castell & D.W. White, Hampshire v Lancashire (Manchester)	1970

Hat-tricks: J.D.F. Larter, Northamptonshire v Sussex (Northampton) 1963. D.A.D. Sydenham, Surrey v Cheshire (Hoylake) 1964. R.N.S. Hobbs, Essex v Middlesex (Lord's) 1968. N.M. McVicker, Warwickshire v Lincolnshire (Birmingham) 1971.

Seven wickets in an innings: 7-15 A.L. Dixon, Kent v Surrey (The Oval) 1968. P.J. Sainsbury, Hampshire v Norfolk (Southampton) 7-30 in 1965 and R.D. Jackman, Surrey v Yorkshire (Harrogate) 7-33 in 1970 have also achieved this feat.

Most 'Man of the Match' awards: 7 C.H. Lloyd (Lancashire); 6 B.L. D'Oliveira (Worcestershire) and B. Wood (Lancashire); 5 M.C. Cowdrey (Kent), A.W. Greig (Sussex) and R.D.V. Knight (Gloucestershire and Surrey).

Congratulations, Derbyshire, on being the first to win it.

🔁 NatWest Bank Trophy

SOMERSET TAKE
THE BENSON & HEDGES

Benson & Hedges, who have never had a great deal of luck with their Finals, must have hoped for a more exciting contest this time between Surrey and Somerset. It just happened that, despite a valiant effort by Roger Knight, Surrey's captain, who battled on to score 92, Somerset had the big guns (and very big ones) in Joel Garner, who took 5 for 14, and the great master, Viv Richards, who treated the crowd to a superb 132 not out. So at least the ingredients were of high quality; not so the competitive element – Surrey were never really in it. They began as if they had a sizeable mountain to climb and the score after 15 overs was 16 for 1, not the sort of progress to give any sort of foundation for a worthwhile score. Knight totally lacked genuine support and Surrey's final score of 194 for 8 in the prescribed 55 overs was never likely to be enough. The picture changed, momentarily, however, when Denning was out for nought and Rose for 5 – 5 for 2. Enter Richards and, with Roebuck and Botham performing minor roles the great man helped himself to 132. Surrey were never in the hunt and the score went from 5 for 2 to 110 for 3 and 197 for 3 off 44.3 overs when the end came, an inevitable end long since predicted as an absolute matter of course.

If Surrey failed to stretch their opposition in the Final and produce a hair-raising finish, they did so in their semi-final against Leicestershire at The Oval. Surrey's 191 for 9 scarcely looked enough especially when Leicester were 153 for 5. Wickets then went down at 153, 163, 163, and 165 and it looked all over – a dramatic change almost in a single breath. But here Parsons and Higgs battled on and crept nearer and nearer. At 188, when it looked as though they might have done the job, Higgs was run out. Surrey won by 3 runs and went to Lord's with high hopes never to be fulfilled – they lost their third Final in three years. It was a fine effort to get to three Finals in successive seasons but very frustrating for the players. Somerset had had a fairly easy run-up to the Final in their semi-final against Kent.

Disagreeable weather early in the competition disrupted a number of games. Middlesex, for instance, failed to win one of their four matches. They first lost to Hampshire. This was followed by three abandoned matches, against Minor Counties, Sussex and Surrey. To have had three no-results in four must have been sickening for players and supporters alike. Middlesex were thus eliminated without a chance.

1981 RESULTS

9 MAY

Glamorgan v Essex at Swansea
Glamorgan 206-9 in 55 overs
Essex 124 in 42.2 overs
Result: Glamorgan won by 82 runs
Gold Award: Javed Miandad

Northants v Notts at Northampton
Nottinghamshire 155-9 in 54.3 overs
Northamptonshire 152 in 53.5 overs
Result: Nottinghamshire won by 1 wicket
Gold Award: C.E.B. Rice

Leicestershire v Glos at Leicester
Leicestershire 256-6 in 55 overs
Gloucestershire 195-7 in 55 overs
Result: Leicestershire won by 61 runs
Gold Award: J.C. Balderstone

Middlesex v Hampshire at Lord's
Hampshire 176-9 in 54.3 overs
Middlesex 175 in 54 overs
Result: Hampshire won by 1 wicket
Gold Award: D.R. Turner

9 & 11 MAY

Derbyshire v Yorkshire at Derby
Yorkshire 203-9 in 53.4 overs
Derbyshire 202-8 in 55 overs
Result: Yorkshire won by 1 wicket
Gold Award: D.L. Bairstow

11 MAY

Lancs v Warwickshire at Manchester
Warwickshire 291-5 in 54.3 overs
Lancashire 288-9 in 55 overs
Result: Warwickshire won by 5 wickets
Gold Award: G.W. Humpage

Sussex v Surrey at Hove
Sussex 143-7 in 52.4 overs
Surrey 142-7 in 55 overs
Result: Sussex won by 3 wickets
Gold Award: C.S. Clinton

Kent v Combined U. at Canterbury
Kent 108-2 in 28 overs
Combined Universities 104 in 53.4 overs
Result: Kent won by 8 wickets
Gold Award: R.A. Woolmer

13 MAY

Hants v Minor Co. at Southampton
Minor Counties 182-7 in 55 overs
Hampshire 179 in 54.3 overs
Result: Minor Counties won by 3 runs
Gold Award: S.G. Plumb

16 MAY

Essex v Somerset at Chelmsford
Essex 278-5 in 55 overs
Somerset 240 in 50.2 overs
Result: Essex won by 38 runs
Gold Award: G.A. Gooch

Notts v Worcs at Trent Bridge
Nottinghamshire 217-4 in 52.5 overs
Worcestershire 214-8 in 55 overs
Result: Nottinghamshire won by 6 wickets
Gold Award: R.T. Robinson

Scotland v Lancashire at Titwood
Lancashire 116-4 in 43.1 overs
Scotland 112-7 in 48 overs
Result: Lancashire won by 6 wickets
Gold Award: D.P. Hughes

16 & 18 MAY – Matches Abandoned (points shared)

Warwickshire v Derbys at Edgbaston
Warwickshire 23-1 in 11.1 overs

Hampshire v Surrey at Bournemouth
Hampshire 143-5 in 49 overs

Glos v Northants at Bristol

Combined U. v Glamorgan at Oxford

Minor Counties v Middlesex at Slough

19 MAY

Worcs v Glos at Worcester
Gloucestershire 247-6 in 55 overs
Worcestershire 178 in 50.2 overs
Result: Glos won by 69 runs
Gold Award: Sadiq Mohammad

Derbyshire v Scotland at Derby
Derbyshire 98-3 in 32.2 overs
Scotland 97 in 50.3 overs
Result: Derbyshire won by 7 wickets
Gold Award: M. Hendrick

Warwickshire v Yorks at Edgbaston
Yorkshire 221 in 54.3 overs
Warwickshire 211 in 54.3 overs
Result: Yorkshire won by 10 runs
Gold Award: R.G.D. Willis

Combined U. v Somerset at Cambridge
Somerset 114-3 in 33 overs
Combined Universities 111-9 in 55 overs
Result: Somerset won by 7 wickets
Gold Award: J. Garner

19 & 20 MAY

Glamorgan v Kent at Cardiff
Kent 80-8 in 15 overs
Glamorgan 71-9 in 15 overs
Result: Kent won by 9 runs
Gold Award: E.A. Moseley

Matches Abandoned (points shared)
Northants v Leics at Northampton
Leicestershire 20-2 in 11.2 overs

Middlesex v Sussex at Lord's

21 MAY

Somerset v Kent at Taunton
Somerset 173-5 in 48.4 overs
Kent 172 in 54.1 overs
Result: Somerset won by 5 wickets
Gold Award: I.T. Botham

21 & 22 MAY

Glos v Notts at Gloucester
Nottinghamshire 191-9 in 55 overs
Gloucestershire 127 in 49 overs
Result: Notts won by 84 runs
Gold Award: C.E.B. Rice

Leics v Worcs at Leicester
Leicestershire 238-7 in 55 overs
Worcestershire 190 in 51.5 overs
Result: Leicestershire won by 48 runs
Gold Award: J.C. Balderstone

Lancs v Derbys at Old Trafford
Derbyshire 181-8 in 54.3 overs
Lancashire 179-7 in 55 overs
Result: Derbyshire won by 2 wickets
Gold Award: G. Miller

Yorkshire v Scotland at Bradford
Yorkshire 228-6 in 55 overs
Scotland 186 in 51.3 overs
Result: Yorkshire won by 42 runs
Gold Award: J.D. Love

Essex v Combined U. at Chelmsford
Essex 121-2 in 23 overs
Combined U. 120 in 48.4 overs
Result: Essex won by 8 wickets
Gold Award: S. Turner

Minor Counties v Sussex at Slough
Sussex 154-5 in 23 overs
Minor Counties 108 in 22 overs
Result: Sussex won by 46 runs
Gold Award: P.W.G. Parker

Match Abandoned (points shared)

Surrey v Middlesex at The Oval
Middlesex 54-5 in 23 overs

30 MAY

Notts v Leics at Trent Bridge
Nottinghamshire 117-4 in 36.3 overs
Leicestershire 114-8 in 55 overs
Result: Notts won by 6 wickets
Gold Award: R.J. Hadlee

Worcs v Northants at Worcester
Northamptonshire 127-1 in 46.2 overs
Worcestershire 123 in 53.3 overs
Result: Northants won by 9 wickets
Gold Award: G. Cook

Scotland v Warwickshire at Titwood
Warwickshire 221-5 in 55 overs
Scotland 203 in 53.5 overs
Result: Warwickshire won by 18 runs
Gold Award: G.W. Humpage

Kent v Essex at Dartford
Kent 162-2 in 41.4 overs
Essex 161 in 51.4 overs
Result: Kent won by 8 wickets
Gold Award: R.A. Woolmer

Somerset v Glamorgan at Taunton
Somerset 170-6 in 50.1 overs
Glamorgan 169-8 in 55 overs
Result: Somerset won by 4 wickets
Gold Award: I.V.A. Richards

Surrey v Minor Counties at The Oval
Surrey 226 in 54.4 overs
Minor Counties 98 in 41.2 overs
Result: Surrey won by 128 runs
Gold Award: N.T. O'Brien

30 MAY, 1 JUNE

Sussex v Hampshire at Hove
Sussex 198-7 in 54.5 overs
Hampshire 194 in 54.2 overs
Result: Sussex won by 3 wickets
Gold Award: I.A. Greig

Match Abandoned (points shared)

Yorkshire v Lancashire at Headingley

ZONAL POINTS TABLE

Group A	P	W	L	NR	Pts	Group C	P	W	L	NR	Pts
Nottinghamshire	4	4	0	0	8	Kent	4	3	1	0	6
Leicestershire	4	2	1	1	5	Somerset	4	3	1	0	6
Northamptonshire	4	1	1	2	4	Essex	4	2	2	0	4
Gloucestershire	4	1	2	1	3	Glamorgan	4	1	2	1	3
Worcestershire	4	0	4	0	0	Combined U	4	0	3	1	1
Group B						Group D					
Yorkshire	4	3	0	1	7	Sussex	4	3	0	1	7
Warwickshire	4	2	1	1	5	Surrey	4	1	1	2	4
Derbyshire	4	2	1	1	5	Hampshire	4	1	2	1	3
Lancashire	4	1	2	1	3	Middlesex	4	0	1	3	3
Scotland	4	0	4	0	0	Minor Counties	4	1	2	1	3

QUARTER-FINALS – 24 JUNE
Notts v Surrey at Trent Bridge
Surrey 226-7 in 55 overs
Nottinghamshire 179 in 49.4 overs
Result: Surrey won by 47 runs
Gold Award: R.D.V. Knight

Yorkshire v Somerset at Headingley
Somerset 223-7 in 53.5 overs
Yorkshire 221-9 in 55 overs
Result: Somerset won by 3 wickets
Gold Award: B.C. Rose

24 & 25 JUNE

Sussex v Leicestershire at Hove
Leicestershire 199-6 in 54.1 overs
Sussex 196-9 in 55 overs
Result: Leicestershire won by 4
wickets
Gold Award: C.P. Phillipson

Kent v Warwickshire at Canterbury
No play, transferred to The Oval

26 JUNE

Kent v Warwickshire at The Oval
Kent 193-8 in 50 overs
Warwickshire 179 in 49.1 overs
Result: Kent won by 14 runs
Gold Award: C.J. Tavaré

SEMI-FINALS – 8 JULY

Surrey v Leicestershire at The Oval
Surrey 191-9 in 55 overs
Leicestershire 188 in 54.5 overs
Result: Surrey won by 3 runs
Gold Award: I.R. Payne

Somerset v Kent at Taunton
Kent 154 in 52.1 overs
Somerset 157-5 in 48.3 overs
Result: Somerset won by 5 wickets
Gold Award: N.F.M. Popplewell

THE BENSON & HEDGES CUP FINAL
PLAYED AT LORD'S, 25 JULY
SOMERSET WON BY 7 WICKETS

SURREY

G.S. Clinton	c Roebuck b Marks	6
C.J. Richards	b Garner	1
R.D.V. Knight	c Taylor b Garner	92
G.P. Howarth	c Roebuck b Marks	16
M.A. Lynch	c Garner b Popplewell	22
D.M. Smith	b Garner	7
S.T. Clarke	c Popplewell b Garner	15
G.R.J. Roope	not out	14
D.J. Thomas	b Garner	0
R.D. Jackman	not out	2
P.I. Pocock	did not bat	
Extras (B2, LB14, W2, NB1)		19
Total (55 overs) (8 wkts)		194

SOMERSET

B.C. Rose	b Jackman	5
P.W. Denning	b Clarke	0
I.V.A. Richards	not out	132
P.M. Roebuck	c Smith b Knight	22
I.T. Botham	not out	37
V.J. Marks	did not bat	
N.F.M. Popplewell	did not bat	
D. Breakwell	did not bat	
J. Garner	did not bat	
D.J.S. Taylor	did not bat	
C.H. Dredge	did not bat	
Extras (NB1)		1
Total (44.3 overs) (3 wkts)		197

Gold Award: I.V.A. Richards.

BOWLING

SOMERSET	O	M	R	W	FALL OF WICKETS		
						SUR	SOM
Garner	11	5	14	5			
Botham	11	2	44	0	1st	4	5
Dredge	11	0	48	0	2nd	16	5
Marks	11	5	24	2	3rd	63	110
Popplewell	11	0	45	1	4th	98	—
SURREY					5th	132	—
Clarke	8	1	24	1	6th	166	—
Jackman	11	1	53	1	7th	182	—
Thomas	5.3	0	32	0	8th	183	—
Pocock	11	1	46	0	9th	—	—
Knight	9	0	41	1	10th	—	—

BENSON & HEDGES CUP
PRINCIPAL RECORDS

Highest innings total: 350-3 off 55 overs, Essex v Combined Universities (Chelmsford) 1979.

Highest innings total by a side batting second: 291-5 off 53.5 overs, Warwickshire v Lancashire (Manchester) 1981.

Highest innings total by a side batting first and losing: 288-9 off 55 overs, Lancashire v Warwickshire (Manchester) 1981.

Lowest completed innings total: 61 off 26 overs, Sussex v Middlesex (Hove) 1978.

Highest individual innings: 173* C.G. Greenidge, Hampshire v Minor Counties (South) (Amersham) 1973.

82 centuries have been scored in the competition.

Record Wicket Partnership

1st	241	S.M. Gavaskar & B.C. Rose, Somerset v Kent (Canterbury)	1980
2nd	285*	C.G. Greenidge & D.R. Turner, Hampshire v Minor Counties (South) (Amersham)	1973
3rd	227	M.E.J.C. Norman & B.F. Davison, Leicestershire v Warwickshire (Coventry)	1972
	227	D. Lloyd & F.C. Hayes, Lancashire v Minor Counties (North) (Manchester)	1973
4th	184*	D. Lloyd & B.W. Reidy, Lancashire v Derbyshire (Chesterfield)	1980
5th	134	M. Maslin & D.N.F. Slade, Minor Counties (East) v Nottinghamshire (Nottingham)	1976
6th	114	M.J. Khan & G.P. Ellis, Glamorgan v Gloucestershire (Bristol)	1975
7th	149*	J.D. Love & C.M. Old, Yorkshire v Scotland (Bradford)	1977
8th	109	R.E. East & N. Smith, Essex v Northamptonshire (Chelmsford)	1977
9th	81	J.N. Shepherd & D.L. Underwood, Kent v Middlesex (Lord's)	1975
10th	80*	D.L. Bairstow & M. Johnson, Yorkshire v Derbyshire (Derby)	1981

Hat-tricks: G.D. McKenzie, Leicestershire v Worcestershire (Worcester) 1972. K. Higgs, Leicestershire v Surrey (Lord's) 1974. A.A. Jones, Middlesex v Essex (Lord's) 1977. M.J. Procter, Gloucestershire v Hampshire (Southampton) 1977. W. Larkins, Northamptonshire v Combined Universities (Northampton) 1980. E.A. Moseley, Glamorgan v Kent (Cardiff) 1981.

Seven wickets in an innings: 7-12 W.W. Daniel, Middlesex v Minor Counties (East) (Ipswich) 1978, 7-22 J.R. Thomson, Middlesex v Hampshire (Lord's) 1981, 7-32 R.G.D. Willis, Warwickshire v Yorkshire (Birmingham) 1981.

Most 'Gold' awards: 10 B. Wood (all for Lancashire), 9 J.H. Edrich (Surrey).

BENSON & HEDGES CUP WINNERS

1972 Leicestershire	1977 Gloucestershire
1973 Kent	1978 Kent
1974 Surrey	1979 Essex
1975 Leicestershire	1980 Northamptonshire
1976 Kent	1981 Somerset

ESSEX WIN THE JOHN PLAYER

Essex, who went a very long time without winning anything, did a double in 1979 when they won the Schweppes County Championship and the Benson & Hedges Cup; now, in 1981, they have added the John Player League Championship to their laurels. They never did win the Gillette Cup or even reach a Final, but presumably now they will be turning their attention to the NatWest Bank Trophy. It is interesting that Essex won the John Player without a single representative in the first dozen, batting or bowling, in the averages. Keith Fletcher explained that their success was totally a team effort and not dependent on one or two key players. Overseas players figure prominently in the records but at least there was some consolation for those who believe that one-day cricket is eliminating spinners. Underwood, Hemmings and Pocock were the first nine in the averages conceding at no more than 3.6 an over. Essex, fourteenth the previous season, were, no doubt, surprising winners. In reverse, Middlesex sank from third place in 1980 to fifteenth. Northants took a tumble, too, from sixth to seventeenth, losing eleven games, by far the worst record. Zaheer made the highest score of the season with 129 not out against Middlesex at Lord's and Colin Tunnicliffe's 5 for 24 was the best bowling for Derbyshire against Northants.

JOHN PLAYER LEAGUE FINAL TABLE

	P	W	L	NR	TIE	Pts
Essex (14)	16	12	3	1	0	50
Somerset (2)	16	11	5	0	0	44
Warwickshire (1)	16	10	4	2	0	44
Derbyshire (6)	16	10	5	1	0	42
Sussex (9)	16	8	5	3	0	38
Hampshire (11)	16	8	7	1	0	34
Kent (11)	16	7	7	1	1	32
Surrey (5)	16	7	7	2	0	32
Yorkshire (14)	16	6	6	4	0	32
Glamorgan (17)	16	6	8	2	0	28
Lancashire (13)	16	6	8	1	1	28
Nottinghamshire (14)	16	6	8	2	0	28
Worcestershire (6)	16	7	9	0	0	28
Leicestershire (4)	16	5	9	2	0	24
Middlesex (3)	16	4	9	3	0	22
Gloucestershire (10)	16	3	9	4	0	20
Northamptonshire (6)	16	4	11	1	0	18

1980 positions in brackets

JOHN PLAYER LEAGUE
PRINCIPAL RECORDS

Highest innings total: 307-4 off 38 overs. Worcs v Derbyshire (Worcester) 1975.

Highest innings total by a side batting second: 261-8 off 39.1 overs. Warwickshire v Nottinghamshire (Birmingham) 1976; 261 off 36.2 overs, Worcestershire v Sussex (Horsham) 1980.

Highest innings total by a side batting first and losing: 260-5 off 40 overs, Nottinghamshire v Warwickshire (Birmingham) 1976.

Lowest completed innings total: 23 off 19.4 overs, Middlesex v Yorkshire (Leeds) 1974.

Highest individual innings: 163* C.G. Greenidge, Hampshire v Warwickshire (Birmingham) 1979.

168 centuries have been scored in the League.

Record Wicket Partnerships

1st	218	A.R. Butcher & G.P. Howarth, Surrey v Glos (Oval)	1976
2nd	179	B.W. Luckhurst & M.H. Denness, Kent v Somerset (Canterbury)	1973
3rd	188	A.J. Lamb & R.G. Williams, Northamptonshire v Worcestershire (Worcester)	1981
4th	175	M.J.K. Smith & D.L. Amiss, Warwickshire v Yorkshire (Birmingham)	1970
5th	163	A.G.E. Ealham & B.D. Julien, Kent v Leicestershire (Leicester)	1977
6th	121	C.P. Wilkins & A.J. Borrington, Derbyshire v Warwickshire (Chesterfield)	1972
7th	101	S.J. Windaybank & D.A. Graveney, Gloucestershire v Nottinghamshire (Nottingham)	1981
8th	95*	D. Breakwell & K.F. Jennings, Somerset v Nottinghamshire (Nottingham)	1976
9th	86	D.P. Hughes & P. Lever, Lancashire v Essex (Leyton)	1973
10th	57	D.A. Graveney & J.B. Mortimore, Gloucestershire v Lancashire (Tewkesbury)	1973

Four wickets in four balls: A. Ward, Derbyshire v Sussex (Derby) 1970.

Hat-tricks (excluding above): R. Palmer, Somerset v Gloucestershire (Bristol) 1970. K.D. Boyce, Essex v Somerset (Westcliff) 1971. G.D. McKenzie, Leicestershire v Essex (Leicester) 1972. R.G.D. Willis, Warwickshire v Yorkshire (Birmingham) 1973. W. Blenkiron, Warwickshire v Derbyshire (Buxton) 1974. A. Buss, Sussex v Worcestershire (Hastings) 1974. J.M. Rice, Hampshire v Northamptonshire (Southampton) 1975. M.A. Nash, Glamorgan v Worcestershire (Worcester) 1975. A. Hodgson, Northamptonshire v Sussex (Northampton) 1976. A.E. Cordle, Glamorgan v Hampshire (Portsmouth) 1979. C.J. Tunnicliffe, Derbyshire v Worcestershire (Derby) 1979. M.D. Marshall, Hampshire v Surrey (Southampton) 1981.

Eight wickets in an innings: 8-26 K.D. Boyce, Essex v Lancashire (Manchester) 1971.

JOHN PLAYER LEAGUE CHAMPIONS

1969	Lancashire	1976	Kent
1970	Lancashire	1977	Leicestershire
1971	Worcestershire	1978	Hampshire
1972	Kent	1979	Somerset
1973	Kent	1980	Warwickshire
1974	Leicestershire	1981	Essex
1975	Hampshire		

NOTTS, AT LAST!
ARE COUNTY CHAMPIONS

Nottinghamshire were Schweppes County Champions in 1981 for the first time since 1929, when they won the Championship (no Schweppes then!) with such players as Harold Larwood and Bill Voce, George Gunn and Arthur Carr. Sussex, who have never won the County Championship, were Runners-Up as they were in 1902, 1903, 1932, 1933, 1934, and 1953. So it will be seen that in three successive years they were in second place to Yorkshire, twice, and Lancashire. Now, it's Notts for a change. Somerset were third, and like Sussex they have never won the Championship and, moreover, have never been Runners-Up; they were third in 1892, 1958, 1963 and 1966. Middlesex, in fourth place, are steeped in Championship honours – Champions seven times and Joint-Champions twice.

It was Stuart Surridge during his successful reign as Captain of Surrey who was always quoted as saying that 'Bowlers win matches'. With Bedser, Loader, Lock and Laker it was not difficult to appreciate his point, which could apply again to Notts. Hadlee 105 Championship wickets at 14.89; Rice 65 at 19.20 and Hemmings 84 at 20.71. Of course they had batting, too. The remarkable Rice, tremendous all-rounder, who headed their batting averages with 1462 runs at an average of 56.23, and Randall, almost the forgotten man of English Test cricket, scored 1093 at 45.54. Overall, six Notts players scored Championship centuries, making a total of thirteen hundreds during the Championship season. No-one, anywhere, not even in sixteen other Counties could begrudge Notts their success. Many have a great affection for their wonderful old ground at Trent Bridge which for years was the best pitch in England (or anywhere else for that matter) and success is long overdue here.

Sussex did not quite have the bowling resources, though in LeRoux, Ian Greig and Imran Khan they were not very far behind. Greig had a particularly good season with 60 wickets at 21.06 and a batting average of 30.34. John Barclay, the Captain, was not as successful with his off-spin as he might have been – his 28 wickets costing him nearly 30 apiece. Paul Parker with the highly commendable average of 55.08 had his best season and was suitably rewarded.

If we are talking about successes, the lesser performance of Hampshire in coming seventh is worthy of mention since in 1980 they were seventeenth. Greenidge, of course, dominated their batting, and Marshall, the other West Indian, their bowling, but it was a greatly improved performance all round. Kent had a disappointing season, though even that was an improvement on 1980 when they finished sixteenth; this time they were ninth, so mathematically still in the bottom half of the table.

It is perhaps surprising to look at the bottom three – Northamptonshire, Lancashire and Warwickshire – and to think that the same three were very nearly in the same position last time, except that Hampshire, Glamorgan and Kent were beneath them. Every team in every sport suffers its periods of transition, though Lancashire and Warwickshire would seem to be going through this rather more than do Northants. The mighty Clive Lloyd still headed the Lancashire averages with 1324 runs at an average of 45.65, and Fowler and David Lloyd both scored over 1,000 runs, but the bowling lacked penetration. Holding bowled only 271.1 overs and took 40 wickets for 17.87. Allott bowled well to take 74 at 23.55, but behind this – some way behind – was Simmons with 28 at 25.17 and Lee with 24 wickets at 32.41. Warwickshire, too, suffered very much in the bowling department. Willis, missing so often, of course, bowled only 138.3 overs and took 13 wickets at 28.46, so your best bowler bowling just over 100 overs would be a severe handicap for any side. No other bowler had a bowling average of under 30 with Hogg taking most wickets; he took 50 but they cost 33.88. So for the fourth successive year the Championship has produced a different winner – Kent, Essex, Middlesex, Notts. What next?

SCHWEPPES COUNTY CHAMPIONSHIP FINAL TABLE

	P	W	L	D	Bonus points Bt	Bw	Pts
1—Nottinghamshire (3)	22	11	4	7	56	72	304
2—Sussex (4)	22	11	3	8	58	63	302
3—Somerset (5)	22	10	2	10	54	65	279
4—Middlesex (1)	22	9	3	10	49	64	257
5—Essex (8)	22	8	4	10	62	64	254
6—Surrey (2)	22	7	5	10	52	72	236
7—Hampshire (17)	22	6	7	9	45	64	206
8—Leicestershire (9)	22	6	6	10	45	58	199
9—Kent (16)	22	5	7	10	51	58	189
10—Yorkshire (6)	22	5	9	8	41	66	187
11—Worcestershire (11)	22	5	9	8	44	52	172
12—Derbyshire (9)	22	4	7	11	51	57	172
13—Gloucestershire (7)	22	4	3	15	51	55	170
14—Glamorgan (13)	22	3	10	9	50	69	167
15—Northamptonshire (12)	22	3	6	13	51	67	166
16—Lancashire (15)	22	4	7	11	47	57	164
17—Warwickshire (14)	22	2	11	9	56	47	135

1980 positions in brackets.
Worcestershire and Lancashire totals include 12pts for wins in matches reduced to 1 innings.

COUNTY CHAMPIONS

The earliest winners of the title were decided usually by the least matches lost. In 1888 an unofficial points table was introduced and in 1890 the Championship was constituted officially. Since 1977 it has been sponsored by Schweppes.

Year	County	Year	County	Year	County
1864	Surrey	1897	Lancashire	1946	Yorkshire
1865	Nottinghamshire	1898	Yorkshire	1947	Middlesex
1866	Middlesex	1899	Surrey	1948	Glamorgan
1867	Yorkshire	1900	Yorkshire	1949 {	Middlesex
1868	Nottinghamshire	1901	Yorkshire		Yorkshire
1869 {	Nottinghamshire	1902	Yorkshire	1950 {	Lancashire
	Yorkshire	1903	Middlesex		Surrey
1870	Yorkshire	1904	Lancashire	1951	Warwickshire
1871	Nottinghamshire	1905	Yorkshire	1952	Surrey
1872	Nottinghamshire	1906	Kent	1953	Surrey
1873 {	Gloucestershire	1907	Nottinghamshire	1954	Surrey
	Nottinghamshire	1908	Yorkshire	1955	Surrey
1874	Gloucestershire	1909	Kent	1956	Surrey
1875	Nottinghamshire	1910	Kent	1957	Surrey
1876	Gloucestershire	1911	Warwickshire	1958	Surrey
1877	Gloucestershire	1912	Yorkshire	1959	Yorkshire
1878	Undecided	1913	Kent	1960	Yorkshire
1879 {	Nottinghamshire	1914	Surrey	1961	Hampshire
	Lancashire	1919	Yorkshire	1962	Yorkshire
1880	Nottinghamshire	1920	Middlesex	1963	Yorkshire
1881	Lancashire	1921	Middlesex	1964	Worcestershire
1882 {	Nottinghamshire	1922	Yorkshire	1965	Worcestershire
	Lancashire	1923	Yorkshire	1966	Yorkshire
1883	Nottinghamshire	1924	Yorkshire	1967	Yorkshire
1884	Nottinghamshire	1925	Yorkshire	1968	Yorkshire
1885	Nottinghamshire	1926	Lancashire	1969	Glamorgan
1886	Nottinghamshire	1927	Lancashire	1970	Kent
1887	Surrey	1928	Lancashire	1971	Surrey
1888	Surrey	1929	Nottinghamshire	1972	Warwickshire
1889 {	Surrey	1930	Lancashire	1973	Hampshire
	Lancashire	1931	Yorkshire	1974	Worcestershire
	Nottinghamshire	1932	Yorkshire	1975	Leicestershire
1890	Surrey	1933	Yorkshire	1976	Middlesex
1891	Surrey	1934	Lancashire	1977 {	Kent
1892	Surrey	1935	Yorkshire		Middlesex
1893	Yorkshire	1936	Derbyshire	1978	Kent
1894	Surrey	1937	Yorkshire	1979	Essex
1895	Surrey	1938	Yorkshire	1980	Middlesex
1896	Yorkshire	1939	Yorkshire	1981	Nottinghamshire

THE COUNTIES AND
THEIR PLAYERS

Compiled by Michael Fordham

Abbreviations

B	Born	HSGC/	Highest score in
RHB	Right-hand bat	NW	former Gillette Cup if
LHB	Left-hand bat		higher than NatWest
RF	Right-arm fast		Trophy
RFM	Right-arm fast medium	HSJPL	Highest score John Player
RM	Right-arm medium		League
LF	Left-arm fast	HSBH	Highest score Benson &
LFM	Left-arm fast medium		Hedges Cup
LM	Left-arm medium	BB	Best bowling figures
OB	Off-break	BBUK	Best bowling figures in this
LB	Leg-break		country
LBG	Leg-break and googly	BBTC	Best bowling figures in Test
SLA	Slow left-arm orthodox		cricket if different from
SLC	Slow left-arm 'chinaman'		above
WK	Wicket-keeper	BBC	Best bowling figures for
*	Not out or unfinished stand		County if different from
HS	Highest score		above
HSUK	Highest score in this	BBNW	Best bowling figures
	country		NatWest Trophy
HSTC	Highest score in Test	BBGC/	Best bowling figures in
	cricket if different from	NW	former Gillette Cup if
	above		better than NatWest
HSC	Highest score for County if		Trophy
	different from highest	BBJPL	Best bowling figures John
	first-class score		Player League
HSNW	Highest score NatWest	BBBH	Best bowling figures Benson
	Trophy		& Hedges Cup

When a player is known by a name other than his first name, the name in question has been underlined.

All Test appearances are complete to 1st September 1981.

'Debut' denotes 'first-class debut' and 'Cap' means '1st XI county cap'.

Wisden 1981 indicates that a player was selected as one of *Wisden*'s Five Cricketers of the Year for his achievements in 1981.

Owing to the increasing number of privately arranged overseas tours of short duration, only those which may be regarded as major tours have been included.

DERBYSHIRE

Formation of present club: 1870.
Colours: Chocolate, amber, and pale blue.
Badge: Rose and crown.
County Champions: 1936.
NatWest Trophy Winners: 1981.
Gillette Cup Finalists: 1969.
Best final position in John Player League: 3rd in 1970.
Benson & Hedges Cup Finalists: 1978.
NatWest Trophy Man of the Match Awards: 3.
Gillette Man of the Match Awards: 15.
Benson & Hedges Gold Awards: 27.

Secretary: R. Pearman, County Cricket Ground,
Nottingham Road, Derby DE2 6DA.
Captain: B. Wood.
Prospects of Play Telephone No: Derby (0332) 44849.

Iain Stuart ANDERSON (Dovecliff GS and Wulfric School, Burton-on-Trent) B
Derby 24/4/1960. RHB, OB. Debut 1978. HS: 75 v Worcs (Worcester) 1978.
HSJPL: 21 v Middlesex (Lord's) 1978. BB: 4-35 v Australians (Derby) 1981.

Kim John BARNETT (Leek HS) B Stoke-on-Trent 17/7/1960. RHB, LB. Played
for county and Northants 2nd XIs and Staffordshire in 1976 and for Warwickshire
2nd XI in 1977 and 1978. Toured Australia with England under-19 team in 1978-79.
Debut 1979. NatWest Man of the Match Awards: 1. HS: 96 v Lancs (Chesterfield)
1979. HSNW: 59 v Essex (Derby) 1981. HSJPL: 48* v Lancs (Buxton) 1980. HSBH:
34 v Notts (Nottingham) 1980. BB: 4-76 v Warwickshire (Birmingham) 1980.
BBJPL: 3-39 v Yorks (Chesterfield) 1979.

Anthony John (Tony) BORRINGTON (Spondon Park GS) B Derby 8/12/1948.
RHB, LB. Played for MCC Schools at Lord's in 1967. Played in one John Player
League match in 1970. Debut 1971. Cap 1977. Played in one NatWest Trophy match
only in 1981. Benson & Hedges Gold Awards: 4. HS: 137 v Yorks (Sheffield) 1978.
HSGCNW: 29 v Somerset (Taunton) 1979. HSJPL: 101 v Somerset (Taunton) 1977.
HSBH: 81 v Notts (Nottingham) 1974. Trained as a teacher at Loughborough
College of Education.

Kevin Graham BROOKS (Clarks GS, Bristol, Monkseaton GS, Whitley Bay) B
Reading 15/10/1959. RHB, RM. Played for Hants 2nd XI 1979. Debut 1980. Played
in one Benson & Hedges Cup match and one John Player League match in 1981.
HS: 8 v Warwickshire (Birmingham) 1980. HSJPL: 12 v Lancs (Manchester) 1981.
HSBH: 10 v Notts (Nottingham) 1980.

Michael John DEAKIN (Priesthorpe School, Pudsey) B Bury (Lancs) 5/5/1957.
RHB, WK. Debut 1981 through absence of R.W. Taylor for Test Matches. HS: 15
v Somerset (Taunton) 1981.

Peter John HACKER B Lenton Abbey, Nottingham 16/7/1952. RHB, LFM.
Debut 1974. Played for Orange Free State in 1979-80 Castle Bowl competition. Cap
1980. Has joined Derbyshire for 1982. HS: 35 Notts v Kent (Canterbury) 1977. BB:
6-35 Notts v Hants (Nottingham) 1980. BBGC/NW: 4-30 Notts v Durham
(Nottingham) 1980. BBJPL: 6-16 Notts v Essex (Chelmsford) 1980.

John Harry HAMPSHIRE (Oakwood Technical HS, Rotherham) B Thurnscoe, Yorks 10/2/1941. Son of J. Hampshire who played for Yorks in 1937. RHB, LB. Debut for Yorks 1961. Cap 1963. Played for Tasmania in 1967-68, 1968-69, 1977-78 and 1978-79. Benefit (£28,425) in 1976. County captain in 1979 and 1980. Left county after 1981 season and has joined Derbyshire for 1982. Tests: 8 between 1969 and 1975. Scored 107 in his first Test v West Indies (Lord's) and is only English player to have scored a century on debut in Test cricket when this has occurred at Lord's. Tour: Australia and New Zealand 1970-71. 1,000 runs (14) – 1,596 runs (av. 53.20) in 1978 best. Gillette Man of Match Awards: 4. Benson & Hedges Gold Awards: 2. HS: 183* Yorks v Sussex (Hove) 1971. HSTC: 107 v West Indies (Lord's) 1969. HSGC/NW: 110 Yorks v Durham (Middlesbrough) 1978. HSJPL: 119 Yorks v Leics (Hull) 1971. HSBH: 85 Yorks v Warwickshire (Leeds) 1980. BB: 7-52 Yorks v Glamorgan (Cardiff) 1963).

Alan HILL (New Mills GS) B Buxworth (Derbyshire) 29/6/1950. RHB, OB. Joined staff 1969. Debut 1972. Cap 1976. Played for Orange Free State in 1976-77 Currie Cup competition. Gillette Man of the Match Awards: 1. Benson & Hedges Gold Awards: 1. 1,000 runs (2)—1,303 runs (av. 34.28) in 1976 best. HS: 160* v Warwickshire (Coventry) 1976. HSGC/NW: 72 v Middlesex (Derby) 1978. HSJPL: 120 v Northants (Buxton) 1976. HSBH: 102* v Warwickshire (Ilkeston) 1978. BB: 3-5 Orange Free State v Northern Transvaal (Pretoria) 1976-77.

Peter Noel KIRSTEN (South African College School, Cape Town) B Pietermaritzburg, Natal, South Africa 14/5/1955, RHB, OB. Debut for Western Province in Currie Cup 1973-74. Played for Sussex v Australians 1975 as well as playing for County 2nd XI. Played for Derbyshire 2nd XI in 1977 and made debut for County in 1978. Cap 1978. Scored 4 centuries in 4 consecutive innings and 6 in 7 innings including 2 in match—173* and 103 Western Province v Eastern Province (Cape Town) 1976-77. 1,000 runs (4)—1,895 runs (av. 63.16) in 1980 best. Also scored 1,074 runs (av. 76.71) in 1976-77. Scored 6 centuries (including 3 double centuries) in 1980 to equal county record. Shared 3rd wkt partnership record for county, 291 with D.S. Steele v Somerset (Taunton) 1981. NatWest Man of the Match Awards: 1. Benson & Hedges Gold Awards: 1. HS: 228 v Somerset (Taunton) 1981. HSNW: 84* v Worcs (Worcester) 1981. HSJPL: 102 v Glamorgan (Swansea) 1979. HSBH: 70 v Surrey (Derby) 1979. BB: 4-44 v Middlesex (Derby) 1979. BBJPL: 5-34 v Northants (Long Eaton) 1979.

Bernard Joseph Michael MAHER (Abbotsfield and Bishopshalt Schools, Hillingdon) B Hillingdon (Middlesex) 11/2/1958. RHB, WK. Played for Middlesex 2nd XI 1977. Debut 1981 through absence of R.W. Taylor for Test Match. Played two matches and one John Player League match. HS: 4* v Glos (Derby) 1981.

Geoffrey (Geoff) MILLER (Chesterfield GS) B Chesterfield 8/9/1952. RHB, OB. Toured India 1970-71 and West Indies 1972 with England Young Cricketers. Won Sir Frank Worrell Trophy as Outstanding Boy Cricketer of 1972. Debut 1973. Cap 1976. Elected Best Young Cricketer of the Year in 1976 by the Cricket Writers Club. Appointed county captain in 1979. Relinquished appointment in 1981. Tests: 25 between 1976 and 1980-81. Tours: India, Sri Lanka and Australia 1976-77, Pakistan and New Zealand 1977-78. Australia 1978-79, and 1979-80 (returning early through injury), West Indies 1980-81 (became vice-captain after return home of R.G.D. Willis). Benson & Hedges Gold Awards: 3. HS: 98* England v Pakistan (Lahore) 1977-78. HSUK: 95 v Lancs (Manchester) 1978. HSGC/NW: 59* v Worcs (Worcester) 1978. HSJPL: 84 v Somerset (Chesterfield) 1980. HSBH: 75 v

DERBYSHIRE

Warwickshire (Derby) 1977. BB: 7-54 v Sussex (Hove) 1977. BBTC: 5-44 v Australia (Sydney) 1978-79. BBJPL: 4-22 v Yorks (Huddersfield) 1978. BBBH: 3-23 v Surrey (Derby) 1979.

Dallas Gordon MOIR (Aberdeen GS) B Mtarfa, Malta 13/4/1957. 6ft 8ins tall. RHB, SLA. Debut for Scotland v Ireland 1980. Debut for county 1981. HS: 44 Scotland v Ireland (Coatbridge) 1980. HSC: 16 v Lancs (Blackpool) 1981. BB: 4-43 Scotland v Ireland (Coatbridge) 1980.

Paul Geoffrey NEWMAN (Alderman Newton's GS, Leicester) B Leicester 10/1/1959. RHB, RFM. Played for Leics 2nd XI in 1978 and 1979. Debut 1980. HS: 29* v Sussex (Derby) 1980. BB: 5-51 v Essex (Derby) 1981. BBNW: 3-23 v Notts (Derby) 1981. BBJPL: 4-30 v Sussex (Derby) 1980.

Stephen (Steve) OLDHAM B High Green, Sheffield 26/7/1948. RHB, RFM. Debut for Yorkshire 1974. Left county after 1979 season and made debut for Derbyshire in 1980. Cap 1980. Benson & Hedges Gold Awards: 1 (for Yorks). HS: 50 Yorks v Sussex (Hove) 1979. HSC: 33 v Kent (Derby) 1981. HSJPL: 38* Yorks v Glamorgan (Cardiff) 1977. BB: 5-40 Yorks v Surrey (Oval) 1978. BBC: 4-41 v Surrey (Derby) 1980. BBNW: 3-29 v Notts (Derby) 1981. BBJPL: 4-21 Yorks v Notts (Scarborough) 1974. BBBH: 5-32 Yorks v Minor Counties (North) (Scunthorpe) 1975.

Philip Edgar (Phil) RUSSELL (Ilkeston GS) B Ilkeston 9/5/1944. RHB, RM/OB. Debut 1965. Not re-engaged after 1972 season, but rejoined staff in 1974 and is now county coach. Cap 1975. Played in one Benson & Hedges Cup match and one John Player League match in 1980. Did not play in 1981. HS: 72 v Glamorgan (Swansea) 1970. HSGC/NW: 27* v Middlesex (Derby) 1978. HSJPL: 47* v Glamorgan (Buxton) 1975. HSBH: 22* v Lancs (Southport) 1976. BB: 7-46 v Yorks (Sheffield) 1976. BBGC/NW: 3-44 v Somerset (Taunton) 1975. BBJPL: 6-10 v Northants (Buxton) 1976. BBBH: 3-28 v Kent (Lord's) 1978.

Robert William (Bob) TAYLOR B Stoke 17/7/1941. RHB, WK. Played for Bignall End (N. Staffs and S. Cheshire League) when only 15 and for Staffordshire from 1958 to 1960. Debut 1960 for Minor Counties v South Africans (Stoke-on-Trent). Debut for county 1961. Cap 1962. Testimonial (£6,672) in 1973. Appointed county captain during 1975 season. Relinquished post during 1976 season. *Wisden* 1976. 2nd testimonial in 1981. Tests: 29 between 1970–71 and 1981. Tours: Australia and New Zealand 1970-71, 1974-75, Australia with Rest of the World team 1971-72, West Indies 1973-74, Pakistan and New Zealand 1977-78, Australia 1978-79, Australia and India 1979-80, India and Sri Lanka 1981-82. Withdrew from India, Sri Lanka and Pakistan tour 1972-73. Dismissed 80 batsmen (77 ct 3 st) in 1962, 83 batsmen (81 ct 2 st) in 1963, and 86 batsmen (79 ct 7 st) in 1965. Dismissed 7 batsmen in innings (equals Test record) and 10 batsmen in match (all caught) for Test record v India (Bombay) 1979-80. Dismissed 10 batsmen in match, all caught v Hants (Chesterfield) 1963 and 7 in innings, all caught v Glamorgan (Derby) 1966. Gillette Man of the Match Awards: 1. Benson & Hedges Gold Awards: 1. HS: 100 v Yorks (Sheffield) 1981. HSTC: 97 v Australia (Adelaide) 1978-79. HSGC/NW: 53* v Middlesex (Lord's) 1965. HSJPL: 43* v Glos (Burton-on-Trent) 1969. HSBH: 31* v Hants (Southampton) 1974. Awarded M.B.E. in 1981 Birthday Honours List.

Colin John TUNNICLIFFE B Derby 11/8/1951. RHB, LFM. Debut 1973. Left staff after 1974 season. Re-appeared in 1976. Cap 1977. Hat-trick in John Player League v Worcs (Derby) 1979. HS: 82* v Middlesex (Ilkeston) 1977. HSNW: 14* v Northants (Lord's) 1981. HSJPL: 42 v Yorks (Huddersfield) 1978. HSBH: 28 v

Warwickshire (Birmingham) 1979. BB: 7-36 v Essex (Chesterfield) 1980. BBNW: 5-50 v Worcs (Worcester) 1981. BBJPL: 5-24 v Northants (Derby) 1981. BBBH: 5-24 v Yorks (Derby) 1981.

Barry WOOD B Ossett (Yorks) 26/12/1942. RHB, RM. Brother of R. Wood who played occasionally for Yorkshire some years ago. Debut for Yorks 1964. Joined Lancs by special registration, making debut for county in 1966. Cap 1968. Played for Eastern Province in Currie Cup in 1971-72 and 1973-74. Testimonial (£62,429) in 1979. Left county after 1979 season and made debut for Derbyshire in 1980. Cap 1980. Appointed County Captain during 1981 season. Tests: 12 between 1972 and 1978. Tours: India, Pakistan and Sri Lanka 1972-73, New Zealand 1974-75 (flown out as reinforcement). 1,000 runs (7)—1,492 runs (av. 38.25) in 1971 best. Gillette Man of the Match Awards: 6 (for Lancs). Benson & Hedges Gold Awards: 10 (for Lancs). HS: 198 Lancs v Glamorgan (Liverpool) 1976. HSC: 153 v Worcs (Chesterfield) 1981. HSTC: 90 v Australia (Oval) 1972. HSGC/NW: 116 Lancs v Kent (Canterbury) 1979. HSJPL: 90* Lancs v Notts (Manchester) 1977 and 90* v Hants (Southampton) 1980. HSBH: 79 Lancs v Minor Counties (North) (Longton) 1975. BB: 7-52 Lancs v Middlesex (Manchester) 1968. BBC: 3-22 v Sussex (Derby) 1980. BBGC/NW: 4-17 Lancs v Hants (Manchester) 1975. BBJPL: 5-19 Lancs v Kent (Manchester) 1971. BBBH: 5-12 Lancs v Derbyshire (Stockport) 1976.

John Geoffrey WRIGHT (Christ's College, Christchurch and Otago University) B Darfield, New Zealand 5/7/1954. LHB, RM. Debut for Northern Districts in Shell Cup in 1975-76. Debut for county 1977. Cap 1977. Tests: 17 for New Zealand between 1977-78 and 1980-81. Tours: New Zealand to England 1978, Australia 1980-81. 1,000 runs (4) – 1,504 runs (av. 48.51) in 1980 best. Benson & Hedges Gold Awards: 3. HS: 166* v Lancs (Manchester) 1980. HSTC: 110 New Zealand v India (Auckland) 1980-81. HSGC/NW: 87* v Sussex (Hove) 1977. HSJPL: 92* v Worcs (Worcester) 1980. HSBH: 102 v Worcs (Chesterfield) 1977.

N.B. The following player whose particulars appeared in the 1980 Annual has been omitted: J. Walters (left staff through injury).

In addition M. Hendrick and D.S. Steele have joined Nottinghamshire and Northamptonshire respectively and their particulars will be found under those counties.

County Averages

Schweppes County Championship: Played 22, won 4, drawn 10, lost 7, abandoned 1. All first-class matches: Played 23, won 4, drawn 11, lost 7, abandoned 1.

BATTING AND FIELDING

Cap		M	I	NO	Runs	HS	Avge	100	50	Ct	St
1978	P.N. Kirsten	21	35	6	1605	228	55.34	3	7	11	—
1980	B. Wood	22	37	6	1439	153	46.41	3	8	13	—
1977	J.G. Wright	20	32	1	1257	150	40.34	4	6	9	—
1976	A. Hill	22	32	8	940	107	39.16	2	5	6	—
1979	D.S. Steele	21	32	3	902	137	31.10	1	5	15	—
—	K.J. Barnett	17	23	4	443	67*	23.31	—	3	11	—
1976	G. Miller	21	31	3	552	81	19.71	—	5	19	—

DERBYSHIRE

Cap		M	I	NO	Runs	HS	Avge	100	50	Ct	St
1962	R.W. Taylor	16	16	4	236	100	19.66	1	—	33	12
1972	M. Hendrick	11	9	3	81	21	13.50	—	—	8	—
1977	C.J. Tunnicliffe	21	25	1	246	39	10.25	—	—	9	—
1980	S. Oldham	15	14	5	92	33	10.22	—	—	3	—
—	I.S. Anderson	11	15	4	96	44	8.72	—	—	8	—
—	D.G. Moir	3	4	1	26	16	8.66	—	—	—	—
—	P.G. Newman	15	15	4	93	27	8.45	—	—	5	—
—	M.J. Deakin	4	6	0	45	15	7.50	—	—	9	—

Played in two matches: B.J.M. Maher 4*, 0, 2 (6 ct 2 st).

BOWLING

	Type	O	M	R	W	Avge	Best	5 wI	10 wM
D.S. Steele	SLA	403	141	1019	46	22.15	7-53	4	—
P.G. Newman	RFM	341.5	63	1143	47	24.31	5-51	1	—
M. Hendrick	RFM	325.2	91	792	30	26.40	5-41	1	—
I.S. Anderson	OB	73	16	257	7	36.71	4-35	—	—
C.J. Tunnicliffe	LFM	499.2	111	1563	42	37.21	5-34	3	—
G. Miller	OB	466.2	137	1281	33	38.81	4-27	—	—
S. Oldham	RFM	314.2	55	1025	23	44.56	3-35	—	—
B. Wood	RM	254.3	58	815	17	47.94	2-12	—	—

Also bowled: K.J. Barnett 117.3-21-435-4; A. Hill 1.1-0-5-0; P.N. Kirsten 32-6-98-2; D.G. Moir 62.2-14-203-2; J.G. Wright 2-1-4-0.

County Records

First-class cricket

Highest innings	For	645 v Hampshire (Derby)	1898
totals:	Agst	662 by Yorkshire (Chesterfield)	1898
Lowest innings	For	16 v Nottinghamshire (Nottingham)	1879
totals:	Agst	23 by Hampshire (Burton-on-Trent)	1958
Highest indi-	For	274 G. Davidson v Lancashire (Manchester)	1896
vidual innings:	Agst	343* P.A. Perrin for Essex (Chesterfield)	1904
Best bowling	For	10-40 W. Bestwick v Glamorgan (Cardiff)	1921
in an innings:	Agst	10-74 T.F. Smailes for Yorkshire (Sheffield)	1939
Best bowling	For	16-84 C. Gladwin v Worcs (Stourbridge)	1952
in a match:	Agst	16-101 G. Giffen for Australians (Derby)	1886
Most runs in a season:		2165 (av. 48.1) D.B. Carr	1959
runs in a career:		20516 (av. 31.41) D. Smith	1927-1952
100s in a season:		6 by L.F. Townsend	1933
		6 by P.N. Kirsten	1980
100s in a career:		30 by D. Smith	1927-1952
wickets in a season:		168 (av. 19.55) T.B. Mitchell	1935
wickets in a career:		1670 (av. 17.11) H.L. Jackson	1947-1963

RECORD WICKET STANDS

1st	322	H. Storer & J. Bowden v Essex (Derby)	1929
2nd	349	C.S. Elliot & J.D. Eggar v Notts (Nottingham)	1947
3rd	291	P.N. Kirsten & D.S. Steele v Somerset (Taunton)	1981
4th	328	P. Vaulkhard & D. Smith v Notts (Nottingham)	1946
5th	203	C.P. Wilkins & I.R. Buxton v Lancashire (Manchester)	1971
6th	212	G.M. Lee & T.S. Worthington v Essex (Chesterfield)	1932
7th	241*	G.H. Pope & A.E.G. Rhodes v Hampshire (Portsmouth)	1948
8th	182	A.H.M. Jackson & W. Carter v Leicestershire (Leicester)	1922
9th	283	A.R. Warren & J. Chapman v Warwickshire (Blackwell)	1910
10th	93	J. Humphries & J. Horsley v Lancashire (Derby)	1914

One-day cricket

Highest innings totals:	NatWest Trophy	270–6 v Suffolk (Bury St. Edmund's)	1981
	John Player League	260–6 v Glos (Derby)	1972
	Benson & Hedges Cup	225–6 v Notts (Nottingham)	1974
Lowest innings totals:	Gillette Cup/NatWest Trophy	79 v Surrey (Oval)	1967
	John Player League	70 v Surrey (Derby)	1972
	Benson & Hedges Cup	102 v Yorks (Bradford)	1975
Highest individual innings:	NatWest Trophy	89* D.S. Steele v Suffolk (Bury St. Edmund's)	1981
	John Player League	120 A. Hill v Northants (Buxton)	1976
	Benson & Hedges Cup	111* P.J. Sharpe v Glamorgan (Chesterfield)	1976
Best bowling figures:	Gillette Cup/NatWest Trophy	6–18 T.J.P. Eyre v Sussex (Chesterfield)	1969
	John Player League	6–7 M. Hendrick v Notts (Nottingham)	1972
	Benson & Hedges Cup	6–33 E.J. Barlow v Glos (Bristol)	1978

ESSEX

Formation of present club: 1876.
Colours: Blue, gold and red.
Badge: Three seaxes with word 'Essex' underneath.
County Champions: 1979.
Gillette Cup semi-finalists: 1978.
NatWest Trophy semi-finalists: 1981
John Player League Champions: 1981.
Benson & Hedges Cup winners: 1979.
Benson & Hedges Cup Finalists: 1980.
Gillette Man of the Match Awards: 14.
NatWest Trophy Man of the Match Awards: 3.
Benson & Hedges Gold Awards: 30.

Secretary: P.J. Edwards, The County Ground, New Writtle Street, Chelmsford CM2 0PG.
Captain: K.W.R. Fletcher.
Prospects of Play Telephone No: Chelmsford matches only. Chelmsford (0245) 66794.

David Laurence ACFIELD (Brentwood School & Cambridge) B Chelmsford 24/7/1947. RHB, OB. Debut 1966. Blue 1967-68. Cap 1970. Benefit in 1981. HS: 42 Cambridge U v Leics (Leicester) 1967. HSC: 38 v Notts (Chelmsford) 1973. BB: 8-55 v Kent (Canterbury) 1981. BBJPL: 5-14 v Northants (Northampton) 1970. Also obtained Blue for fencing (sabre). Has appeared in internationals in this sport and represented Great Britain in Olympic Games at Mexico City and Munich. Obtained degree in History.

David Edward EAST (Hackney Downs School) B Clapton 27/7/1959. No relation to R.E. East. RHB, WK. Played for 2nd XI in 1976 and 1977 and for Northants 2nd XI in 1980. Debut 1981. NatWest Man of the Match Awards: 1. HS: 28 v Northants (Southend) 1981. HSNW: 18 v Derbyshire (Derby) 1981. Studied at University of East Anglia.

Raymond Eric (Ray) EAST B Manningtree (Essex) 20/6/1947. RHB, SLA. Debut 1965. Cap 1967. Benefit (£29,000) in 1978. Hat-trick: The Rest v MCC Tour XI (Hove) 1973. Benson & Hedges Gold Awards: 3. HS: 113 v Hants (Chelmsford) 1976. HSGC/NW: 38* v Glos (Chelmsford) 1973. HSJPL: 25* v Glamorgan (Colchester) 1976. HSBH: 54 v Northants (Chelmsford) 1977. BB: 8-30 v Notts (Ilford) 1977. BBGC/NW: 4-28 v Herts (Hitchin) 1976. BBJPL: 6-18 v Yorks (Hull) 1969. BBBH: 5-33 v Kent (Chelmsford) 1975.

Keith William Robert FLETCHER B Worcester 20/5/1944. RHB, LB. Debut 1962. Cap 1963. Appointed county vice-captain in 1971 and county captain in 1974. Benefit (£13,000) in 1973. *Wisden* 1974. Testimonial in 1982. Tests: 52 between 1968 and 1976-77. Also played in 4 matches v Rest of the World in 1970. Tours: Pakistan 1966-67, Ceylon and Pakistan 1968-69, Australia and New Zealand, 1970-71, 1974-75, India, Sri Lanka and Pakistan 1972-73, West Indies 1973-74, India, Sri Lanka and Australia 1976-77, India and Sri Lanka 1981-82 (captain). 1,000 runs (17)—1,890 runs (av. 41.08) in 1968 best. Scored two centuries in match (111 and 102*) v Notts (Nottingham) 1976. Gillette Man of the Match Awards: 1. Benson & Hedges Gold Awards: 5. HS: 228* v Sussex (Hastings) 1968. HSTC: 216 v New Zealand (Auckland) 1974-75. HSGC/NW: 74 v Notts (Nottingham) 1969. HSJPL: 99* v

74

Notts (Ilford) 1974. HSBH: 90 v Surrey (Oval) 1974. BB: 5-41 v Middlesex (Colchester) 1979.

Neil Alan FOSTER (Philip Morant School, Colchester) B Colchester 6/5/1962. 6ft. 3in. tall. RHB, RM. Played for 2nd XI in 1979. Toured West Indies with England Young Cricketers 1980. Debut 1980. One match v Kent (Ilford) and played one match in 1981 v Cambridge U (Cambridge). HS: 8* v Kent (Ilford) 1980 and 8* v Cambridge U (Cambridge) 1981. BB: 3-51 v Kent (Ilford) 1980.

Christopher GLADWIN (Langdon School, Newham) B East Ham 10/5/1962. LHB, RM. Played for 2nd XI from 1978. Toured West Indies with England Young Cricketers 1980. Debut 1981. One match v Lancs (Southend). HS: 53 v Lancs (Southend) 1981.

Graham Alan GOOCH (Norlington Junior HS, Leyton) B Leytonstone 23/7/1953. Cousin of G.J. Saville, former Essex player and assistant secretary of club. RHB, RM. Toured West Indies with England Young Cricketers 1972. Debut 1973. Cap 1975. *Wisden* 1979. Tests: 35 between 1975 and 1980. Tours: Australia 1978-79, Australia and India 1979-80, West Indies 1980-81, India and Sri Lanka 1981-82. 1,000 runs (5)—1,437 runs (av. 47.90) in 1980 best. Shared 2nd wicket partnership record for county, 321 with K.S. McEwan v Northants (Ilford) 1978. Scored record aggregate of runs in limited overs competitions in 1979 – 1,137 runs (av. 54.14). NatWest Man of the Match Awards: 1. Benson & Hedges Gold Awards: 7. HS: 205 v Cambridge U (Cambridge) 1980. HSTC: 153 v West Indies (Kingston) 1980-81. HSNW: 101 v Herts (Hitchin) 1981. HSJPL: 100 v Yorks (Chelmsford) 1981. HSBH: 138 v Warwickshire (Chelmsford) 1979 and 138 v Somerset (Chelmsford) 1981. BB: 5-40 v West Indians (Chelmsford) 1976. BBJPL: 3-14 v Derbyshire (Derby) 1978.

Brian Ross HARDIE (Larbert HS) B Stenhousemuir 14/1/1950. RHB, RM. Has played for Stenhousemuir in East of Scotland League. Debut for Scotland 1970. His father and elder brother K.M. Hardie have also played for Scotland. Debut for Essex by special registration in 1973. Cap 1974. 1,000 (6) – 1,522 runs (av. 43.48) in 1975 best. Scored two centuries in match for Scotland v MCC, Aberdeen 1971, a match not regarded as first-class. HS: 162 v Warwickshire (Birmingham) 1975. HSGC/NW: 83 v Staffs (Stone) 1976. HSJPL: 108* v Yorks (Chelmsford) 1981. HSBH: 53 v Glos (Bristol) 1981.

Robert James LEIPER (Chigwell School) B Woodford Green (Essex) 30/8/1961. Son of J.M. Leiper who played for county in 1950. LHB, RM. Played for 2nd XI since 1977. Toured India in 1977 and West Indies in 1980 with England Young Cricketers. Debut 1981. One match v Australians (Chelmsford). HS: 49 v Australians (Chelmsford) 1981.

John Kenneth LEVER B Stepney 24/2/1949. RHB, LFM. Debut 1967. Cap 1970. *Wisden* 1978. Benefit (£66,110) in 1980. Tests: 18 between 1976-77 and 1980. Tours: India, Sri Lanka and Australia 1976-77, Pakistan and New Zealand 1977-78, Australia 1978-79, Australia and India 1979-80, India and Sri Lanka 1981-82. 100 wkts (2) – 106 wkts (av. 15.18) in 1978 and 106 wkts (av. 17.30) in 1979. Gillette Man of the Match Awards: 3, NatWest Man of the Match Awards: 1. Benson & Hedges Gold Awards: 1 HS: 91 v Glamorgan (Cardiff) 1970. HSTC: 53 v India (Delhi) 1976-77 (on debut). HSNW: 10* v Sussex (Hove) 1981. HSJPL: 23 v Worcs (Worcester) 1974. HSBH: 12* v Warwickshire (Birmingham) 1975. BB: 8-49 (13-87 match) v Warwickshire (Birmingham) 1979 and 8-49 v Yorks (Leeds) 1981. BBTC: 7-46 v India (Delhi) 1976-77 (on debut). BBGC/NW: 5-8 v Middlesex (Westcliff)

ESSEX

1972. BBJPL: 5-13 v Glamorgan (Ebbw Vale) 1975. BBBH: 5-16 v Middlesex (Chelmsford) 1976.

Alan William LILLEY (Caterham Secondary High School, Ilford) B Ilford 8/5/1959. RHB, WK. Debut 1978. Scored century in second innings of debut match v Notts (Nottingham). Benson & Hedges Gold Awards: 1 HS: 100* v Notts (Nottingham) 1978. HSNW: 40 v Glos (Bristol) 1981. HJPL: 60 v Northants (Chelmsford) 1980. HSBH: 119 v Combined Universities (Chelmsford) 1979.

Kenneth Scott (Ken) McEWAN (Queen's College, Queenstown) B Bedford, Cape Province, South Africa 16/7/1952. RHB, OB. Debut for Eastern Province in 1972-73 Currie Cup competition. Played for T.N. Pearce's XI v West Indians (Scarborough) 1973. Debut for county and cap 1974. *Wisden* 1977. Played for Western Australia in 1979-80 and 1980-81. 1,000 runs (8) — 1,821 runs (av. 49.21) in 1976 best. Scored 4 consecutive centuries in 1977 including two centuries in match (102 and 116) v Warwickshire (Birmingham). Shared 2nd wicket partnership record for county. 321 with G.A. Gooch v Northants (Ilford) 1978. Gillette Man of the Match Awards: 1. Benson & Hedges Gold Awards: 5. HS: 218 v Sussex (Chelmsford) 1977. HSGC/NW: 119 v Leics (Leicester) 1980. HSJPL: 136 v Sussex (Hastings) 1980. HSBH: 133 v Notts (Chelmsford) 1978.

Norbert PHILLIP (Dominica GS, Roseau) B Bioche, Dominica 12/6/1948. RHB, RFM. Debut 1969-70 for Windward Islands v Glamorgan and has played subsequently for Combined Islands in Shell Shield competition. Debut for county and cap 1978. Tests: 9 for West Indies between 1977-78 and 1978-79. Tour: West Indies to India and Sri Lanka 1978-79. Had match double of 100 runs and 10 wickets (160 and 10-130), Combined Islands v Guyana (Georgetown) 1977-78. HS: 134 v Glos (Gloucester) 1978. HSTC: 47 West Indies v India (Calcutta) 1978-79. HSGC/NW: 45 v Surrey (Chelmsford) 1980. HSJPL: 83* v Northants (Milton Keynes) 1981. HSBH: 32* v Northants (Lord's) 1980 and 32 v Glamorgan (Swansea) 1981. BB: 6-33 v Pakistanis (Chelmsford) 1978. BBTC: 4-48 West Indies v India (Madras) 1978-79. BBNW: 3-12 v Glos (Bristol) 1981. BBJPL: 4-19 v Northants (Chelmsford) 1980. BBBH: 4-32 v Glamorgan (Chelmsford) 1980.

Keith Rupert PONT B Wanstead 16/1/1953. RHB, RM. Debut 1970. Cap 1976. Benson & Hedges Gold Awards: 2. HS: 113 v Warwickshire (Birmingham) 1973. HSGC/NW: 39 v Somerset (Taunton) 1978. HSJPL: 55* v Warwickshire (Birmingham) 1981. HSBH: 60* v Notts (Ilford) 1976. BB: 5-33 v Middlesex (Southend) 1980. BBJPL: 4-22 v Warwickshire (Birmingham) 1981. BBBH: 4-60 v Northants (Lord's) 1980.

Derek Raymond PRINGLE (Felsted School and Cambridge) B Nairobi, Kenya 18/9/1958. 6ft. 4½in. tall. Son of late Donald Pringle who played for East Africa in 1975 Prudential Cup. RHB, RM. Toured India with England Schools C.A. 1977-78. Debut 1978. Blue 1979-80-81. University captain for 1982. HS: 127* Camb U v Worcs (Cambridge) 1981. HSC: 50* v Cambridge U (Cambridge) 1978. HSNW: 17 v Sussex (Hove) 1981. HSJPL: 42* v Derbyshire (Chelmsford) 1981. HSBH: 58 Combined Universities v Essex (Chelmsford) 1979. BB: 6-90 Cambridge U. v Warwickshire (Cambridge) 1980. BBC: 3-34 v Glos (Gloucester) 1980. BBNW: 3-12 v Glos (Bristol) 1981. BBJPL: 3-29 v Hants (Southampton) 1981.

Gary Edward SAINSBURY (Beal HS, Ilford) B Wanstead 17/1/1958. RHB, LM. Played for 2nd XI since 1977. Debut 1979. Did not play in 1981. BB: 4-85 v Surrey (Oval) 1980. Obtained degree in Statistics at University of Bath.

Neil SMITH (Ossett GS) B Dewsbury 1/4/1949. RHB, WK. Debut for Yorks 1970. Debut for county by special registration in 1973. Cap 1975. HS: 126 v Somerset (Leyton) 1976. HSGC/NW: 12 v Leics (Southend) 1977. HSJPL: 60 v Middlesex (Lord's) 1980. HSBH: 61 v Northants (Chelmsford) 1977.

Stuart TURNER B Chester 18/7/1943. RHB, RFM. Debut 1965. Cap 1970. Played for Natal in 1976-77 and 1977-78 Currie Cup competition. Benefit (£37,288) in 1979. Hat-trick: v Surrey (Oval) 1971. Benson & Hedges Gold Awards: 1. HS: 121 v Somerset (Taunton) 1970. HSGC/NW: 50 v Lancs (Chelmsford) 1971. HSJPL: 87 v Worcs (Chelmsford) 1975. HSBH: 41* v Minor Counties (East) (Chelmsford) 1977. BB: 6-26 v Northants (Northampton) 1977. BBGC/NW: 3-16 v Glamorgan (Ilford) 1971. BBJPL: 5-35 v Hants (Chelmsford) 1978. BBBH: 4-19 v Combined Universities (Chelmsford) 1981.

NB The following players whose particulars appeared in the 1981 Annual have been omitted: R. Herbert (not re-engaged) and M.S.A. McEvoy (not re-engaged). The career record of McEvoy will be found elsewhere in this annual.

County Averages

Schweppes County Championship: Played 21, won 8, drawn 9, lost 4, abandoned 1. All first-class matches: Played 23, won 8, drawn 11, lost 4, abandoned 1.

BATTING AND FIELDING

Cap		M	I	NO	Runs	HS	Avge	100	50	Ct	St
1975	G.A. Gooch	10	19	0	1184	164	62.31	5	5	9	—
1963	K.W.R. Fletcher	18	29	4	1180	165*	47.20	4	5	18	—
1974	K.S. McEwan	22	37	1	1420	141	39.44	6	6	17	—
1970	S. Turner	20	30	10	782	73*	39.10	—	4	13	—
1974	B.R. Hardie	23	39	4	1339	129	38.25	3	7	17	—
—	A.W. Lilley	12	21	0	616	90	29.33	—	5	8	—
1976	K.R. Pont	16	27	3	692	89	28.83	—	5	5	—
1975	N. Smith	10	12	4	191	41	23.87	—	—	23	4
1978	N. Phillip	22	37	3	720	80*	21.81	—	3	10	—
—	M.S.A. McEvoy	11	19	0	367	56	19.31	—	3	10	—
—	D.R. Pringle	9	13	4	150	28	16.66	—	—	2	—
1967	R.E. East	20	25	4	333	47	15.85	—	—	9	—
—	D.E. East	13	17	3	144	28	10.28	—	—	21	5
1970	J.K. Lever	22	20	4	147	21	9.18	—	—	6	—
1970	D.L. Acfield	22	18	11	40	8*	5.71	—	—	5	—

Played in one match: N.A. Foster 8*; C. Gladwin 53; R.J. Leiper 1, 49.

BOWLING

	Type	O	M	R	W	Avge	Best	5 wI	10 wM
D.L. Acfield	OB	769.5	232	1719	76	22.61	8-55	4	1
J.K. Lever	LFM	680.5	149	2049	80	25.61	8-49	4	1
S. Turner	RFM	483	132	1203	44	27.34	5-55	1	—
R.E. East	SLA	680.2	190	1513	53	28.54	7-49	3	1
G.A. Gooch	RM	65	19	191	6	31.83	3-47	—	—
N. Phillip	RFM	521.1	87	1725	51	33.82	6-40	1	—
D.R. Pringle	RM	164	31	554	10	55.40	2-20	—	—

Also bowled: N.A. Foster 25-5-90-1; M.S.A. McEvoy 27-7-99-3; K.S. McEwan 9.5-1-66-0; K.R. Pont 45-10-137-1.

County Records

First-Class Cricket

Highest innings totals:	For	692 v Somerset (Taunton)	1895
	Agst	803-4 by Kent (Brentwood)	1934
Lowest innings totals	For	30 v Yorkshire (Leyton)	1901
	Agst	31 by Derbyshire (Derby) and by Yorkshire (Huddersfield)	1914 & 1935
Highest individual innings	For	343* P.A. Perrin v Derbyshire (Chesterfield)	1904
	Agst	332 W.H. Ashdown for Kent (Brentwood)	1934
Best bowling in an innings	For	10-32 H. Pickett v Leicestershire (Leyton)	1895
	Agst	10-40 E.G. Dennett for Gloucestershire (Bristol)	1906
Best bowling in a match	For	17-119 W. Mead v Hampshire (Southampton)	1895
	Agst	17-56 C.W.L. Parker for Glos (Gloucester)	1925
Most runs in a season:		2308 (av. 56.29) J. O'Connor	1934
runs in a career:		29162 (av. 36.18) P.A. Perrin	1896-1928
100s in a season:		9 by J. O'Connor and D.J. Insole	1934 & 1955
100s in a career:		71 by J. O'Connor	1921-1939
wickets in a season:		172 (av. 27.13) T.P.B. Smith	1947
wickets in a career		1611 (av. 26.26) T.P.B. Smith	1929-1951

RECORD WICKET STANDS

1st	270	A.V. Avery & T.C. Dodds v Surrey (Oval)	1946
2nd	321	G.A. Gooch & K.S. McEwan v Northamptonshire (Ilford)	1978
3rd	343	P.A. Gibb & R. Horsfall v Kent (Blackheath)	1951
4th	298	A.V. Avery & R. Horsfall v Worcestershire (Clacton)	1948
5th	287	C.T. Ashton & J. O'Connor v Surrey (Brentwood)	1934
6th	206	J.W.H.T. Douglas & J. O'Connor v Glos (Cheltenham)	1923
		B.R. Knight & R.A.G. Luckin v Middlesex (Brentwood)	1962
7th	261	J.W.H.T. Douglas & J. Freeman v Lancashire (Leyton)	1914
8th	263	D.R. Wilcox & R.M. Taylor v Warwickshire (Southend)	1946
9th	251	J.W.H.T. Douglas & S.N. Hare v Derbyshire (Leyton)	1921
10th	218	F.H. Vigar & T.P.B. Smith v Derbyshire (Chesterfield)	1947

One-day cricket

Highest innings totals:	Gillette Cup/NatWest Trophy	316-6 v Staffordshire (Stone)	1976
	John Player League	283-6 v Gloucestershire (Cheltenham)	1975
	Benson & Hedges Cup	350-3 v Combined Universities (Chelmsford)	1979
Lowest innings totals:	Gillette Cup/NatWest Trophy	100 v Derbyshire (Brentwood)	1965
	John Player League	69 v Derbyshire (Chesterfield)	1974
	Benson & Hedges Cup	123 v Kent (Canterbury)	1973
Highest individual innings:	Gillette Cup/NatWest Trophy	119 K.S. McEwan v Leicestershire (Leicester)	1980
	John Player League	136 K.S. McEwan v Sussex (Hastings)	1980
	Benson & Hedges Cup	138 G.A. Gooch v Warwickshire (Chelmsford)	1979
		138 G.A. Gooch v Somerset (Chelmsford)	1981
Best bowling figures:	Gillette Cup/NatWest Trophy	5-8 J.K. Lever v Middlesex (Westcliff)	1972
	John Player League	8-26 K.D. Boyce v Lancs (Manchester)	1971
	Benson & Hedges Cup	5-16 J.K. Lever v Middlesex (Chelmsford)	1976

GLAMORGAN

Formation of present club: 1888.
Colours: Blue and gold.
Badge: Gold daffodil.
County Champions (2): 1948 and 1969.
Gillette Cup finalists: 1977.
NatWest Trophy Second Round: 1981.
Best final position in John Player League: 8th in 1977.
Benson & Hedges Cup quarter-finalists (5): 1972, 1973, 1977, 1978 and 1979.
Gillette Man of the Match Awards: 13.
NatWest Man of the Match Awards: Nil.
Benson & Hedges Gold Awards: 22

Secretary: P.B. Clift, 6 High Street, Cardiff CF1 2PW.
Cricket Manager: T.W. Cartwright.
Captain: M.A. Nash.
Prospects of Play Telephone Nos: Cardiff (0222) 29956 or 387367
Swansea (0792) 466321

Stephen Royston BARWICK (Cwrt Sart and Dwr-y-Felin Comprehensive Schools, Neath) B Neath 6/9/1960. RHB, RM. Debut 1981. HS: 11* v Sussex (Hove) 1981. BBNW: 4-14 v Hants (Bournemouth) 1981. BBJPL: 3-39 v Sussex (Ebbw Vale) 1981. BBBH: 3-38 v Somerset (Taunton) 1981.

Simon Antony Brewis DANIELS (Sedbergh School) B Darlington 23/8/1958. 6ft 3ins tall. RHB, RFM. Played for Durham in 1979 and 1980 and also for Derbyshire 2nd XI in 1980. Debut 1981. HS: 10 v Middlesex (Lord's) and 10* v Leics (Cardiff) 1981. BB: 3-33 v Essex (Colchester) 1981. Studied at Newcastle-upon-Tyne Polytechnic.

Terry DAVIES B St Albans (Herts) 25//10/1960. 5ft 4ins tall. RHB, WK. Played for 2nd XI in 1978. Debut 1979. One match v Sri Lankans (Swansea). Did not play in 1980. Re-appeared against Sri Lankans (Cardiff) 1981.

Norman George FEATHERSTONE (King Edward VII High School, Johannesburg) B Que Que, Rhodesia 20/8/1949. RHB, OB. Debut for Transvaal B 1967-68 and for Middlesex 1968. Cap 1971. Benefit (£30,000) in 1979. Left county after 1979 season and made debut for Glamorgan 1980. Cap 1980. Is regarded as an English player for qualification purposes. 1,000 runs in season (4) – 1,156 runs (av. 35.03) in 1975 best. Scored two centuries in match (127* and 100*) Middlesex v Kent (Canterbury) 1975. Gillette Man of the Match Awards: 1 (for Middlesex). Benson & Hedges Gold Awards: 1 (for Middlesex). HS: 147 Middlesex v Yorks (Scarborough) 1975. HSC: 113* v Hants (Bournemouth) 1981. HSGC/NW: 72* Middlesex v Worcs (Worcester) 1975. HSJPL: 82* Middlesex v Notts (Lord's) 1976. HSBH: 56* Middlesex v Sussex (Hove) 1975 and 56 Middlesex v Kent (Lord's) 1975. BB: 5-32 Middlesex v Notts (Nottingham) 1978. BBC: 5-90 v Somerset (Taunton) 1980. BBGC/NW: 3-17 Middlesex v Glamorgan (Lord's) 1977. BBJPL: 4-10 Middlesex v Worcs (Worcester) 1978. BBBH: 4-33 Middlesex v Minor Counties (East) (Lord's) 1976.

David Arthur FRANCIS (Cwmtawe Comprehensive School, Pontardawe) B Clydach (Glamorgan) 29/11/1953. RHB, OB. Debut 1973 after playing for 2nd XI in 1971 and 1972. HS: 110 v Warwickshire (Nuneaton) 1977. HSGC/NW: 62* v Worcs (Worcester) 1977. HSJPL: 101* v Warwickshire (Birmingham) 1980. HSBH: 59 v Warwickshire (Birmingham) 1977.

Geoffrey Clark HOLMES (West Denton HS, Newcastle-upon-Tyne) B Newcastle-upon-Tyne 16/9/1958. RHB, RM. Debut 1978. HS: 100* v Glos (Bristol) 1979. HSNW: 11 v Hants (Bournemouth) 1981. HSJPL: 43* v Hants (Portsmouth) 1979. HSBH: 30 v Glos (Bristol) 1980. BB: 5–86 v Surrey (Oval) 1980. BBJPL: 3-17 v Notts (Swansea) 1980.

John Anthony HOPKINS B Maesteg 16/6/1953. Younger brother of J. D. Hopkins, formerly on staff and who appeared for Middlesex. RHB, WK. Debut 1970. Cap 1977. 1,000 runs (5) – 1,371 runs (av. 33.43) in 1978 best. Gillette Man of the Match Awards: 1. Benson & Hedges Gold Awards: 3. HS: 230 v Worcs (Worcester) 1977 – the fourth highest score for the county. HSGC/NW: 63 v Leics (Swansea) 1977. HSJPL: 75 v Warwickshire (Swansea) 1981. HSBH: 103* v Minor Counties (Swansea) 1980. Trained as a teacher at Trinity College of Education, Carmarthen.

JAVED MIANDAD KHAN B Karachi 12/6/1957. RHB, LBG. Debut 1973-74 for Karachi Whites in Patron Trophy tournament aged 16 years 5 months. Has subsequently played for various Karachi, Sind and Habib Bank sides. Vice-captain of Pakistan Under-19 side in England in 1974 and captain of Under-19 side in Sri Lanka 1974-75. Scored 227 for Sussex 2nd XI v Hants (Hove) 1975 whilst qualifying for county. Debut for Sussex 1976. Cap 1977. Left county after end of 1979 season and made debut for Glamorgan in 1980. Cap 1980 *Wisden* 1981. Tests: 34 for Pakistan between 1976-77 and 1980-81, captaining Pakistan in 7 tests. Tours: Pakistan to Australia and West Indies 1976-77, England 1978, New Zealand and Australia 1978-79, India 1979-80, Australia 1981-82 (captain). 1,000 runs (3) – 2,083 runs (av. 69.43) in 1981 best, scoring 8 centuries, both being county records. Scored 163 for Pakistan v New Zealand (Lahore) 1976-77 on Test Debut and 206 v New Zealand (Karachi) in third Test becoming youngest double-century maker in Test cricket at age of 19 years 141 days. Scored two centuries in match twice (107 and 123) Habib Bank v National Bank (Lahore) 1980-81, (137 and 106) v Somerset (Swansea) 1981. Gillette Man of the Match Awards: 1 (for Sussex). Benson & Hedges Gold Awards: 1. HS: 311 Karachi Whites v National Bank (Karachi) 1974-75. HSUK: 200* v Somerset (Taunton) 1981 and 200* v Essex (Colchester) 1981. HSTC: 206 Pakistan v New Zealand (Karachi) 1976-77. HSGC/NW: 75 Sussex v Lancs (Hove) 1978. HSJPL: 107* v Leics (Leicester) 1981. HSBH: 76 Sussex v Surrey (Oval) 1977. BB: 7-39 Habib Bank v Industrial Development Bank of Pakistan (Lahore) 1980-81. BBUK: 4-10 Sussex v Northants (Northampton) 1977. BBTC: 3-74 Pakistan v New Zealand (Hyderabad) 1976-77.

Alan JONES B Velindre, Swansea 4/11/1938. LHB, OB. Joined staff in 1955. Debut 1957. Cap 1962. Played for Western Australia in 1963-64, for Northern Transvaal in 1975-76 and for Natal in 1976-77. Benefit (£10,000) in 1972. County captain from 1976 to 1978. *Wisden* 1977. Testimonial (£35,000) in 1980. Played one match v Rest of World 1970, 1,000 runs (21) – 1,865 runs (av. 34.53) in 1966 and 1,862 runs (av. 38.00) in 1968 best. Scored two centuries in match (187* and 105*) v Somerset (Glastonbury) 1963, (132 and 156*) v Yorks (Middlesbrough) 1976 and (147 and 100) v Hants (Swansea) 1978. Shared in record partnership for any wicket for county, 330 for 1st wicket with R.C. Fredericks v Northants (Swansea) 1972. Shared in 2nd wicket partnership record for county, 238 with A.R. Lewis v Sussex (Hastings) 1962. Completed 30,000 runs in 1979. Has scored more runs and centuries for county than any other player. Gillette Man of the Match Awards: 2. Benson & Hedges Gold Awards: 1. HS: 204* v Hants (Basingstoke) 1980. HSGC/NW: 124* v Warwickshire (Birmingham) 1976. HSJPL: 110* v Glos (Cardiff) 1978. HSBH: 89 v Worcs (Cardiff) 1979. BBJPL: 3-21 v Northants (Wellingborough) 1975.

Alan Lewis JONES (Ystalyfera GS and Cwmtawe Comprehensive School) B Alltwen, Glamorgan 1/6/1957. No relation to A. and E.W. Jones. LHB. Played for 2nd XI in 1972. Debut 1973 at age of 16 years 99 days. Toured West Indies with England Young Cricketers 1976. HS: 83 v Worcs (Worcester) 1979. HSGC/NW: 11 v Hants (Southampton) 1975. HSJPL: 62 v Hants (Cardiff) 1975. HSBH: 36 v Worcs (Cardiff) 1979. Trained as a teacher at Cardiff College of Education.

Eifion Wyn JONES B Velindre, Swansea 25/6/1942. Brother of A. Jones. RHB, WK. Debut 1961. Cap 1967. Benefit (£17,000) in 1975. Dismissed 94 batsmen (85 ct 9 st) in 1970. Dismissed 7 batsmen (6 ct 1 st) in innings v Cambridge U (Cambridge) 1970. Benson & Hedges Gold Awards: 1. HS: 146* v Sussex (Hove) 1968. HSGC/NW: 67* v Herts (Swansea) 1969. HSJPL: 48 v Hants (Cardiff) 1971. HSBH: 39* v Minor Counties (West) (Amersham) 1977.

Peter John LAWLOR (Gowerton Comprehens : School) B. Gowerton 8/5/1960. RHB, OB. Played for 2nd XI in 1980. Debut 1981. One match v Sri Lankans (Cardiff).

Michael John (Mike) LLEWELLYN B Clydach (Glamorgan) 27/11/1953. LHB, OB. Debut 1970 at age of 16 years 202 days. Cap 1977. Gillette Man of the Match Awards: 1. Benson & Hedges Gold Awards: 2. HS: 129* v Oxford U (Oxford) 1977. HSGC/NW: 62 v Middlesex (Lord's) 1977. HSJPL: 79* v Glos (Bristol) 1977. HSBH: 63 v Hants (Swansea) 1973. BB: 4-35 v Oxford U (Oxford) 1970.

Barry John LLOYD B Neath 6/9/1953. RHB, OB. Formerly on MCC groundstaff. Debut 1972. HS: 45* v Hants (Portsmouth) 1973. HSJPL: 14 v Worcs (Worcester) 1980. BB: 8-70 v Lancs (Cardiff) 1981. BBJPL: 3-22 v Derbyshire (Derby) 1980. Trained as a teacher at Bangor Normal College.

Hugh MORRIS (Blundell's School, Tiverton) B Cardiff 5/10/1963. LHB. Captained MCC Schools and ESCA sides in 1981. Debut 1981. One match v Leics (Cardiff). HS: 16 v Leics (Cardiff) 1981.

Ezra Alphonsa MOSELEY (Christ Church High School) B Christ Church, Barbados 5/1/1958. RHB, RFM. Debut 1980 taking 6-102 v Essex (Swansea) in debut match. Cap 1981. Hat-trick in Benson & Hedges Cup v Kent (Cardiff) 1981. Benson & Hedges Gold Awards: 1. HS: 70* v Kent (Canterbury) 1980. HSJPL: 20 v Worcs (Abergavenny) 1981. BB: 6-23 v Australians (Swansea) 1981. BBJPL: 4-22 v Leics (Leicester) 1981. BBBH: 4-8 v Kent (Cardiff) 1981.

Malcolm Andrew NASH (Wells Cathedral School) B Abergavenny (Monmouthshire) 9/5/1945. LHB, LM. Debut 1966. Cap 1969. Benefit (£18,000) in 1978. Appointed County Captain in 1980. Benson & Hedges Gold Awards: 3. Hat-trick in John Player League v Worcs (Worcester) 1975. HS: 130 v Surrey (Oval) 1976. HSGC/NW: 51 v Lincs (Swansea) 1974. HSJPL: 68 v Essex (Purfleet) 1972. HSBH: 103* v Hants (Swansea) 1976. BB: 9-56 (14-137 match) v Hants (Basingstoke) 1975. BBNW: 5-31 v Oxfordshire (Oxford) 1981. BBJPL: 6-29 v Worcs (Worcester) 1975. BBBH: 4-12 v Surrey (Cardiff) 1975.

Rodney Craig ONTONG (Selborne College, East London) B Johannesburg, South Africa 9/9/1955. RHB, RFM. Debut 1972-73 for Border in Currie Cup competition. Debut for county 1975 after being on MCC staff. Transferred to Transvaal for 1976-77 season. Cap 1979. Scored 1,157 runs (av. 34.02) in 1979. Is regarded as an English player for qualification purposes. Shared in 10th wkt partnership record for county with R.N.S. Hobbs, 140* v Hants (Swansea) 1981. Benson & Hedges Gold Awards: 1. HS: 151* v Hants (Swansea) 1981. HSGC/NW: 64 v Somerset (Cardiff) 1978. HSJPL: 55 v Lancs (Cardiff) 1979. HSBH: 50* v Glos (Swansea) 1979. BB: 7-60 Border v Northern Transvaal (Pretoria) 1975-76. BBUK: 6-62 v Sri Lankans (Cardiff) 1981. BBJPL: 4-31 v Middlesex (Lord's) 1979. BBBH: 4-28 v Worcs (Cardiff) 1979.

John Gregory THOMAS (Cwmtawe School, Swansea) B Garnswilt (Glamorgan) 12/8/1960. 6ft 3ins tall. RHB, RM. Debut 1979. HS: 34 v Sri Lankans (Swansea) 1979. HSJPL: 10* v Lancs (Cardiff) 1981. BB: 4-65 v Lancs (Cardiff) 1981. BBJPL: 3-33 v Somerset (Cardiff) 1981. Training as a teacher at Cardiff College of Education.

NB. The following players whose particulars appeared in the 1981 Annual have been omitted: R.N.S. Hobbs (not re-engaged) and A.A. Jones (retired). Their career records will be found elsewhere in this annual.

County Averages

Schweppes County Championship: Played 22, won 3, drawn 8, lost 10, abandoned 1.
First-class matches: Played 24, won 3, drawn 11, lost 10, abandoned 1.

BATTING AND FIELDING

Cap		M	I	NO	Runs	HS	Avge	100	50	Ct	St
1980	Javed Miandad	22	37	3	2083	200*	69.43	8	7	11	—
1980	N.G. Featherstone	23	39	5	1105	113*	32.50	2	9	27	—
1962	A. Jones	23	41	2	1192	109	30.56	1	5	5	—
1977	J.A. Hopkins	23	41	1	1217	135	30.42	4	5	15	—
1979	R.C. Ontong	23	40	5	968	151*	27.65	2	2	7	—
—	G.C. Holmes	14	23	8	394	70*	26.26	—	2	6	—
1979	R.N.S. Hobbs	15	15	10	101	49*	20.20	—	—	7	—
—	S.R. Barwick	5	4	3	20	11*	20.00	—	—	1	—
1981	E.A. Moseley	15	19	3	306	57	19.12	—	2	5	—
—	A.L. Jones	6	12	1	204	81	18.54	—	1	3	—
—	A.A. Jones	3	3	2	14	9	14.00	—	—	1	—
—	D.A. Francis	3	5	0	67	28	13.40	—	—	2	—
1969	M.A. Nash	23	31	5	282	36*	10.84	—	—	12	—
—	J.G. Thomas	5	8	3	53	13*	10.60	—	—	3	—
—	B.J. Lloyd	22	28	2	242	31	9.30	—	—	19	—
1967	E.W. Jones	23	31	2	232	33	8.00	—	—	46	10
—	S.A.B. Daniels	5	8	4	30	10*	7.50	—	—	4	—
1977	M.J. Llewellyn	9	9	1	43	15	5.37	—	—	8	—

Played in one match: T. Davies 1 1 0 (5 ct 1 st); P.J. Lawlor 0, 8 (1 ct); H. Morris 5, 16; N.J. Perry 0 (1 ct).

BOWLING

	Type	O	M	R	W	Avge	Best	5 wI	10 wM
E.A. Moseley	RFM	355.4	87	942	52	18.11	6-23	3	—
S.R. Barwick	RM	71	33	133	7	19.00	2-10	—	—
M.A. Nash	LM	565.4	153	1728	71	24.33	7-62	2	—
G.C. Holmes	RM	49	9	193	7	27.57	2-22	—	—
R.C. Ontong	RFM	457.5	97	1369	49	27.93	6-62	1	—
A.A. Jones	RFM	69	14	237	6	29.62	3-23	—	—
B.J. Lloyd	OB	619.3	142	1717	53	32.39	8-70	1	—
R.N.S. Hobbs	LBG	390.3	99	1151	35	32.88	5-67	2	—
J.G. Thomas	RM	80.3	10	355	10	35.50	4-65	—	—
S.A.B. Daniels	RFM	89	18	326	8	40.75	3-33	—	—

Also bowled: N.G. Featherstone 16-7-38-1; Javed Miandad 37-7-108-3; A. Jones 1.1-1-4-0; P.J. Lawlor 13-2-50-1; N.J. Perry 19-1-89-2.

County Records

First-class cricket

Highest innings totals:	For	587-8d v Derbyshire (Cardiff)	1951
	Agst	653-6d by Gloucestershire (Bristol)	1928
Lowest innings totals:	For	22 v Lancashire (Liverpool)	1924
	Agst	33 by Leicestershire (Ebbw Vale)	1965
Highest individual innings:	For	287* D.E. Davies v Gloucestershire (Newport)	1939
	Agst	302* W.R. Hammond for Glos (Bristol)	1934
		302 W.R. Hammond for Glos (Newport)	1939
Best bowling in an innings:	For	10-51 J. Mercer v Worcs (Worcester)	1936
	Agst	10-18 G. Geary for Leics (Pontypridd)	1929
Best bowling in a match:	For	17-212 J.C. Clay v Worcs (Swansea)	1937
	Agst	16-96 G. Geary for Leics (Pontypridd)	1929
Most runs in a season:		2,083 (av. 69.43) Javed Miandad	1981
runs in a career:		31,506 (av. 33.02) A. Jones	1957-1981
100s in a season:		8 by Javed Miandad	1981
100s in a career:		47 by A. Jones	1957-1981
wickets in a season:		176 (av. 17.34) J.C. Clay	1937
wickets in a career:		2,174 (av. 20.95) D.J. Shepherd	1950-1972

RECORD WICKET STANDS

1st	330	A. Jones & R.C. Fredericks v Northamptonshire (Swansea)	1972
2nd	238	A. Jones & A.R. Lewis v Sussex (Hastings)	1962
3rd	313	D.E. Davies & W.E. Jones v Essex (Brentwood)	1948
4th	263	G. Lavis & C. Smart v Worcestershire (Cardiff)	1934
5th	264	M. Robinson & S.W. Montgomery v Hampshire (Bournemouth)	1949
6th	230	W.E. Jones & B.L. Muncer v Worcestershire (Worcester)	1953
7th	195*	W. Wooller & W.E. Jones v Lancashire (Liverpool)	1947
8th	202	D. Davies & J.J. Hills v Sussex (Eastbourne)	1928
9th	203*	J.J. Hills & J.C. Clay v Worcestershire (Swansea)	1929
10th	140*	R.C. Ontong & R.N.S. Hobbs v Hampshire (Swansea)	1981

One-day cricket

Highest innings totals:	Gillette Cup/ NatWest Trophy	283-3 v Warwickshire (Birmingham)	1976
	John Player League	266-6 v Northants (Wellingborough)	1975
	Benson & Hedges Cup	245-7 v Hampshire (Swansea)	1976
Lowest innings totals:	Gillette Cup/ NatWest Trophy	76 v Northants (Northampton)	1968
	John Player League	42 v Derbyshire (Swansea)	1979
	Benson & Hedges Cup	68 v Lancs (Manchester)	1973
Highest individual innings:	Gillette Cup/ NatWest Trophy	124* A. Jones v Warwickshire (Birmingham)	1976
	John Player League	110* A. Jones v Glos (Cardiff)	1978
	Benson & Hedges Cup	103* M.A. Nash v Hants (Swansea)	1976
		103* J.A. Hopkins v Minor Counties (Swansea)	1980
Best bowling figures:	Gillette Cup/ NatWest Trophy	5-21 P.M. Walker v Cornwall (Truro)	1970
	John Player League	6-29 M.A. Nash v Worcs (Worcester)	1975
	Benson & Hedges Cup	5-17 A.H. Wilkins v Worcs (Worcester)	1978

GLOUCESTERSHIRE

Formation of present club: 1871.
Colours: Blue, gold, brown, silver, green and red.
Badge: Coat of Arms of the City and County of Bristol.
County Champions (3): 1874, 1876 and 1877.
Joint Champions: 1873.
Gillette Cup Winners: 1973.
NatWest Trophy Second Round: 1981.
Best Position in John Player League: 6th in 1969, 1973 and 1977.
Benson & Hedges Cup Winners: 1977.
Gillette Man of the Match Awards: 17.
NatWest Man of the Match Awards: 1.
Benson & Hedges Gold Awards: 21.

Secretary: A.S. Brown, County Ground, Nevil Road, Bristol BS7 9EJ.
Captain: D.A. Graveney.
Prospects of Play Telephone Nos: Bristol (0272) 48461
Cheltenham (0242) 22000
Gloucester (0452) 24621

Philip BAINBRIDGE (Hanley HS and Stoke-on-Trent Sixth Form College) B Stoke-on-Trent 16/4/1958. RHB, RM. Played for four 2nd XIs in 1976 – Derbyshire, Glos, Northants and Warwickshire. Debut 1977. Cap 1981. Scored 1,019 runs (av. 40.76) in 1981. HS: 105* v Middlesex (Lord's) 1981. HSNW: 61* v Ireland (Dublin) 1981. HSJPL: 35 v Sussex (Moreton-in-Marsh) 1980 and 35 v Sussex (Hove) 1981. HSBH: 16* v Essex (Bristol) 1980. BB: 5-68 v Somerset (Bath) 1981. BBJPL: 4-27 v Middlesex (Cheltenham) 1980. BBBH: 3-21 v Notts (Gloucester) 1981. Trained as a teacher at Borough Road College of Education.

Andrew James (Andy) BRASSINGTON B Bagnall (Staffordshire) 9/8/1954. RHB, WK. Debut 1974. Cap 1978. HS: 28 v Glamorgan (Cardiff) 1975. HSGC/NW: 20 v Hants (Bristol) 1979. Plays soccer as a goalkeeper.

Brian Christopher (Chris) BROAD (Colston's School, Bristol) B Bristol 29/9/1957. 6ft 4ins tall. LHB, RM. Played for 2nd XI since 1976. Debut 1979. Cap 1981. Scored 1,117 runs (av. 31.02) in 1981. Shared in first wkt partnerships of 126 and 89 with S.J. Windaybank in their debut match v Cambridge U (Cambridge). Scored century before lunch against Oxford U (Oxford) on opening day of 1980 season. HS: 129 v Northants (Bristol) 1979. HSJPL: 58 v Lancs (Bristol) 1981. HSBH: 40 v Sussex (Hove) 1980. Trained as a teacher at St Paul's College, Cheltenham.

John Henry CHILDS B Plymouth 15/8/1951. LHB, SLA. Played for Devon 1973-74. Debut 1975. Cap 1977. HS: 20 v Northants (Bristol) 1981. HSJPL: 16* v Notts (Nottingham) 1981. HSBH: 10 v Somerset (Bristol) 1979. BB: 9-56 v Somerset (Bristol) 1981. BBJPL: 4-15 v Northants (Northampton) 1976.

John Henry DIXON (Monkton Coombe School and Oxford) B. Bournemouth 3/3/1954. 6ft 5ins tall. RHB, RM. Played for University in Benson & Hedges Cup in 1973. Debut for County 1973. Not re-engaged after 1976 season. Re-appeared in one match v Oxford U (Oxford) in 1981. HS: 13* v Northants (Bristol) 1975. BB: 5-44 v Glamorgan (Cardiff) 1975.

Richard James DOUGHTY (Scarborough College) B Bridlington (Yorks) 17/11/1960. RHB, RM. Played for Northants 2nd XI in 1980. Debut 1981. One match v Somerset (Bristol) and also played in two John Player League matches. HS: 10 v Somerset (Bristol) 1981.

Barry DUDLESTON (Stockport School) B Bebington (Cheshire) 16/7/1945. RHB, SLA. Debut for Leics 1966. Cap 1969. Played for Rhodesia from 1976-77 to 1979-80 in Currie Cup competitions. Benefit (£25,000) in 1980. Not re-engaged after 1980 season and made debut for Glos in 1981. Is coach and 2nd XI captain. 1,000 runs (8) – 1,374 runs (av. 31.22) in 1970 best. Shared in 1st wkt partnership record for Leics, 390 with J.F. Steele v Derbyshire (Leicester) 1979. Also shared in 7th wkt partnership record for county, 206 with J. Birkenshaw v Kent (Canterbury) 1969. Gillette Man of the Match Awards: 2. Benson & Hedges Gold Awards: 4. HS: 202 Leics v Derbyshire (Leicester) 1979. HSC: 99 v Oxford U (Oxford) 1981. HSGC/NW: 125 Leics v Worcs (Leicester) 1979. HSJPL: 152 Leics v Lancs (Manchester) 1975. HSBH: 90 Leics v Warwickshire (Leicester) 1973. BB: 4-6 Leics v Surrey (Leicester) 1972.

David Anthony GRAVENEY (Millfield School) B Bristol 2/1/1953. Son of J.K.R. Graveney. 6ft 4ins tall. RHB, SLA. Debut 1972. Cap 1976. Appointed County Captain during 1981 season. HS: 119 v Oxford U (Oxford) 1980. HSGC/NW: 44 v Surrey (Bristol) 1973. HSJPL: 49 v Notts (Nottingham) 1981. HSBH: 21 v Somerset (Street) 1975. BB: 8-85 v Notts (Cheltenham) 1974. BBNW: 5-11 v Ireland (Dublin) 1981. BBJPL: 4-22 v Hants (Lydney) 1974. BBBH: 3-32 v Middlesex (Bristol) 1977.

Alastair James HIGNELL (Denstone College and Cambridge) B Cambridge 4/9/1955. RHB, LB. Scored 117* and 78* for England Schools v All India Schools (Birmingham) 1973 and 133 for England Young Cricketers v West Indies Young Cricketers (Arundel) 1974. Debut 1974. Cap 1977. Blue 1975-76-77-78. Captain in last two years. 1,000 runs (2) – 1,140 runs (av. 30.81) in 1976 best. Scored two centuries in match (108 and 145) for Cambridge U v Surrey (Cambridge) 1978. Benson & Hedges Gold Awards: 1 (for Combined Universities). HS: 149 Cambridge U v Glamorgan (Cambridge) 1977 and 149* v Northants (Bristol) 1979. HSGC/NW: 85* v Northants (Bristol) 1977. HSJPL: 51 v Northants (Northampton) 1976. HSBH: 63 Combined Universities v Worcs (Worcester) 1978. Blue for rugby 1974-75 (captain)-76-77 (captain). Plays for Bristol. Toured Australia with England Rugby team 1975. 14 caps for England between 1975 and 1978-79.

David Valentine LAWRENCE (Linden Secondary School, Gloucester). B Gloucester 28/1/1964. RHB, RFM. Played for 2nd XI in 1980. Debut 1981. Is first player born in this country of Commonwealth immigrant parents (Jamaican) to appear in county cricket. One match v Glamorgan (Bristol).

Martin David PARTRIDGE (Marling School, Stroud) B Birdlip (Glos) 25/10/1954. LHB, RM. Deubt 1976. Did not play in 1981, but may re-appear on a match contract basis in future. HS: 90 v Notts (Nottingham) 1979. HSGC/NW: 20 v Surrey (Oval) 1980. HSJPL: 33 v Warwickshire (Moreton-in-Marsh) 1979. HSBH: 27 v Warwickshire (Bristol) 1978. BB: 5-29 v Worcs (Worcester) 1979. BBJPL: 5-47 v Kent (Cheltenham) 1977. Studied civil engineering at Bradford University.

Michael John (Mike) PROCTER (Hilton College, Natal) B Durban 15/9/1946. RHB, RF/OB. Vice-captain of South African Schools team to England 1963. Debut for county 1965 in one match v South Africans. Returned home to make debut for Natal in 1965-66 Currie Cup competition. Joined staff in 1968. Cap 1968. *Wisden*

87

1969. Transferred to Western Province for 1969-70 Currie Cup competition, Rhodesia in 1970-71 and Natal 1976-77. Appointed county captain in 1977. Benefit (£15,500) in 1976. Is now regarded as an English player for qualification purposes. Relinquished captaincy during 1981 season and subsequently announced retirement owing to knee injury. May re-appear in one-day matches if knee stands up to season in South Africa. Tests: 7 for South Africa v Australia 1966-67 and 1969-70. Played in 5 matches for Rest of World v England in 1970. 1,000 runs (9) – 1,786 runs (av. 45.79) in 1971 best. 100 wkts (2) – 109 wkts (av. 18.04) in 1977 best. Scored 6 centuries in 6 consecutive innings for Rhodesia 1970-71 to equal world record. Scored two centuries in match (114 and 131) for Rhodesia v International Wanderers (Salisbury) 1972-73. Hat-tricks (4): v Essex (Westcliff) 1972 – all lbw – and also scored a century in the match, v Essex (Southend) 1977, v Leics (Bristol) 1979 and also scored a century, and in next match v Yorks (Cheltenham) 1979 – all lbw. Also v Hants (Southampton) in Benson & Hedges Cup 1977. Had match double of 100 runs and 10 wkts (108 and 13-73) v Worcs (Cheltenham) 1977 and (108 and 14-76) v Worcs (Cheltenham) 1980. Gillette Man of the Match Awards: 2. Benson & Hedges Gold Awards: 6. HS: 254 Rhodesia v Western Province (Salisbury) 1970-71. HSUK: 203 v Essex (Gloucester) 1978. HSTC: 48 South Africa v Australia (Cape Town) 1969-70. HSGC/NW: 107 v Sussex (Hove) 1971. HSJPL: 109 v Warwickshire (Cheltenham) 1972. HSBH: 154* v Somerset (Taunton) 1977. BB: 9-71 Rhodesia v Transvaal (Bulawayo) 1972-73. BBUK: 8-30 v Worcs (Worcester) 1979. BBTC: 6-73 South Africa v Australia (Port Elizabeth) 1969-70. BBGC/NW: 4-21 v Yorks (Leeds) 1976. BBJPL: 5-8 v Middlesex (Gloucester) 1977. BBBH: 6-13 v Hants (Southampton) 1977.

Paul William ROMAINES B Bishop Auckland (Co. Durham) 25/12/1955. RHB. Debut for Northants 1975. Not re-engaged after 1976 season. Played for Durham from 1977 to 1981 and was professional for Darlington in North Yorks and South Durham League. Has joined county for 1982. HS: 17 Northants v Glos (Northampton) 1976. HSGC/NW: 48 Durham v Berks (Durham) 1979. HSJPL: 25* Northants v Lancs (Manchester) 1975.

Robert Charles (Jack) RUSSELL (The Archway School, Stroud) B Stroud 15/8/1963. LHB, WK. Debut 1981. One match v Sri Lankans (Bristol) making 8 dismissals (7 ct 1st) in the match.

SADIQ MOHAMMAD B Junagadh, India 3/5/1945. LHB, LBG. Youngest of family of five cricket-playing brothers which includes Hanif and Mushtaq Mohammad. Debut in Pakistan 1959-60 at age of 14 years 9 months and has played subsequently for various Karachi sides, Pakistan International Airways and United Bank. Played for Northants 2nd XI in 1967 and 1968, for Nelson in Lancs League in 1968, and subsequently for Poloc, Glasgow in Scottish Western Union. Played for D.H. Robins' XI v Oxford U 1969 and for Essex v Jamaica XI in 1970. Debut for county 1972. Cap 1973. Played for Tasmania against MCC in 1974-75. Benefit in 1982. Tests: 41 for Pakistan between 1969-70 and 1980-81. Tours: Pakistan to England 1971, 1974 and 1978, Australia and New Zealand 1972-73, Australia and West Indies 1976-77, India 1979-80. 1,000 runs (7) – 1,759 runs (av. 47.54) in 1976 best. Scored 1,169 runs (av. 41.75) in Australia and New Zealand 1972-73. Scored 4 centuries in 4 consecutive innings in 1976 including two centuries in match (163* and 150) v Derbyshire (Bristol). Also scored two centuries in match (171 and 103) v Glamorgan (Bristol) 1979. Gillette Man of the Match Awards: 1. Benson & Hedges Gold Awards: 4. HS: 203 v Sri Lankans (Bristol) 1981. HSTC: 166 Pakistan v New Zealand (Wellington) 1972-73. HSGC/NW: 122 v Lancs (Manchester) 1975. HSJPL: 131 v Somerset (Imperial Ground, Bristol) 1975. HSBH: 128 v Minor

Counties (South) (Bristol) 1974. BB: 7-34 United Bank v Universities (Peshawar) 1978-79. BBUK: 5-37 v Kent (Bristol) 1973. BBGC/NW: 3-19 v Oxfordshire (Bristol) 1975. BBJPL: 3-27 v Hants (Bristol) 1972. BBBH: 3-20 v Minor Counties (South) (Bristol) 1972.

John Neil SHEPHERD (Alleyn's School, Barbados) B St. Andrew, Barbados 9/11/1943. RHB, RM. Debut 1964-65 in one match for Barbados v Cavaliers and has played subsequently for Barbados in Shell Shield competition. Debut for Kent 1966. Cap 1967. Played for Rhodesia in 1975-76 Currie Cup competition. *Wisden* 1978. Benefit (£58,537) in 1979. Is regarded as an English player for qualification purposes. Not re-engaged after 1981 season and has joined Glos in 1982. Tests: 5 for West Indies in 1969 and 1970-71. Tour: West Indies to England 1969. Scored 1,157 runs (av. 29.66) and took 96 wkts (av. 18.72) in 1968. Gillette Man of the Match Awards: 1 (for Kent). Benson & Hedges Gold Awards: 2 (for Kent). HS: 170 Kent v Northants (Folkestone) 1968. HSTC: 32 West Indies v England (Lord's) 1969. HSGC/NW: 101 Kent v Middlesex (Canterbury) 1977. HSJPL: 94 Kent v Hants (Southampton) 1978. HSBH: 96 Kent v Middlesex (Lord's) 1975. BB: 8-40 West Indians v Glos (Bristol) 1969. BBTC: 5-104 West Indies v England (Manchester) 1969. BBGC/NW: 4-23 Kent v Essex (Leyton) 1972. BBJPL: 4-17 Kent v Middlesex (Lord's) 1978. BBBH: 4-25 Kent v Derbyshire (Lord's) 1978.

Andrew Willis STOVOLD (Filton HS) B Bristol 19/3/1953. RHB, WK. Toured West Indies with England Young Cricketers 1972. Played for 2nd XI since 1971. Debut 1973. Cap 1976. Played for Orange Free State in 1974-75 and 1975-76 Currie Cup competition. 1,000 runs (3) – 1,388 runs (av. 36.52) in 1979 best. NatWest Man of the Match Awards: 1. Benson & Hedges Gold Awards: 5. HS: 196 v Notts (Nottingham) 1977. HSNW: 70 v Ireland (Dublin) 1981. HSJPL: 98* v Kent (Cheltenham) 1977. HSBH: 104 v Leics (Leicester) 1977.

Martin Willis STOVOLD (Thornbury GS) B Bristol 28/12/1955. Younger brother of A.W. Stovold. LHB. Played in one John Player League match v Essex (Gloucester) 1978. Debut 1979. HS: 75* v Oxford U (Oxford) 1980. HSNW: 17 v Essex (Bristol) 1981. HSJPL: 27 v Somerset (Bristol) 1980. HSBH: 32 v Essex (Bristol) 1980. Trained as a teacher at Loughborough College.

David SURRIDGE (Richard Hale School, Hertford, Southampton and Cambridge Universities) B Bishops Stortford, Herts 6/1/1956. RHB, RFM. Played for Hertfordshire from 1976 to 1979. Debut for Cambridge U and Blue 1979. Debut for county 1980. HS: 14 Cambridge U v Yorks (Cambridge) 1979. HSBH: 11* Combined Universities v Northants (Cambridge) 1979. BB: 4-22 Cambridge U v Oxford U (Lord's) 1979. BBC: 3-24 v Oxford U (Oxford) 1980.

Michael Roy WHITNEY (South Sydney Boys' HS) B Sydney 24/2/1959. RHB, LFM. Played for Surrey 2nd XI 1978. Debut 1980-81 for New South Wales. Played as professional for Fleetwood in Northern League in 1981, subsequently making debut for county. Was chosen for Australian team following injuries to fast bowlers. Test: 2 for Australia in 1981. HS: 4 Australia v England (Oval) 1981. BB: 5-60 Australians v Sussex (Hove) 1981. BBC: 4-86 v Sri Lankans (Bristol) 1981.

Alan Haydn WILKINS (Whitchurch HS, Cardiff) B Cardiff 22/8/1953. RHB, LM. Played in two John Player League matches for Glamorgan in 1975. Debut for county 1976, Left county after 1979 season and made debut for Glos in 1980. HS: 70 Glamorgan v Notts (Worksop) 1977. HSC: 44 v West Indians (Bristol) 1980. HSGC/NW: 18* Glamorgan v Somerset (Cardiff) 1978. HSJPL: 19* v Derbyshire

89

GLOUCESTERSHIRE

(Gloucester) 1981. HSBH: 27 v Minor Counties (Chippenham) 1980. BB: 8-57 v Lancs (Manchester) 1981. BBJPL: 5-23 Glamorgan v Warwickshire (Birmingham) 1978. BBBH: 5-17 Glamorgan v Worcs (Worcester) 1978. Trained as a teacher at Loughborough College of Education.

Stephen James WINDAYBANK (Cotham GS) B Pinner, Middlesex 20/10/1956. RHB. Played for 2nd XI in 1978. Debut 1979. Shared in first wkt partnerships of 126 and 89 with B.C. Broad in their debut match v Cambridge U (Cambridge). HS: 53 v Cambridge U (Cambridge) 1979. HSNW: 18 v Essex (Bristol) 1981. HSJPL: 56* v Notts (Nottingham) 1981.

Anthony John WRIGHT (Alleyne's GS, Stevenage) B Stevenage, Herts 27/6/1962. RHB, RM. Played for 2nd XI since 1979. Played in two John Player League matches in 1980. Did not play in 1981 and has yet to appear in first-class cricket.

Syed ZAHEER ABBAS B Sialkot, Pakistan 24/7/1947. RHB, OB. Wears glasses. Debut for Karachi Whites 1965-66, subsequently playing for Pakistan International Airways. *Wisden* 1971. Debut for county 1972. Cap 1975. Tests: 43 for Pakistan between 1969-70 and 1980-81. Played in 5 matches for Rest of the World v Australia 1971-72. Tours: Pakistan to England 1971 and 1974, Australia and New Zealand 1972-73, Australia and West Indies 1976-77, New Zealand and Australia 1978-79, India 1979-80, Australia 1981-82, Rest of World to Australia 1971-72. 1,000 runs (10) – 2,554 runs (av. 75.11) in 1976 best. Scored 1,597 runs (av. 84.05) in Pakistan 1973-74 – the record aggregate for a Pakistan season. Scored 4 centuries in 4 consecutive innings in 1970-71. Scored two centuries in a match on six occasions including record of double-century and century on four occasions – 216* and 156* v Surrey (Oval) 1976, 230* and 104* v Kent (Canterbury) 1976, 205* and 108* v Sussex (Cheltenham) 1977, 100* and 100* Pakistan International Airways v Railways (Lahore) 1980-81, 215* and 150* v Somerset (Bath) 1981 and 135* and 128 v Northants (Northampton) 1981. Scored 1,016 runs (av. 112.88) in June 1981 after not having batted in a first-class match in May. Was dismissed, hit the ball twice, for Pakistan International Airways v Karachi Blues (Karachi) 1969-70. Gillette Man of the Match Awards: 4. HS: 274 Pakistan v England (Birmingham) 1971. HSC: 230* v Kent (Canterbury) 1976. HSGC/NW: 131* v Leics (Leicester) 1975. HSJPL: 129* v Middlesex (Lord's) 1981. HSBH: 98 v Surrey (Oval) 1975. BB: 5-15 Dawood Club v Railways (Lahore) 1975-76. BBUK: 3-32 v Warwickshire (Gloucester) 1981.

NB. The following players whose particulars appeared in the 1980 Annual have been omitted: B.M. Brain (retired) and I. Broome (not re-engaged). The career record of Brain will be found elsewhere in this annual.

County Averages

Schweppes County Championship: Played 22, won 4, drawn 11, lost 4, abandoned 3.
First-class matches: Played 25, won 5, drawn 13, lost 4, abandoned 3.

BATTING AND FIELDING

Cap		M	I	NO	Runs	HS	Avge	100	50	Ct	St
1975	Zaheer Abbas	21	36	10	2306	215*	88.69	10	10	9	—
1981	P. Bainbridge	22	36	11	1019	105*	40.76	2	8	8	—

Cap		M	I	NO	Runs	HS	Avge	100	50	Ct	St
1977	A.J. Hignell	22	33	5	979	102*	34.96	1	5	20	—
1981	B.C. Broad	22	40	4	1117	115	31.02	1	6	15	—
1976	A.W. Stovold	21	35	5	927	104	30.90	1	6	27	18
1973	Sadiq Mohammad	18	32	1	917	203	29.58	2	2	16	—
1976	D.A. Graveney	20	22	7	427	105*	28.46	1	—	10	—
	S.J. Windaybank	11	12	3	203	46*	22.55	—	—	2	—
1968	M.J. Procter	7	11	0	225	46	20.46	—	—	6	—
	M.W. Stovold	8	10	3	142	39	20.28	—	—	4	—
1977	J.H. Childs	22	18	10	120	20	15.00	—	—	13	—
1977	B.M. Brain	9	6	2	59	42	14.75	—	—	3	—
	A.H. Wilkins	21	23	3	117	31	5.85	—	—	7	—
1978	A.J. Brassington	4	3	1	10	9	5.00	—	—	3	1
	D. Surridge	6	3	3	2	2*	0.00	—	—	1	—
	M.R. Whitney	3	2	0	0	0	0.00	—	—	2	—

Played in one match: J.H. Dixon did not bat; B. Dudleston 99 (2 ct); R.J. Doughty 7, 10; D. Lawrence did not bat; R. Russell 1* (7 ct 1 st).

BOWLING

	Type	O	M	R	W	Avge	Best	5 wI	10 wM
D.A. Graveney	SLA	486.3	148	1078	48	22.45	6-54	3	1
J.H. Childs	SLA	768.4	228	1962	75	26.16	9-56	7	—
M.J. Procter	RF/OB	172.5	45	513	19	27.00	5-80	1	—
P. Bainbridge	RM	355.1	85	1009	33	30.57	5-68	1	—
M.R. Whitney	LFM	121	30	399	13	30.69	4-86	—	—
A.H. Wilkins	LM	630	146	1892	52	36.38	8-57	1	—
Sadiq Mohammad	LBG	102.4	15	412	11	37.45	3-34	—	—
B.M. Brain	RFM	205	49	609	16	38.06	3-34	—	—
D. Surridge	RFM	139.5	23	476	9	52.88	2-47	—	—
B.C. Broad	RM	120	31	443	6	73.83	2-70	—	—

Also bowled: J. Dixon 24-5-79-1; R.T. Doughty 27-10-55-2; B. Dudleston 7-0-30-0; A.J. Hignell 4.1-0-23-2; D. Lawrence 19-4-86-0; M.W. Stovold 2-0-6-0; Zaheer Abbas 12-2-42-3.

County Records

First-class cricket

Highest innings	For	653-6d v Glamorgan (Bristol)	1928
totals:	Agst	774-7d by Australians (Bristol)	1948
Lowest innings	For	17 v Australians (Cheltenham)	1896
totals:	Agst	12 by Northamptonshire (Gloucester)	1907
Highest indi-	For	318* W.G. Grace v Yorkshire (Cheltenham)	1876
vidual innings:	Agst	296 A.O. Jones for Notts (Nottingham)	1903
Best bowling	For	10-40 E.G. Dennett v Essex (Bristol)	1906
in an innings:	Agst	10-66 A.A. Mailey for Aust. (Cheltenham)	1921
		and K. Smales for Notts (Stroud)	1956

GLOUCESTERSHIRE

Best bowling in a match:	For	17-56 C.W.L. Parker v Essex (Gloucester)	1925
	Agst	15-87 A.J. Conway for Worcestershire (Moreton-in-Marsh)	1914
Most runs in a season:		2,860 (av. 69.75) W.R. Hammond	1933
runs in a career:		33,664 (av. 57.05) W.R. Hammond	1920-1951
100s in a season:		13 by W.R. Hammond	1938
100s in a career:		113 by W.R. Hammond	1920-1951
wickets in a season:		222 (av. 16.80 & 16.37) T.W.J. Goddard	1937 & 1947
wickets in a career:		3,170 (av. 19.44) C.W.L. Parker	1903-1935

RECORD WICKET STANDS

1st	395	D.M. Young & R.B. Nicholls v Oxford U (Oxford)	1962
2nd	256	C.T.M. Pugh & T.W. Graveney v Derbyshire (Chesterfield)	1960
3rd	336	W.R. Hammond & B.H. Lyon v Leicestershire (Leicester)	1933
4th	321	W.R. Hammond & W.L. Neale v Leicestershire (Gloucester)	1937
5th	261	W.G. Grace & W.O. Moberley v Yorkshire (Cheltenham)	1876
6th	320	G.L. Jessop & J.H. Board v Sussex (Hove)	1902
7th	248	W.G. Grace & E.L. Thomas v Sussex (Hove)	1896
8th	239	W.R. Hammond & A.E. Wilson v Lancashire (Bristol)	1938
9th	193	W.G. Grace & S.A. Kitcat v Sussex (Bristol)	1896
10th	131	W.R. Gouldsworthy & J.G. Bessant v Somerset (Bristol)	1923

One-day cricket

Highest innings totals:	Gillette Cup/NatWest Trophy	327-7 v Berkshire (Reading)	1966
	John Player League	255 v Somerset (Imperial Ground, Bristol)	1975
	Benson & Hedges Cup	282 v Hants (Bristol)	1974
Lowest innings totals:	NatWest Trophy	85 v Essex (Bristol)	1981
	John Player League	49 v Middlesex (Bristol)	1978
	Benson & Hedges Cup	62 v Hants (Bristol)	1975
Highest individual innings:	Gillette Cup/NatWest Trophy	131* Zaheer Abbas v Leics (Leicester)	1975
	John Player League	131 Sadiq Mohammad v Somerset (Imperial Ground, Bristol)	1975
	Benson & Hedges Cup	154* M.J. Procter v Somerset (Taunton)	1972
Best bowling figures:	NatWest Trophy	5-11 D.A. Graveney v Ireland (Dublin)	1981
	John Player League	5-8 M.J. Procter v Middlesex (Gloucester)	1977
	Benson & Hedges Cup	6-13 M.J. Procter v Hampshire (Southampton)	1977

HAMPSHIRE

Formation of present club: 1863.
Colours: Blue, gold and white.
Badge: Tudor rose and crown.
County Champions (2): 1961 and 1973.
Gillette Cup Semi-Finalists (2): 1966 and 1976.
NatWest Trophy Third Round: 1981.
John Player League Champions (2): 1975 and 1978.
Benson & Hedges Cup Semi-Finalists (2): 1975 and 1977.
Fenner Trophy Winners (3): 1975, 1976 and 1977.
Gillette Man of the Match Awards: 25.
NatWest Man of the Match Awards: 2.
Benson & Hedges Gold Award: 24

Secretary: A.K. James, County Cricket Ground,
Northlands Road, Southampton SO9 2TY.
Captain: N.E.J. Pocock.
Prospects of Play Telephone Nos: Southampton (0703) 333788/9
Bournemouth (0202) 25872
Basingstoke (0256) 3646

Michael John BAILEY (Cheltenham GS) B Cheltenham 1/8/1954. LHB, OB. Played for Glos 2nd XI 1974 and for county 2nd XI in 1978. Debut 1979. HS: 24 v Surrey (Portsmouth) 1979 and 24 v Northants (Wellingborough) 1980. BB: 5-89 v Northants (Wellingborough) 1980.

Nigel Geoffrey COWLEY B Shaftesbury (Dorset) 1/3/1953. RHB, OB. Debut 1974. Cap 1978. HS: 109* v Somerset (Taunton) 1977. HSGC/NW: 63* v Glos (Bristol) 1979. HSJPL: 74 v Warwickshire (Birmingham) 1981. HSBH: 59 v Glos (Southampton) 1977. BB: 5-44 v Derbyshire (Basingstoke) 1979. BBGC/NW: 4-20 v Midlesex (Lord's) 1979. BBJPL: 4-46 v Sussex (Hove) 1980.

Christopher Colin CURZON B Lenton, Nottingham 22/12/1958. RHB, WK. Debut for Notts 1978. Not re-engaged by county after 1980 season and made debut for Hants in 1981. One match v Sri Lankans (Bournemouth). HS: 45 Notts v Glamorgan (Swansea) 1980 HSC: 31* v Sri Lankans (Bournemouth) 1981. HSJPL: 28* Notts v Kent (Nottingham) 1980. HSBH: 15 Notts v Northants (Northampton) 1980.

Cuthbert Gordon GREENIDGE B St. Peter, Barbados 1/5/1951. RHB, RM. Debut 1970. Cap 1972. Has subsequently played for Barbados. *Wisden* 1976. Tests: 34 for West Indies between 1974–75 and 1980-81. Tours: West Indies to India, Sri Lanka and Pakistan 1974-75, Australia 1975-76 and 1981-82, England 1976 and 1980, Australia and New Zealand 1979-80, Pakistan 1980-81. 1,000 runs (10) – 1,952 runs (av. 55.77) in 1976 best. Scored two centuries in match (134 and 101) West Indies v England (Manchester) 1976, and (136 and 120) v Kent (Bournemouth) 1978. Gillette Man of the Match Awards: 3. NatWest Man of the Match Awards: 1. Benson & Hedges Gold Awards: 4 HS: 273* D.H. Robins' XI v Pakistanis (Eastbourne) 1974. HSC: 259 v Sussex (Southampton) 1975. HSTC: 134 West Indies v England (Manchester) 1976. HSGC/NW: 177 v Glamorgan (Southampton) 1975 – record for all one-day competitions. HSJPL: 163* v Warwickshire (Birmingham) 1979 – record for competition. HSBH: 173* v Minor Counties (South) (Amersham) 1973 – record for competition – and shared in partnership of 285* for second wicket

93

with D.R. Turner – the record partnership for all one-day competitions. BB: 5–49 v Surrey (Southampton) 1971.

Jonathan James Ean HARDY B Nakuru, Kenya 2/10/1960. LHB. Played for 2nd XI since 1980 and is on county staff. Has not yet appeared in first-class cricket.

Richard Edward HAYWARD (Latymer Upper School, Hammersmith) B Hillingdon (Middlesex) 15/2/1954. LHB, LM. Played for Middlesex 2nd XI in 1977 and for Buckinghamshire in 1978 and 1979. Debut for Minor Counties v Indians (Wellington) 1979. Joined county in 1980. Debut 1981 scoring 101* and 53 in first match. HS: 101* v Sri Lankans (Bournemouth) 1981. HSNW: 33 v Lancs (Southampton) 1981.

Trevor Edward JESTY B Gosport 2/6/1948. RHB, RM. Debut 1966. Cap 1971. Played for Border in 1973–74 and Griqualand West in 1974-75 and 1975-76 Currie Cup competitions. Played for Canterbury in Shell Trophy in 1979-80 and for Griqualand West in 1980–81 South African Breweries Bowl Competition. Benefit in 1982. 1,000 runs (4) – 1,288 runs (av. 35.77) in 1976 best. Gillette Man of the Match Awards: 3. NatWest Man of the Match Awards: 1. Benson & Hedges Gold Awards: 6. Took 3 wkts in 4 balls v Somerset (Portsmouth) 1969. HS: 159* v Somerset (Bournemouth) 1976. HSGC/NW: 118 v Derbyshire (Derby) 1980. HSJPL: 107 v Surrey (Southampton) 1977. HSBH: 105 v Glamorgan (Swansea) 1977. BB: 7-75 v Worcs (Southampton) 1976. BBGC/NW: 6-46 v Glos (Bristol) 1979. BBJPL: 6-20 v Glamorgan (Cardiff) 1976. BBBH: 4-28 v Somerset (Taunton) 1974.

Steven John MALONE (King's School, Ely) B Chelmsford 19/10/1953. RHB, RM. Debut for Essex 1975 playing in one match v Cambridge U (Cambridge). Reappeared in corresponding match in 1978. Did not play in 1979 and made debut for Hants in 1980. HS: 23 v Kent (Bournemouth) 1981. BB: 3-56 v Lancs (Portsmouth) 1980. BBNW: 5-34 v Cheshire (Southampton) 1981. BBJPL: 4-39 v Yorks (Basingstoke) 1980.

Malcolm Denzil MARSHALL (Parkinson Comprehensive School, Barbados) B St. Michael, Barbados 18/4/1958. RHB, RF. Debut for Barbados 1977-78 in last match of Shell Shield competition. Debut for county 1979. Cap 1981. Tests: 12 between 1978-79 and 1980-81. Tours: West Indies to India and Sri Lanka 1978-79, Australia and New Zealand 1979-80, England 1980, Pakistan 1980-81, Zimbabwe 1981-82, Australia 1981-82. Hat-trick in John Player League v Surrey (Southampton) 1981. HS: 109 West Indian XI v Zimbabwe (Bulawayo) 1980. HSUK: 75* v Essex (Southampton) 1981. HSTC: 45 West Indies v England (Oval) 1980. HSGC/NW: 21* v Middlesex (Lord's) 1979. HSJPL: 20 v Middlesex (Lord's) 1979 and 20 v Somerset (Taunton) 1981. HSBH: 18 v Sussex (Hove) 1981. BB: 7-56 West Indians v Worcs (Worcester) 1980. BBC: 6-57 v Leics (Leicester) 1981. BBTC: 4-25 West Indies v Pakistan (Faisalabad) 1980-81. BBJPL: 5-13 v Glamorgan (Portsmouth) 1979. BBBH: 3-11 v Sussex (Hove) 1981.

Simon Nigel Craig MASSEY B Newcastle-under-Lyme (Staffs) 14/10/1961. RHB, OB. Played for 2nd XI since 1979 and is on county staff. Has not yet appeared in first-class cricket.

Mark Charles Jefford NICHOLAS (Bradfield College) B London 29/9/1957. RHB. RM. Debut 1978. HS: 112 v Somerset (Bournemouth) 1980. HSGC/NW: 28 v Yorks (Southampton) 1980. HSJPL: 62 v Derbyshire (Southampton) 1980. HSBH: 26 v Surrey (Bournemouth) 1981. BBBH: 3-29 v Surrey (Oval) 1980.

Robert James (Bobby) PARKS (Eastbourne GS) B Cuckfield, Sussex 15/6/1959. Son of J.M. Parks and grandson of J.H. Parks. RHB, WK. Played for 2nd XI since 1976. Debut 1980. Dismissed 10 batsmen (all ct.) in match v Derbyshire (Portsmouth) 1981. HS: 64* v Essex (Chelmsford) 1980. HSNW: 19* v Glamorgan (Cardiff) 1981. HSJPL: 32 v Somerset (Taunton) 1981. HSBH: 11 v Middlesex (Lord's) 1981.

Nicholas Edward Julian (Nick) POCOCK (Shrewsbury School) B Maracaibo, Venezuela 15/12/1951. RHB, LM. Debut 1976. Appointed county captain in 1980. Cap 1980. HS: 143* v Middlesex (Portsmouth) 1979. HSGC/NW: 73* v Derbyshire (Derby) 1980. HSJPL: 53* v Northants (Northampton) 1978. HSBH: 41 v Somerset (Bournemouth) 1980.

John Michael RICE (Brockley CGS, London) B Chandler's Ford, Hants 23/10/1949. 6ft 3ins tall. RHB, RM. On Surrey staff 1970, but not re-engaged. Debut 1971. Cap 1975. Hat-trick in John Player League v Northants (Southampton) 1975. Gillette Cup Man of the Match Awards: 1. Benson & Hedges Gold Awards: 1. HS: 161* v Warwickshire (Birmingham) 1981. HSGC/NW: 40 v Glos (Bristol) 1979. HSJPL: 91 v Yorks (Leeds) 1979. HSBH: 49 v Sussex (Hove) 1981. BB: 7-48 v Worcs (Worcester) 1977. BBGC/NW: 5-35 v Yorks (Bournemouth) 1977. BBJPL: 5-14 v Northants (Southampton) 1975. BBBH: 3-20 v Somerset (Bournemouth) 1975.

Christopher Lyall (Kippy) SMITH (Northlands HS, Durban) B Durban, South Africa 15/10/1958. RHB, OB. Debut for Natal B 1977-78. One match v Rhodesia B (Pinetown). Debut for Glamorgan 1979. One match v Sri Lankans (Swansea). Debut for Hants 1980. Cap 1981. Will be regarded as an English player for qualification purposes in May 1983. Scored 1,048 runs (av. 31.75) in 1980. HS: 130 v Kent (Bournemouth) 1980. HSJPL: 66 v Middlesex (Bournemouth) 1980. HSBH: 48 v Kent (Canterbury) 1980.

Robin Arnold SMITH B Durban, South Africa 13/9/1963. Younger brother of C.L. Smith. RHB. Played for 2nd XI in 1981 and is on county staff. Scored 206 against Glos 2nd XI (Bristol) 1981. Will be regarded as an English player for qualification purposes in 1985. Has not yet appeared in first-class cricket.

John William SOUTHERN (The William Ellis School, Highgate) B King's Cross, London 2/9/1952. 6ft 3½ins tall. RHB, SLA. Debut 1975. Cap 1978. HS: 61* v Yorks (Bradford) 1979. HSBH: 14 v Somerset (Bournemouth) 1980. BB: 6-46 v Glos (Bournemouth) 1975. Obtained B.Sc degree in Chemistry at Southampton University.

Keith STEVENSON (Bemrose GS, Derby) B Derby 6/10/1950. RHB, RFM. Debut for Derbyshire 1974. Left county after 1977 season and made debut for Hants in 1978. Cap 1979. HS: 33 Derbyshire v Northants (Chesterfield) 1974. HSC: 31 v Derbyshire (Portsmouth) 1981. HSGC/NW: 14 Derbyshire v Surrey (Ilkeston) 1976. HSJPL: 11* v Somerset (Taunton) 1981. BB: 7-22 v Oxford U (Oxford) 1979. BBGC/NW: 4-21 Derbyshire v Surrey (Ilkeston) 1976. BBJPL: 3-22 v Essex (Chelmsford) 1980. BBBH: 4-18 v Middlesex (Lord's) 1981.

Vivian Paul TERRY (Millfield School) B Osnabruck, West Germany 14/1/1959. RHB, RM. Played for 2nd XI since 1976. Debut 1978. HS: 94* v Northants (Southampton) 1981. HSGC/NW: 11 v Middlesex (Lord's) 1979. HSJPL: 33 v Glos (Basingstoke) 1979.

Timothy Maurice (Tim) TREMLETT (Richard Taunton College, Southampton)
B Wellington, Somerset 26/7/1956. Son of M.F. Tremlett, former Somerset player.
RHB, RM. Debut 1976. HS: 88 v Lancs (Manchester) 1981. HSJPL: 28 v Glos
(Cheltenham) 1980, HSBH: 29 v Surrey (Bournemouth) 1981. BB: 5-30 v Notts
(Nottingham) 1980. BBJPL: 4-22 v Lancs (Manchester) 1981. BBBH: 3-21 v
Combined Universities (Cambridge) 1978.

David Roy TURNER B Chippenham, Wilts 5/2/1949. LHB, RM. Played for
Wiltshire in 1965. Debut 1966. Cap 1970. Played for Western Province in 1977-78
Currie Cup competition. Benefit in 1981. 1,000 runs (6) – 1,269 runs (av. 36.25) in
1976 best. Gillette Man of the Match Awards: 1. Benson & Hedges Gold Awards:
4. HS: 181* v Surrey (Oval) 1969. HSGC/NW: 86 v Northants (Southampton) 1976.
HSJPL: 109 v Surrey (Oval) 1980. HSBH: 123* v Minor Counties (South)
(Amersham) 1973.

N.B. The following player whose particulars appeared in the 1981 Annual has been
omitted: S.F. Graf.

County Averages

**Schweppes County Championship: Played 22, won 6, drawn 8, lost 7, abandoned 1.
All first-class matches: Played 25, won 6, drawn 11, lost 7, abandoned 1.**

BATTING AND FIELDING

Cap		M	I	NO	Runs	HS	Avge	100	50	Ct	St
1972	C.G. Greenidge	19	30	1	1442	140	49.72	4	9	24	—
1975	J.M. Rice	11	19	3	639	161*	39.93	2	2	7	—
1981	C.L. Smith	8	15	2	428	81*	32.92	—	3	5	—
1978	J.W. Southern	13	13	6	230	46	32.85	—	—	5	—
1971	T.E. Jesty	23	35	6	891	99	30.72	—	5	13	—
1970	D.R. Turner	22	30	6	704	106	29.33	1	4	4	—
—	R.E. Hayward	7	13	3	285	101*	28.50	1	1	3	—
1980	N.E.J. Pocock	15	15	1	393	63	28.07	—	2	10	—
—	V.P. Terry	5	7	2	139	94*	27.80	—	1	2	—
—	M.C.J.Nicholas	19	32	5	721	101*	26.70	1	3	9	—
—	T.M. Tremlett	16	25	1	636	88	26.50	—	4	5	—
1981	M.D. Marshall	17	23	3	425	75*	21.25	—	1	6	—
1979	K. Stevenson	24	23	9	232	31	16.57	—	—	7	—
1978	N.G. Cowley	23	29	1	451	67	16.10	—	2	4	—
—	R.J. Parks	23	29	8	330	37	15.71	—	—	49	3
—	S.J. Malone	8	6	1	44	23	8.80	—	—	3	—
—	M.J. Bailey	10	13	3	67	14	6.70	—	—	6	—

Played in one match C.C. Curzon 31*, 22 (1 ct).

BOWLING

	Type	O	M	R	W	Avge	Best	5 wI	10 wM
M.D. Marshall	**RF**	531.3	166	1321	68	19.42	6-57	5	—
T.E. Jesty	**RM**	437.4	136	1033	52	19.86	6-25	3	—
T.M. Tremlett	**RM**	196	68	383	14	27.35	4-11	—	—
K. Stevenson	**RFM**	595.5	119	1966	57	34.49	5-32	3	—
S.J. Malone	**RM**	147	27	518	14	37.00	3-88	—	—
N.G. Cowley	**OB**	368.5	92	1134	27	42.00	4-134	—	—
J.W. Southern	**SLA**	362.1	98	952	20	47.60	5-108	1	—
J.M. Rice	**RM**	64.5	13	258	5	51.60	2-25	—	—
M.J. Bailey	**OB**	140	24	489	8	61.12	4-138	—	—

Also bowled: C.G. Greenidge 0.4-0-1-0; R.E. Hayward 2-0-5-0; M.C.J. Nicholas 1.5-0-4-1; R.J. Parks 0.3-0-0-0; P.I. Pocock 7.3-3-36-1; C.L. Smith 41-7-149-2; V.P. Terry 13.5-4-39-0; D.R. Turner 23.1-7-88-4.

County Records

First-class cricket

Highest innings	For	672-7d v Somerset (Taunton)	1899
totals:	Agst	742 by Surrey (The Oval)	1909
Lowest innings	For	15 v Warwickshire (Birmingham)	1922
totals:	Agst	23 by Yorkshire (Middlesbrough)	1965
Highest individual innings:	For	316 R.H. Moore v Warwickshire (Bournemouth)	1937
	Agst	302* P. Holmes for Yorkshire (Portsmouth)	1920
Best bowling	For	9-25 R.M.H. Cottam v Lancs (Manchester)	1965
in an innings:	Agst	9-21 L.B. Richmond for Notts (Nottingham)	1921
Best bowling	For	16-88 J.A. Newman v Somerset	1927
in a match:		(Weston-super-Mare)	
	Agst	17-119 W. Mead for Essex (Southampton)	1895
Most runs in a season:		2,854 (av. 79.27) C.P. Mead	1928
runs in a career:		48,892 (av. 48.84) C.P. Mead	1905-1936
100s in a season:		12 by C.P. Mead	1928
100s in a career:		138 by C.P. Mead	1905-1936
wickets in a season:		190 (av. 15.61) A.S. Kennedy	1922
wickets in a career:		2,669 (av. 18.22) D. Shackleton	1948-1969

RECORD WICKET STANDS

1st	249	R.E. Marshall & J.R. Gray v Middlesex (Portsmouth)	1960
2nd	321	G. Brown & E.I.M. Barrett v Gloucestershire (Southampton)	1920
3rd	344	C.P. Mead & G. Brown v Yorkshire (Portsmouth)	1927
4th	263	R.E. Marshall & D.A. Livingstone v Middlesex (Lord's)	1970
5th	235	G. Hill & D.F. Walker v Sussex (Portsmouth)	1937
6th	411	R.M. Poore & E.G. Wynyard v Somerset (Taunton)	1899
7th	325	G. Brown & C.H. Abercrombie v Essex (Leyton)	1913
8th	178	C.P. Mead & C.P. Brutton v Worcestershire (Bournemouth)	1925
9th	230	D.A. Livingstone & A.T. Castell v Surrey (Southampton)	1962
10th	192	A. Bowell & W.H. Livsey v Worcestershire (Bournemouth)	1921

NB. A partnership of 334 for the first wicket by B.A. Richards, C.G. Greenidge and D.R. Turner occurred against Kent at Southampton in 1973. Richards retired hurt after 241 runs had been scored and, in the absence of any official ruling on the matter, it is a matter of opinion as to whether it should be regarded as the first-wicket record for the county.

One-day cricket

Highest inning totals:	Gillette Cup/ NatWest Trophy	371-4 v Glamorgan (Southampton)	1975
	John Player League	288-5 v Somerset (Weston-super-Mare)	1975
	Benson & Hedges Cup	321-1 v Minor Counties (South) (Amersham)	1973
Lowest innings totals:	Gillette Cup/ NatWest Trophy	98 v Lancashire (Manchester)	1975
	John Player League	43 v Essex (Basingstoke)	1972
	Benson & Hedges Cup	94 v Glamorgan (Swansea)	1973
Highest indi-vidual innings:	Gillette Cup/ NatWest Trophy	177 C.G. Greenidge v Glamorgan (Southampton)	1975
	John Player League	163* C.G. Greenidge v Warwickshire (Birmingham)	1979
	Benson & Hedges Cup	173* C.G. Greenidge v Minor Counties (South) (Amersham)	1973
Best bowling figures:	Gillette Cup/ NatWest Trophy	7-30 P.J. Sainsbury v Norfolk (Southampton)	1965
	John Player League	6-20 T.E. Jesty v Glamorgan (Cardiff)	1975
	Benson & Hedges Cup	5-24 R.S. Herman v Gloucestershire (Bristol)	1975

KENT

Formation of present club: 1859, re-organised 1870.
Colours: Red and white.
Badge: White horse.
County Champions (6): 1906, 1909, 1910, 1913, 1970 and 1978.
Joint Champions: 1977.
Gillette Cup Winners (2): 1967 and 1974.
Gillette Cup Finalists: 1971.
NatWest Trophy Second Round: 1981.
John Player League Champions (3): 1972, 1973 and 1976.
Benson & Hedges Cup Winners (3): 1973, 1976 and 1978.
Benson & Hedges Cup Finalists: 1977.
Fenner Trophy Winners (2): 1971 and 1973.
Gillette Man of the Match Awards: 23.
NatWest Trophy Man of the Match Awards: 1.
Benson & Hedges Gold Awards: 32.

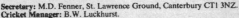

Secretary: M.D. Fenner, St. Lawrence Ground, Canterbury CT1 3NZ.
Cricket Manager: B.W. Luckhurst.
Captain: Asif Iqbal.
Prospects of Play Telephone No: Canterbury matches only, Canterbury (0227) 57323.

ASIF IQBAL RAZVI (Osmania University, Hyderabad, India) B Hyderabad, India 6/6/1943. Nephew of Ghulam Ahmed, former Indian off-break bowler and Test cricketer. RHB, RM. Debut 1959-60 for Hyderabad in Ranji Trophy. Migrated to Pakistan in 1961 and has since appeared for various Karachi teams, Pakistan International Airways and National Bank. Captained Pakistan under-25 v England under-25 in 1966-67. Debut for county and cap 1968. *Wisden* 1967. County Captain in 1977. Benefit 1981. Re-appointed County Captain in 1981. Tests: 58 for Pakistan between 1964-65 and 1979-80 captaining Pakistan in 6 Tests. Tours: Pakistan to Australia and New Zealand 1964-65, 1972-73 (vice-captain), England 1967, 1971 (vice-captain) and 1974 (vice-captain). Australia and West Indies 1976-77, India 1979-80 (captain), Pakistan Eaglets to England 1963, Pakistan 'A' to Ceylon 1964, Pakistan International Airways to East Africa 1964. 1,000 runs (7) – 1,379 runs (av. 39.40) in 1970 best. Scored 1,029 runs (av. 41.16) in Australia and New Zealand 1972-73. Scored two centuries in match (104 and 110*) Pakistan International Airways v Habib Bank (Lahore) 1979-80. Scored 146 v England (Oval) 1967 sharing in 9th-wkt partnership of 190 with Intikhab Alam after Pakistan were 65-8 – record 9th-wicket stand in Test cricket. Gillette Man of the Match Awards: 3. Benson & Hedges Gold Awards: 4. HS: 196 National Bank v Pakistan International Airways (Lahore) 1976-77. HSTC: 175 Pakistan v New Zealand (Dunedin) 1972-73. HSUK: 171 v Glos (Folkstone) 1978. HSGC/NW: 89 v Lancs (Lord's) 1971. HSJPL: 106 v Glos (Maidstone) 1976. HSBH: 75 v Middlesex (Canterbury) 1973. BB: 6-45 Pakistan Eaglets v Cambridge U (Cambridge) 1963. BBTC: 5-48 Pakistan v New Zealand (Wellington) 1964-65. BBC: 4-11 v Lancs (Canterbury) 1968. BBGC/NW: 4-18 v Lancs (Canterbury) 1979. BBJPL: 3-3 v Northants (Tring) 1977. BBBH: 5-42 v Middlesex (Lord's) 1980.

Derek George ASLETT (Dover Grammar School for Boys) B Dover 12/2/1958. RHB, LB. Played for 2nd XI since 1978. Debut 1981 scoring 146* in debut match, the second highest score by a player making his first-class debut in a county championship match. HS: 146* v Hants (Bournemouth) 1981. HSJPL: 25 v Middlesex (Canterbury) 1981. Obtained B.A. Degree of Leicester University.

Eldine Asworth BAPTISTE B St. John's, Antigua 12/3/1960. RHB, RFM. Joined staff 1980. Debut 1981. HS: 37* v Lancs (Maidstone) 1981. HSJPL: 22 v Glos (Cheltenham) 1981. BB: 5-37 v Lancs (Maidstone) 1981. BBJPL: 3-32 v Sussex (Eastbourne) 1981.

Mark Richard BENSON (Sutton Valence School) B Shoreham, Sussex 6/7/1958. LHB, OB. Played for 2nd XI since 1978. Debut 1980. Cap 1981. Scored 1,063 runs (av. 32.21) in 1981. HS: 114 v Warwickshire (Nuneaton) 1981. HSNW: 57 v Yorks (Canterbury) 1981. HSJPL: 88 v Worcs (Canterbury) 1981. HSBH: 33* v Essex (Dartford) 1981.

Christopher Stuart (Chris) COWDREY (Tonbridge School) B Farnborough, Kent 20/10/1957. Eldest son of M.C. Cowdrey. RHB, RM. Played for 2nd XI at age of 15. Captain of England Young Cricketers team to West Indies 1976. Played in one John Player League match in 1976. Debut 1977. Cap 1979. Benson & Hedges Gold Awards: 1. HS: 101* v Glamorgan (Swansea) 1977. HSNW: 25 v Notts (Canterbury) 1981. HSJPL: 74 v Worcs (Worcester) 1978. HSBH: 114 v Sussex (Canterbury) 1977. BB: 3-17 v Hants (Bournemouth) 1980. BBNW: 4-41 v Yorks (Canterbury) 1981.

Graham Roy DILLEY B Dartford 18/5/1959. 6ft 3ins tall. LHB RF. Debut 1977. Cap 1980. Elected Best Young Cricketer of the Year in 1980 by the Cricket Writers' Club. Tests: 12 between 1979-80 and 1981-. Tours: Australia and India 1979-80, West Indies 1980-81, India and Sri Lanka 1981-82. HS: 81 v Northants (Northampton) 1979. HSTC: 56 v Australia (Leeds) 1981. HSJPL: 17 v Derbyshire (Canterbury) 1980. HSBH: 13* v Hants (Canterbury) 1980. BB: 6-66 v Middlesex (Lord's) 1979. BBTC: 4-24 v Australia (Nottingham) 1981. BBJPL: 4-20 v Glos (Canterbury) 1980. BBBH: 4-14 v Combined Universities (Canterbury) 1981.

Alan George Ernest EALHAM B Ashford (Kent) 30/8/1944. RHB, OB. Debut 1966. Cap 1970. County Captain from 1978 to 1980. Benefit in 1982. 1,000 runs (3) – 1,363 runs (av.34.94) in 1971 best. Held 5 catches in innings v Glos (Folkestone) 1966, all in outfield off D.L. Underwood. Gillette Man of the Match Awards: 1. Benson & Hedges Gold Awards: 4. HS: 153 v Worcs (Canterbury) 1979. HSGC/NW: 85* v Glamorgan (Swansea) 1979. HSJPL: 83 v Leics (Leicester) 1977. HSBH: 94* v Sussex (Canterbury) 1977.

Richard Mark ELLISON (Tonbridge School) B Ashford (Kent) 21/9/1959. LHB, RM. Played for 2nd XI since 1979. Debut 1981. HS: 61* v Somerset (Folkestone) 1981. HSJPL: 16* v Glos (Cheltenham) 1981. Is studying at Exeter University.

Simon Graham HINKS B Northfleet 12/10/1960. LHB. Joined staff 1980. Has yet to appear in first-class cricket.

Kevin Bertram Sidney JARVIS (Springhead School, Northfleet) B Dartford 23/4/1953. 6ft 3in tall. RHB, RFM. Debut 1975. Cap 1977. Benson & Hedges Gold Awards: 1. HS: 12* v Cambridge U (Canterbury) 1977, 12 v Sussex (Hove) 1978 and 12 v Leics (Leicester) 1981. BB: 8-97 v Worcs (Worcester) 1978. BBGC/NW: 3-53 v Sussex (Canterbury) 1976. BBJPL: 4-27 v Surrey (Maidstone) 1977. BBBH: 4-34 v Worcs (Lord's) 1976.

100

Graham William JOHNSON (Shooters Hill GS) B Beckenham 8/11/1946. RHB, OB. Debut 1965. Cap 1970. 1,000 runs (3) – 1,438 runs (av. 31.26) in 1973 and 1,438 runs (av. 35.95) in 1975 best. Gillette Man of the Match Awards: 1. Benson & Hedges Gold Awards: 3. HS: 168 v Surrey (Oval) 1976. HSGC/NW: 120* v Bucks (Canterbury) 1974. HSJPL: 89 v Sussex (Hove) 1976. HSBH: 85* v Minor Counties (South) (Canterbury) 1975. BB: 6-32 v Surrey (Tunbridge Wells) 1978. BBJPL: 5-26 v Surrey (Oval) 1974. Studied at London School of Economics.

Alan Philip Eric KNOTT B Belvedere (Kent) 9/4/1946. RHB, WK. Can bowl OB. Debut 1964. Cap 1965. Elected Best Young Cricketer of the Year in 1965 by Cricket Writers Club. *Wisden* 1969. Played for Tasmania 1969-70 whilst coaching there. Benefit (£27,037) in 1976. Tests: 95 between 1967 and 1981. Played in 5 matches against Rest of World in 1970. Tours: Pakistan 1966-67, West Indies 1967-68 and 1973-74, Ceylon and Pakistan 1968-69, Australia and New Zealand 1970-71, 1974-75, India, Sri Lanka and Pakistan 1972-73, India, Sri Lanka and Australia 1976-77. 1,000 runs (2) – 1,209 runs (av. 41.68) in 1971 best. Scored two centuries in match (127* and 118*) v Surrey (Maidstone) 1972. Gillette Man of the Match Awards: 2. Benson & Hedges Gold Awards: 1. HS: 156 MCC v South Zone (Bangalore) 1972-73. HSUK: 144 v Sussex (Canterbury) 1976. HSTC: 135 v Australia (Nottingham) 1977. HSGC/NW: 46 v Notts (Nottingham) 1975. HSJPL: 60 v Hants (Canterbury) 1969. HSBH: 65 v Combined Universities (Oxford) 1976. Dismissed 84 batsmen (74 ct 10 st) in 1965. 81 batsmen (73 ct 7 st) in 1966, and 98 batsmen (90 ct 8 st) in 1967. Dismissed 7 batsmen (7 ct) on debut in Test cricket v Pakistan (Nottingham) 1967.

Christopher PENN (Dover Grammar School for Boys) B Dover 19/6/1963. RHB, RM. Played for 2nd XI in 1981, but has not yet appeared in first-class cricket. Has joined staff for 1982.

Laurie POTTER (Kelmscott HS, Perth, Western Australia) B Bexleyheath 7/11/1962. RHB, LM. Emigrated to Australia with parents at age of four. Captained Australian Under-19 team on tour of Pakistan in 1980-81, scoring century in final representative match at Karachi. Played for England Young Cricketers v Indian Young Cricketers 1981. Debut 1981. HS: 42* v Oxford U (Oxford) 1981. BBJPL: 4-27 v Somerset (Bath) 1981.

Guy Dennis SPELMAN (Sevenoaks School) B Westminster 18/10/1958. 6ft 3½ins tall. LHB, RM. Played in three John Player League matches in 1978. Debut 1980. Did not play in 1981. BBJPL: 3-30 v Northants (Luton) 1980. Studied at Nottingham University.

Christopher James (Chris) TAVARÉ (Sevenoaks School and Oxford) B Orpington 27/10/1954. RHB, RM. Scored 124* for England Schools v All-India Schools (Birmingham) 1973. Debut 1974. Blue 1975-76-77. Cap 1978. Tests: 4 in 1980 and 1981. Tour: India and Sri Lanka 1981-82. 1,000 runs (5) – 1,770 runs (av. 53.63) in 1981 best. NatWest Man of the Match Awards: 1. Benson & Hedges Gold Awards: 3 (2 for Combined Universities). HS: 156 v Derbyshire (Derby) 1981. HSTC: 149 v India (Delhi) 1981-82. HSNW: 118* v Yorks (Canterbury) 1981. HSJPL: 136* v Glos (Canterbury) 1978. HSBH: 95 v Surrey (Oval) 1980.

Neil Royston TAYLOR (Cray Technical School) B Orpington 21/7/1959. RHB, OB. Played for 2nd XI since 1977. Debut 1979 scoring 110 v Sri Lankans

(Canterbury) in debut match. HS: 110.as above. HSJPL: 49 v Glos (Cheltenham) 1981.

Derek Leslie UNDERWOOD (Beckenham and Penge GS) B Bromley 8/6/1945. RHB, LM. Debut 1963, taking 100 wkts and being the youngest player ever to do so in debut season. Cap 1964 (second youngest Kent player to have received this award). Elected Best Young Cricketer of the Year in 1966 by the Cricket Writers Club. *Wisden* 1968. Benefit (£24,114) in 1975. Awarded MBE in 1981 New Year's Honours List. Took 1,000th wkt in first-class cricket in New Zealand 1970-71 at age of 25 years 264 days – only W. Rhodes (in 1902) and G.A. Lohmann (in 1890) have achieved the feat at a younger age – and 2,000th wkt in 1981. Took 200th wkt in Test cricket against Australia in 1975. Tests: 79 between 1966 and 1980. Played in 3 matches against Rest of World in 1970. Tours: Pakistan 1966-67, Ceylon and Pakistan 1968-69, Australia and New Zealand 1970-71, 1974-75, India, Sri Lanka and Pakistan 1972-73, West Indies 1973-74, India, Sri Lanka and Australia 1976-77, Australia and India 1979-80, India and Sri Lanka 1981-82. 100 wkts (9) – 157 wkts (av. 13.80) in 1966 best. Hat-trick v Sussex (Hove) 1977. HS: 80 v Lancs (Manchester) 1969. HSTC: 45* v Australia (Leeds) 1968. HSGC/NW: 28 v Sussex (Tunbridge Wells) 1963. HSJPL: 22 v Worcs (Dudley) 1969. HSBH: 17 v Essex (Canterbury) 1973. BB: 9-28 v Sussex (Hastings) 1964 and 9-32 v Surrey (Oval) 1978. BBTC: 8-51 v Pakistan (Lord's) 1974. BBGC/NW: 4-57 v Leics (Canterbury) 1974. BBJPL: 5-19 v Glos (Maidstone) 1972. BBBH: 5-35 v Surrey (Oval) 1976.

Stuart Nicholas Varney WATERTON (Gravesend School for Boys) B Dartford 6/12/1960. RHB, WK. Debut 1980. HS: 40* v Surrey (Maidstone) 1980. Is studying at London University.

Lindsay Jonathan WOOD (Simon Langton School for Boys, Canterbury) B Ruislip (Middlesex) 12/5/1961. LHB, SLA. Played for 2nd XI since 1979. Debut 1981. One match v Essex (Chelmsford) 1981. BB: 4-124 v Essex (Chelmsford) 1981. Is training as a teacher at King Alfred's College, Winchester.

Robert Andrew WOOLMER (Skinners' School, Tunbridge Wells) B Kanpur, India 14/5/1948. RHB, RM. Debut 1968. Cap 1970. *Wisden* 1975. Played for Natal between 1973-74 and 1975-76 in Currie Cup competition and for Western Province in 1980-81. Tests: 19 between 1975 and 1981. Tour: India, Sri Lanka and Australia 1976-77. 1,000 runs (5) – 1,749 runs (av. 47.27) in 1976 best. Hat-trick for MCC v Australians (Lord's) 1975. Gillette Man of the Match Awards: 2. Benson & Hedges Gold Awards: 5. HS: 171 v Sussex (Hove) 1980. HSTC: 149 England v Australia (Oval) 1975. HSGC/NW: 91 v Yorks (Leeds) 1980. HSJPL: 112* v Notts (Nottingham) 1980. HSBH: 79 v Derbyshire (Lord's) 1978 and 79* v Essex (Dartford) 1981. BB: 7-47 v Sussex (Canterbury) 1969. BBGC/NW: 4-28 v Somerset (Taunton) 1979. BBJPL: 6-9 v Derbyshire (Chesterfield) 1979. BBBH: 4-14 v Sussex (Tunbridge Wells) 1972.

N.B. The following players whose particulars appeared in the 1980 annual have been omitted: N.J. Kemp (not re-engaged) and C.J.C. Rowe (not re-engaged). In addition J.N. Shepherd who was also not re-engaged has joined Gloucestershire and his particulars will be found under that county.

The career records of all these players will be found elsewhere in the annual.

County Averages

Schweppes County Championship: Played 22; Won 5, Drawn 10, Lost 7
All first-class matches: Played 24: Won 6, Drawn 12, Lost 6

BATTING AND FIELDING

Cap		M	I	NO	Runs	HS	Avge	100	50	Ct	St
1978	C.J. Tavaré	20	36	7	1591	156	54.86	4	10	17	—
	R.M. Ellison	7	11	6	237	61*	47.40	—	3	3	—
1968	Asif Iqbal	19	31	3	1252	112	44.71	2	9	5	—
1979	C.S. Cowdrey	17	27	4	757	97	32.91	—	6	15	—
1981	M.R. Benson	21	36	3	1063	114	32.21	2	6	9	—
1970	A.G.E. Ealham	3	5	0	141	48	28.20	—	—	2	—
1970	R.A. Woolmer	19	34	1	904	119*	27.39	1	4	13	—
1965	A.P.E. Knott	19	28	4	617	65	25.70	—	4	39	8
1970	G.W. Johnson	24	38	8	698	107	23.26	1	1	15	—
	N.R. Taylor	11	19	2	385	99	22.64	—	3	12	—
1967	J.N. Shepherd	15	20	6	310	59*	22.14	—	2	4	—
	E.A. Baptiste	15	22	4	359	37*	19.94	—	—	8	—
	L. Potter	3	6	1	99	42*	19.80	—	—	3	—
1964	D.L. Underwood	23	21	10	162	50	14.72	—	1	10	—
1977	C.J.C. Rowe	5	10	0	142	54	14.20	—	1	2	—
	S.N.V. Waterton	5	5	1	50	28	12.50	—	—	10	3
1980	G.R. Dilley	11	8	4	39	17*	9.75	—	—	6	—
1977	K.B.S. Jarvis	23	17	4	26	12	2.00	—	—	7	—

Played in two matches: D.G. Aslett 146*, 20*, 11, 11 (1 ct).
Played in one match: N.J. Kemp 5*; L.J. Wood 0, 5.

BOWLING

	Type	O	M	R	W	Avge	Best	5 wI	10 wM
D.L. Underwood	LM	774.3	282	1788	78	22.92	7-93	5	1
K.B.S. Jarvis	RFM	586.3	137	1885	81	23.27	7-65	5	2
G.W. Johnson	OB	625.3	177	1572	57	27.57	6-33	2	—
E.A. Baptiste	RFM	280.2	64	844	29	29.10	5-37	1	—
J.N. Shepherd	RM	424.3	111	1136	28	40.57	5-61	1	—
C.S. Cowdrey	RM	75.1	14	271	6	45.16	2-14	—	—
G.R. Dilley	RF	183.5	33	661	14	47.21	3-57	—	—

Also bowled: Asif Iqbal 9.4-2-61-1; M.R. Benson 4-0-28-0; R.M. Ellison 70.2-18-144-4; N.J. Kemp 7-1-32-0; A.P.E. Knott 2-2-0-0; C.J.C. Rowe 21-3-89-0; C.J. Tavaré 11-2-96-0; N. Taylor 4-0-23-0; L.J. Wood 43-11-124-4; R.A. Woolmer 47-11-141-4.

County Records

First-class cricket

Highest innings	For	803-4d v Essex (Brentwood)		1934
totals:	Agst	676 by Australians (Canterbury)		1921

KENT

Lowest innings	For	18 v Sussex (Gravesend)	1867
totals:	Agst	16 by Warwickshire (Tonbridge)	1913
Highest indi-	For	332 W.H. Ashdown v Essex (Brentwood)	1934
vidual innings:	Agst	344 W.G. Grace for MCC (Canterbury)	1876
Best bowling	For	10-30 C. Blythe v Northamptonshire	
in an innings:		(Northampton)	1907
	Agst	10-48 C.H.G. Bland for Sussex (Tonbridge)	1899
Best bowling	For	17-47 C. Blythe v Northamptonshire	
in a match:		(Northampton)	1907
	Agst	17-106 T.W. J. Goddard for Gloucestershire	
		(Bristol)	1939
Most runs in a season:		2,894 (av. 59.06) F.E. Woolley	1928
runs in a career:		47,868 (av. 41.77) F.E. Woolley	1906-1938
100s in a season:		10 by F.E. Woolley	1928 & 1934
100s in a career:		122 by F.E. Woolley	1906-1938
wickets in a season:		262 (av. 14.74) A.P. Freeman	1933
wickets in a career:		3,340 (av. 17.64) A.P. Freeman	1914-1936

RECORD WICKET STANDS

1st	283	A.E. Fagg & P.R. Sunnucks v Essex (Colchester)	1938
2nd	352	W.H. Ashdown & F.E. Woolley v Essex (Brentwood)	1934
3rd	321*	A. Hearne & J.R. Mason v Nottinghamshire (Nottingham)	1899
4th	297	H.T.W. Hardinge & A.P.F. Chapman v Hampshire (Southampton)	1926
5th	277	F.E. Woolley & L.E.G. Ames v New Zealanders (Canterbury)	1931
6th	284	A.P.F. Chapman & G.B. Legge v Lancashire (Maidstone)	1927
7th	248	A.P. Day & E. Humphreys v Somerset (Taunton)	1908
8th	157	A.L. Hilder & C. Wright v Essex (Gravesend)	1924
9th	161	B.R. Edrich & F. Ridgway v Sussex (Tunbridge Wells)	1949
10th	235	F.E. Woolley & A. Fielder v Worcestershire (Stourbridge)	1909

One-day cricket

Highest innings totals:	Gillette Cup/ NatWest Trophy	297-3 v Worcestershire (Canterbury)	1970
	John Player League	278-5 v Gloucestershire (Maidstone)	1976
	Benson & Hedges Cup	280-3 v Surrey (Oval)	1976
Lowest innings totals:	Gillette Cup/ NatWest Trophy	60 v Somerset (Taunton)	1979
	John Player League	84 v Gloucestershire (Folkestone)	1969
	Benson & Hedges Cup	73 v Middlesex (Canterbury)	1979
Highest indi- vidual innings:	Gillette Cup/ NatWest Trophy	129 B.W. Luckhurst v Durham (Canterbury)	1974
	John Player League	142 B.W. Luckhurst v Somerset (Weston-super-Mare)	1970
	Benson & Hedges Cup	114 (C.S. Cowdrey v Sussex (Canterbury)	1977
Best bowling figures:	Gillette Cup/ NatWest Trophy	7-15 A.L. Dixon v Surrey (Oval)	1967
	John Player League	6-9 R.A. Woolmer v Derbyshire (Chesterfield)	1979
	Benson & Hedges Cup	5-21 B.D. Julien v Surrey (Oval)	1973

104

LANCASHIRE

Formation of present club: 1864.
Colours: Red, green and blue.
Badge: Red rose.
County Champions (8): 1881, 1897, 1904, 1926, 1927, 1928, 1930 and 1934.
Joint Champions (4): 1879, 1882, 1889 and 1950.
Gillette Cup Winners (4): 1970, 1971, 1972 and 1975.
Gillette Cup Finalists (2): 1974 and 1976.
NatWest Trophy Semi-Finalists: 1981.
John Player League Champions (2): 1969 and 1970.
Benson & Hedges Cup Semi-Finalists (2): 1973 and 1974.
Gillette Man of the Match Awards: 35.
NatWest Man of the Match Awards: 3.
Benson & Hedges Gold Awards: 26.

Secretary: C.D. Hassell, Old Trafford, Manchester M16 0PX.
Cricket Manager: J.D. Bond.
Captain: C.H. Lloyd.
Prospects of Play Telephone No: 061-872 0261.

John ABRAHAMS (Heywood GS) B Cape Town, South Africa 21/7/1952. LHB, OB. Son of Cecil J. Abrahams, former professional for Milnrow and Radcliffe in Central Lancashire League. Has lived in this country since 1962. Debut 1973. HS: 126 v Cambridge U (Cambridge) 1978. HSGC/NW: 46 v Northants (Lord's) 1976. HSJPL: 59 v Hants (Manchester) 1979. HSBH: 47 v Leics (Leicester) 1980. BB: 3-27 v Worcs (Manchester) 1981.

Paul John Walter ALLOTT (Altrincham County Grammar School for Boys) B Altrincham (Cheshire) 14/9/1956. 6ft 4ins tall. RHB, RFM. Played for Cheshire in 1976 and for county 2nd XI in 1977. Debut 1978. Cap 1981. Tests: 1 in 1981. Tour: India and Sri Lanka 1981-82. HS: 52* v Australia (Manchester) 1981. HSGC/NW: 19* v Worcs (Worcester) 1980. HSJPL: 22* v Middlesex (Manchester) 1979. BB: 8-48 v Northants (Northampton) 1981. BBNW: 3-22 v Durham (Manchester) 1981. BBJPL: 3-15 v Warwickshire (Birmingham) 1979. BBBH: 3-34 v Derbyshire (Manchester) 1981. Studied at Durham University.

Douglas Keith BECKETT (Cheadle Hulme School) B Hampton Court (Surrey) 29/8/1959. RHB, RM. Played for Cheshire in 1978 and 1979 and for Derbyshire 2nd XI in 1979. Played for county in two John Player League matches and one Gillette Cup match in 1980 and three John Player League matches in 1981. Has yet to appear in first-class cricket. HSJPL: 30 v Glos (Bristol) 1981. Studied at Manchester University.

Ian COCKBAIN (Bootle GS) B Bootle 19/4/1958. RHB, SLA. Played for 2nd XI since 1976. Debut 1979. HS: 85 v Glos (Manchester) 1981. HSJPL: 34 v Warwickshire (Liverpool) 1980. HSBH: 53 v Worcs (Manchester) 1980.

Colin Everton Hunte CROFT (Central High School, Georgetown) B Lancaster Village, Demerara, British Guiana 15/3/1953. 6ft 4ins tall. RHB, RF. Debut for Guyana in 1971-72 Shell Shield Competition. Played for Warwickshire 2nd XI in 1972. Debut for county 1977. Not re-engaged after 1978 season, but has rejoined county for 1982, his registration having been retained. Professional for Royston in

LANCASHIRE

Central Lancashire League in 1979. Tests: 24 for West Indies between 1976-77 and 1980-81. Tours: West Indies to Australia and New Zealand 1979-89, England 1980, Pakistan 1980-81, Australia 1981-82. HS: 46* v Worcs (Worcester) 1977. HSTC: 33 West Indies v England (Bridgetown) 1980-81. HSJPL: 10* v Surrey (Oval) 1977. BB: 8-29 West Indies v Pakistan (Port of Spain) 1976-77. BBUK: 7-54 v Notts (Nottingham) 1977. BBGC/NW: 3-52 v Sussex (Hove) 1978. BBJPL: 4-29 v Essex (Manchester) 1978. BBBH: 3-22 v Glos (Liverpool) 1978

Philip Andrew DAVIS (Birkenhead School) B Neston (Cheshire) 16/1/1961. RHB, RM. Played for 2nd XI since 1980 and is on county staff. Has not yet appeared in first-class cricket.

Ian FOLLEY B Burnley 9/1/1963. RHB, LM. Played for 2nd XI since 1980 and is on county staff. Has not yet appeared in first-class cricket.

Graeme FOWLER (Accrington GS) B Accrington 20/4/1957. LHB, WK. Played for 2nd XI since 1973. Played in one John Player League match v Derbyshire (Chesterfield) 1978. Debut 1979. Cap 1981. Scored 1,560 runs (av. 39.00) in 1981. HS: 143 v Cambridge U (Cambridge) 1981. HSNW: 57 v Northants (Northampton) 1981. HSJPL: 65 v Worcs (Manchester) 1981. HSBH: 34 v Scotland (Glasgow) 1981. Studied at Durham University.

Frank Charles HAYES (De La Salle College, Salford) B Preston 6/12/1946. RHB, RM. Debut 1970 scoring 94 and 99 in first two matches after scoring 203* for 2nd XI v Warwickshire 2nd XI (Birmingham). Cap 1972. County Captain from 1978 to 1980. Tests: 9 between 1973 and 1976. Tour: West Indies 1973-74. 1,000 runs (6) – 1,311 runs (av. 35.43) in 1974 best. Scored 34 in one over (6 4 6 6 6 6) off M.A. Nash v Glamorgan (Swansea) 1977. Gillette Man of the Match Awards: 1. Benson & Hedges Gold Awards: 2. HS: 187 v Indians (Manchester) 1974. HSTC: 106* v West Indies (Oval) 1973 in second innings on Test debut. HSGC/NW: 93 v Warwickshire (Birmingham) 1976. HSJPL: 84* v Somerset (Bath) 1980. HSBH: 102 v Minor Counties (North) (Manchester) 1973. Amateur soccer player. Studied at Sheffield University.

Kevin Anthony HAYES (Queen Elizabeth's GS, Blackburn and Oxford) B Mexborough (Yorks) 26/9/1962. No relation to F.C. Hayes. Has lived in Lancs since 1969. RHB, RM. Played for 2nd XI in 1979. Plays for East Lancashire in Lancashire League. Debut 1980. Blue 1981. University Secretary for 1982. HS: 59 Oxford U v Glos (Oxford) 1981. HSC: 27 v Oxford U (Oxford) 1981. HSBH: 17 Combined Universities v Essex (Chelmsford) 1981. Soccer Blues 1980-81, 1981-82.

Michael Anthony HOLDING (Kingston College HS) B Kingston, Jamaica 16/2/1954. 6ft 3ins tall. RHB, RF. Debut for Jamaica in 1972-73 Shell Shield Competition. *Wisden* 1976. Debut for county 1981 whilst playing as professional for Rishton in Lancashire League. Tests: 28 for West Indies between 1975-76 and 1980-81. Tours: West Indies to Australia 1975-76, 1981-82, England 1976 and 1980, Australia and New Zealand 1979-80, Pakistan 1980-81. HS: 62 West Indies v New South Wales (Sydney) 1975-76. HSUK: 42 West Indians v MCC (Lord's) 1976. HSC: 32 v Glos (Manchester) 1981. HSTC: 58* West Indians v England (St John's) 1980-81. HSNW: 12* v Northants (Northampton) 1981. BB: 8-92 (14-149 match) West Indies v England (Oval) 1976. BBC: 6-74 v Glos (Manchester) 1981. BBNW: 3-35 v Hants (Southampton) 1981.

David Paul HUGHES (Newton-le-Willows GS) B Newton-le-Willows (Lancs)

106

13/5/1947. RHB, SLA. Debut 1967. Cap 1970. Played for Tasmania in 1975-76 and 1976-77 whilst coaching there. Testimonial in 1981. Scored 1,002 runs (av. 29.47) in 1981. Gillette Man of the Match Awards: 1. Benson & Hedges Gold Awards: 1. HS: 126 v Warwickshire (Manchester) 1981. HSGC/NW: 42* v Middlesex (Lord's) 1974. HSJPL: 84 v Essex (Leyton) 1973. HSBH: 52 v Derbyshire (Manchester) 1981. BB: 7-24 v Oxford U (Oxford) 1970. BBGC/NW: 4-61 v Somerset (Manchester) 1972. BBJPL: 6-29 v Somerset (Manchester) 1977. BBBH: 5-23 v Minor Counties (West) (Watford) 1978.

Andrew KENNEDY (Nelson GS) B Blackburn 4/11/1949. LHB, RM. Debut 1970. Cap 1975. Elected Best Young Cricketer of the Year in 1975 by the Cricket Writers' Club. 1,000 runs (3) – 1,194 runs (av. 34.11) in 1980 best. Gillette Man of the Match Awards: 1. NatWest Man of the Match Awards: 1. HS: 180 v Derbyshire (Chesterfield) 1981. HSGC/NW: 131 v Middlesex (Manchester) 1978. HSJPL: 89 v Yorks (Manchester) 1978. HSBH: 91 v Notts (Manchester) 1980. BB: 3-58 v/ Warwickshire (Liverpool) 1980.

Peter Granville LEE B Arthingworth (Northants) 27/8/1945. RHB, RFM. Debut for Northants 1967. Joined Lancs in 1972. Cap 1972. *Wisden* 1975. 100 wkts (2) – 112 wkts (av. 18.45) in 1975 best. HS: 26 Northants v Glos (Northampton) 1969. HSC: 25 v Australians (Manchester) 1977. HSGC/NW: 10* v Middlesex (Lord's) 1974. HSJPL: 27* Northants v Derbyshire (Chesterfield) 1971. BB: 8-34 v Oxford U (Oxford) 1980. BBGC/NW: 4-7 v Cornwall (Truro) 1977. BBJPL: 4-17 v Derbyshire (Chesterfield) 1972. BBBH: 4-32 v Worcs (Manchester) 1973.

Clive Hubert LLOYD (Chatham HS, Georgetown) B Georgetown, British Guiana 31/8/1944. 6ft 4½ins tall. Cousin of L.R. Gibbs. LHB, RM. Wears glasses. Debut 1963-64 for Guyana (then Britian Guiana). Played for Haslingden in Lancashire League in 1967 and also for Rest of World XI in 1967 and 1968. Debut for county v Australians 1968. Cap 1969. *Wisden* 1970. Testimonial (£27,199) in 1977. Appointed County Captain in 1981. Tests: 82 for West Indies between 1966-67 and 1980-81, captaining West Indies in 46 Tests, the record for all countries. Played in 5 matches for Rest of World 1970 and 2 in 1971-72. Scored 118 on debut v England (Port of Spain) 1967-68, 129 on debut v Australia (Brisbane) 1968-69, and 82 and 78* on debut v India (Bombay) 1966-67. Tours: West Indies to India and Ceylon 1966-67, Australia and New Zealand 1968-69, 1979-80 (captain), England 1969, 1973, 1976 (captain), and 1980 (captain), Rest of World to Australia 1971-72 (returning early owing to back injury), India, Sri Lanka and Pakistan 1974-75 (captain), Australia 1975-76 (captain), 1981-82 (captain), Pakistan 1980-81 (captain). 1,000 runs (9) – 1,603 runs (av. 47.14) in 1970 best. Also scored 1,000 runs in Australia and New Zealand 1968-69 and in India, Sri Lanka and Pakistan 1974-75. Scored 201* in 120 minutes for West Indies v Glamorgan (Swansea) 1976 to equal record for fastest double-century in first-class cricket. Gillette Man of the Match Awards: 6. NatWest Man of the Match Awards: 1. HS: 242* West Indies v India (Bombay) 1974-75. HSUK: 217* v Warwickshire (Manchester) 1971. HSGC/NW: 126 v Warwickshire (Lord's) 1972. HSJPL: 134* v Somerset (Manchester) 1970. HSBH: 124 v Warwickshire (Manchester) 1981. BB: 4-48 v Leics (Manchester) 1970. BBGC/NW: 3-39 v Somerset (Taunton) 1970. BBJPL: 4-33 v Middlesex (Lord's) 1971. BBBH: 3-23 v Derbyshire (Manchester) 1974.

David LLOYD (Accrington Secondary TS) B Accrington 18/3/1947. LHB, SLA. Debut 1965. Cap 1968. County Captain from 1973 to 1977. Testimonial (£40,171) in 1978. Tests: 9 in 1974 and 1974-75. Tour: Australia and New Zealand 1974-75. 1,000 runs (10) – 1,510 runs (av. 47.18) in 1972 best. Scored two centuries in match (116

107

and 104* v Worcs (Southport) 1979. Gillette Man of the Match Awards: 3. NatWest Man of the Match Awards: 1. Benson & Hedges Gold Awards: 2. HS: 214* England v India (Birmingham) 1974. HSC: 195 v Glos (Manchester) 1973. HSGC/NW: 121* v Glos (Manchester) 1978. HSJPL: 103* v Northants (Bedford) 1971. HSBH: 113 v Minor Counties (North) (Manchester) 1973 and 113 v Scotland (Manchester) 1980. BB: 7–38 v Glos (Lydney) 1966. BBNW: 3-22 v Durham (Manchester) 1981. BBJPL: 3-23 v Glos (Manchester) 1980. BBBH: 4-17 v Notts (Manchester) 1980.

Steven Joseph (Steve) O'SHAUGHNESSY B Bury 9/9/1961. RHB, RM. Debut 1980. HS: 50 v Oxford U (Oxford) 1980. HSNW: 13* v Middlesex (Manchester) 1981. HSJPL: 38 v Hants (Southampton) 1980. BB: 3-17 v Surrey (Oval) 1981. BBJPL: 3-23 v Hants (Southampton) 1980.

Harry PILLING (Ashton TS) B Ashton-under-Lyne (Lancs) 23/2/1943. 5ft 3ins tall. RHB, OB. Debut 1962. Cap 1965. Testimonial (£9,500) in 1974. Did not play in 1981. 1,000 runs (8) – 1,606 runs (av. 36.50) in 1967 best. Scored two centuries in match (119* and 104*) v Warwickshire (Manchester) 1970. Gillette Man of the Match Awards: 3. Benson & Hedges Gold Awards: 3. HS: 149* v Glamorgan (Liverpool) 1976. HSGC/NW: 90 v Middlesex (Lord's) 1973. HSJPL: 85 v Sussex (Hove) 1970. HSBH: 109* v Glamorgan (Manchester) 1973.

Neal Victor RADFORD (Athlone High School, Johannesburg) B Luanshya, Northern Rhodesia (now Zambia) 7/6/1957. RHB, RFM. Played for Glamorgan 2nd XI and for Burnley in Lancashire League in 1978. Played for county 2nd XI in 1979 and as professional for Bacup in Lancashire League in 1979 and 1980. Debut for Transvaal B in President's competition 1978-79. Debut for county 1980. Will be qualified as an English player in April 1983. HS: 76* v Derbyshire (Blackpool) 1981. HSJPL: 48* v Glamorgan (Cardiff) 1981. BB: 6-41 Transvaal B v Griqualand West (Kimberley) 1980-81. BBUK: 5-107 v Notts (Nottingham) 1981. BBNW: 3-20 v Middlesex (Manchester) 1981. BBJPL: 3-16 v Hants (Manchester) 1981.

Bernard Wilfrid REIDY (St. Mary's College, Blackburn) B Bramley Meade, Whalley (Lancs) 18/9/1953. LHB, LM. Toured West Indies with England Young Cricketers 1972. Played for 2nd XI since 1971. Debut 1973. Cap 1980. Benson & Hedges Gold Awards: 3. HS: 131* v Derbyshire (Chesterfield) 1979. HSGC/NW: 18 v Glos (Manchester) 1975. HSJPL: 74 v Glamorgan (Manchester) 1980. HSBH: 109* v Derbyshire (Chesterfield) 1980. BB: 5-61 v Worcs (Worcester) 1979. BBNW: 3-22 v Northants (Northampton) 1981. BBJPL: 3-33 v Surrey (Manchester) 1978.

Christopher John SCOTT (Ellesmere Park HS) B Swinton, Manchester 16/9/1959. LHB, WK. Played for 2nd XI since 1975. Debut 1977 aged 17 years 8 months. HS: 27* v Notts (Nottingham) 1981. HSBH: 18 v Leics (Leicester) 1980.

Jack SIMMONS (Accrington Secondary TS) B Claydon-le-moors (Lancs) 28/3/1941. RHB, OB. Debut for 2nd XI 1959. Played for Blackpool in Northern League as professional. Debut 1968. Cap 1971. Played for Tasmania from 1972-73 to 1978-79 whilst coaching there. Benefit (£128,000) in 1980. Hat-trick v Notts (Liverpool) 1977. Gillette Man of the Match Awards: 1. Benson & Hedges Gold Awards: 2. HS: 112 v Sussex (Hove) 1970. HSGC/NW: 54* v Essex (Manchester) 1979. HSJPL: 65 v Essex (Manchester) 1980. HSBH: 64 v Derbyshire (Manchester) 1978. BB: 7-59 Tasmania v Queensland (Brisbane) 1978-79. BBUK: 7-64 v Hants (Southport) 1973. BBGC/NW: 5-49 v Worcs (Worcester) 1974. BBJPL: 5-28 v Northants (Peterborough) 1972. BBBH: 4-31 v Yorks (Manchester) 1975. Has played soccer in Lancs Combination.

Gary John SPEAK (Rivington & Blackrod HS, Horwich, Bolton) B Chorley 26/4/1962. RHB, RFM. Debut 1981 (two matches).

Timothy John TAYLOR (Stockport GS and Oxford) B Romiley (Cheshire) 28/3/1961. RHB, SLA. Played for Cheshire 1980. Debut for both county and university in 1981. Also played for Minor Counties v Sri Lankans (Reading). Blue 1981. HS: 28* Oxford U v Kent (Oxford) 1981. BB: 5-81 Oxford U v Middlesex (Oxford) 1981.

Mark Andrew WALLWORK B Salford 14/12/1960. RHB, WK. Plays for Farnworth in Bolton League. Joined staff in 1981. Has yet to appear in first-class cricket. Is studying dentistry at Newcastle University.

Roger Graeme WATSON B Rawtenstall 14/1/1964. LHB, OB. Joined staff in 1981. Has yet to appear in first-class cricket.

NB. The following player whose particulars appeared in the 1981 annual has been omitted: M.F. Malone (left staff).

County Averages

Schweppes County Championship. Played 22, won 4, drawn 11, lost 7.
All first-class matches: Played 24, won 4, drawn 13, lost 7.

BATTING AND FIELDING

Cap		M	I	NO	Runs	HS	Avgr	100	50	W	St
1969	C.H. Lloyd	18	31	2	1324	145	45.65	1	10	13	—
1981	G. Fowler	24	42	3	1560	143	40.00	3	9	24	3
1968	D. Lloyd	21	35	3	1122	146*	35.06	3	3	13	—
1980	B.W. Reidy	15	23	2	624	96	29.71	—	5	16	—
1970	D.P. Hughes	24	39	5	1002	126	29.47	1	5	19	—
—	I. Cockbain	6	10	1	262	85	29.11	—	2	4	—
1972	F.C. Hayes	12	20	3	470	126	27.64	1	2	3	—
—	N.V. Radford	15	19	7	330	76*	27.50	—	2	8	—
1975	A. Kennedy	24	42	0	1044	180	24.85	1	3	5	—
—	J. Abrahams	14	22	4	438	74	24.33	—	2	8	—
1971	J. Simmons	16	22	6	340	65*	21.25	—	1	14	—
—	S.J. O'Shaughnessy	14	18	2	223	38	13.93	—	—	3	—
—	M.A. Holding	7	8	2	66	32	11.00	—	—	2	—
1981	P.J.W. Allott	20	26	7	177	27	9.31	—	—	6	—
—	C.J. Scott	14	16	5	99	27*	9.00	—	—	25	4
1972	P.G. Lee	13	14	4	64	12*	6.40	—	—	—	—

Played in three matches: T.J. Taylor 2, 0, 0*, 0
Played in two matches: K.A. Hayes 11, 0; G. Speak 0*, 0*

BOWLING

	Type	O	M	R	W	Avge	Best	5 wI	10 wM
M.A. Holding	**RF**	271.1	75	715	40	17.87	6-74	4	1
P.J.W. Allott	**RFM**	621.3	165	1791	75	23.88	8-48	3	—
J. Simmons	**OB**	332.5	111	740	29	25.51	5-39	1	—
S.J. O'Shaughnessy	**RM**	103.2	20	345	11	31.36	3-17	—	—
P.G. Lee	**RFM**	285.1	81	816	25	32.64	6-44	2	1
D.P. Hughes	**SLA**	292.5	83	780	21	37.14	4-40	—	—
J. Abrahams	**OB**	203.5	52	567	14	40.50	3-27	—	—
D. Lloyd	**SLA**	205.2	49	586	12	48.83	2-18	—	—
N.V. Radford	**RFM**	303.2	58	1140	21	54.28	5-107	1	—
B.W. Reidy	**LM**	129	25	436	8	54.50	3-67	—	—

Also bowled: I. Cockbain 6-1-14-0; G. Fowler 1-0-12-0; A. Kennedy 33-7-102-2;
G. Speak 15-1-54-0; T.J. Taylor 68-17-166-4

County Records

First-class cricket

Highest innings	For	801 v Somerset (Taunton)	1895
totals:	Agst	634 by Surrey (The Oval)	1898
Lowest innings	For	25 v Derbyshire (Manchester)	1871
totals:	Agst	22 by Glamorgan (Liverpool)	1924
Highest indi-	For	424 A.C. MacLaren v Somerset (Taunton)	1895
vidual innings:	Agst	315* T.W. Hayward for Surrey (The Oval)	1898
Best bowling	For	10-55 J. Briggs v Worcestershire (Manchester)	1900
in innings:	Agst	10-40 G.O.B. Allen for Middlesex (Lord's)	1929
Best bowling	For	17-91 H. Dean v Yorkshire (Liverpool)	1913
in a match:	Agst	16-65 G. Giffen for Australians (Manchester)	1886
Most runs in a season:		2,633 (av. 56.02) J.T. Tyldesley	1901
runs in a career:		34,222 (av. 45.02) G.E. Tyldesley	1909-1936
100s in a season:		11 by C. Hallows	1928
100s in a career:		90 by G.E. Tyldesley	1909-1936
wickets in a season:		198 (av. 18.55) E.A. McDonald	1925
wickets in a career:		1,816 (av. 15.12) J.B. Statham	1950-1968

RECORD WICKET STANDS

1st	368	A.C. MacLaren & R.H. Spooner v Gloucestershire (Liverpool)	1903
2nd	371	F.B. Watson & G.E. Tyldesley v Surrey (Manchester)	1928
3rd	306	E. Paynter & N. Oldfield v Hampshire (Southampton)	1938
4th	324	A.C. MacLaren & J.T. Tyldesley v Notts (Nottingham)	1904
5th	249	B. Wood & A. Kennedy v Warwickshire (Birmingham)	1975
6th	278	J. Iddon & H.R.W. Butterworth v Sussex (Manchester)	1932
7th	245	A.H. Hornby & J. Sharp v Leicestershire (Manchester)	1912
8th	158	J. Lyon & R.M. Ratcliffe v Warwickshire (Manchester)	1979
9th	142	L.O.S. Poidevin & A. Kermode v Sussex (Eastbourne)	1907
10th	173	J. Briggs & R. Pilling v Surrey (Liverpool)	1885

One-day cricket

Highest innings totals:	Gillette Cup/ NatWest Trophy	304-9 v Leics (Manchester)	1963
	John Player League	255-5 v Somerset (Manchester)	1970
	Benson & Hedges Cup	288-9 v Warwickshire (Manchester)	1981
Lowest innings totals:	Gillette Cup/ NatWest Trophy	59 v Worcs (Worcester)	1963
	John Player League	76 v Somerset (Manchester)	1972
	Benson & Hedges Cup	82 v Yorks (Bradford)	1972
Highest individual innings:	Gillette Cup/ NatWest Trophy	131 A. Kennedy v Middlesex (Manchester)	1978
	John Player League	134* C.H. Lloyd v Somerset (Manchester)	1970
	Benson & Hedges Cup	124 C.H. Lloyd v Warwickshire (Manchester)	1981
Best bowling figures:	Gillette Cup/ NatWest Trophy	5-28 J.B. Statham v Leics (Manchester)	1963
	John Player League	6-29 D.P. Hughes v Somerset (Manchester)	1977
	Benson & Hedges Cup	5-12 B. Wood v Derbyshire (Southport)	1976

LEICESTERSHIRE

Formation of present club: 1879.
Colours: Scarlet and dark green.
Badge: Running fox (gold) on green background.
County Champions: 1975.
Gillette Cup Semi-Finalists: 1977.
NatWest Trophy Third Round: 1981.
John Player League Champions (2): 1974 and 1977.
Benson & Hedges Cup Winners (2): 1972 and 1975.
Benson & Hedges Cup Finalists: 1974.
Fenner Trophy Winners: 1979.
Gillette Man of the Match Awards: 15.
NatWest Man of the Match Awards: 1.
Benson & Hedges Gold Awards: 32.

Secretary/Manager: F.M. Turner, County Ground, Grace Road, Leicester LE2 8AD.
Captain: R.W. Tolchard.
Prospects of Play Telephone No: Leicester (0533) 836236.

Jonathan Philip AGNEW (Uppingham School) B Macclesfield (Cheshire) 4/4/1960. 6ft 3½ins tall. RHB, RF. Played for Surrey 2nd XI in 1976 and 1977. Debut 1978. HS: 31 v Glamorgan (Leicester) 1980. BB: 6-70 v Zimbabwe (Salisbury) 1980-81. BBUK: 5-72 v Yorks (Bradford) 1981.

John Christopher (Chris) BALDERSTONE B Huddersfield 16/11/1940. RHB, SLA. Played for Yorks from 1961 to 1970. Specially registered and made debut for Leics in 1971. Cap 1973. Tests: 2 in 1976. 1,000 runs (7) – 1,472 runs (av. 43.29) in 1980 best. Shared in 2nd wkt partnership record for county, 289* with D.I. Gower v Essex (Leicester) 1981. Hat-trick v Sussex (Eastbourne) 1976. Gillette Man of the Match Awards: 2. Benson & Hedges Gold Awards: 7. HS: 178* v Notts (Nottingham) 1977. HSTC: 35 v West Indies (Leeds) 1976. HSGC/NW: 119* v Somerset (Taunton) 1973. HSJPL: 96 v Northants (Leicester) 1976. HSBH: 113* v Glos (Leicester) 1981. BB: 6-25 v Hants (Southampton) 1978. BBGC/NW: 4-33 v Herts (Leicester) 1977. BBJPL: 3-29 v Worcs (Leicester) 1971. Soccer for Huddersfield Town, Carlisle United, Doncaster Rovers and Queen of the South.

Timothy James (Tim) BOON (Edlington Comprehensive School, Doncaster) B Doncaster 1/11/1961. RHB, RM. Played for Yorks 2nd XI in 1978 and 1979. Captained England Young Cricketers in West Indies 1980. Debut 1980. HS: 83 v Warwickshire (Coventry) 1981. HSJPL: 39 v Surrey (Leicester) 1981.

Nigel Edwin BRIERS (Lutterworth GS) B Leicester 15/1/1955. RHB. Cousin of N. Briers who played once for county in 1967. Debut 1971 at age of 16 years 103 days. Youngest player ever to appear for county. Cap 1981. Scored 1,194 runs (av. 36.18) in 1981. Shared in 5th wicket partnership record for county, 235 with R.W. Tolchard v Somerset (Leicester) 1979. Benson & Hedges Gold Awards: 1. HS: 119 v Warwickshire (Birmingham) 1981. BSGC/NW: 20 v Worcs (Leicester) 1979. HSJPL: 119* v Hants (Bournemouth) 1981. HSBH: 71* v Hants (Southampton) 1979.

Ian Paul BUTCHER (John Ruskin HS, Croydon) B Farnborough, Kent 1/7/1962. RHB, WK. Brother of A.R. Butcher of Surrey. Played in last two John Player

League matches of 1979. Debut 1980. Played one match v Oxford U (Oxford) and in one John Player League match. Played in one match in 1981 v Sri Lankans (Leicester). HS: 42 v Sri Lankans (Leicester) 1981. HSJPL: 16 v Surrey (Leicester) 1979.

Patrick Bernard (Paddy) CLIFT (St. George's College, Salisbury) B Salisbury, Rhodesia 14/7/1953. RHB, RM. Debut for Rhodesia 1971-72. Debut for county 1975. Cap 1976. Hat-trick v Yorks (Leicester) 1976. HS: 88* v Oxford U (Oxford) 1979. HSGC/NW: 48* v Worcs (Leicester) 1979. HSJPL: 51* v Somerset (Leicester) 1979. HSBH: 91 v Notts (Leicester) 1980. BB: 8-17 v MCC (Lord's) 1976. BBGC: 3-36 v Worcs (Leicester) 1979. BBJPL: 4-14 v Lancs (Leicester) 1978. BBBH: 4-13 v Minor Counties (East) (Amersham) 1978.

Russell Alan COBB (Trent College) B Leicester 18/5/1961. RHB, LM. Played for 2nd XI since 1977. Toured Australia 1979 and West Indies 1980 with England Young Cricketers. Debut 1980. HS: 54 v Northants (Leicester) 1981. HSJPL: 24 v Worcs (Leicester) 1981.

Nicholas Grant Billson (Nick) COOK (Lutterworth GS) B Leicester 17/6/1956. RHB, SLA. Played for 2nd XI since 1974. Debut 1978. HS: 75 v Somerset (Taunton) 1980. HSJPL: 13* v Kent (Leicester) 1979 and 13* v Middlesex (Lord's) 1981. BB: 7-81 v Sussex (Leicester) 1981.

Brian Fettes DAVISON (Gifford Technical HS, Rhodesia) B Bulawayo, Rhodesia 21/12/1946. RHB, RM. Debut for Rhodesia 1967-68 in Currie Cup competition. Debut for county 1970 after having played for International Cavaliers. Cap 1971. County Captain in 1980. Played for Tasmania from 1979-80 to 1981-82. Is now regarded as an English player for qualification purposes. Benefit in 1982. 1,000 runs (11) – 1,818 runs (av. 56.81) in 1976 best. Gillette Man of the Match Awards: 1. NatWest Man of the Match Awards: 1. Benson & Hedges Gold Awards: 6. HS: 189 v Australians (Leicester) 1975. HSGC/NW: 99 v Essex (Southend) 1977. HSJPL: 85* v Glamorgan (Cardiff) 1974. HSBH: 158* v Warwickshire (Coventry) 1972. BB: 5-52 Rhodesia v Griqualand West (Bulawayo) 1967-68. BBUK: 4-99 v Northants (Leicester) 1970. BBJPL: 4-29 v Glamorgan (Neath) 1971. Has played hockey for Rhodesia.

Grant FORSTER (Seaham Comprehensive School) B Seaham, Co. Durham 27/5/1961. LHB, OB. Played for Northants 2nd XI from 1978 to 1980. Debut for Northants 1980. One match v Cambridge U (Cambridge). Joined Leics in 1981, but did not appear for 1st XI.

Michael Anthony (Mike) GARNHAM (Camberwell GS, Melbourne, Scotch College, Perth, Australia, Park School, Barnstaple) B Johannesburg 20/8/1960. RHB, WK. Played for Devon and Glos 2nd XI in 1976 and 1977. Toured India with English Schools Cricket Association in 1977. Played for Glos in last John Player League match of 1978 v Warwickshire (Birmingham). Debut for Glos 1979. Left county and made debut for Leics in 1980. HS: 74 v Kent (Leicester) 1981. HSGC/NW: 25 v Essex (Leicester) 1980. HSJPL: 37 v Lancs (Manchester) 1981. HSBH: 47 v Sussex (Hove) 1981. Studied at East Anglia University.

David Ivon GOWER (King's School, Canterbury) B Tunbridge Wells 1/4/1957. LHB, OB. Toured South Africa with England Schools XI 1974-75 and West Indies with England Young Cricketers 1976. Debut 1975. Cap 1977. *Wisden* 1978. Elected Best Young Cricketer of the Year in 1978 by Cricket Writers' Club. Tests: 31 between 1978 and 1981. Tours: Australia 1978-79, Australia and India 1979-80,

113

LEICESTERSHIRE

West Indies 1980-81, India and Sri Lanka 1981-82. 1,000 runs (3) – 1,418 runs (av. 48.49) in 1981 best. Shared in 2nd wkt partnership record for county, 289* with J.C. Balderstone v Essex (Leicester) 1981. Gillette Man of the Match Awards: 1. Benson & Hedges Gold Awards: 1. HS: 200* England v India (Birmingham) 1979. HSC: 156* v Essex (Leicester) 1981. HSGC/NW: 117* v Herts (Leicester) 1977. HSJPL: 135* v Warwickshire (Leicester) 1977. HSBH: 114* v Derbyshire (Derby) 1980. BB: 3-47 v Essex (Leicester) 1977.

Kenneth (Ken) HIGGS B Sandyford (Staffordshire) 14/1/1937. LHB, RM. Played for Staffordshire 1957. Debut for Lancs 1958. Cap 1959. Benefit (£8,390) in 1968. Retired after 1969 season. Re-appeared for Leics in 1972. Cap 1972. Appointed County Vice-Captain in 1973 and County Captain for 1979 relinquishing post at end of season. Is now county coach. Played only in one-day matches in 1981. Tests: 15 between 1965 and 1968. Shared in 10th wkt partnership of 128 with J.A. Snow v West Indies (Oval) 1966 – 2 runs short of then record 10th wkt partnership in Test cricket. Also shared in 10th wkt partnership record for county, 228 with R. Illingworth v Northants (Leicester) 1977. Tours: Australia and New Zealand 1965-66, West Indies 1967-68. 100 wkts (5) – 132 wkts (av. 19.42) in 1960 best. Hat-tricks (3) – Lancs v Essex (Blackpool) 1960, Lancs v Yorks (Leeds) 1968 and v Hants (Leicester) 1977. Hat-trick also in Benson & Hedges Cup Final v Surrey (Lord's) 1974. Benson & Hedges Gold Awards: 1. HS: 98 v Northants (Leicester) 1977. HSTC: 63 England v West Indies (Oval) 1966. HSGC/NW: 25 Lancs v Somerset (Taunton) 1966. HSJPL: 17* v Notts (Nottingham) 1975. HSBH: 10 v Surrey (Oval) 1981. BB: 7-19 Lancs v Leics (Manchester) 1965. BBTC: 6-91 v West Indies (Lord's) 1966. BBC: 7-44 v Middlesex (Lord's) 1978. BBGC/NW: 6-20 v Staffs (Longton) 1975. BBJPL: 6-17 v Glamorgan (Leicester) 1973. BBBH: 4-10 v Surrey (Lord's) 1974. Soccer for Port Vale.

Gordon James PARSONS B Slough (Bucks) 17/10/1959. LHB, RM. Played for county 2nd XI since 1976 and also for Buckinghamshire in 1977. Debut 1978. HS: 50 v Kent (Leicester) 1981. HSGC/NW: 22 v Essex (Leicester) 1980. HSBH: 14* v Surrey (Oval) 1981. BB: 4-38 v Essex (Chelmsford) 1980. BBJPL: 3-19 v Northants (Northampton) 1981. BBBH: 4-33 v Worcs (Leicester) 1981.

Anderson Montgomery Everton (Andy) ROBERTS B Antigua 29/1/1951. RHB, RF. Debut for Leeward Islands v Windward Islands 1969-70 and played subsequently for Combined Islands in Shell Shield competition. Debut for Hants 1973. Cap 1974. *Wisden* 1974. Played for New South Wales in 1976-77 Sheffield Shield competition. Left Hants in 1978. Debut for Leics 1981 whilst playing as professional for Haslingden in Lancashire League. Tests: 38 for West Indies between 1973-74 and 1980-81. Tours: West Indies to India, Sri Lanka and Pakistan 1974-75, Australia 1975-76, 1981-82, England 1976 and 1980, Australia and New Zealand 1979-80. Took 100th wkt in Test cricket in 1976 in then record time of 2 years 142 days. Took 119 wkts (av. 13.62) in 1974. Hat-trick for Combined Islands v Jamaica (St. Kitts) 1980-81. Benson & Hedges Gold Awards: 1 (for Hants). HS: 63 Combined Islands v Guyana (Grenada) 1980-81. HSUK: 57 v Essex (Colchester) 1981. HSTC: 54 West Indies v Australia (Melbourne) 1979-80. HSGC/NW: 15 Hants v Leics (Leicester) 1978. HSJPL: 59* v Somerset (Leicester) 1981. HSBH: 29 Hants v Glos (Bristol) 1975 and 29 v Surrey (Oval) 1981. BB: 8-47 Hants v Glamorgan (Cardiff) 1974. BBC: 5-49 v Glamorgan (Cardiff) 1981. BBTC: 7-54 West Indies v Australia (Perth) 1975-76. BBGC/NW: 3-17 Hants v Glamorgan (Southampton) 1975. BBJPL: 5-13 Hants v Sussex (Hove) 1974. BBBH: 4-12 Hants v Somerset (Bournemouth) 1975.

John Frederick STEELE B Stafford 23/7/1946. Younger brother of D.S. Steele of Northamptonshire. RHB, SLA. Debut 1970. Was 12th man for England v Rest of World (Lord's) a month after making debut. Cap 1971. Played for Natal in 1973-74 and 1977-78 Currie Cup competition. 1,000 runs (6) – 1,347 runs (av. 31.32) in 1972 best. Shared in 1st wkt partnership record for county, 390 with B. Dudleston v Derbyshire (Leicester) 1979. Gillette Man of the Match Awards: 3. Benson & Hedges Gold Awards: 4. HS: 195 v Derbyshire (Leicester) 1971. HSGC/NW: 108* v Staffs (Longton) 1975. HSJPL: 92 v Essex (Leicester) 1973. HSBH: 91 v Somerset (Leicester) 1974. BB: 7-29 Natal B v Griqualand West (Umzinto) 1973-74 and 7-29 v Glos (Leicester) 1980. BBGC/NW: 5-19 v Essex (Southend) 1977. BBJPL: 5-22 v Glamorgan (Leicester) 1979. BBBH: 3-17 v Cambridge U (Leicester) 1972.

Leslie Brian (Les) TAYLOR (Heathfield HS, Earl Shilton) B Earl Shilton (Leics) 25/10/1953. 6ft 3½ins tall. RHB, RFM. Debut 1977. Cap 1981. Played for Natal in 1981-82 Currie Cup competition. Hat-trick v Middlesex (Leicester) 1979. HS: 22 v Derbyshire (Derby) 1981. HSJPL: 15* v Somerset (Taunton) 1980. BB: 7-28 v Derbyshire (Leicester) 1981. BBGC/NW: 3-11 v Hants (Leicester) 1978. BBJPL: 5-23 v Notts (Nottingham) 1978. BBBH: 3-39 v Glos (Leicester) 1981.

Roger William TOLCHARD (Malvern College) B Torquay 15/6/1946. RHB, WK. Played for Devon in 1963 and 1964. Also played for Hants.2nd XI and Public Schools v Combined Services (Lord's) in 1964. Debut 1965. Cap 1966. Appointed Vice-Captain in 1970. Relinquished appointment in 1973. Appointed County Captain in 1981. Tests: 4 in 1976-77. Tours: India, Pakistan and Sri Lanka 1972-73, India, Sri Lanka and Australia 1976-77, Australia 1978-79. Scored 998 runs (av. 30.24) in 1970. Shared in 5th-wicket partnership record for county, 235 with N.E. Briers v Somerset (Leicester) 1979. Benson & Hedges Gold Awards: 4. HS: 126* v Cambridge U (Cambridge) 1970. HSGC/NW: 86* v Glos (Leicester) 1975. HSJPL: 103 v Middlesex (Lord's) 1972 and was dismissed obstructing the field. HSBH: 92* v Worcs (Worcester) 1976. Had soccer trial for Leicester City.

David Alan WENLOCK (Lutterworth GS) B Leicester 16/4/1959. RHB, RM. Played for 2nd XI in 1979. Debut 1980. HS: 62 v Sri Lankans (Leicester) 1981. HSJPL: 22 v Glamorgan (Leicester) 1981. HSBH: 15 v Lancs (Leicester) 1980.

NB. The following players whose particulars appeared in the 1981 annual have been omitted: P. Booth (not re-engaged), D.J. Munden (not re-engaged).
The career record of Booth will be found elsewhere in this annual.

County Averages

Schweppes County Championship: Played 22, won 6, drawn 9, lost 6, abandoned 1
All first-class matches: Played 25, won 7, drawn 11, lost 6, abandoned 1

BATTING AND FIELDING

Cap		M	I	NO	Runs	HS	Avge	100	50	Ct	St
1977	D. I. Gower	13	21	3	1009	156*	56.05	4	5	17	—
1971	B.F. Davison	22	35	4	1198	123*	39.93	1	9	21	—
1981	N.E. Briers	23	36	3	1194	116	36.18	3	5	7	—
1973	J.C. Balderstone	23	39	3	1266	150*	35.16	3	5	16	—
1966	R.W. Tolchard	17	24	8	535	104*	33.43	1	2	15	1
1976	P.B. Clift	11	17	2	430	73	28.66	—	8	2	—

LEICESTERSHIRE

Cap		M	I	NO	Runs	HS	Avge	100	50	Ct	St
1971	J.F. Steele	19	32	2	819	116	27.30	1	6	11	—
—	A.M.E. Roberts	11	17	2	347	57	23.13	—	2	2	—
—	R.A. Cobb	8	12	0	275	54	22.91	—	1	5	—
—	T.J. Boon	15	26	2	542	83	22.58	—	2	7	—
—	M.A. Garnham	18	27	4	513	74	22.30	—	1	45	7
1976	P. Booth	5	7	1	116	35*	19.33	—	—	1	—
—	G.J. Parsons	19	23	7	252	50	15.75	—	1	5	—
—	J.P. Agnew	12	16	6	143	26	14.30	—	—	9	—
—	N.G.B. Cook	24	24	7	183	62	10.76	—	1	18	—
1981	L.B. Taylor	21	16	9	74	22	10.57	—	—	7	—

Played in two matches: D.A. Wenlock 0, 29, 62 (1 ct).
Played in one match: I.P. Butcher 14, 42.

BOWLING

	Type	O	M	R	W	Avge	Best	5 wI	10 wM
L.B. Taylor	RFM	547.1	131	1628	75	21.70	7-28	2	—
A.M.E. Roberts	RF	310.1	80	923	37	24.94	5-49	2	1
P.B. Clift	RM	308.2	82	799	29	27.55	6-47	2	1
J.F. Steele	SLA	323.3	86	787	27	29.14	4-31	—	—
N.G.B. Cook	SLA	791	263	1974	63	31.33	7-81	2	—
J.C. Balderstone	SLA	159.3	43	444	14	31.71	4-17	—	—
G.J. Parsons	RM	462.3	94	1452	45	32.26	4-44	—	—
J.P. Agnew	RF	221	45	775	24	32.29	5-72	1	—
N.E. Briers	RM	64.2	15	171	5	34.20	2-32	—	—
P. Booth	RFM	76	21	207	6	34.50	3-52	—	—

Also bowled: T.J. Boon 3-0-7-0; R.W. Tolchard 2-0-14-0; D.A. Wenlock 15-3-47-1.

County Records

First-class cricket

Highest innings	For	701-4d v Worcestershire (Worcester)	1906
totals:	Agst	739-7d by Nottinghamshire (Nottingham)	1903
Lowest innings	For	25 v Kent (Leicester)	1912
totals:	Agst	24 by Glamorgan (Leicester)	1971
Highest indi-	For	252* S. Coe v Northants (Leicester)	1914
vidual innings	Agst	341 G.H. Hirst for Yorkshire (Leicester)	1905
Best bowling	For	10-18 G. Geary v Glamorgan (Pontypridd)	1929
in an innings:	Agst	10-32 H. Pickett for Essex (Leyton)	1895
Best bowling	For	16-96 G. Geary v Glamorgan (Pontypridd)	1929
in a match:	Agst	16-102 C. Blythe for Kent (Leicester)	1909
Most runs in a season:		2,446 (av. 52.04) G.L. Berry	1937
runs in a career:		30,143 (av. 30.32) G.L. Berry	1924-1951
100s in a season:		7 by G.L. Berry and W. Watson	1937 and 1959
100s in a career:		45 by G.L. Berry	1924-1951
wickets in a season:		170 (av. 18.96) J.E. Walsh	1948
wickets in a career:		2,130 (av. 23.19) W.E. Astill	1906-1939

RECORD WICKET STANDS

1st	390	B. Dudleston & J.F. Steele v Derbyshire (Leicester)	1979
2nd	289*	J.C. Balderstone & D.I. Gower v Essex (Leicester)	1981
3rd	316	W. Watson & A. Wharton v Somerset (Taunton)	1961
4th	270	C.S. Dempster & G.S. Watson v Yorkshire (Hull)	1937
5th	235	N.E. Briers & R.W. Tolchard v Somerset (Leicester)	1979
6th	262	A.T. Sharpe & G.H.S. Fowke v Derbyshire (Chesterfield)	1911
7th	206	B. Dudleston & J. Birkenshaw v Kent (Canterbury)	1969
8th	164	M.R. Hallam & C.T. Spencer v Essex (Leicester)	1964
9th	160	W.W. Odell & R.T. Crawford v Worcestershire (Leicester)	1902
10th	228	R. Illingworth & K. Higgs v Northamptonshire (Leicester)	1977

One-day cricket

Highest innings totals:	Gillette Cup/ NatWest Trophy	326-6 v Worcestershire (Leicester)	1979
	John Player League	262-6 v Somerset (Frome)	1970
	Benson & Hedges Cup	327-4 v Warwickshire (Coventry)	1972
Lowest innings totals:	Gillette Cup/ NatWest Trophy	56 v Northamptonshire (Leicester)	1964
	John Player League	36 v Sussex (Leicester)	1973
	Benson & Hedges Cup	82 v Hampshire (Leicester)	1973
Highest individual innings:	Gillette Cup/ NatWest Trophy	125 B. Dudleston v Worcestershire (Leicester)	1979
	John Player League	152 B. Dudleston v Lancs (Manchester)	1975
	Benson & Hedges Cup	158* B.F. Davison v Warwickshire (Coventry)	1972
Best bowling figures:	Gillette Cup/ NatWest Trophy	6-20 K. Higgs v Staffs (Longton)	1975
	John Player League	6-17 K. Higgs v Glamorgan (Leicester)	1973
	Benson & Hedges Cup	5-20 R. Illingworth v Somerset (Leicester)	1974

MIDDLESEX

Formation of present club: 1863.
Colours: Blue.
Badge: Three seaxes.
County Champions (7): 1866, 1903, 1920, 1921, 1947, 1976 and 1980.
Joint Champions (2): 1949 and 1977.
Gillette Cup Winners (2): 1977 and 1980.
Gillette Cup Finalists: 1975.
NatWest Trophy Second Round: 1981.
Best Position in John Player League: 3rd in 1977 and 1980.
Benson & Hedges Cup Finalists: 1975.
Gillette Man of the Match Awards: 27.
NatWest Man of the Match Awards: Nil.
Benson & Hedges Gold Awards: 21.

Secretary: A.J. Wright, Lord's Cricket Ground, St. John's Wood Road, London NW8 8QN.
Captain: J.M. Brearley, OBE.
Prospects of Play Telephone No: 01-286 8011.

Graham Derek BARLOW (Ealing GS) B Folkestone 26/3/1950. LHB, RM. Played in MCC Schools matches at Lord's 1968. Debut 1969. Cap 1976. Tests: 3 in 1976-77 and 1977. Tour: India, Sri Lanka and Australia 1976-77. 1,000 runs (5) – 1,478 runs (av. 49.26) in 1976 best. Shared in 1st wkt partnership record for county, 367* with W.N. Slack v Kent (Lord's) 1981. Gillette Man of the Match Awards: 1. Benson & Hedges Gold Awards: 2. HS: 177 v Lancs (Southport) 1981. HSTC: 7* v India (Calcutta) 1976-77. HSGC/NW: 76* v Warwickshire (Birmingham) 1975. HSJPL: 114 v Warwickshire (Lord's) 1979. HSBH: 129 v Northants (Northampton) 1977. Studied at Loughborough College for whom he played rugby.

John Michael (Mike) BREARLEY (City of London School and Cambridge) B Harrow 28/4/1942. RHB. Occasional WK. Debut 1961 scoring 1,222 runs (av. 35.94) in first season. Blue 1961-62-63-64 (capt 1963-64). Cap 1964. Elected Best Young Cricketer of the Year in 1964 by the Cricket Writers' Club. Did not play in 1966 or 1967, but re-appeared in latter half of each season between 1968 and 1970. Appointed County Captain in 1971. *Wisden* 1976. Awarded OBE in 1978 New Year Honours List. Benefit (£31,000) in 1978. Tests: 39 between 1976 and 1981, captaining England in 31 Tests between 1977 and 1981. Tours: South Africa 1964-65, Pakistan 1966-67 (captain), India, Sri Lanka and Australia (vice-captain) 1976-77, Pakistan and New Zealand 1977-78 (captain), returned home early owing to injury, Australia 1978-79 (captain), Australia and India 1979-80 (captain). 1,000 runs (10) – 2,178 runs (av. 44.44) in 1964 best. Holds record for most runs scored for Cambridge University (4,310 runs, av. 38.48). Gillette Man of the Match Awards: 4. Benson & Hedges Gold Awards: 3. HS: 312* MCC Under-25 v North Zone (Peshawar) 1966-67. HSUK: 173* v Glamorgan (Cardiff) 1974. HSTC: 91 v India (Bombay) 1976-77. HSGC/NW: 124* v Bucks (Lord's) 1975. HSJPL 109* v Somerset (Taunton) 1980. HSBH: 100* v Surrey (Lord's) 1980.

Roland Orlando BUTCHER B East Point, St. Philip, Barbados 14/10/1953. RHB, RM. Debut 1974. Played for Barbados in 1974-75 Shell Shield competition. Cap 1979. Tests: 3 v West Indies in 1980-81. Tour: West Indies 1980-81. HS: 179 v Yorks (Scarborough) 1980. HSTC: 32 v West Indies (Kingston) 1980-81.

118

HSGC/NW: 50* v Surrey (Lord's) 1980. HSJPL: 94 v Surrey (Oval) 1979. HSBH: 27 v Hants (Lord's) 1981.

Colin Roy COOK (Merchant Taylor's School, Northwood) B Edgware 11/1/1960. RHB. Toured Australia with England Young Cricketers 1978-79. Debut 1981. HS: 79 v Lancs (Southport) 1981 in debut match. HSJPL: 73 v Glos (Lord's) 1981 in only appearance. Studied at Durham University.

Norman George COWANS B Enfield St. Mary, Jamaica 17/4/1961. 6ft 3ins tall. RHB, RFM. Played for 2nd XI since 1978. Debut 1980. HS: 10 v Oxford U (Oxford) 1981. BB: 5-58 v Leics (Leicester) 1981.

Wayne Wendell DANIEL B St. Philip, Barbados 16/1/1956. RHB, RF. Toured England with West Indies Schoolboys team 1974. Played for 2nd XI in 1975. Debut for Barbados 1975-76. Debut for county and cap 1977. Tests: 5 for West Indies in 1975-76 and 1976. Tour: West Indies to England 1976. Hat-trick v Lancs (Southport) 1981. Gillette Man of the Match Awards: 2. Benson & Hedges Gold Awards: 2. Took 51 wickets (av. 13.72) in limited-overs matches in 1980 to equal record of R.J. Clapp of Somerset in 1974. HS: 53* Barbados v Jamaica (Bridgetown) 1979-80 and 53* v Yorks (Lord's) 1981. HSTC: 11 West Indies v India (Kingston) 1975-76. HSGC/NW: 14 v Lancs (Manchester) 1978. HSJPL: 14 v Kent (Lord's) 1980. HSBH: 20* v Derbyshire (Derby) 1978. BB: 7-95 Barbados v Guyana (Georgetown) 1979-80. BBC: 6-33 v Sussex (Lord's) 1977. BBTC: 4-53 West Indies v England (Nottingham) 1976. BBGC/NW: 6-15 v Sussex (Hove) 1980. BBJPL: 4-12 v Worcs (Worcester) 1980. BBBH: 7-12 v Minor Counties (East) (Ipswich) 1978 – record for competition.

Paul Rupert DOWNTON (Sevenoaks School) B Farnborough (Kent) 4/4/1957. Son of G. Downton, former Kent player. RHB, WK. Played for Kent 2nd XI at age of 16. Vice-captain of England Young Cricketers team to West Indies 1976. Debut for Kent 1977. Cap 1979. Left county after 1979 season and made debut for Middlesex in 1980. Cap 1981. Tests: 4 in 1980-81 and 1981. Tours: Pakistan and New Zealand 1977-78, West Indies 1980-81. HS: 90* v Derbyshire (Uxbridge) 1980. HSTC: 26* v West Indies (Kingston) 1980-81. HSGC/NW: 10 v Sussex (Hove) 1980. HSJPL: 24 v Glamorgan (Lord's) 1981. HSBH: 11 v Hants (Lord's) 1981. Studied Law at Exeter University.

Phillipe Henri (Phil) EDMONDS (Gilbert Rennie HS, Lusaka, Skinner's School, Tunbridge Wells, Cranbrook School and Cambridge) B Lusaka, Northern Rhodesia (now Zambia) 8/3/1951. RHB, SLA. Debut for Cambridge U and county 1971. Blue 1971-73 (capt in 1973). Cap 1974. Elected Best Young Cricketer of the Year in 1974 by the Cricket Writers' Club. Played for Eastern Province in 1975-76 Currie Cup competition. Tests: 18 between 1975 and 1979. Tours: Pakistan and New Zealand 1977-78, Australia 1978-79. Hat-trick v Leics (Leicester) 1981. Benson & Hedges Gold Awards: 1. HS: 141* v Glamorgan (Lord's) 1979. HSTC: 50 v New Zealand (Christchurch) 1977-78. HSGC/NW: 63* v Somerset (Lord's) 1979. HSJPL: 52 v Somerset (Taunton) 1980. HSBH: 44* v Notts (Newark) 1976. BB: 8-132 (14-150 match) v Glos (Lord's) 1977. BBTC: 7-66 v Pakistan (Karachi) 1977-78. BBGC/NW: 3-28 v Sussex (Lord's) 1979. BBJPL: 3-19 v Leics (Lord's) 1973. BBBH: 4-11 v Kent (Lord's) 1975. Also played rugby for University and narrowly missed obtaining Blue.

Richard Gary Peter ELLIS (Haileybury College and Oxford) B Paddington 20/10/1960. RHB, OB. Joined staff 1979. Debut for Oxford U 1981. Blue 1981.

MIDDLESEX

Played in one John Player League match in 1981 v Leics (Lord's). University captain for 1982. HS: 63 Oxford U v Middlesex (Oxford) 1981. HSBH: 32 Combined Universities v Essex (Chelmsford) 1981.

John Ernest EMBUREY B Peckham 20/8/1952. RHB, OB. Played for Surrey Young Cricketers 1969-70. Joined county staff 1972. Debut 1973. Cap 1977. Tests: 18 between 1978 and 1981. Tours: Australia 1978-79, Australia and India 1979-80 (as replacement for G. Miller), West Indies 1980-81, India and Sri Lanka 1981-82. Benson & Hedges Gold Awards: 1. HS: 91* v Surrey (Oval) 1979. HSTC: 57 v Australia (Manchester) 1981. HSGC/NW: 36* v Lancs (Manchester) 1978. HSJPL: 35* v Warwickshire (Lord's) 1981. HSBH: 34* v Sussex (Lord's) 1980. BB: 7-36 v Cambridge U (Cambridge) 1977. BBTC: 5-124 v West Indies (Port of Spain) 1980–81. BBJPL: 4-41 v Notts (Nottingham) 1981. BBBH: 3-35 v Kent (Lord's) 1980.

Michael William (Mike) GATTING (John Kelly Boys HS, Cricklewood) B Kingsbury (Middlesex) 6/6/1957. RHB, RM. Represented England Young Cricketers 1974. Debut 1975. Toured West Indies with England Young Cricketers 1976. Cap 1977. Elected Best Young Cricketer of the Year in 1981 by the Cricket Writers' Club. Tests: 14 between 1977-78 and 1981. Tours: Pakistan and New Zealand 1977-78, West Indies 1980-81, India and Sri Lanka 1981-82. 1,000 runs (3) – 1,492 runs (av. 55.25) in 1981 best. Gillette Man of the Match Awards: 1. Benson & Hedges Gold Awards: 2. HS: 186* v Derbyshire (Derby) 1981. HSTC: 59 v Australia (Lord's) 1981. HSGC/NW: 95* v Notts (Nottingham) 1980. HSJPL: 85 v Notts (Lord's) 1978. HSBH: 95* v Somerset (Taunton) 1980. BB: 5-59 v Leics (Lord's) 1978. BBJPL: 4-32 v Kent (Lord's) 1978. BBBH: 3-19 v Kent (Lord's) 1980.

Simon Peter HUGHES (Latymer Upper School, Hammersmith) B Kingston-upon-Thames 20/12/1959. RHB, RFM. Played for 2nd XI in 1979. Debut 1980. Cap 1981. Gillette Man of the Match Awards: 1. HS: 18 v Kent (Maidstone) 1981. BB: 6-75 v Lancs (Southport) 1981. BBGC/NW: 3-23 v Worcs (Worcester) 1981. Studied Geography at Durham University.

Kevan David JAMES (Edmonton Comprehensive School) B Lambeth 18/3/1961. LHB, LM. Played for 2nd XI since 1978. Toured Australia in 1979 and West Indies in 1980 with England Young Cricketers. Debut 1980. Played in one match v Oxford U (Oxford) 1980, one Benson & Hedges match and one John Player League match, and in one match and one John Player League match in 1981. HS: 16 v Oxford U (Oxford) 1980. HSJPL: 13 v Kent (Canterbury) 1981. BB: 3-14 v Oxford U (Oxford) 1980.

Rajesh Jaman MARU (Pinner VIth Form College) B Nairobi, Kenya 28/10/1962. RHB, SLA. Played for 2nd XI in 1979. Toured West Indies in 1980 with England Young Cricketers. Debut 1980. Did not play in 1981. HS: 25 v Zimbabwe (Bulawayo) 1980-81. HSUK: 13 v Essex (Lord's) 1980. BB: 3-29 v Warwickshire (Birmingham) 1980.

William Gerald (Bill) MERRY B Newbury (Berks) 8/8/1955. RHB, RM. Played for Leics 2nd XI in 1976 and for Hertfordshire between 1976 and 1978. Debut 1979. HS: 14* v Oxford U (Oxford) 1981. BB: 4-24 v Somerset (Taunton) 1980. BBJPL: 3-29 v Lancs (Manchester) 1979. BBBH: 3-19 Minor Counties (West) v Derbyshire (Derby) 1978.

Colin Peter METSON (Enfield GS, Stanborough School, Welwyn Garden City)

B Cuffley (Herts) 2/7/1963. 5ft 5½ins tall. RHB, WK. Played for 2nd XI in 1980. Debut 1981. One match v Derbyshire (Derby) and also played in two John Player League matches. HS: 38* v Derbyshire (Derby) 1981.

James Dermot MONTEITH (Royal Belfast Academical Institute) B Lisburn (Co Antrim, Northern Ireland) 2/6/1943. RHB, SLA. Debut for Ireland 1966. Debut for county 1981. Had match double of 100 runs and 10 wickets (26 and 78, 7-38 and 5-57) Ireland v Scotland (Cork) 1973. HS: 78 Ireland v Scotland (Cork) 1973. HSC: 16* v Lancs (Southport) 1981. HSJPL: 10 v Warwickshire (Lord's) 1981. BB: 7-38 Ireland v Scotland (Cork) 1973. BBC: 5-68 v Northants (Northampton) 1981.

Clive Thornton RADLEY (King Edward VI GS, Norwich) B Hertford 13/5/1944. RHB, LB. Debut 1964. Cap 1967. Benefit (£26,000) in 1977. *Wisden* 1978. Tests: 8 in 1977-78 and 1978. Tours: Pakistan and New Zealand 1977-78 (as replacement for J.M. Brearley), Australia 1978-79. 1,000 runs (14) – 1,491 runs (av. 57.34) in 1980 best. Shared in 6th wicket partnership record for county, 227 with F.J. Titmus v South Africans (Lord's) 1965. Gillette Man of the Match Awards: 2. Benson & Hedges Gold Awards: 2. HS: 171 v Cambridge U (Cambridge) 1976. HSTC: 158 v New Zealand (Auckland) 1977-78. HSGC/NW: 105* v Worcs (Worcester) 1975. HSJPL: 133* v Glamorgan (Lord's) 1969. HSBH: 121* v Minor Counties (East) (Lord's) 1976.

Michael Walter William (Mike) SELVEY (Battersea GS and Manchester and Cambridge Universities) B Chiswick 25/4/1948. RHB, RFM. Debut for Surrey 1968. Debut for Cambridge U and Blue 1971. Debut for Middlesex 1972. Cap 1973. Played for Orange Free State in 1973-74 Currie Cup competition. Benefit in 1982. Tests: 3 in 1976 and 1976-77. Tour: India, Sri Lanka and Australia 1976-77. Took 101 wkts (av. 19.09) in 1978. Benson & Hedges Gold Awards: 1. HS: 67 v Zimbabwe (Bulawayo) 1980-81. HSUK: 57 v Essex (Ilford) 1981. HSGC/NW: 14 v Derbyshire (Derby) 1978. HSJPL: 38 v Essex (Southend) 1977 and 38* v Essex (Chelmsford) 1979. HSBH: 27* v Surrey (Lord's) 1973. BB: 7-20 v Glos (Gloucester) 1976. BBTC: 4-41 v West Indies (Manchester) 1976. BBGC/NW: 3-32 v Somerset (Lord's) 1977. BBJPL: 5-18 v Glamorgan (Cardiff) 1975. BBBH: 5-39 v Glos (Lord's) 1972. Played soccer for University.

Wilfred Norris SLACK B Troumaca, St. Vincent 12/12/1954. LHB, RM. Played for Buckinghamshire in 1976. Debut 1977. Cap 1981. Scored 1,372 runs (av. 47.31) in 1981. Shared in 1st wicket partnership record for county, 367* with G.D. Barlow v Kent (Lord's) 1981. HS: 248* v Worcs (Lord's) 1981. HSNW: 53* v Lancs (Manchester) 1981. HSJPL: 57 v Kent (Lord's) 1978. HSBH: 42 v Northants (Lord's) 1980.

Andrew Geoffrey SMITH B Muswell Hill 10/6/1957. RHB. Joined staff 1980. Has yet to appear in first-class cricket.

Chilton Richard Vernon TAYLOR (Birkenhead School and Cambridge) B Birkenhead 3/10/1951. RHB, WK. Played for Cheshire from 1969 to 1972. Debut for Warwickshire 1970, playing one match v Cambridge University. Cambridge Blue 1971-72-73. Had trial with Glos whilst at Cambridge, but never played for 1st XI. Made debut for Middlesex in 1981 (two matches) and played against Essex (Ilford) without having been registered with TCCB. HS: 25 Cambridge U v Warwickshire (Cambridge) 1972. HSC: 19 v Oxford U (Oxford) 1981.

Jeffrey Robert (Jeff) THOMSON (Punchbowl Boys' HS, Sydney) B Sydney

MIDDLESEX

16/8/1950. RHB, RF. Debut for New South Wales 1972-73, transferring to Queensland 1974-75. Debut for county 1981, missing part of season through injury. Tests: 34 for Australia between 1972-73 and 1979-80. Tours: Australia to England 1975, 1977 and 1980, West Indies 1977-78 (vice-captain). HS: 61 Queensland v Victoria (Brisbane) 1974-75. HSTC: 49 Australia v England (Birmingham) 1975. HSC: 35 v Essex (Lord's) 1981. BB: 7-33 Queensland v New South Wales (Brisbane) 1976-77. BBTC: 6-46 Australia v England (Brisbane) 1974-75. BBUK: 5-38 Australia v England (Birmingham) 1975. BBC: 4-66 v Essex (Lord's) 1981. BBBH: 7-22 v Hants (Lord's) 1981.

Keith Patrick TOMLINS (St. Benedict's School, Ealing) B Kingston-upon-Thames 23/10/1957. RHB, RM. Debut 1977. HS: 94 v Worcs (Worcester) 1978. HSJPL: 34 v Kent (Canterbury) 1981. BBJPL: 4-24 v Notts (Lord's) 1978. Studied at Durham University.

NB. The following players whose particulars appeared in the 1981 annual have been omitted: M.F. Cohen (not re-engaged) and V.A.P. Van der Bijl (returned to South Africa).

The career record of Van der Bijl will be found elsewhere in this annual.

County Averages

Schweppes County Championship: Played 22, won 8, drawn 10, lost 3, abandoned 1
All first-class matches: Played 25, won 8, drawn 13, lost 3, abandoned 1

BATTING AND FIELDING

Cap		M	I	NO	Runs	HS	Avge	100	50	Ct	St
1977	M.W. Gatting	12	19	4	1026	186*	68.40	4	2	14	—
1964	J.M. Brearley	15	25	1	1304	145	54.33	6	4	10	—
1981	W.N. Slack	18	32	3	1372	248*	47.31	3	9	6	—
1976	G.D. Barlow	22	38	5	1313	177	39.78	4	3	9	—
1967	C.T. Radley	23	40	7	1177	101*	35.66	1	7	19	—
—	K.P. Tomlins	10	16	3	403	79*	31.00	—	3	7	—
—	C.R. Cook	6	12	2	249	79	24.90	—	1	5	—
—	W.G. Merry	7	5	4	24	14*	24.00	—	—	1	—
1979	R.O. Butcher	20	33	3	695	106*	23.16	1	5	32	—
1977	W.W. Daniel	21	22	11	195	53*	17.72	—	1	2	—
—	P.R. Downton	21	27	6	371	44	17.66	—	—	41	8
1977	J.E. Emburey	13	14	2	196	38	16.33	—	—	17	—
1974	P.H. Edmonds	23	31	6	391	93	15.64	—	1	24	—
1973	M.W.W. Selvey	17	18	1	242	57	14.23	—	2	7	—
—	J.R. Thomson	8	6	1	63	35	12.60	—	—	4	—
—	N.G. Cowans	3	1	0	10	10	10.00	—	—	2	—
—	J.D. Monteith	8	11	2	61	16*	6.77	—	—	1	—
—	S.P. Hughes	12	14	5	57	18	6.33	—	—	3	—

Played in two matches: C.R.V. Taylor 19, 1, 5 (6 ct).
Played in one match: K.D. James 5* (1 ct); C.P. Metson 38* (1 ct); V.A.P. Van der Bijl did not bat.

BOWLING

	Type	O	M	R	W	Avge	Best	5 wI	10 wM
N.G. Cowans	RFM	54	9	155	8	19.37	5-58	1	—
J.E. Emburey	OB	566.5	164	1256	59	21.28	7-88	8	3
W.W. Daniel	RF	514.2	103	1494	67	22.29	6-64	2	—
J.R. Thomson	RF	162.3	30	522	23	22.69	4-66	—	—
J.D. Monteith	SLA	222.3	58	596	24	24.83	5-60	2	—
P.H. Edmonds	SLA	899	280	1814	73	24.84	6-93	3	—
S.P. Hughes	RFM	336.1	67	1056	42	25.14	6-75	3	—
W.G. Merry	RM	125	27	378	13	29.07	2-17	—	—
M.W.W. Selvey	RFM	388.3	114	1054	35	30.11	5-79	2	—

Also bowled: G.D. Barlow 0.3-0-7-0; M.W. Gatting 36-12-88-3; K.D. James 14-3-34-0; C.T. Radley 5-0-21-0; W.N. Slack 10-1-33-0; K.P. Tomlins 30-7-84-2; V.A.P. Van der Bijl 29-12-38-1.

County Records

First-class cricket

Highest innings totals:	For	642-3d v Hampshire (Southampton)	1923
	Agst	665 by West Indians (Lord's)	1939
Lowest innings totals:	For	20 v MCC (Lord's)	1864
	Agst	31 by Gloucestershire (Bristol)	1924
Highest individual innings:	For	331* J.D.B. Robertson v Worcs (Worcester)	1949
	Agst	316* J.B. Hobbs for Surrey (Lord's)	1926
Best bowling in an innings:	For	10-40 G.O.B. Allen v Lancs (Lord's)	1929
	Agst	9-38 R.C. Robertson-Glasgow for Somerset (Lord's)	1924
Best bowling in a match:	For	16-114 { G. Burton v Yorks (Sheffield) / J.T. Hearne v Lancs (Manchester) }	1888 / 1898
	Agst	16-109 C.W.L. Parker for Glos (Cheltenham)	1930
Most runs in a season:		2,650 (av. 85.48) W.J. Edrich	1947
runs in a career:		40,302 (av. 49.81) E.H. Hendren	1907-1937
100s in a season:		13 by D.C.S. Compton	1947
100s in a career:		119 by E.H. Hendren	1907-1937
wickets in a season:		158 (av. 14.63) F.J. Titmus	1955
wickets in a career:		2,358 (av. 21.25) F.J. Titmus	1949-1980

RECORD WICKET STANDS

1st	367*	G.D. Barlow & W.N. Slack v Kent (Lord's)	1981
2nd	380	F.A. Tarrant & J.W. Hearne v Lancashire (Lord's)	1914
3rd	424*	W.J. Edrich & D.C.S. Compton v Somerset (Lord's)	1948
4th	325	J.W. Hearne & E.H. Hendren v Hampshire (Lord's)	1919
5th	338	R.S. Lucas & T.C. O'Brien v Sussex (Hove)	1895
6th	227	C.T. Radley & F.J. Titmus v South Africans (Lord's)	1965
7th	271*	E.H. Hendren & F.T. Mann v Nottinghamshire (Nottingham)	1925
8th	182*	M.H.C. Doll & H.R. Murrell v Nottinghamshire (Lord's)	1913
9th	160*	E.H. Hendren & T.J. Durston v Essex (Leyton)	1927
10th	230	R.W. Nicholls & W. Roche v Kent (Lord's)	1899

One-day cricket

Highest innings totals:	Gillette Cup/ NatWest Trophy	280-8 v Sussex (Lord's)	1965
	John Player League	256-9 v Worcs (Worcester)	1976
	Benson & Hedges Cup	303-7 v Northants (Northampton)	1977
Lowest innings totals:	Gillette Cup/ NatWest Trophy	41 v Essex (Westcliff)	1972
	John Player League	23 v Yorkshire (Leeds)	1974
	Benson & Hedges Cup	97 v Northants (Lord's)	1976
Highest individual innings:	Gillette Cup/ NatWest Trophy	124* J.M. Brearley v Buckinghamshire (Lord's)	1975
	John Player League	133* C.T. Radley v Glamorgan (Lord's)	1969
	Benson & Hedges Cup	129 G.D. Barlow v Northants (Northampton)	1977
Best bowling figures:	Gillette Cup/ NatWest Trophy	6-15 W.W. Daniel v Sussex (Hove)	1980
	John Player League	6-6 R.W. Hooker v Surrey (Lord's)	1969
	Benson & Hedges Cup	7-12 W.W. Daniel v Minor Counties (East) (Ipswich)	1978

124

NORTHAMPTONSHIRE

Formation of present club: 1820, reorganised 1878.
Colours: Maroon.
Badge: Tudor Rose.
County Championship Runners-up (4): 1912, 1957, 1965 and 1976.
Gillette Cup Winners: 1976.
Gillette Cup Finalists: 1979.
NatWest Trophy Finalists: 1981.
Best final position in John Player League: 4th in 1974.
Benson & Hedges Cup Winners: 1980.
Fenner Trophy Winners: 1978.
Gillette Man of the Match Awards: 17.
NatWest Man of the Match Awards: 4.
Benson & Hedges Gold Awards: 16.

Secretary: K.C. Turner, County Ground, Wantage Rd, Northampton, NN1 4TJ.
Captain: G. Cook.
Prospects of Play Telephone No: Northampton (0604) 37040.

Robin James BOYD-MOSS (Bedford School and Cambridge) B Hattoh, Ceylon (now Sri Lanka) 16/12/1959. RHB, SLA. Played for Bedfordshire from 1977 to 1979 and for County 2nd XI in 1979. Debut for Cambridge U and County in 1980. Blue 1980-81. HS: 84 Cambridge U v Lancs (Cambridge) 1981. HSC: 56 v Essex (Northampton) 1980. HSJPL: 62 v Warwickshire (Northampton) 1981. HSBH: 58 Combined Universities v Northants (Northampton) 1980. Rugby Blue 1980-81, 1981-82.

David John CAPEL (Roade Comprehensive School, Northampton) B Northampton 6/2/1963. RHB, RM. Played for 2nd XI since 1979. Debut 1981. One match v Sri Lankans. HS: 37 v Sri Lankans (Northampton) 1981.

Robert Michael (Bob) CARTER B King's Lynn 25/5/1960. RHB, RM. Played for 2nd XI since 1976. Debut 1978. HS: 42* v Kent (Northampton) 1981. HSNW: 14 v Lancs (Northampton) 1981. HSJPL: 21* v Surrey (Oval) 1979. BB: 4-27 v Glos (Bristol) 1980. BBJPL: 3-35 v Worcs (Milton Keynes) 1978. Has played soccer for Norwich City.

Geoffrey (Geoff) COOK (Middlesbrough HS) B Middlesbrough 9/10/1951. RHB, SLA. Debut 1971. Cap 1975. Played for Eastern Province from 1978-79 to 1980-81 in Currie Cup competition. Appointed County Captain in 1981. Tour: India and Sri Lanka 1981-82. 1,000 runs (6) – 1,759 runs (av. 43.97) in 1981 best. Gillette Man of Match Awards: 2. NatWest Man of the Match Awards: 2. Benson & Hedges Gold Awards: 2. HS: 172 Eastern Province v Northern Transvaal (Port Elizabeth) 1979-80. HSUK: 155 v Derbyshire (Northampton) 1978. HSGC/NW: 114* v Surrey (Northampton) 1979. HSJPL: 85 v Leics (Leicester) 1976. HSBH: 96 v Minor Counties (East) (Northampton) 1978. Has played soccer for Wellingborough Town in Southern League.

Brian James (Jim) GRIFFITHS B Wellingborough 13/6/1949. RHB, RFM. Debut 1974. Cap 1978. HS: 11 v Middlesex (Lord's) 1978. BB: 8-50 v Glamorgan (Northampton) 1981. BBGC/NW: 3-39 v Leics (Northampton) 1979. BBJPL: 4-22 v Somerset (Weston-super-Mare) 1977. BBBH: 5-43 v Sussex (Eastbourne) 1979.

125

NORTHAMPTONSHIRE

KAPIL DEV NIKHANJ B Chandigarh, India 6/1/1959. RHB, RFM. Debut for Haryana in Ranji Trophy 1975-76 aged 16 years 10 months taking 6-39 in debut match v Punjab (Rohtak). Debut for county 1981 whilst playing as professional for Nelson in Lancashire League. Tests: 32 for India between 1978-79 and 1980-81. Tours: India to England 1979, Australia and New Zealand 1980-81. Is youngest player to take 100 wkts in Test cricket (21 years 25 days) and score 1,000 runs (21 years 27 days). Took 100 wkts in 1 year 107 days to beat record held previously by I.T. Botham. Hat-trick North Zone v West Zone (Delhi) 1978-79. HS: 193 Haryana v Punjab (Chandigarh) 1979-80. HSTC: 126* India v West Indies (Delhi) 1978-79. HSUK: 102 Indians v Northants (Northampton) 1979. HSC: 79 v Worcs (Stourbridge) 1981. BB: 8-38 Haryana v Services (Rohtak) 1977-78. BBTC: 7-56 India v Pakistan (Madras) 1979-80. BBUK: 5-146 India v England (Birmingham) 1979.

Allan Joseph LAMB (Wynberg Boys' High School) B Langebaanweg, Cape Province, South Africa 20/6/1954. RHB, RM. Debut for Western Province in Currie Cup 1972-73. Debut for county and cap 1978. *Wisden* 1980. Is regarded as an English player for qualification purposes. 1,000 runs (3) – 2,049 runs (av. 60.26) in 1981 best. Benson & Hedges Gold Awards: 2. HS: 178 v Leics (Leicester) 1979. HSGC/NW: 101 v Sussex (Hove) 1979. HSJPL: 127* v Worcs (Worcester) 1981. HSBH: 77 v Essex (Northampton) 1979.

Hon. Timothy Michael (Tim) LAMB (Shrewsbury School and Oxford) B Hartford (Cheshire) 24/3/1953. Younger son of Lord Rochester. RHB, RM. Debut for Oxford U 1973. Blue 1973-74. Debut for Middlesex 1974. Left county and made debut for Northants in 1978. Cap 1978. NatWest Man of the Match Awards: 1. Benson & Hedges Gold Awards: 1. HS: 77 Middlesex v Notts (Lord's) 1976. HSC: 33 v Notts (Northampton) 1978. HSGC/NW: 12 v Surrey (Oval) 1980. HSJPL: 27 Middlesex v Hants (Basingstoke) 1976. HSBH: 10* v Combined Universities (Northampton) 1980. BB: 7-56 v Cambridge U (Cambridge) 1980. BBGC/NW: 4-52 v Sussex (Hove) 1979. BBJPL: 5-13 v Notts (Northampton) 1979. BBBH: 5-44 Middlesex v Yorks (Lord's) 1975.

Wayne LARKINS B Roxton (Beds) 22/11/1953. RHB, RM. Joined staff 1969. Debut 1972. Cap 1976. Tests: 6 between 1979-80 and 1981. Tour: Australia and India 1979-80. 1,000 runs (4) – 1,772 runs (av. 45.43) in 1980 best. Shared in 2nd wkt partnership record for county, 322 with R.G. Williams v Leics (Leicester) 1980. Hat-trick in Benson & Hedges Cup v Combined Universities (Northampton) 1980. NatWest Man of the Match Awards: 1. Benson & Hedges Gold Awards: 2. HS: 170* v Worcs (Northampton) 1978. HSTC: 34 v Australia (Oval) 1981. HSGC/NW: 92* v Leics (Northampton) 1979. HSJPL: 111 v Leics (Wellingborough) 1979. HSBH: 108 v Warwickshire (Birmingham) 1980. BB: 3-34 v Somerset (Northampton) 1976. BBJPL: 5-32 v Essex (Ilford) 1978. BBBH: 4-37 v Combined Universities (Northampton) 1980.

Neil Alan MALLENDER (Beverley GS) B Kirk Sandall (Yorks) 13/8/1961. RHB, RFM. Toured West Indies in 1980 with England Young Cricketers. Debut 1980. HS: 18 v Glamorgan (Northampton) 1981. HSJPL: 22 v Warwickshire (Northampton) 1981. BB: 6-37 v Yorks (Wellingborough) 1981. BBNW: 3-35 v Derbyshire (Lord's) 1981. BBJPL: 5-34 v Middlesex (Tring) 1981. BBBH: 3-13 v Worcs (Worcester) 1981.

John Peter Crispin MILLS (Oundle School and Cambridge) B Kettering 6/12/1958. Son of J.M. Mills, former Cambridge captain and Warwickshire player.

RHB, RM. Played for 2nd XI since 1977. Debut for Cambridge U 1979. Blues 1979-80-81. University secretary for 1981. Debut for county 1981. HS: 111 Combined Universities v Sri Lankans (Oxford) 1981. HSC: 68 v Sri Lankans (Northampton) 1981. HSBH: 19 Combined Universities v Kent (Canterbury) 1981.

Neil PRIESTLEY (John Leggott VIth Form College, Scunthorpe) B Blyborough (Lincs) 23/6/1961. LHB, WK. Played for 2nd XI in 1980. Debut 1981. One match v Sri Lankans (Northampton). HS: 20* v Sri Lankans (Northampton) 1981.

Sarfraz NAWAZ (Government College, Lahore) B Lahore, Pakistan 1/12/1948. RHB, RFM. Debut 1967-68 for West Pakistan Governor's XI v Punjab University at Lahore and subsequently played for various Lahore sides and United Bank. Debut for county 1969. Not re-engaged after 1971 season, but rejoined staff in 1974. Cap 1975. Tests: 39 for Pakistan between 1968-69 and 1980-81. Tours: Pakistan to England 1971, 1974 and 1978, Australia and New Zealand 1972-73, Australia and West Indies 1976-77, New Zealand and Australia 1978-79, Australia 1981-82. Took 101 wkts (av. 20.30) in 1975. Gillette Man of Match Awards: 1. Benson & Hedges Gold Awards: 1. HS: 90 v Sri Lankans (Northampton) 1981. HSTC: 55 Pakistan v West Indies (Lahore) 1980-81. HSGC/NW: 39* v Surrey (Oval) 1980. HSJPL: 59* v Yorks (Scarborough) 1980. HSBH: 50 v Kent (Northampton) 1977. BB: 9-86 Pakistan v Australia (Melbourne) 1978-79. BBUK: 8-27 Pakistanis v Notts (Nottingham) 1974. BBC: 7-37 v Somerset (Weston-super-Mare) 1977. BBGC/NW: 4-17 v Herts (Northampton) 1976. BBJPL: 5-15 v Yorks (Northampton) 1975. BBBH: 5-21 v Middlesex (Lord's) 1980.

George SHARP B West Hartlepool 12/3/1950. RHB, WK. Can also bowl SLA. Debut 1968. Cap 1973. Benefit in 1982. HS: 94 v Lancs (Southport) 1980. HSGC/NW: 35* v Durham (Northampton) 1977. HSJPL: 47 v Sussex (Hove) 1974 and 47* v Worcs (Milton Keynes) 1978. HSBH: 43 v Surrey (Northampton) 1979.

David Stanley STEELE B Stoke-on-Trent 29/9/1941. Elder brother of J.F. Steele of Leics and cousin of B.S. Crump, former Northants player. Wears glasses. RHB, SLA. Played for Staffordshire from 1958 to 1962. Debut for Northants 1963. Cap 1965. Benefit (£25,500) in 1975. *Wisden* 1975. Transferred to Derbyshire in 1979 as county captain. Relinquished post during season. Cap 1979. Rejoined Northants for 1982. Tests: 8 in 1975 and 1976. 1,000 runs (10) – 1,756 runs (av. 48.77) in 1975 best. Hat-trick v Glamorgan (Derby) 1980. Had match double of 100 runs and 10 wkts (130, 6-36 and 5-39) v Derbyshire (Northampton) 1978. Gillette Man of the Match Awards: 1. NatWest Man of the Match Awards: 1 (for Derbyshire). HS: 140* v Worcs (Worcester) 1971. HSTC: 106 v West Indies (Nottingham) 1976. HSGC/NW: 109 v Cambs (March) 1975. HSJPL: 76 v Sussex (Hove) 1974. HSBH: 71 Derbyshire v Notts (Nottingham) 1966. BB: 8-29 v Lancs (Northampton) 1966. BBNW: 3-23 Derbyshire v Suffolk (Bury St. Edmunds) 1981. BBJPL: 4-21 Derbyshire v Notts (Derby) 1979.

Duncan James WILD (Northampton GS) B Northampton 28/11/1962. Son of J. Wild, former Northants player. LHB, RM. Played for 2nd XI since 1978. Toured West Indies with England Young Cricketers in 1980. Debut 1980. HS: 30 v Essex (Southend) 1981. HSJPL: 18 v Derbyshire (Derby) 1981.

Peter WILLEY B Sedgefield, County Durham 6/12/1949. RHB, OB. Debut 1966 aged 16 years 180 days scoring 78 in second innings of first match v Cambridge U (Cambridge). Cap 1971. Benefit (£31,400) in 1981. Tests: 20 between 1976 and 1981. Tours: Australia and India 1979-80, West Indies 1980-81. 1,000 runs (2) – 1,115 runs

127

(av. 41.29) in 1976 best. Shared in 4th wkt partnership record for county, 370 with R.T. Virgin v Somerset (Northampton) 1976. Gillette Man of Match Awards: 4. Benson & Hedges Gold Awards: 1. HS: 227 v Somerset (Northampton) 1976. HSTC: 102* v West Indies (St. John's) 1980-81. HSGC/NW: 89 v Sussex (Hove) 1979. HSJPL: 107 v Warwickshire (Birmingham) 1975 and 107 v Hants (Tring) 1976. HSBH: 66* v Warwickshire (Birmingham) 1980. BB: 7-37 v Oxford U (Oxford) 1975. BBGC/NW: 3-37 v Cambs (March) 1975. BBJPL: 4-38 v Leics (Leicester) 1980. BBBH: 3-12 v Minor Counties (East) (Horton) 1977.

Richard Grenville WILLIAMS (Ellesmere Port GS) B Bangor, Caernarvonshire 10/8/1957. RHB, OB. 5ft 6½ins tall. Debut for 2nd XI in 1972, aged 14 years 11 months. Debut 1974 aged 16 years 313 days. Toured West Indies with England Young Cricketers 1976. Cap 1979. 1,000 runs (3) – 1,262 runs (av. 34.10) in 1980 best. Scored two centuries in match (109 and 151*) v Warwickshire (Northampton) 1979. Shared in 2nd wkt partnership record for county, 322 with W. Larkins v Leics (Leicester) 1980. Hat-trick v Glos (Northampton) 1980. Gillette Man of Match Awards: 1. Benson & Hedges Gold Awards: 2. HS: 175* v Leics (Leicester) 1980. HSGC/NW: 51 v Durham (Northampton) 1977. HSJPL: 81 v Worcs (Worcester) 1981. HSBH: 83 v Yorks (Bradford) 1980. BB: 7-73 v Cambridge U (Cambridge) 1980. BBGC/NW: 3-15 v Leics (Northampton) 1979. BBJPL: 4-22 v Yorks (Scarborough) 1980.

Thomas James (Jim) YARDLEY (King Charles I GS, Kidderminster) B Chaddesley Corbett, Worcs 27/10/1946. LHB, RM. Occasional WK. Debut for Worcs 1967. Cap 1972. Not re-engaged after 1975 season and made debut for Northants in 1976. Cap 1978. Scored 1,066 runs (av. 30.45) in 1971. HS: 135 Worcs v Notts (Worcester) 1973. HSC: 100* v Glos (Northampton) 1980. HSGC/NW: 52 Worcs v Warwickshire (Birmingham) 1972 and 52* Worcs v Warwickshire (Birmingham) 1973. HSJPL: 66* v Middlesex (Lord's) 1977. HSBH: 75* Worcs v Warwickshire (Worcester) 1972.

NB. The following players whose particulars appeared in the 1981 annual have been omitted: C.D. Booden (not re-engaged), I.G. Peck and R.M. Tindall (not re-engaged).

The career records of all of these players will be found elsewhere in the annual.

County Averages

Schweppes County Championship: Played 22, won 3, drawn 12, lost 6, abandoned 1.
All first class matches: Played 25, won 4, drawn 14, lost 6, abandoned 1.

BATTING AND FIELDING

Cap		M	I	NO	Runs	HS	Avge	100	50	Ct	St
1978	A.J. Lamb	24	43	9	2049	162	60.26	5	14	20	—
1975	G. Cook	24	43	3	1759	146*	43.97	5	11	23	—
1976	W. Larkins	20	35	1	1369	157	40.26	4	7	2	—
—	Kapil Dev	3	5	0	175	79	35.00	—	1	1	—
1979	R.G. Williams	23	38	2	1197	142*	33.25	3	6	15	—
1978	T.J. Yardley	23	35	8	803	96*	29.74	—	4	23	—
1975	Sarfraz Nawaz	11	16	3	366	90	28.15	—	1	9	—
1971	P. Willey	9	13	1	316	79	26.33	—	2	6	—

NORTHAMPTONSHIRE

Cap		M	I	NO	Runs	HS	Avge	100	50	Ct	St
1973	G. Sharp	21	29	5	544	69*	22.66	—	2	45	2
—	J.P.C. Mills	3	6	0	135	68	22.50	—	1	1	—
—	R.M. Tindall	6	8	1	126	29*	18.00	—	—	3	—
—	D.J. Wild	6	10	3	106	30	15.14	—	—	1	—
—	R.J. Boyd-Moss	7	14	2	165	25	13.75	—	—	4	—
1978	T.M. Lamb	24	21	8	126	31	9.69	—	—	8	—
—	R.M. Carter	15	17	3	132	42*	9.42	—	—	9	—
—	N.A. Mallender	17	20	6	123	18	8.78	—	—	9	—
1978	B.J. Griffiths	23	16	5	30	8	2.72	—	—	4	—

Played in two matches: C.D. Booden 0, 4* (1 ct).
Played in one match: D. Capel 37, 0* (1 ct); I.G. Peck 13*, 2 (1 ct, 1 st); N. Priestley 20* (1 ct, 2 st).

BOWLING

	Type	O	M	R	W	Avge	Best	5 wI	10 wM
N.A. Mallender	RFM	396.5	94	1170	49	23.87	6-37	1	—
Sarfraz Nawaz	RFM	251.4	46	815	33	24.69	6-84	1	—
P. Willey	OB	281	95	554	22	25.18	5-46	2	1
B.J. Griffiths	RFM	681.5	196	1841	70	26.30	8-50	2	—
T.M. Lamb	RM	674.1	183	1701	59	28.83	4-31	—	—
R.G. Williams	OB	612.2	163	1686	48	35.12	5-88	2	—
R.M. Carter	RM	184.4	32	676	18	37.55	4-52	—	—
Kapil Dev	RFM	96	25	316	6	52.66	2-24	—	—

Also bowled: C.D. Booden 51-11-147-3; D. Capel 3-0-6-0; R.J. Boyd-Moss 42-9-156-4; G. Cook 36.4-10-145-2; A.J. Lamb 8-1-35-0; W. Larkins 21.2-5-91-4; R.M. Tindall 44-10-169-2; D.J. Wild 80-15-306-3; T.J. Yardley 1-0-3-0.

County Records

First-class cricket

Highest innings	For	557-6d v Sussex (Hove)	1914
totals:	Agst	670-9d by Sussex (Hove)	1921
Lowest innings	For	12 v Gloucestershire (Gloucester)	1907
totals:	Agst	33 by Lancashire (Northampton)	1977
Highest indi-	For	300 R. Subba Row v Surrey (The Oval)	1958
vidual innings	Agst	333 K.S. Duleepsinhji for Sussex (Hove)	1930
Best bowling	For	10-127 V.W.C. Jupp v Kent (Tunbridge Wells)	1932
in an innings:	Agst	10-30 C. Blythe for Kent (Northampton)	1907
Best bowling	For	15-31 G.E. Tribe v Yorkshire (Northampton)	1958
in a match:	Agst	17-48 C. Blythe for Kent (Northampton)	1907
Most runs in a season:		2198 (av. 51.11) D. Brookes	1952
runs in a career:		28980 (av. 36.13) D. Brookes	1934-1959
100s in a season:		8 by R.A. Haywood	1921
100s in a career:		67 by D. Brookes	1934-1959
wickets in a season:		175 (av. 18.70) G.E. Tribe	1955
wickets in a career:		1097 (av. 21.31) E.W. Clark	1922-1947

RECORD WICKET STANDS

1st	361	N. Oldfield & V. Broderick v Scotland (Peterborough)	1953
2nd	322	W. Larkins & R.G. Williams v Leicestershire (Leicester)	1980
3rd	320	L. Livingston & F. Jakeman v South Africans (Northampton)	1951
4th	370	R.T. Virgin & P. Willey v Somerset (Northampton)	1976
5th	347	D. Brookes & D. Barrick v Essex (Northampton)	1952
6th	376	R. Subba Row & A. Lightfoot v Surrey (The Oval)	1958
7th	229	W.W. Timms & F.A. Walden v Warwickshire (Northampton)	1926
8th	155	F.R. Brown & A.E. Nutter v Glamorgan (Northampton)	1952
9th	156	R. Subba Row & S. Starkie v Lancashire (Northampton)	1955
10th	148	B.W. Bellamy & V. Murdin v Glamorgan (Northampton)	1925

One-day cricket

Highest innings totals:	Gillette Cup/ NatWest Trophy	275-5 v Notts (Nottingham)	1976
	John Player League	259 v Warwickshire (Northampton)	1979
	Benson & Hedges Cup	249-3 v Warwickshire (Northampton)	1974
Lowest innings totals:	Gillette Cup/ NatWest Trophy	62 v Leics (Leicester)	1974
	John Player League	41 v Middlesex (Northampton)	1972
	Benson & Hedges Cup	85 v Sussex (Northampton)	1978
Highest individual innings:	Gillette Cup/ NatWest Trophy	114* G. Cook v Surrey (Northampton)	1979
	John Player League	127* A.J. Lamb v Worcs (Worcester)	1981
	Benson & Hedges Cup	131 Mushtaq Mohammad v Minor Counties (East) (Longton)	1976
Best bowling figures:	Gillette Cup/ NatWest Trophy	5-24 J.D.F. Larter v Leicestershire (Leicester)	1964
	John Player League	7-39 A. Hodgson v Somerset (Northampton)	1976
	Benson & Hedges Cup	5-21 Sarfraz Nawaz v Middlesex (Lord's)	1980

NOTTINGHAMSHIRE

Formation of present club: 1841, reorganised 1866.
Colours: Green and gold.
Badge: County Badge of Nottinghamshire.
County Champions (13): 1865, 1868, 1871, 1872, 1875, 1880, 1883, 1884, 1885, 1886, 1907, 1929 and 1981.
Joint Champions (5): 1869, 1873, 1879, 1882 and 1889.
Gillette Cup Semi-Finalists: 1969.
NatWest Trophy Third Round: 1981.
Best final position in John Player League: 5th in 1975.
Benson & Hedges Cup Quarter-Finalists (5): 1973, 1976, 1978, 1980 and 1981.
Gillette Man of the Match Awards: 13.
NatWest Man of the Match Awards: 2.
Benson & Hedges Gold Awards: 24.

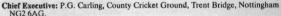

Chief Executive: P.G. Carling, County Cricket Ground, Trent Bridge, Nottingham NG2 6AG.
Cricket Manager: K. Taylor.
Captain: C.E.B. Rice.
Prospects of Play Telephone No: Nottingham (0602) 869681.

John Dennis BIRCH B Nottingham 18/6/1955. RHB, RM. Debut 1973. Cap 1981. Benson & Hedges Gold Awards: 1. HS: 111 v Essex (Chelmsford) 1981. HSGC/NW: 32 v Yorks (Bradford) 1978. HSJPL: 71 v Yorks (Scarborough) 1978. HSBH: 85 v Minor Counties (North) (Nottingham) 1979. BB: 6-64 v Hants (Bournemouth) 1975. BBJPL: 3-29 v Glamorgan (Swansea) 1976.

Michael Kenneth (Mike) BORE B Hull 2/6/1947. RHB, LM. Debut for Yorks 1969. Left county after 1978 season and made debut for Notts in 1979. Cap 1980. Benson & Hedges Gold Awards: 1. HS: 37* Yorks v Notts (Bradford) 1973. HSC: 24* v Yorks (Nottingham) 1980. HSJPL: 28* v Northants (Northampton) 1979. BB: 8-89 v Kent (Folkestone) 1979. BBGC/NW: 3-35 Yorks v Kent (Canterbury) 1971. BBJPL: 4-21 Yorks v Sussex (Middlesbrough) 1970 and 4-21 Yorks v Worcs (Worcester) 1970. BBBH: 6-22 v Leics (Leicester) 1980.

Kevin Edward COOPER B Hucknall (Notts) 27/12/1957. LHB, RFM. Debut 1976. Cap 1980. HS: 27 v Middlesex (Nottingham) 1981. HSJPL: 12 v Northants (Northampton) 1979. BB: 6-32 v Derbyshire (Derby) 1978. BBJPL: 4-25 v Hants (Nottingham) 1976. BBBH: 4-23 v Kent (Canterbury) 1979.

Mark Andrew FELL (Grove Comprehensive School, New Balderton, Newark) B Newark 17/11/1960. RHB, SLA. Played for 2nd XI in 1980. Played in three John Player League matches in 1981. Has yet to appear in first-class cricket. HSJPL: 14 v Warwickshire (Birmingham) 1981.

Bruce Nicholas FRENCH (The Meden Comprehensive School, Warsop) B Warsop (Notts) 13/8/1959. RHB, WK. Debut 1976 aged 16 years 287 days. Cap 1980. HS: 70* v Worcs (Cleethorpes) 1980. HSNW: 33* v Kent (Canterbury) 1981. HGJPL: 25 v Northants (Nottingham) 1978. HSBH: 16 v Surrey (Nottingham) 1981.

Richard John HADLEE (Christchurch Boys' High School!) B Christchurch, New Zealand 3/7/1951. Youngest son of W.A. Hadlee, former New Zealand Test cricketer, and brother of D.R. Hadlee. LHB, RFM. Debut for Canterbury 1971-72 in Plunket Shield competition. Debut for county and cap 1978. Played for Tasmania in 1979-80. *Wisden* 1981. Tests: 35 for New Zealand between 1972-73 and 1980-81. Tours: New Zealand to England 1973 and 1978, Australia 1973-74 and 1980-81, Pakistan and India 1976-77. Took 105 wkts (av. 14.89) in 1981. NatWest Man of the Match Awards: 1. Benson & Hedges Gold Awards: 2. HS: 142* v Yorks (Bradford) 1981. HSTC: 103 New Zealand v West Indies (Christchurch) 1979-80. HSNW: 38* v Kent (Canterbury) 1981. HSJPL: 67* v Surrey (Nottingham) 1981. HSBH: 41 v Kent (Canterbury) 1978. BB: 7-23 New Zealand v India (Wellington) 1975-76 and 7-23 v Sussex (Nottingham) 1979. BBJPL: 6-12 v Lancs (Nottingham) 1980. BBBH: 4-13 v Derbyshire (Nottingham) 1980.

Michael John (Mike, Pasty) HARRIS B St. Just-in-Roseland (Cornwall) 25/5/1944. RHB, WK. Can bowl LBG. Debut for Middlesex 1964. Cap 1967. Left staff after 1968 season and joined Notts by special registration in 1969. Cap 1970. Played for Eastern Province in 1971-72 Currie Cup competition. Played for Wellington in New Zealand Shell Shield competition in 1975-76. Benefit in 1977. 1,000 runs (11) – 2,238 runs (av. 50.86) in 1971 best. Scored 9 centuries in 1971 to equal county record. Scored two centuries in match twice in 1971, 118 and 123 v Leics (Leicester) and 107 and 131* v Essex (Chelmsford) and also in 1979, 133* and 102 v Northants (Nottingham). Benson & Hedges Gold Awards: 2. HS: 201* v Glamorgan (Nottingham) 1973. HSGC/NW: 101 v Somerset (Nottingham) 1970. HSJPL: 104* v Hants (Nottingham) 1970. HSBH: 101 v Yorks (Hull) 1973. BB: 4-16 v Warwickshire (Nottingham) 1969.

Sheikh Basharat HASSAN (City HS, Nairobi) B Nairobi, Kenya 24/3/1944. RHB, RM, occasional WK. Debut for East Africa Invitation XI v MCC 1963-64. Played for Coast Invitation XI v Pakistan International Airways 1964. Also played for Kenya against these and other touring sides. Debut for county 1966. Cap 1970. Benefit in 1978. 1,000 runs (5) – 1,395 runs (av. 32.44) in 1970 best. Scored century with aid of a runner v Kent (Canterbury) 1977 – a rare achievement in first-class cricket. HS: 182* v Glos (Nottingham) 1977. HSGC/NW: 79 v Hants (Southampton) 1977. HSJPL: 120* v Warwickshire (Birmingham) 1981. HSBH: 98* v Minor Counties (North) (Nottingham) 1973. BB: 3-33 v Lancs (Manchester) 1976. BBGC/NW: 3-20 v Durham (Chester-le-Street) 1967.

Edward Ernest (Eddie) HEMMINGS (Campion School, Leamington Spa) B Leamington Spa 20/2/1949. RHB, OB. Debut for Warwickshire 1966. Cap 1974. Left staff after 1978 season and made debut for Notts in 1979. Cap 1980. Hat-trick Warwickshire v Worcs (Birmingham) 1977. HS: 86 v Worcs (Worcester) 1980. HSGC/NW: 20 Warwickshire v Worcs (Birmingham) 1973. HSJPL: 44* Warwickshire v Kent (Birmingham) 1971. HSBH: 61* Warwickshire v Leics (Birmingham) 1974. BB: 7-33 (12-64 match) Warwickshire v Cambridge U (Cambridge) 1975. BBC: 7-59 (13-129 match) v Derbyshire (Nottingham) 1981. BBJPL: 5-22 Warwickshire v Northants (Birmingham) 1974. BBBH: 3-18 Warwickshire v Oxford and Cambridge Universities (Coventry) 1975.

Michael (Mike) HENDRICK B Darley Dale (Derbyshire) 22/10/1948. RHB, RFM. Debut for Derbyshire 1969. Cap 1972. Elected Best Young Cricketer of the Year in 1973 by the Cricket Writers' Club. *Wisden* 1977. Benefit (£36,050) in 1980. Left county after 1981 season and has joined Notts for 1982. Tests: 30 between 1974 and 1981. Tours: West Indies 1973-74, Australia and New Zealand 1974-75, Pakistan and New Zealand 1977-78, Australia 1978-79, Australia (returned home early through injury) 1979-80. Hat-trick Derbyshire v West Indians (Derby) 1980. Gillette

Man of the Match Awards: 1 (for Derbyshire). Benson & Hedges Gold Awards: 3 (for Derbyshire). HS: 46 Derbyshire v Essex (Chelmsford) 1973. HSTC: 15 v Australia (Oval) 1977. HSGC/NW: 17 Derbyshire v Middlesex (Derby) 1978. HSJPL: 21 Derbyshire v Warwickshire (Buxton) 1974. HSBH: 32 Derbyshire v Notts (Chesterfield) 1973. BB: 8-45 Derbyshire v Warwickshire (Chesterfield) 1973. BBTC: 4-28 v India (Birmingham) 1974. BBGC/NW: 4-16 Derbyshire v Middlesex (Chesterfield) 1975. BBJPL: 6-7 Derbyshire v Notts (Nottingham) 1972. BBBH: 5-30 Derbyshire v Notts (Chesterfield) 1975 and 5-30 Derbyshire v Lancashire (Southport) 1976.

Nigel John Bartle ILLINGWORTH (Denstone College) B Chesterfield 23/11/1960. RHB, RM. Played for 2nd XI in 1980. Debut 1981. One match v Cambridge (Cambridge) and also played in seven John Player League matches. BBJPL: 4-39 v Glamorgan (Nottingham) 1981.

Paul JOHNSON (Grove Comprehensive School, New Balderton, Newark) B Newark 24/4/1965. RHB, RM. Joined staff 1981. Played in one John Player League match v Warwickshire (Nottingham). Has yet to appear in first-class cricket.

Ian Leslie PONT (Brentwood School) B Brentwood (Essex) 28/8/1961. Younger brother of K.R. Pont of Essex. RHB, RM. Played for Essex 2nd XI in 1978 and for Warwickshire 2nd XI in 1980. Joined staff 1981. Played in last two John Player League matches of 1981 season. Has yet to appear in first-class cricket.

Derek William RANDALL B Retford 24/2/1951. RHB, RM. Played in one John Player League match in 1971. Debut 1972. Cap 1973. *Wisden* 1979. Tests: 27 between 1976-77 and 1979-80. Tours: India, Sri Lanka and Australia 1976-77, Pakistan and New Zealand 1977-78, Australia 1978-79, Australia and India 1979-80. 1,000 runs (7) – 1,546 runs (av. 42.94) in 1976 best. Scored two centuries in match (209 and 146) v Middlesex (Nottingham) 1979. Gillette Man of Match Awards: 1. Benson & Hedges Gold Awards: 3. HS: 209 v Middlesex (Nottingham) 1979. HSTC: 174 v Australia (Melbourne) 1976-77. HSGC/NW: 75 v Sussex (Hove) 1979. HSJPL: 107* v Middlesex (Lord's) 1976. HSBH: 103* v Minor Counties (North) (Nottingham) 1979.

Clive Edward Butler RICE (St. John's College, Johannesburg) B Johannesburg 23/7/1949. RHB, RFM. Debut for Transvaal 1969-70. Professional for Ramsbottom in Lancashire League in 1973. Played for D.H. Robins' XI v West Indians 1973 and Pakistanis 1974. Debut for county and cap 1975. Appointed county captain for 1978, but was relieved of appointment when his signing for World Series Cricket was announced. Re-appointed county captain during 1979 season. *Wisden* 1980. 1,000 runs (7) – 1,871 runs (av. 66.82) in 1978 best. Scored two centuries in match (131* and 114*) v Somerset (Nottingham) 1980. Scored 105* out of innings total of 143 v Hants (Bournemouth) 1981 – lowest innings total in first-class cricket to contain a century. Benson & Hedges Gold Awards: 4. HS: 246 v Sussex (Hove) 1976. HSGC/NW: 71 v Yorks (Bradford) 1978. Scored 157 for Transvaal v Orange Free State (Bloemfontein) 1975-76 in South African Gillette Cup competition. HSJPL: 120* v Glamorgan (Swansea) 1978. HSBH: 96 v Glos (Gloucester) 1981. BB: 7-62 Transvaal v Western Province (Johannesburg) 1975-76. BBUK: 6-16 v Worcs (Worcester) 1977. BBNW: 3-21 v Kent (Canterbury) 1981. BBJPL: 4-15 v Hants (Nottingham) 1980. BBBH: 6-22 v Northants (Northampton) 1981.

Robert Timothy (Tim) ROBINSON (High Pavement College, Nottingham) B Sutton-in-Ashfield (Notts) 21/11/1958. RHB, RM. Played for Northants 2nd XI in

NOTTINGHAMSHIRE

1974 and 1975 and for county 2nd XI in 1977. Debut 1978. Benson & Hedges Gold Awards: 1. HS: 138 v Leics (Nottingham) 1980. HSGC/NW: 32 v Middlesex (Nottingham) 1980. HSJPL: 48* v Glamorgan (Nottingham) 1981. HSBH: 77* v Worcs (Nottingham) 1981. Obtained Degree in Accountancy and Financial Management from Sheffield University.

Kevin SAXELBY (Magnus GS, Newark) B Worksop 23/2/1959. RHB, RM. Debut 1978. HS: 15 v Surrey (Oval) 1980. BB: 4-64 v Glos (Nottingham) 1981. BBJPL: 4-37 v Yorks (Nottingham) 1981.

Christopher William SCOTT (The Robert Pattinson School, North Rykeham, Lincs) B Thorpe-on-the-Hill (Lincs) 23/1/1964. RHB, WK. Debut 1981 (two matches). HS: 8 v Hants (Bournemouth) 1981.

Paul Adrian TODD B Morton (Notts) 12/3/1953. RHB, RM. Debut 1972. Cap 1977. Gillette Man of Match Awards: 1. NatWest Man of the Match Awards: 1. Benson & Hedges Gold Awards: 1. 1,000 runs (3) – 1,181 runs (av. 29.52) in 1978 best. HS: 178 v Glos (Nottingham) 1975. HSGC/NW: 105 v Warwickshire (Birmingham) 1979. HSJPL: 79 v Hants (Nottingham) 1978. HSBH: 59 v Kent (Canterbury) 1979.

Neil Ivan WEIGHTMAN (Magnus GS, Newark) B Normanton-on-Trent (Notts) 5/10/1960. LHB, OB. Played for 2nd XI since 1977. Played in last two John Player League matches of 1980. Debut 1981. HS: 105 v Leics (Hinckley) 1981. HSJPL: 17 v Yorks (Nottingham) 1981.

Robert Arthur (Bob) WHITE (Chiswick GS) B Fulham 6/10/1936. LHB, OB. Debut for Middlesex 1958. Cap 1963. Debut for Notts after special registration in 1966 and developed into useful off-break bowler. Cap 1966. Benefit (£11,000) in 1974. Is now 2nd XI coach. Did not play in 1981. Scored 1,355 runs (av. 33.87) in 1963. HS: 116* v Surrey (Oval) 1967, sharing in 7th wicket partnership record for county, 204 with M.J. Smedley. HSGC/NW: 39 v Worcs (Worcester) 1966. HSJPL: 86* v Surrey (Guildford) 1973. HSBH: 52* v Worcs (Worcester) 1973. BB: 7-41 v Derbyshire (Ilkeston) 1971. BBGC/NW: 3-43 v Worcs (Worcester) 1968. BBJPL: 4-15 v Somerset (Bath) 1975. BBBH: 3-27 v Northants (Northampton) 1976.

Peter George WOOD B Heaton Park, Manchester 29/9/1951. RHB, RM. Played for Lancs 2nd XI in 1974 and has captained Rawtenstall in Lancashire League. Has also played in South Africa. Played in two John Player League matches in 1981. Has yet to appear in first-class cricket. HSJPL: 15 v Glamorgan (Nottingham) 1981.

NB. The following players who appeared in the 1981 annual have been omitted: R.E. Dexter (left staff), N. Nanan (left staff) and W.K. Watson. In addition P.J. Hacker has joined Derbyshire and his particulars will be found under that county.

The career records of Dexter and Hacker will be found elsewhere in this annual.

County Averages

Schweppes County Championship: Played 22, won 11, drawn 6, lost 4, abandoned 1.
All first-class matches: Played 23, won 12, drawn 6, lost 4, abandoned 1.

BATTING AND FIELDING

Cap		M	I	NO	Runs	HS	Avge	100	50	Ct	St
1975	C.E.B. Rice	21	30	4	1462	172*	56.23	6	6	25	—
1973	D.W. Randall	18	29	5	1093	162*	45.54	3	6	21	—
1970	S.B. Hassan	13	20	5	641	97*	42.73	—	6	15	—
1981	J.D. Birch	20	27	6	757	111	36.04	1	5	18	—
1978	R.J. Hadlee	21	26	3	745	142*	32.39	1	3	14	—
—	N.I. Weightman	3	5	0	139	105	27.80	1	—	3	—
1977	P.A. Todd	21	37	4	899	112	27.24	1	4	8	—
1970	M.J. Harris	8	10	4	162	44*	27.00	—	—	8	—
—	R.T. Robinson	19	33	7	687	91	26.42	—	3	12	—
—	R.E. Dexter	8	14	3	209	57	19.00	—	1	13	—
1980	P.J. Hacker	7	5	4	18	8*	18.00	—	—	2	—
1980	E.E. Hemmings	22	23	4	257	44	13.52	—	—	6	—
—	K. Saxelby	4	4	2	23	10*	11.50	—	—	3	—
1980	B.N. French	20	23	0	261	31	11.34	—	—	51	2
1980	K.E. Cooper	19	20	2	132	27	7.33	—	—	8	—
1980	M.K. Bore	15	14	5	60	11*	6.66	—	—	4	—

Played in two matches: C.W. Scott 6, 8 (2 ct, 1 st).
Played in one match: N.J.B. Illingworth did not bat (1 ct).

BOWLING

	Type	O	M	R	W	Avge	Best	5 wI	10 wM
R.J. Hadlee	RFM	708.4	231	1564	105	14.89	7-25	4	—
C.E.B. Rice	RFM	494.5	142	1248	65	19.20	6-44	1	—
P.J. Hacker	LFM	175.5	53	446	23	19.39	4-34	—	—
E.E. Hemmings	OB	804.2	262	1857	90	20.63	7-59	6	2
K. Saxelby	RM	99.4	24	293	12	24.41	4-64	—	—
K.E. Cooper	RM	423.3	125	1081	43	25.13	4-13	—	—
M.K. Bore	LM	474.5	158	1075	36	29.86	4-46	—	—

Also bowled: M.J. Harris 8-1-39-0; N.J.B. Illingworth 7-3-16-1; R.T. Robinson 1-0-5-0.

County Records

First-class cricket

Highest innings totals:	For	739-7d v Leicestershire (Nottingham)	1903
	Agst	706-4d by Surrey (Nottingham)	1947
Lowest innings totals:	For	13 v Yorkshire (Nottingham)	1901
	Agst	16 by Derbyshire (Nottingham) and Surrey (The Oval)	1879 & 1880
Highest individual innings:	For	312* W.W. Keeton v Middlesex (The Oval)	1939
	Agst	345 C.G. Macartney for Australians (Nottingham)	1921
Best bowling in an innings:	For	10-66 K. Smales v Gloucestershire (Stroud)	1956
	Agst	10-10 H. Verity for Yorkshire (Leeds)	1932

135

Best bowling	For	17-89 F.C.L. Matthews v Northants (Nottingham)	1923
in a match:	Agst	17-89 W.G. Grace for Glos (Cheltenham)	1877
Most runs in a season:		2,620 (av. 53.46) W.W. Whysall	1929
runs in a career:		31,592 (av. 35.70) G. Gunn	1902-1932
100s in a season:		9 by W.W. Whysall	1928
		and M.J. Harris	1971
100s in a career:		65 by J. Hardstaff	1930-1955
wickets in a season:		181 (av. 14.96) B. Dooland	1954
wickets in a career:		1,653 (av. 20.34) T. Wass	1896-1914

RECORD WICKET STANDS

1st	391	A.O. Jones & A. Shrewsbury v Gloucestershire (Bristol)	1899
2nd	398	W. Gunn & A. Shrewsbury v Sussex (Nottingham)	1890
3rd	369	J.R. Gunn & W. Gunn v Leicestershire (Nottingham)	1903
4th	361	A.O. Jones & J.R. Gunn v Essex (Leyton)	1905
5th	266	A. Shrewsbury & W. Gunn v Sussex (Hove)	1884
6th	303*	H. Winrow & P.F. Harvey v Derbyshire (Nottingham)	1947
7th	204	M.J. Smedley & R.A. White v Surrey (Oval)	1967
8th	220	G.F.H. Heane & R. Winrow v Somerset (Nottingham)	1933
9th	167	W. McIntyre & G. Wootton v Kent (Nottingham)	1869
10th	152	E. Alletson & W. Riley v Sussex (Hove)	1911

One-day cricket

Highest innings totals:	Gillette Cup/ NatWest Trophy	271 v Gloucestershire (Nottingham)	1968
	John Player League	260-5 v Warwickshire (Birmingham)	1976
	Benson & Hedges Cup	269-5 v Derbyshire (Nottingham)	1980
Lowest innings totals:	Gillette Cup/ NatWest Trophy	123 v Yorkshire (Scarborough)	1969
	John Player League	66 v Yorks (Bradford)	1969
	Benson & Hedges Cup	94 v Lancashire (Nottingham)	1975
Highest individual innings:	Gillette Cup/ NatWest Trophy	107 M. Hill v Somerset (Taunton)	1964
	John Player League	120* C.E.B. Rice v Glamorgan (Swansea)	1978
		120* S.B. Hassan v Warwickshire (Birmingham)	1981
	Benson & Hedges Cup	103* D.W. Randall v Minor Counties (North) (Nottingham)	1979
Best bowling figures:	Gillette Cup/ NatWest Trophy	5-44 B. Stead v Worcestershire (Worcester)	1974
	John Player League	6-12 R.J. Hadlee v Lancashire (Nottingham)	1980
	Benson & Hedges Cup	6-22 M.K. Bore v Leicestershire (Leicester)	1980
		6-22 C.E.B. Rice v Northamptonshire (Northampton)	1981

SOMERSET

Formation of present club: 1875, reorganised 1885.
Colours: Black, silver and maroon.
Badge: Wessex Wyvern.
Best final position in Championship: Third (5): 1892, 1958, 1963, 1966 and 1981.
Gillette Cup Winners: 1979.
Gillette Cup Finalists (2): 1967 and 1978.
NatWest Trophy Second Round: 1981.
John Player League Champions: 1979.
Benson & Hedges Cup Winners: 1981.
Gillette Man of the Match Awards: 26.
NatWest Man of the Match Awards: Nil.
Benson & Hedges Gold Awards: 28.

Secretary and Chief Executive: D.G. Seward, County Cricket Ground, St. James's Street, Taunton TA1 1JT.
Captain: B.C. Rose.
Prospects of Play Telephone No: Taunton (0823) 70007.

Ian Terrence BOTHAM B Heswall (Cheshire) 24/11/1955. RHB, RFM. Played for 2nd XI in 1971. On MCC staff 1972-73. Played for county in last two John Player League matches of 1973. Debut 1974. Cap 1976. Elected Best Young Cricketer of the Year in 1977 by the Cricket Writers' Club. *Wisden* 1977. Tests: 41 between 1977 and 1981, captaining England in 12 Tests. Tours: Pakistan and New Zealand 1977-78, Australia 1978-79, Australia and India 1979-80, West Indies 1980-81 (Captain), India and Sri Lanka 1981-82. 1,000 runs (2) – 1,149 runs (av. 42.55) in 1980 best. Took 100 wkts (av. 16.40) in 1978. Became first player ever to score a century and take 8 wkts in innings in a Test match, v Pakistan (Lord's) 1978, and to score a century and take 10 wkts in a match, v India (Bombay) 1979-80. Took 100th wkt in Test cricket in 1979 in record time of 2 years 9 days. Achieved double of 1,000 runs and 100 wkts in Tests in 1979 to create records of fewest Tests (21), shortest time (2 years 33 days) and at youngest age (23 years 279 days). These records, with exception of fewest Tests, were beaten by Kapil Dev for India in 1979-80. Took 200th wkt in 1981 in record time of 4 years 34 days and at youngest age of 25 years 280 days. Became third player in Test cricket to achieve double of 2,000 runs and 200 wkts in 1981-82 in fewest Tests (42), shortest time (4 years 126 days) and youngest age (26 years 7 days). Scored centuries against Australia in 1981 off 87 balls (Leeds) and 86 balls (Manchester). Hat-trick for MCC v Middlesex (Lord's) 1978. Gillette Man of Match Awards: 1. Benson & Hedges Gold Awards: 4. HS: 228 v Glos (Taunton) 1980 in 184 minutes with 10 6's and 27 4's, scoring 182 between lunch and tea, and sharing in 4th wkt partnership record for county, 310 with P.W. Denning. HSTC: 149* v Australia (Leeds) 1981. HSGC/NW: 91* v Northumberland (Taunton) 1977. HSJPL: 106 v Hants (Taunton) 1981. HSBH: 57* v Kent (Taunton) 1981. BB: 8-34 v Pakistan (Lord's) 1978. BBC: 7-61 v Glamorgan (Cardiff) 1978. BBGC/NW: 3-15 v Kent (Taunton) 1979. BBJPL: 4-10 v Yorks (Scarborough) 1979. BBBH: 4-16 v Combined Universities (Taunton) 1978. Has played soccer for Scunthorpe United.

Mark DAVIS (West Somerset School, Minehead) B Kilve (Somerset) 26/2/1962. LHB, LFM. Played for 2nd XI since 1980 and joined staff in 1981. Has not yet appeared in first-class cricket.

137

Peter William (Pete) DENNING (Millfield School) B Chewton Mendip (Somerset) 16/12/1949. LHB, OB. Debut 1969. Cap 1973. 1,000 runs (6) – 1,222 runs (Av. 42.13) in 1979 best. Scored two centuries in match (122 and 107) v Glos (Taunton) 1977. Shared in 4th wkt partnership record for county, 310 with I.T. Botham v Glos (Taunton) 1980. Gillette Man of Match Awards: 4. Benson & Hedges Gold Awards: 2. HS: 184 v Notts (Nottingham) 1980. HSGC/NW: 145 v Glamorgan (Cardiff) 1978. HSJPL: 100 v Northants (Brackley) 1974. HSBH: 87 v Glos (Taunton) 1974. Trained as a teacher at St. Luke's College, Exeter.

Colin Herbert DREDGE B Frome 4/8/1954. LHB, RM. 6ft 5ins tall. Debut 1976. Cap 1978. Gillette Man of Match Awards: 1. HS: 56* v Yorks (Harrogate) 1977. HSJPL: 14 v Essex (Taunton) 1978. HSBH: 10* v Worcs (Taunton) 1978. BB: 6-37 v Glos (Bristol) 1981. BBGC/NW: 4-23 v Kent (Canterbury) 1978. BBJPL: 5-35 v Middlesex (Lord's) 1981. BBBH: 4-10 v Hants (Bournemouth) 1980. Played soccer for Bristol City Reserves.

Trevor GARD (Huish Episcopi School, Langport) B West Lambrook, near South Petheron (Somerset) 2/6/1957. RHB, WK. Played for 2nd XI since 1972. Debut 1976. Did not play in 1981. HS: 51* v Indians (Taunton) 1979.

Joel GARNER B Barbados 16/12/1952. RHB, RF. 6ft 8ins tall. Debut for Barbados in Shell Shield competition 1975-76. Debut for county 1977 playing in mid-week matches whilst playing as a professional for Littleborough in Central Lancashire League. Cap 1979. *Wisden* 1979. Tests: 25 for West Indies between 1976-77 and 1980-81. Tours: West Indies to Australia and New Zealand 1979-80, England 1980, Pakistan 1980-81, Australia 1981-82. Gillette Man of Match Awards: 1. Benson & Hedges Gold Awards: 1. HS: 104 West Indians v Glos (Bristol) 1980. HSTC: 60 West Indies v Australia (Brisbane) 1979-80. HSC: 90 v Glos (Bath) 1981. HSGC/NW: 38* v Glamorgan (Cardiff) 1978. HSJPL: 32 v Kent (Taunton) 1979. HSBH: 17 v Sussex (Hove) 1978. BB: 8-31 v England (Kingston) 1980-81. BBTC: 6-56 West Indies v New Zealand (Auckland) 1979-80. BBGC/NW: 6-29 v Northants (Lord's) 1979. BBJPL: 4-21 v Glos (Bath) 1981. BBBH: 5-14 v Surrey (Lord's) 1981.

Jeremy William LLOYDS (Blundell's School) B Penang, Malaya 17/11/1954. LHB, OB. Played for 2nd XI from 1973 to 1977. Played for Hants, Middlesex and Worcs 2nd XIs in 1978. Debut 1979. HS: 127 v Lancs (Manchester) 1981. HSJPL: 33 v Surrey (Oval) 1981. HSBH: 12 v Glamorgan (Taunton) 1981. BB: 6-61 v Worcs (Weston-super-Mare) 1980.

Victor James (Vic) MARKS (Blundell's School, Tiverton and Oxford) B Middle Chinnock (Somerset) 25/6/1955. RHB, OB. Debut for both Oxford U and county 1975. Blue 1975-76-77-78 (Captain in 1976-77). Cap 1979. Benson & Hedges Gold Awards: 2. Scored 215 for Oxford U v Army (Aldershot) in non-first class match. HS: 105 Oxford U v Worcs (Oxford) 1976. HSC: 98 v Essex (Leyton) 1976. HSGC/NW: 33* v Essex (Taunton) 1978. HSJPL: 71* v Surrey (Taunton) 1980. HSBH: 81* v Hants (Bournemouth) 1980. BB: 6-33 v Northants (Taunton) 1979. BBJPL: 3-19 v Derbyshire (Taunton) 1979, and 3-19 v Glos (Bristol) 1980. Half-blue for Rugby Fives.

Hallam Reynold MOSELEY B Christ Church, Barbados 28/5/1948. RHB, RFM. Toured England with Barbados team in 1969 and made debut v Notts (Nottingham). Subsequently played for Barbados in Shell Shield. Joined county in 1970 and made debut in 1971. Cap 1972. Testimonial (£24,085) in 1979. Is now regarded as an

138

English player for qualification purposes. HS: 67 v Leics (Taunton) 1972. HSGC/NW: 15 v Lancs (Manchester) 1972. HSJPL: 24 v Notts (Torquay) 1972 and 24 v Hants (Weston-super-Mare) 1975. HSBH: 33 v Hants (Bournemouth) 1973. BB: 6-34 v Derbyshire (Bath) 1975 and 6-35 v Glos (Taunton) 1978. BBGC/NW: 4-31 v Surrey (Taunton) 1974. BBJPL: 5-30 v Middlesex (Lord's) 1973. BBBH: 3-17 v Leics (Taunton) 1977.

Martin OLIVE (Millfield School) B Watford (Herts) 18/4/1958. RHB, RM. Played for 2nd XI since 1974. Debut 1977. HS: 50 v Yorks (Weston-super-Mare) 1980.

Richard Leslie OLLIS (Wellsway School, Keynsham) B Clifton (Glos) 14/1/1961. LHB, RM. Played for 2nd XI since 1979. Debut 1981 (two matches). HS: 22 v Warwickshire (Birmingham) 1981.

Nigel Francis Mark POPPLEWELL (Radley College and Cambridge) B Chislehurst (Kent) 8/8/1957. Son of O.B. Popplewell, Q.C., former Cambridge Blue. RHB, RM. Played for Buckinghamshire in 1975 and 1978 and for Hants 2nd XI in 1976 and 1977. Debut for Cambridge U 1977. Blue 1977-78-79 (secretary). Debut for county 1979. Benson & Hedges Gold Awards: 1. HS: 135* v Kent (Taunton) 1980. HSNW: 57 v Northants (Northampton) 1981. HSJPL: 55 v Surrey (Taunton) 1980. HSBH: 42 v Kent (Taunton) 1981. BB: 5-33 v Northants (Weston-super-Mare) 1981.

Isaac Vivian Alexander (Viv) RICHARDS (Antigua Grammar School) B St. John's, Antigua 7/3/1952. RHB, OB. Debut 1971-72 for Leeward Islands v Windward Islands and subsequently played for Combined Islands in Shell Shield tournament. Debut for county and cap 1974. *Wisden* 1976. Played for Queensland in 1976-77 Sheffield Shield competition. Benefit in 1982. Tests: 44 for West Indies between 1974-75 and 1980-81, captaining West Indies in 1 Test in 1980. Tours: West Indies to India, Sri Lanka and Pakistan 1974-75, Australia 1975-76, 1979-80, 1981-82 (Vice-Captain), England 1976 and 1980 (Vice-Captain), Pakistan 1980-81 (Vice-Captain). 1,000 runs (8) – 2,161 runs (av. 65.48) in 1977 best. Also scored 1,267 runs (av. 60.33) on 1974-75 tour and 1,107 runs (av. 58.26) on 1975-76 tour. Scored 1,710 in 11 Test matches in 1976 including 829 runs in 4 Tests against England – record aggregate for a year and fourth highest aggregate for a Test Series. Scored 99 and 110 v Leics (Taunton) 1978. Gillette Man of Match Awards: 3, Benson & Hedges Gold Awards: 5. HS: 291 West Indies v England (Oval) 1976. HSC: 241* v Glos (Bristol) 1977. HSGC/NW: 139* v Warwickshire (Taunton) 1978. HSJPL: 126* v Glos (Bristol, Imperial Ground) 1975. HSBH: 132* v Surrey (Lord's) 1981. BB: 5-88 West Indians v Queensland (Brisbane) 1981-82. BBUK: 4-55 v Glamorgan (Taunton) 1981. BBJPL: 3-32 v Glos (Bristol) 1978.

Peter Michael ROEBUCK (Millfield School and Cambridge) B Oxford 6/3/1956. RHB, OB. Played for 2nd XI in 1969 at age of 13. Debut 1974. Blue 1975-76-77. Cap 1978. 1,000 runs (2) – 1,273 runs (av. 47.14) in 1979 best. Benson & Hedges Gold Awards: 1. HS: 158 Cambridge U v Oxford U (Lord's) 1975. HSC: 131* v New Zealanders (Taunton) 1978. HSGC/NW: 57 v Essex (Taunton) 1978. HSJPL: 73* v Kent (Taunton) 1981. HSBH: 51* v Kent (Taunton) 1981. BB: 6-50 Cambridge U v Kent (Canterbury) 1977.

Brian Charles ROSE (Weston-super-Mare GS) B Dartford (Kent) 4/6/1950. LHB, LM. Wears spectacles. Played for English Schools CA at Lord's 1968. Debut 1969. Cap 1975. Appointed county captain in 1978. *Wisden* 1979. Tests: 9 between

SOMERSET

1977-78 and 1980-81. Tours: Pakistan and New Zealand 1977-78, West Indies 1980-81 (returned early through eyesight problem). 1,000 runs (7) – 1,624 runs (av. 46.40) in 1976 best. Scored two centuries in match (124 and 150*) v Worcs (Worcester) 1980. Gillette Man of Match Awards: 2. Benson & Hedges Gold Awards: 2. HS: 205 v Northants (Weston-super-Mare) 1977. HSTC: 70 v West Indies (Manchester) 1980. HSGC/NW: 128 v Derbyshire (Ilkeston) 1977. HSJPL: 112* v Essex (Ilford) 1980. HSBH: 137* v Kent (Canterbury) 1980. BB: 3-9 v Glos (Taunton) 1975. BBJPL: 3-25 v Lancs (Manchester) 1975. Trained as a teacher at Borough Road College, Isleworth.

Neil RUSSOM (Huish's GS, Taunton and Cambridge) B Finchley (London) 3/12/1958. RHB, RM. Played for 2nd XI since 1975. Played in one Fenner Trophy match v Northants (Scarborough) 1978. Debut for Cambridge U 1979. Blues 1980-81. Debut for county 1980, one match v Glamorgan (Taunton). Benson & Hedges Gold Awards: 1 (for Combined Universities). HS: 79* Cambridge U v Northants (Cambridge) 1980. HSBH: 22 Combined Universities v Kent (Canterbury) 1981. BB: 4-84 Cambridge U v Leics (Cambridge) 1980. BBBH: 5-40 Combined Universities v Northants (Northampton) 1980.

Philip Anthony (Phil) SLOCOMBE (Weston-super-Mare GS and Millfield School) B Weston-super-Mare 6/9/1954. RHB, RM. Played for 2nd XI in 1969 at age of 14. Joined staff 1974. Debut 1975. Cap 1978. 1,000 runs (2) – 1,221 runs (av. 38.15) in 1978 best. Scored 106* & 98 v Worcs (Worcester) 1978. HS: 132 v Notts (Taunton) 1975. HSGC/NW: 42 v Surrey (Oval) 1975. HSJPL: 42 v Leics (Leicester) 1981. HSBH: 42 v Middlesex (Taunton) 1980. Plays soccer for Weston-super-Mare in Western League.

Derek John Somerset TAYLOR (Amersham College) B Amersham (Bucks) 12/11/1942. Twin brother of M.N.S. Taylor of Hants, RHB, WK. Debut for Surrey 1966. Cap 1969. Left staff after 1969 season and made debut for Somerset in 1970. Cap 1971. Testimonial (£20,764) in 1978. Played for Griqualand West in Currie Cup competition 1970-71 and 1971-72. Scored 1,121 runs (av. 28.02) in 1975. Was dismissed obstructing the field in John Player League match v Warwickshire (Birmingham) 1980. HS: 179 v Glamorgan (Swansea) 1974. HSGC/NW: 49 v Kent (Canterbury) 1974. HSJPL: 93 v Surrey (Guildford) 1975. HSBH: 83* v Glos (Street) 1975. Has played soccer for Corinthian Casuals.

NB. The following players whose particulars appeared in the 1981 annual have been omitted: D. Breakwell (become county coach), S.M. Gavaskar, H.E.I. Gore and K.F. Jennings (not re-engaged).

The career records of Breakwell and Jennings will be found elsewhere in the annual.

County Averages

Schweppes County Championship: Played 22, Won 10, Drawn 10, Lost 2.
All first-class matches: Played 24, Won 11, Drawn 11, Lost 2.

BATTING AND FIELDING

Cap		M	I	NO	Runs	HS	Avge	100	50	Ct	St
1974	I.V.A. Richards	20	33	3	1718	196	57.26	7	5	18	—
1976	I.T. Botham	10	12	1	526	123*	47.81	1	3	6	—
1978	P.A. Slocombe	4	6	2	173	62*	43.25	—	2	1	—
1978	P.M. Roebuck	22	34	8	1057	91	40.65	—	9	13	—
1973	P.W. Denning	24	36	6	1087	102*	36.23	1	8	14	—
1975	B.C. Rose	23	39	4	1005	107	28.71	1	5	21	—
1976	D. Breakwell	12	13	2	284	58	25.81	—	3	1	—
1979	V.J. Marks	22	30	7	589	81*	25.60	—	3	9	—
—	J.W. Lloyds	21	35	2	837	127	25.36	1	5	11	—
—	N.F.M. Popplewell	17	25	2	513	51*	22.30	—	1	20	—
1979	J. Garner	18	18	2	324	90	20.25	—	2	10	—
1971	D.J.S. Taylor	24	28	7	370	48*	17.61	—	—	56	6
1972	H.R. Moseley	20	21	8	162	36*	12.46	—	—	9	—
—	M. Olive	3	6	0	72	19	12.00	—	—	1	—
1978	C.H. Dredge	19	16	10	51	14	8.50	—	—	9	—

Played in two matches: K.F. Jennings 4 (2 ct); R.L. Ollis 20, 18, 22, 0 (1 ct).
Played in one match: N. Russom 12, 12* (1 ct).

BOWLING

	Type	O	M	R	W	Avge	Best	5 wI	10 wM
J. Garner	RF	605.4	182	1349	88	15.32	7-25	7	4
C.H. Dredge	RM	498.2	129	1286	54	23.81	6-37	2	—
H.R. Moseley	RFM	436	100	1291	49	26.34	4-16	—	—
I.T. Botham	RFM	301.5	75	1012	33	30.66	6-90	1	—
V.J. Marks	OB	633.5	187	1528	48	31.83	5-34	2	—
N.F.M. Popplewell	RM	194.2	42	598	18	33.22	5-33	1	—
D. Breakwell	SLA	24	44	719	19	37.84	6-38	1	—
I.V.A. Richards	OB	185.5	38	585	13	45.00	4-55	—	—
J.W. Lloyds	OB	144.2	29	482	10	48.20	3-12	—	—

Also bowled: P.W. Denning 3-0 18-0; K.F. Jennings 29-4 74-4; B.C. Rose 2-5-0-9-0; N. Russom 10-3 29-2.

County Records

First-class cricket

Highest innings totals:	For	675-9d v Hampshire (Bath)	1924
	Agst	811 by Surrey (The Oval)	1899
Lowest innings totals:	For	25 v Gloucester (Bristol)	1947
	Agst	22 by Gloucestershire (Bristol)	1920
Highest individual innings:	For	310 H. Gimblett v Sussex (Eastbourne)	1948
	Agst	424 A.C. MacLaren for Lancs (Taunton)	1895

SOMERSET

Best bowling:	For	10-49 E.J. Tyler v Surrey (Taunton)	1895
in an innings:	Agst	10-35 A. Drake for Yorks (Weston-s-Mare)	1914
Best bowling:	For	16-83 J.C. White v Worcestershire (Bath)	1919
in a match:	Agst	17-137 W. Brearley for Lancashire (Manchester)	1905
Most runs in a season:		2,761 (av. 58.74) W.E. Alley	1961
runs in a career:		21,142 (av. 36.96) H. Gimblett	1935-1954
100s in a season:		10 by W.E. Alley	1961
100s in a career:		49 by H. Gimblett	1935-1954
wickets in a season:		169 (av. 19.24) A.W. Wellard	1938
wickets in a career:		2,166 (av. 18.02) J.C. White	1909-1937

RECORD WICKET STANDS

1st	346	H.T. Hewett & L.C.H. Palairet v Yorkshire (Taunton)		1892
2nd	290	J.C.W. MacBryan & M.D. Lyon v Derbyshire (Buxton)		1924
3rd	300	G. Atkinson & P.B. Wight v Glamorgan (Bath)		1960
4th	310	P.W. Denning & I.T. Botham v Gloucestershire (Taunton)		1980
5th	235	J.C. White & C.C.C. Case v Gloucestershire (Taunton)		1927
6th	265	W.E. Alley & K.E. Palmer v Northants (Northampton)		1961
7th	240	S.M.J. Woods & V.T. Hill v Kent (Taunton)		1898
8th	143*	E.F. Longrigg & C.J.P. Barnwell v Glos (Bristol)		1938
9th	183	C. Greetham & H.W. Stephenson v Leicester (Weston-super-Mare)		1963
10th	143	J.J. Bridges & H. Gibbs v Surrey (Weston-super-Mare)		1919

One-day cricket

Highest innings totals:	Gillette Cup/ NatWest Trophy	330-4 v Glamorgan (Cardiff)	1978
	John Player League	286-7 v Hampshire (Taunton)	1981
	Benson & Hedges Cup	281-8 v Middlesex (Taunton)	1980
Lowest innings totals:	Gillette Cup/ NatWest Trophy	59 v Middlesex (Lord's)	1977
	John Player League	58 v Essex (Chelmsford)	1977
	Benson & Hedges Cup	105 v Hampshire (Bournemouth)	1975
Highest individual innings:	Gillette Cup/ NatWest Trophy	145 P.W. Denning v Glamorgan (Cardiff)	1978
	John Player League	131 D.B. Close v Yorkshire (Bath)	1974
	Benson & Hedges Cup	137* B.C. Rose v Kent (Canterbury)	1980
Best bowling figures:	Gillette Cup/ NatWest Trophy	6-29 J. Garner v Northamptonshire (Lord's)	1979
	John Player League	6-25 G.I. Burgess v Glamorgan (Glastonbury)	1972
	Benson & Hedges Cup	5-14 J. Garner v Surrey (Lord's)	1981

SURREY

Formation of present club: 1845.
Colours: Chocolate.
Badge: Prince of Wales' Feathers.
County Champions (18): 1864, 1887, 1888, 1890,
1891, 1892, 1894, 1895, 1899, 1914, 1952, 1953,
1954, 1955, 1956, 1957, 1958, and 1971.
Joint Champions (2): 1889 and 1950.
Gillette Cup Finalists (2): 1965 and 1980.
NatWest Trophy Second Round: 1981.
Best final position in John Player League: 5th in
1969 and 1980.
Benson & Hedges Cup Winners: 1974.
Benson & Hedges Cup Finalists (2): 1979 and 1981.
Gillette Man of the Match Awards: 18.
NatWest Trophy Man of the Match Awards: Nil.
Benson & Hedges Gold Awards: 29.

Secretary: I. F. B. Scott-Browne, Kennington Oval, London, SE11 5SS.
Cricket manager: M. J. Stewart.
Captain: R. D. V. Knight.
Prospects of Play Telephone No: (01) 735 4911.

Alan Raymond BUTCHER (Heath Clark GS, Croydon) B Croydon 7/1/1954.
LHB, SLA. Played in two John Player League matches in 1971. Debut 1972. Cap
1975. Tests: 1 in 1979. 1,000 runs (3) – 1,713 runs (av 46.29) in 1980 best. Benson
& Hedges Gold Awards: 4 HS: 216* v Cambridge U (Cambridge) 1980. HSTC: 20
v India (Oval) 1979. HSGC/NW: 51 v Derbyshire (Ilkeston) 1976. HSJPL: 113* v
Warwickshire (Birmingham) 1978. HSBH: 72 v Somerset (Taunton) 1980. BB: 6-48
v Hants (Guildford) 1972. BBJPL: 5-19 Glos (Bristol) 1975. BBBH: 3-11 v Lancs
(Manchester) 1974.

Robert Giles Lenthall CHEATLE (Stowe School) B London 31/7/1953. LHB,
SLA. Debut for Sussex 1974. Left county after 1979 season and made debut for
Surrey in 1980. Played in one match v Cambridge U (Cambridge) and in one John
Player League match v Leics (Leicester) 1981. HS: 49 Sussex v Kent (Tunbridge
Wells) 1978. HSC: 13* v Yorks (Oval) 1980. HSJPL: 18* Sussex v Warwickshire
(Hove) 1979. HSBH: 16 Sussex v Somerset (Hove) 1978. BB: 6-32 Sussex v Yorks
(Hove) 1979. BBC: 5-28 v Sussex (Oval) 1980. BBJPL: 4-33 Sussex v Glamorgan
(Eastbourne) 1977. BBBH: 3-26 v Hants (Oval) 1980.

Sylvester Theophilus CLARKE B Christ Church, Barbados 11/12/1954. RHB,
RF. Debut for Barbados 1977-78. Debut for county 1979. Cap 1980. Tests: 10 for
West Indies between 1977-78 and 1980-1981. Tours: West Indies to India and Sri
Lanka 1978-79, Pakistan 1980-81, Australia 1981-82. Hat-tricks (2): Barbados v
Trinidad (Bridgetown) 1977-78, v Notts (Oval) 1980. Benson & Hedges Gold
Awards: 1. HS 100* (in 62 minutes) v Glamorgan (Swansea) 1981. HSTC: 35* West
Indies v Pakistan (Faisalabad) 1980-81. HSNW: 45* v Leics (Oval) 1981. HSJPL:
34* v Hants (Oval) 1980. HSBH: 29 v Kent (Oval) 1980. BB: 6-39 Barbados v
Trinidad (Bridgetown) 1977-78. BBUK: 6-61 v Glamorgan (Cardiff) 1979. BBTC:
5-126 West Indies v India (Bangalore) 1978-79. BBGC/NW: 4-38 v Yorks (Oval)
1980. BBJPL: 3-26 v Lancs (Oval) 1979. BBBH: 5-23 v Kent (Oval) 1980.

143

SURREY

Grahame Selvey CLINTON (Chislehurst and Sidcup GS) B Sidcup 5/5/1953. LHB, RM. Toured West Indies with England Young Cricketers 1972. Debut for Kent 1974. Left county after 1978 season and made debut for Surrey in 1979. Played for Zimbabwe/Rhodesia in 1979-80 Currie Cup. Cap 1980. 1,000 runs (3) – 1,240 runs (av. 37.57) in 1980 best. Benson & Hedges Gold Awards: 2 (1 for Kent). HS: 134 v Kent (Oval) 1979. HSGC/NW: 58 v Essex (Chelmsford) 1980. HSJPL: 105* v Yorks (Scarborough) 1981. HSBH: 66 Kent v Surrey (Canterbury) 1976.

Geoffrey Philip (Geoff) HOWARTH (Auckland GS) B Auckland 29/3/1951. Younger brother of H. J. Howarth, New Zealand Test cricketer. RHB, OB. Debut for New Zealand under-23 XI v Auckland (Auckland) 1968-69. Joined Surrey staff 1969. Debut 1971. Cap 1974. Awarded M.B.E. in 1981 Birthday Honours List. Tests: 25 for New Zealand between 1974-75 and 1980-81 captaining New Zealand in 8 tests. Tours: New Zealand to Pakistan and India 1976-77, England 1978, Australia 1980-81 (Captain). 1,000 runs (3) – 1,554 runs (av. 37.90) in 1976 best. Scored two centuries in match (122 and 102) New Zealand v England (Auckland) 1977-78. Benson & Hedges Gold Awards: 3. HS: 183 v Hants (Oval) 1979. HSTC: 147 New Zealand v West Indies (Christchurch) 1979-80. HSGC/NW: 34 v Lancs (Manchester) 1977 and 34 v Northants (Northampton) 1979. HSJPL: 122 v Glos (Oval) 1976. HSBH: 80 v Yorks (Oval) 1974. BB: 5-32 Auckland v Central Districts (Auckland) 1973-74. BBUK: 3-20 v Northants (Northampton) 1976. BBJPL: 4-16 v Warwickshire (Byfleet) 1979.

INTIKHAB ALAM B Hoshiarpur, India 28/12/1941. RHB, LBG. Debut for Karachi 1957-58 aged 16 years 9 months and has played continuously for various Karachi sides and Pakistan International Airways since. Professional for West of Scotland Club in Scottish Western Union for some seasons. Debut for county and cap 1969. Benefit (£20,000) in 1978. Retired after 1981 season but may re-appear a few matches in 1982. Tests: 47 for Pakistan between 1959-60 and 1976-77, captaining country in 17 Tests. Played in 5 matches for Rest of World in 1970 and 5 in 1971-72. Took wkt of C. C. McDonald with first ball he bowled in Test cricket. Tours: Pakistan to India 1960-61, England 1962, 1967, 1971 and 1974 (captain on last two tours), Ceylon 1964, Australia and New Zealand 1964-65, 1972-73 (captain), Australia and West Indies 1976-77, Pakistan Eaglets to England 1963, Pakistan International Airways to East Africa 1964, Rest of World to Australia 1971-72 (vice-captain). Took 104 wkts (av. 28.36) in 1971. Hat-trick v Yorks (Oval) 1972. Benson & Hedges Gold Awards: 1. HS: 182 Karachi Blues v Pakistan International Airways B (Karachi) 1970-71. HSUK: 139 v Glos (Oval) 1973. HSTC: 138 Pakistan v England (Hyderabad) 1972-73. HSGC/NW: 50 v Somerset (Oval) 1975. HSJPL: 62 v Northants (Tolworth) 1973 and 62 v Middlesex (Oval) 1977. HSBH: 32 v Middlesex (Lord's) 1973. BB: 8-54 Pakistanis v Tasmania (Hobart) 1972-73. BBUK: 8-61 Pakistanis v Minor Counties (Swindon) 1967. BBTC: 7-52 Pakistan v New Zealand (Dunedin) 1972-73. BBC: 8-74 v Middlesex (Oval) 1970. BBJPL: 6-25 v Derbyshire (Oval) 1974. BBBH: 3-42 v Essex (Chelmsford) 1973.

Robin David JACKMAN (St Edmund's School, Canterbury) B Simla, India 13/8/1945. RHB, RFM. Debut 1964. Cap 1970. Played for Western Province in 1971-72 and Rhodesia from 1972-73 to 1979-80 in Currie Cup competition. *Wisden* 1980. Benefit in 1981. Tests: 2 in 1980-81. Tour: West Indies 1980-81 (as replacement for R. G. D. Willis). Took 121 wkts (av 15.40) in 1980. Hat-tricks (3): v Kent (Canterbury) 1971, Western Province v Natal (Pietermaritzburg) 1971-72 and v Yorks (Leeds) 1973. Gillette Man of Match Awards: 3. Benson & Hedges Gold Awards: 1. HS: 92* v Kent (Oval) 1974. HSTC: 7 v West Indies (Bridgetown) 1980-81. HSGC/NW: 31 v Glos (Oval) 1980. HSJPL: 43 v Kent (Maidstone) 1977.

144

HSBH: 36 v Leics (Lord's) 1974. BB: 8-40 Rhodesia v Natal (Durban) 1972-73. BBUK: 8-58 v Lancs (Manchester) 1980. BBTC: 3-65 v West Indies (Bridgetown) 1980-81. BBGC/NW: 7-33 v Yorks (Harrogate) 1970. BBJPL: 6-34 v Derbyshire (Derby) 1973. BBBH: 4-24 v Notts (Nottingham) 1981.

Roger David Verdon KNIGHT (Dulwich College and Cambridge) B Streatham 6/9/1946. LHB, RM, Debut for Cambridge U 1967. Blue 1967-68-69-70. Debut for Surrey 1968. Left county after 1970 season and made debut for Glos by special registration 1971. Cap 1971. Left county after 1975 season and made debut for Sussex in 1976. Cap 1976. Left county after 1977 season and rejoined Surrey for 1978 as county captain. Cap 1978. 1,000 runs (10) – 1,350 runs (av. 38.57) in 1974 best. Gillette Man of the Match Awards: 5 (3 for Glos). Benson & Hedges Gold Awards: 5 (1 for Sussex, 2 for Glos). HS: 165* Sussex v Middlesex (Hove) 1976. HSC: 132 v Lancs (Oval) 1980. HSGC/NW: 75 Glos v Glamorgan (Cardiff) 1973. HSJPL: 127 Sussex v Hants (Hove) 1976. HSBH: 117 Sussex v Surrey (Oval) 1977. BB: 6-44 Glos v Northants (Northampton) 1974. BBC: 5-44 Glos v Cheltenham) 1979. BBGC/NW: 5-39 Glos v Surrey (Bristol) 1971. BBJPL: 5-42 Sussex v Notts (Nottingham) 1977. BBBH: 3-19 Sussex v Surrey (Oval) 1977.

Monte Alan LYNCH (Ryden's School, Walton-on-Thames) B Georgetown, British Guiana 21/5/1958. RHB, RM/OB. Debut 1977. HS: 120* v Essex (Oval) 1981. HSGC/NW: 25* v Yorks (Oval) 1981. HSJPL: 80* v Warwickshire (Oval) 1981. HSBH: 67 v Worcs (Worcester) 1979. BB: 3-6 v Glamorgan (Swansea) 1981.

Kevin Scott MACKINTOSH (Kingston-upon-Thames GS) B Surbiton (Surrey) 30/8/1957. RHB, RM. Played for 2nd XI from 1975 to 1977. Made debut for Notts in 1978. Not re-engaged after 1980 season and re-joined county in 1981, making debut in last match of season. Also appeared in last two John Player League matches of season. HS: 23* Notts v Essex (Nottingham) 1978. HSJPL: 12* Notts v Lancs (Nottingham) 1978. BB: 4-49 Notts v Surrey (Oval) 1978. BBJPL: 4-26 Notts v Glos (Nottingham) 1979.

Graham MONKHOUSE (Queen Elizabeth GS, Penrith) B. Carlisle 26/4/1955. RHB, RM. Played for Cumberland from 1972 to 1978. Debut 1981. HS: 28* v Middlesex (Uxbridge) 1981. BB: 3-45 v Kent (Oval) 1981. Has played soccer for Carlisle United and Workington.

Andrew NEEDHAM (Paisley GS and Watford GS) B Calow, (Derbyshire) 23/3/1957. RHB, OB. Debut 1977. Did not play in 1980 and in only one match v Warwickshire (Oval) in 1981. HS: 21 v Sussex (Hove) 1978. HSJPL: 18 v Lancs (Oval) 1979. BB: 3-25 v Oxford U (Oxford) 1977.

Ducan Brian PAULINE (Bishop Fox School, Molesey) B Aberdeen 15/12/1960. RHB, RM. Played for 2nd XI since 1977. Toured Australia with England under-19 side in 1978-79. Debut 1979. HS: 46 v Leics (Leicester) 1980. HSJPL: 92 v Worcs (Oval) 1981.

Ian Roger PAYNE (Emanuel School) B Lambeth Hospital, Kennington 9/5/1958. RHB, RM. Debut 1977. Benson & Hedges Gold Awards: 1. HS: 29 v Kent (Oval) 1977. HSJPL: 33 v Notts (Oval) 1981. BBJPL: 4-31 v Northants (Guildford) 1977. BBBH: 3-20 v Leics (Oval) 1981.

Patrick Ian (Pat) POCOCK (Wimbledon Technical School) B Bangor, Caernarvonshire 24/9/1946. RHB, OB. Debut 1964. Benefit (£18,500) in 1977. Played for

SURREY

Northern Transvaal in 1971-72 Currie Cup competition. Tests: 17 between 1967-68 and 1976. Tours: Pakistan 1966-67, West Indies 1967-68 and 1973-74, Ceylon and Pakistan 1968-69, India, Pakistan and Sri Lanka 1972-73. Took 112 wkts (av. 18.22) in 1967. Took 4 wkts in 4 balls, 5 in 6, 6 in 9, and 7 in 11 (the last two being first-class records) v Sussex (Eastbourne) 1972. Hat-tricks (2): as above and v Worcs (Guildford) 1971. Benson & Hedges Gold Awards: 2. HS: 75* v Notts (Oval) 1968. HSTC: 33 v Pakistan (Hyderabad) 1972-73. HSGC/NW: 14 v Essex (Colchester) 1978. HSJPL: 22 v Notts (Nottingham) 1971. HSBH: 19 v Middlesex (Oval) 1972. BB: 9-57 v Glamorgan (Cardiff) 1979. BBTC: 6-79 v Australia (Manchester) 1968. BBGC/NW: 3-34 v Somerset (Oval) 1975. BBJPL: 4-27 v Essex (Chelmsford) 1974. BBBH: 4-11 v Yorks (Barnsley) 1978.

Clifton James (Jack) RICHARDS (Humphrey Davy GS, Penzance) B Penzance 10/8/1958. RHB, WK. Debut 1976. Cap 1978. Tour: India and Sri Lanka 1981-82. HS: 63 v Leics (Oval) 1981. HSGC/NW: 14 v Essex (Colchester) 1978. HSJPL: 23* v Essex (Chelmsford) 1980. HSBH: 32 v Leics (Oval) 1981.

Graham Richard James ROOPE (Bradfield College) B Fareham, Hants 12/7/1946. RHB, RM, occasional WK. Played for Public Schools XI v Comb. Services (Lord's) 1963 and 1964. Played for Berkshire 1963 scoring century against Wiltshire. Joined county staff and debut 1964. Cap 1969. Played for Griqualand West in 1973-74 Currie Cup competition. Benefit in season 1980. Tests: 21 between 1972-73 and 1978. Tours: India, Pakistan and Sri Lanka 1972-73, Pakistan and New Zealand 1977-78. 1,000 runs (8) – 1,641 runs (av. 44.35) in 1971 best. Scored two centuries in match (109 and 103*) v Leics (Leicester) 1971. Held 59 catches in 1971. Benson & Hedges Gold Awards: 3. HS: 171 v Yorks (Oval) 1971. HSTC: 77 v Australia (Oval) 1975. HSGC/NW: 66 v Somerset (Oval) 1975. HSJPL: 120* v Worcs (Byfleet) 1973. HSBH: 115* v Essex (Chelmsford) 1973. BB: 5-14 v West Indians (Oval) 1969. BBGC/NW: 5-23 v Derbyshire (Oval) 1967. BBJPL: 4-31 v Glamorgan (Oval) 1974. BBBH: 3-31 v Essex (Chelmsford) 1978. Soccer (goal-keeper) for Corinthian Casuals and various Southern League sides.

David Mark SMITH (Battersea GS) B Balham 9/1/1956. LHB, RM. Played for 2nd XI in 1972. Debut 1973 aged 17 years 4 months, whilst still at school. Cap 1980. Benson & Hedges Gold Awards: 1. HS: 115 v Hants (Portsmouth) 1978. HSGC/NW: 61 v Northants (Northampton) 1979. HSJPL: 87* v Hants (Oval) 1980. HSBH: 45* v Northants (Northampton) 1979 and 45* v Hants (Oval) 1980. BB: 3-40 v Sussex (Oval) 1976. BBGC/NW: 3-39 v Derbyshire (Ilkeston) 1976. BBBH: 4-29 v Kent (Oval) 1980.

Alec James STEWART (Tiffin School, Kingston-upon-Thames) B Merton 8/4/1963. Son of M. J. Stewart. RHB, WK. Played for 2nd XI 1980. Joined staff and made debut in 1981. Played in one match and one John Player League match v Glos (Cheltenham).

David James THOMAS (Licensed Victuallers School, Slough) B Solihull (Warwickshire) 30/6/1959. LHB, LM. Debut 1977. Played for Northern Transvaal in 1980-81 Currie Cup competition. HS: 47 v Sussex (Hove) 1981. HSGC/NW: 17 v Essex (Chelmsford) 1980. HSJPL: 56* v Leics (Oval) 1981. HSBH: 13 v Kent (Oval) 1980 and 13 v Notts (Nottingham) 1981. BB: 6-84 v Derbyshire (Oval) 1979. BBJPL: 4-13 v Sussex (Oval) 1978. BBBH: 3-30 v Leics (Oval) 1981.

Peter Hugh L'Estrange WILSON (Wellington College) B Guildford 17/8/1958. 6ft 5ins tall. RHB. RFM. Played for Hants 2nd XI 1976-77. Debut 1978. Played for

Northern Transvaal in 1979-80 Currie Cup competition. HS: 29 Northern Transvaal v Transvaal (Pretoria) 1979-80. HSUK: 15 v Worcs (Guildford) 1979. HSJPL: 18* v Worcs (Oval) 1979. BB: 5-36 Northern Transvaal v Eastern Province (Pretoria) 1979-80. BBUK: 4-39 v Warwickshire (Oval) 1979. BBGC/NW: 3-59 v Essex (Colchester) 1978. BBJPL: 4-32 v Middlesex (Oval) 1979. BBBH: 5-21 v Combined Universities (Oval) 1979.

County Averages

Schweppes County Championship: Played 22, Won 7, Drawn 9, Lost 5, Abandoned 1.
All first-class matches: Played 23, Won 6, Drawn 10, Lost 5, Abandoned 1.

BATTING AND FIELDING

Cap		M	I	NO	Runs	HS	Avge	100	50	Ct	St
1975	A.R. Butcher	19	38	6	1444	154*	45.12	4	5	14	—
1974	G.P. Howarth	8	16	1	480	110*	32.00	1	3	3	—
—	M.A. Lynch	19	37	6	958	120*	30.90	2	3	8	—
1980	G.S. Clinton	22	44	2	1191	123	28.35	3	6	7	—
1980	S.T. Clarke	10	14	1	342	100*	26.30	1	—	8	—
1978	R.D.V. Knight	21	41	1	1041	96	26.02	—	6	16	—
1978	C.J. Richards	19	31	4	680	63	25.18	—	4	30	7
1969	G.R.J. Roope	20	37	4	829	96*	25.12	—	5	44	1
1980	D.M. Smith	17	32	4	684	84*	24.42	—	3	16	—
1970	R.D. Jackman	19	26	10	331	51	20.68	—	1	6	—
—	G. Monkhouse	4	6	4	37	28*	18.50	—	—	2	—
—	D.J. Thomas	14	24	5	323	47	17.00	—	—	7	—
1969	Intikhab Alam	17	31	3	469	79	16.75	—	2	15	—
1967	P.I. Pocock	18	21	10	154	46	14.00	—	—	9	—
—	I.R. Payne	5	8	0	45	18	5.62	—	—	5	—
—	P.H.L. Wilson	4	4	2	3	2*	1.50	—	—	2	—

Played in two matches: D.B. Pauline 5, 0, 0, 12.
Played in one match: R.G.L. Cheatle 5* (1 ct); K.J. Mackintosh did not bat; A. Needham 6*, 1; A.J. Stewart 2, 8 (3 ct).

BOWLING

	Type	O	M	R	W	Avge	Best	5 wI	10 wM
S.T. Clarke	RF	339.4	98	734	49	14.97	6-66	5	—
R.D. Jackman	RFM	570.3	138	1519	64	23.73	6-70	4	—
Intikhab Alam	LBG	555.4	153	1585	65	24.38	5-44	3	—
A.R. Butcher	SLA	64.3	15	247	10	24.70	2-15	—	—
D.J. Thomas	LM	323.5	77	933	34	27.44	5-31	1	—
I.R. Payne	RM	86	25	250	8	31.25	2-28	—	—
G. Monkhouse	RM	83	17	224	7	32.00	3-45	—	—
P.I. Pocock	OB	603.1	180	1511	46	32.84	4-54	—	—
R.D.V. Knight	RM	269	79	685	16	42.81	7-18	—	—

Also bowled: R.G.L. Cheatle 18-4-52-1; G.P. Howarth 7-2-24-0; M.A. Lynch 28.4-7-97-3; K.S. Mackintosh 19-5-65-2; A. Needham 16-5-57-1; D.B. Pauline 2-0-14-0; G.R.J. Roope 39-9-105-4; D.M. Smith 18-8-38-1; P.H.L. Wilson 48-9-141-2.

County Records

First-class cricket

Highest innings	For	811 v Somerset (The Oval)	1899
totals:	Agst	705-8d by Sussex (Hastings)	1902
Lowest innings	For	16 v Nottinghamshire (The Oval)	1880
totals:	Agst	15 by MCC (Lord's)	1839
Highest Indi-	For	357* R. Abel v Somerset (The Oval)	1899
vidual innings:	Agst	300* F. B. Watson for Lancashire (Manchester)	1928
		300 R. Subba Row for Northants (The Oval)	1958
Best bowling	For	10-43 T. Rushby v Somerset (Taunton)	1921
in an innings:	Agst	10-28 W. P. Howell for Australians (The Oval)	1899
Best bowling	For	16-83 G. A. R. Lock v Kent (Blackheath)	1956
in a match:	Agst	15-57 W. P. Howell for Australians (The Oval)	1899
Most runs in a season:		3,246 (av. 72.13) T. W. Hayward	1906
runs in a career:		43,554 (av. 49.72) J. B. Hobbs	1905-1934
100s in a season:		13 by T. W. Hayward and	1906
		J. B. Hobbs	1925
100s in a career:		144 by J. B. Hobbs	1905-1934
wickets in a season:		250 (av. 14.06) T. Richardson	1895
wickets in a career:		1,775 (av. 17.88) T. Richardson	1892-1905

RECORD WICKET STANDS

1st	428	J. B. Hobbs & A. Sandham v Oxford U (The Oval)	1926
2nd	371	J. B. Hobbs & E. G. Hayes v Hampshire (The Oval)	1909
3rd	353	A. Ducat & E. G. Hayes v Hampshire (Southampton)	1919
4th	448	R. Abel & T. W. Hayward v Yorkshire (The Oval)	1899
5th	308	J. N. Crawford & F. C. Holland v Somerset (The Oval)	1908
6th	298	A. Sandham & H. S. Harrison v Sussex (The Oval)	1913
7th	200	T. F. Shepherd & J. W. Hitch v Kent (Blackheath)	1921
8th	204	T. W. Hayward & L. C. Braund v Lancashire (The Oval)	1898
9th	168	E. R. T. Holmes & E. W. J. Brooks v Hampshire (The Oval)	1936
10th	173	A. Ducat & A. Sandham v Essex (Leyton)	1921

One-day cricket

Highest innings	GC/NatWest Trophy	280-5 v Middlesex (The Oval)	1970
totals:	John Player League	248-2 v Glos (The Oval)	1976
	Benson & Hedges Cup	264 v Kent (The Oval)	1976
Lowest innings	GC/NatWest Trophy	74 v Kent (The Oval)	1967
totals:	John Player League	64 v Worcs (Worcester)	1978
	Benson & Hedges Cup	125 v Sussex (Hove)	1972
Highest indi-	Gillette Cup/	101 M.J. Stewart v Durham	
vidual innings:	NatWest Trophy	(Chester-le-Street)	1972
	John Player League	122 G.P. Howarth v	
		Gloucestershire (The Oval)	1976
	Benson & Hedges Cup	115 G.R.J. Roope v Essex	
		(Chelmsford)	1973
Best bowling	Gillette Cup/	7-33 R.D. Jackman v	
figures:	NatWest Trophy	Yorkshire (Harrogate)	1970
	John Player League	6-25 Intikhab Alam v	
		Derbyshire (The Oval)	1974
	Benson & Hedges Cup	5-21 P.H.L. Wilson v	
		Combined U. (The Oval)	1979

148

SUSSEX

Formation of present club: 1839, reorganised 1857.
Colours: Dark blue, light blue, and gold.
Badge: County Arms of six martlets (in shape of inverted pyramid).
County Championship Runners-up (7): 1902, 1903, 1932, 1933, 1934, 1953 and 1981.
Gillette Cup Winners (3): 1963, 1964, and 1978.
Gillette Cup Finalists (3): 1968, 1970, and 1973.
NatWest Trophy third round: 1981.
John Player League Runners-up: 1976.
Benson & Hedges Cup Quarter-Finalists (4): 1972, 1977, 1980 and 1981.
Gillette Man of the Match Awards: 30.
NatWest Man of the Match Awards: 1.
Benson & Hedges Gold Awards: 25.

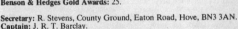

Secretary: R. Stevens, County Ground, Eaton Road, Hove, BN3 3AN.
Captain: J. R. T. Barclay.
Prospects of Play Telephone No: Hove (0273) 772766.

Geoffrey Graham (Geoff) ARNOLD B Earlsfield (Surrey) 3/9/1944. RHB, RFM. Debut for Surrey 1963. Cap 1967. *Wisden* 1971. Benefit (£15,000) in 1976. Played for Orange Free State in 1976-77 Currie Cup competition. Left county after 1977 season and made debut for Sussex in 1978. Cap 1979. Tests: 34 between 1967 and 1975. Tours: Pakistan 1966-67, India, Pakistan, and Sri Lanka 1972-73, West Indies 1973-74, Australia and New Zealand 1974-75. Took 109 wkts (av. 18.22) in 1967. Hat-trick v Leics (Leicester) 1974. Gillette Man of Match Awards: 3 (2 for Surrey). HS: 73 MCC under-25 v Central Zone (Sahiwal) 1966-67. HSUK: 63 Surrey v Warwickshire (Birmingham) 1968. HSC: 51 v Leics (Leicester) 1979. HSTC: 59 v Pakistan (Oval) 1967. HSGC/NW: 18* v Northants (Hove) 1979. HSJPL: 24* Surrey v Notts (Nottingham) 1971. HSBH: 12* Surrey v Combined Universities (Oval) 1976. BB: 8-41 (13-128 match) Surrey v Glos (Oval) 1967. BBC: 7-44 v Lancs (Manchester) 1978. BBTC: 6-45 v India (Delhi) 1972-73. BBGC/NW: 5-9 Surrey v Derbyshire (Oval) 1967. BBJPL: 5-11 Surrey v Glamorgan (Oval) 1969. BBBH: 3-19 Surrey v Yorks (Bradford) 1976. Soccer for Corinthian Casuals.

John Robert Troutbeck BARCLAY (Eton College) B Bonn, West Germany 22/1/1954. RHB, OB. Debut 1970 aged 16 years 205 days, whilst still at school. Was in XI at school from age of 14 and scored the record number of runs for school in a season in 1970. Played in MCC Schools matches at Lord's in 1969-71. Vice-captain of English Schools Cricket Association team to India 1970-71. Captain of England Young Cricketers team to West Indies 1972. Cap 1976. Played for Orange Free State in 1978-79 Castle Bowl Competition. Appointed county captain in 1981. 1,000 runs (4) – 1,093 runs (av. 32.14) in 1979 best. Benson & Hedges Gold Awards: 2. HS: 119 v Leics (Hove) 1980. HSGC/NW: 44 v Derbyshire (Hove) 1977, and 44 v Somerset (Lord's) 1978. HSJPL: 48 v Derbyshire (Derby) 1974. HSBH: 93* v Surrey (Oval) 1976. BB: 6-61 v Sri Lanka (Horsham) 1979. BBGC/NW: 3-27 v Lancs (Hove) 1978. BBJPL: 3-11 v Worcs (Eastbourne) 1978. BBBH: 5-43 v Combined Universities (Oxford) 1973.

Ian James GOULD B Slough (Bucks) 19/8/1957. LHB, WK. Debut for Middlesex 1975. Toured West Indies with England Young Cricketers 1976. Cap 1977. Played

SUSSEX

for Auckland in Shell Trophy in 1979-80. Left county after 1980 season and made debut for Sussex in 1981. Cap 1981. HS: 128 Middlesex v Worcs (Worcester) 1978. HSC: 52 v Surrey (Hove) 1981. HSGC/NW: 58 Middlesex v Derbyshire (Derby) 1978. HSJPL: 69* v Hants (Basingstoke) 1981. HSBH: 32 Middlesex v Notts (Nottingham) 1979.

Allan Michael GREEN (Brighton Sixth Form College) B Pulborough (Sussex) 28/5/1960. RHB, RM. Joined staff 1979. Debut 1980. HS: 38 v Sri Lankans (Hastings) 1981.

Ian Alexander GREIG (Queen's College, Queenstown and Cambridge) B Queenstown, South Africa 8/12/1955. RHB, RM. Younger brother of A.W. Greig. Debut for Border in 1974-75 Currie Cup competition. Played for Griqualand West in 1975-76. Has played for county 2nd XI since 1976. Debut for Cambridge U 1977. Blue 1977-78-79 (captain). Appeared in one John Player League match for county in 1979. Re-appeared for Border in 1979-80 Castle Bowl competition. Debut for county 1980 and is regarded as an English player for qualification purposes. Cap 1981. Had match double of 100 runs and 10 wkts (118*, 6-75, 4-57) v Hants (Hove) 1981. NatWest Man of the Match Awards: 1. Benson & Hedges Gold Awards: 1. HS: 118* v Hants (Hove) 1981. HSNW: 82 v Warwickshire (Birmingham) 1981. HSJPL: 54 v Warwickshire (Horsham) 1981. HSBH: 51 v Hants (Hove) 1981. BB: 7-43 v Cambridge U (Cambridge) 1981. BBNW: 4-31 v Warwickshire (Birmingham) 1981. BBJPL: 3-38 v Lancs (Hove) 1981 and 3-38 v Essex (Southend) 1981. BBBH: 5-35 v Hants (Hove) 1981. Blues for rugby 1977-78.

Jerry Richard Percy HEATH (Imberhorne Comprehensive School, East Grinstead) B Turner's Hill (Sussex) 26/4/1959. LHB. Debut 1980. HS: 101* v Sri Lankans (Hastings) 1981. HSJPL: 35 v Hants (Hove) 1980.

IMRAN KHAN NIAZI (Aitchison College and Cathedral School, Lahore, Worcester RGS and Oxford) B Lahore, Pakistan 25/11/1952. RHB, RF. Cousin of Majid Jahangir Khan. Debut for Lahore A 1969-70 and has played subsequently for various Lahore teams. Debut for Worcs 1971. Blue 1973-74-75 (capt. in 1974). Cap 1976. Left Worcs in 1977 and joined Sussex by special registration. Cap 1978. Tests: 33 for Pakistan between 1971 and 1980-81. Tours: Pakistan to England 1971 and 1974, Australia and West Indies 1976-77, New Zealand and Australia 1978-79, India 1979-80, Australia 1981-82. 1,000 runs (3) – 1,339 runs (av. 41.84) in 1978 best. Scored two centuries in match (117* and 106), Oxford U v Notts (Oxford) 1974. Had match double of 111* and 13-99 (7-53 & 6-46) v Lancs (Worcester) 1976. Gillette Man of Match Awards: 4. (1 for Worcs). Benson & Hedges Gold Awards: 6. (1 for Oxford and Cambridge Universities, 1 for Worcs). HS: 170 Oxford U v Northants (Oxford) 1974. HSC: 167 v Glos (Hove) 1978. HSTC: 123 Pakistan v West Indies (Lahore) 1980-81. HSGC/NW: 63* v Suffolk (Hove) 1980. HSJPL: 75 Worcs v Warwickshire (Worcester) 1976. HSBH: 72 Worcs v Warwickshire (Birmingham) 1976. BB: 7-52 v Glos (Bristol) 1978. BBTC: 6-63 (12-165 match) Pakistan v Australia (Sydney) 1976-77. BBGC/NW 4-27 v Staffs (Stone) 1978. BBJPL: 5-29 Worcs v Leics (Leicester) 1973. BBBH: 5-8 v Northants (Northampton) 1978.

Adrian Nicholas JONES (Seaford College) B Woking (Surrey) 22/7/1961. LHB, RFM. Played for 2nd XI in 1980. Debut 1981. HS: 8 v Australians (Hove) 1981. BB: 4-33 v Yorks (Hove) 1981.

Garth Stirling LE ROUX (Wynberg Boys' High School) B Cape Town 4/9/1955. 6ft 3ins tall. RHB, RF. Debut for Western Province B in 1975-76 Currie Cup competition. Played for Derbyshire 2nd XI in 1977. Debut for county 1978. One match v New Zealanders (Hove). Joined staff in 1979. Cap 1981. "Hat-trick" v Warwickshire (Hove) 1981. HS: 70* Western Province v Northern Transvaal (Cape Town) 1979-80. HSUK: 68* v Leics (Hove) 1980. HSJPL: 34 v Warwickshire (Birmingham) 1980. HSBH: 25* v Leics (Hove) 1981. BB: 8-107 v Somerset (Taunton) 1981. BBNW: 5-35 v Essex (Hove) 1981. BBJPL: 4-26 v Leics (Leicester) 1981. BBBH: 3-38 v Surrey (Hove) 1981.

Gehan Dixon MENDIS (St Thomas College, Colombo and Brighton, Hove and Sussex GS) B Colombo, Ceylon 24/4/1955. RHB, occasional WK. Played for 2nd XI since 1971. Played in one John Player League match in 1973. Debut 1974. Cap 1980. 1,000 runs (2) – 1,522 runs (av. 41.13) in 1981 best. Gillette Man of Match Awards: 2. Benson & Hedges Gold Awards: 2. HS: 204 v Northants (Eastbourne) 1980. HSGC/NW: 141* v Warwickshire (Hove) 1980. HSJPL: 125* v Glos (Hove) 1981. HSBH: 109 v Glos (Hove) 1980. Trained as a teacher at Bede College, Durham University.

Paul William Giles PARKER (Collyers' GS, Horsham and Cambridge) B Bulawayo, Rhodesia 15/1/1956. RHB, RM. Debut for both Cambridge U and county 1976. Blue 1976-77-78. University Secretary for 1977 and 1978. Cap 1979. Elected Best Young Cricketer for the Year in 1979 by Cricket Writers' Club. Tests: 1 in 1981. 1,000 runs (5) – 1,412 runs (av. 45.54) in 1981 best. Gillette Man of Match Awards: 2. Benson & Hedges Gold Awards: 1. HS: 215 Cambridge U v Essex (Cambridge) 1976. HSC: 136 v Lancs (Hove) 1981. HSGC/NW: 69 v Lancs (Hove) 1978. HSJPL: 106* v Worcs (Horsham) 1980. HSBH: 59 v Middlesex (Lord's) 1980. Selected for University rugby match in 1977, but had to withdraw through injury.

Christopher Paul PHILLIPSON (Ardingly College) B Brindaban, India 10/2/1952. RHB, RM. Debut 1970. Cap 1980. Benson & Hedges Gold Awards: 2. HS: 87 v Hants (Hove) 1980. HSGC/NW: 70* v Suffolk (Hove) 1980. HSJPL: 71 v Lancs (Hastings) 1980. HSBH: 59 v Leics (Hove) 1981. BB: 6-56 v Notts (Hove) 1972. BBJPL: 4-25 v Middlesex (Eastbourne) 1972. BBBH: 5-32 v Combined Universities (Oxford) 1977. Trained as a teacher at Loughborough College of Education.

Anthony Charles Shackleton (Tony) PIGOTT (Harrow School) B London 4/6/1958. RHB, RFM. Played for 2nd XI since 1975. Debut 1978. Missed most of 1981 season through injury. Hat-trick v Surrey (Hove) 1978. HS: 55 v Yorks (Hove) 1979. HSGC/NW: 30 v Northants (Hove) 1979. HSJPL: 49 v Warwickshire (Hove) 1979. BB: 4-40 v Cambridge U (Cambridge) 1979. BBGC/NW: 3-43 v Notts (Hove) 1979. BBJPL: 3-29 v Middlesex (Hove) 1980. BBBH: 3-47 v Essex (Chelmsford) 1980.

David James SMITH (Hove County GS) B Brighton 28/4/1962. LHB, WK. Played for 2nd XI since 1979. Debut 1981. One match v Australians (Hove).

Christopher Edward (Chris) WALLER B Guildford 3/10/1948. RHB, SLA. Debut for Surrey 1967. Cap 1972. Left staff after 1973 season and made debut for Sussex in 1974. Cap 1976. HS: 51* v Cambridge U (Cambridge) 1981. HSGC/NW: 14* v Notts (Nottingham) 1975. HSJPL: 18* v Glamorgan (Hove) 1975. HSBH: 11* v Essex (Chelmsford) 1975. BB: 7-64 Surrey v Sussex (Oval) 1971. BBC: 6-40 v Surrey (Hove) 1975. BBJPL: 4-28 v Essex (Hove) 1976. BBBH: 4-25 v Minor Counties (South) (Hove) 1975.

SUSSEX

Alan Peter WELLS (Tideway School, Newhaven) B Newhaven 2/10/1961. Younger brother of C.M. Wells. RHB, RM. Played for 2nd XI since 1978. Debut 1981. Played one match v Cambridge U (Cambridge), one NatWest Trophy match and four John Player League matches. HS: 63 v Cambridge U (Cambridge) 1981. HSJPL: 47* v Northants (Hastings) 1981.

Colin Mark WELLS (Tideway School, Newhaven) B Newhaven 3/3/1960. RHB, RM. Played in three John Player League matches in 1978. Debut 1979. Scored 1,024 runs (av. 44.52) in 1980. HS: 135 v Glamorgan (Swansea) 1980. HSNW: 28 v Warwickshire (Birmingham) 1981. HSJPL: 65* v Essex (Hastings) 1980. HSBH: 32 v Surrey (Hove) 1981. BB: 4-23 v Oxford U (Pagham) 1979. BBJPL: 3-23 v Kent (Eastbourne) 1981. BBBH: 4-21 v Middlesex (Lord's) 1980.

Alan WILLOWS (Portslade Community College and Sixth Form Centre) B Portslade, Sussex 24/4/1961. RHB, SLA. Played for 2nd XI in 1979. Debut 1980 (three matches). Did not play in 1981. BB: 4-33 v Hants (Southampton) 1980.

N.B. The following players whose particulars appeared in the 1981 Annual have been omitted: T.D. Booth Jones (left staff), T.J. Head (not re-engaged) and K.C. Wessels (left staff and is now resident in Australia).

The career records of Booth Jones and Head will be found elsewhere in this Annual.

County Averages

**Schweppes County Championship: Played 20, won 11, drawn 6, lost 3, abandoned 2.
All first-class matches: Played 23, won 13, drawn 6, lost 4, abandoned 2.**

BATTING AND FIELDING

Cap		M	I	NO	Runs	HS	Avge	100	50	Ct	St
1979	P.W.G. Parker	21	37	9	1344	136	48.00	4	6	19	—
—	J.R.P. Heath	4	7	2	215	101*	43.00	1	1	2	—
1980	G.D. Mendis	21	38	3	1457	137	41.62	2	9	6	—
1978	Imran Khan	18	27	6	857	107	40.80	2	3	6	—
—	C.M. Wells	13	21	4	517	111	30.41	1	2	3	—
1981	I.A. Greig	23	34	4	911	118*	30.36	1	4	14	—
1976	J.R.T. Barclay	22	37	4	872	107*	26.42	2	3	29	—
1981	G.S. Le Roux	19	20	7	340	65*	26.15	—	1	6	—
1981	I.J. Gould	21	26	3	594	52	25.82	—	2	59	4
1980	C.P. Phillipson	21	30	10	485	56*	24.25	—	1	28	—
—	A.M. Green	3	5	0	107	38	21.40	—	—	1	—
—	T.D. Booth Jones	16	27	0	541	95	20.03	—	3	6	—
1979	G.G. Arnold	18	17	7	180	46*	18.00	—	—	7	—
1976	C.E. Waller	22	15	6	148	51*	16.44	—	1	11	—
—	A.N. Jones	5	5	2	17	8	5.66	—	—	1	—

Played in two matches: T.J. Head 14, 7, 0, 52*(6ct); A.C.S. Pigutt 7, 39 (1 ct)
Played in one match: D.J. Smith 2, 1; A.P. Wells 63 (1 ct)

BOWLING

	Type	O	M	R	W	Avge	Best	5 wI	10 wM
A.N. Jones	**RFM**	83	11	283	17	16.64	4-33	—	—
I.A. Greig	**RM**	477	100	1469	76	19.32	7-43	4	2
G.S. Le Roux	**RFM**	559.1	133	1582	81	19.53	8-107	3	—
Imran Khan	**RF**	565.1	137	1464	66	22.18	6-52	2	1
C.M. Wells	**RM**	76	18	238	9	26.44	4-48	—	—
J.R.T. Barclay	**OB**	374	93	936	34	27.52	4-47	—	—
G.G. Arnold	**RFM**	458.1	122	1121	40	28.02	6-39	1	—
C.E. Waller	**SLA**	513	152	1264	44	28.72	5-36	2	—

Also bowled: I.J. Gould 3-1-2-0; G.D. Mendis 0.3-0-2-0; P.W.G. Parker 5-3-19-0; A.C.S. Pigott 41-4-135-4; C.P. Phillipson 2-0-15-0.

County Records

First-class cricket

Highest innings	For	705-8d v Surrey (Hastings)	1902
totals:	Agst	726 by Nottinghamshire (Nottingham)	1895
Lowest innings	For	19 v Surrey (Godalming)	1830
totals:		19 v Nottinghamshire (Hove)	1873
	Agst	18 by Kent (Gravesend)	1867
Highest indi-	For	333 by K.S. Duleepsinhji v Northants (Hove)	1930
vidual innings:	Agst	322 E. Paynter for Lancashire (Hove)	1937
Best bowling	For	10-48 C.H.G. Bland v Kent (Tonbridge)	1899
in an innings:	Agst	9-11 A.P. Freeman for Kent (Hove)	1922
Best bowling	For	17-106 G.R. Cox v Warwickshire (Horsham)	1926
in a match:	Agst	17-67 A.P. Freeman for Kent (Hove)	1922
Most runs in a season:		2850 (av. 64.77) John Langridge	1949
runs in a career:		34152 (av. 37.69) John Langridge	1928-1955
100s in a season:		12 by John Langridge	1949
100s in a career:		76 by John Langridge	1928-1955
wickets in a season:		198 (av. 13.45) M.W. Tate	1925
wickets in a career:		2223 (av. 16.34) M.W. Tate	1912-1937

RECORD WICKET STANDS

1st	490	E.H. Bowley & John Langridge v Middlesex (Hove)	1933
2nd	385	E.H. Bowley & M.W. Tate v Northamptonshire (Hove)	1921
3rd	298	K.S. Ranjitsinhji & E.H. Killick v Lancashire (Hove)	1901
4th	326*	G. Cox & James Langridge v Yorkshire (Leeds)	1949
5th	297	J.H. Parks & H.W. Parks v Hampshire (Portsmouth)	1937
6th	255	K.S. Duleepsinhji & M.W. Tate v Northamptonshire (Hove)	1930
7th	344	K.S. Ranjitsinhji & W. Newham v Essex (Leyton)	1902
8th	229*	C.L.A. Smith & G. Brann v Kent (Hove)	1902
9th	178	H.W. Parks & A.F. Wensley v Derbyshire (Horsham)	1930
10th	156	G.R. Cox & H.R. Butt v Cambridge U (Cambridge)	1908

153

One-day cricket

Highest innings totals:	Gillette Cup/ NatWest Trophy	314-7 v Kent (Tunbridge Wells)	1963
	John Player League	293-4 v Worcestershire (Horsham)	1980
	Benson & Hedges Cup	280-5 v Cambridge U (Hove)	1974
Lowest innings totals:	Gillette Cup/ NatWest Trophy	49 v Derbyshire (Chesterfield)	1969
	John Player League	61 v Derbyshire (Derby)	1978
	Benson & Hedges Cup	61 v Middlesex (Hove)	1978
Highest individual innings:	Gillette Cup/ NatWest Trophy	141* G.D. Mendis v Warwickshire (Hove)	1980
	John Player League	129 A.W. Greig v Yorkshire (Scarborough)	1976
	Benson & Hedges Cup	117 R.D.V. Knight v Surrey (The Oval)	1977
Best bowling figures:	Gillette Cup/ NatWest Trophy	6-30 D.L. Bates v Gloucestershire (Hove)	1968
	John Player League	6-14 M.A. Buss v Lancashire (Hove)	1973
	Benson & Hedges Cup	5-8 Imran Khan v Northamptonshire (Northampton)	1978

WARWICKSHIRE

Formation of club: 1882.
Colours: Blue, gold, and silver.
Badge: Bear and ragged staff.
County Champions (3): 1911, 1951 and 1972.
Gillette Cup Winners (2): 1966 and 1968.
Gillette Cup Finalists (2): 1964 and 1972.
NatWest Trophy Second Round: 1981.
John Player League Champions: 1980.
Benson & Hedges Cup Semi-Finalists (4): 1972, 1975, 1976 and 1978.
Gillette Man of the Match Awards: 21.
NatWest Man of the Match Awards: Nil.
Benson & Hedges Gold Awards: 26.

Secretary: A.C. Smith, County Ground, Edgbaston, Birmingham B5 7QU.
Cricket Manager: D.J. Brown.
Captain: R.G.D. Willis, MBE
Prospects of Play Telephone No: (021) 440 3624.

Dennis Leslie AMISS (Oldknow School, Birmingham) B Birmingham 7/4/1943. RHB, SLC. Joined county staff 1958. Debut 1960. Cap 1965. *Wisden* 1974. Benefit (£34,947) in 1975. Tests: 50 between 1966 and 1977. Played in one match v Rest of World in 1970. Tours: Pakistan 1966-67, India, Pakistan, and Sri Lanka 1972-73, West Indies 1973-74, Australia and New Zealand 1974-75, India, Sri Lanka and Australia 1976-77. 1,000 runs (17) – 2,110 runs (av. 65.93) in 1976 best. Also scored 1,120 runs (av. 74.66) in West Indies 1973-74. Scored two centuries in match (155* and 112) v Worcs (Birmingham) 1978 and (109 and 127) v Derbyshire (Derby) 1981. Gillette Man of the Match Awards: 3. Benson & Hedges Gold Awards: 2. HS: 262* England v West Indies (Kingston) 1973-74. HSUK: 232* v Glos (Bristol) 1979. HSGC/NW: 113 v Glamorgan (Swansea) 1966. HSJPL: 117* v Sussex (Horsham) 1981. HSBH: 73* v Minor Counties (West) (Coventry) 1977. BB: 3-21 v Middlesex (Lord's) 1970.

Mohamed ASIF DIN (Ladywood School, Birmingham) B Kampala, Uganda 21/9/1960. RHB, LB. Played for 2nd XI since 1979. Debut 1981, scoring 878 runs (av. 26.60). HS: 73* v Essex (Birmingham) 1981. HSNW: 33 v Sussex (Birmingham) 1981. HSJPL: 51 v Glamorgan (Swansea) 1981 and 51 v Lancs (Birmingham) 1981. HSBH: 37 v Scotland (Glasgow) 1981.

James (Jimmy) CUMBES (Didsbury Secondary Technical School) B East Didsbury (Lancs) 4/5/1944. RHB, RM. Brother-in-law of R. Collins, former Lancs player. Debut for Lancs 1963. Not re-engaged at end of 1967 season and made debut for Surrey in 1968. Not re-engaged after 1970 season and rejoined Lancs in 1971. Made debut for Worcs in 1972 by special registration. Cap 1978. Not re-engaged after 1981 season and has joined Warwickshire for 1982 as player and commercial manager. Hat-trick v Northants (Worcester) 1977. HS: 43 Worcs v Sussex (Hove) 1980. HSJPL: 14* Worcs v Sussex (Eastbourne) 1978. BB: 6-24 Worcs v Yorks (Worcester) 1977. DDGC/NW: 4-23 Worcs v Sussex (Hove) 1974. BBJPL: 3-13 Worcs v Middlesex (Worcester) 1978. BBBH: 3-34 Worcs v Somerset (Taunton) 1978. Soccer (goalkeeper) for Tranmere Rovers, West Bromwich Albion, Aston Villa and Worcester City.

WARWICKSHIRE

Robin Ian Henry Benbow DYER (Wellington College) B Hertford 22/12/1958. 6ft 4ins tall. RHB, RM. Played for 2nd XI since 1977. Toured India with English Schools Cricket Association 1977-78. Debut 1981 (two matches. HS: 9 v Leics (Coventry) 1981.

Anthonie Michal (Yogi) FERREIRA (Hillview High School, Pretoria) B Pretoria, South Africa 13/4/1955. 6ft 3ins tall. RHB, RM. Debut for Northern Transvaal 1974-75. Played for D.H. Robin's XI v both Oxford and Cambridge Universities at Eastbourne in 1978. Debut for county 1979. HS: 106 Northern Transvaal v Eastern Province (Port Elizabeth) 1980-81. HSUK: 90 v Somerset (Taunton) 1980. HSGC/NW: 14 v Oxfordshire (Birmingham) 1980. HSJPL: 43 v Northants (Northampton) 1981. HSBH: 29 v Northants (Birmingham) 1980. BB: 8-38 Northern Transvaal v Transvaal B (Pretoria) 1977-78. BBUK: 5-66 v Somerset (Birmingham) 1979. BBGC/NW: 4-50 v Notts (Birmingham) 1979. BBJPL: 4-26 v Sussex (Horsham) 1981. BBBH: 3-38 v Kent (Oval) 1981.

William (Willie) HOGG (Ulverston Comprehensive School) B Ulverston (Lancs) 12/7/1955. RHB, RFM. Debut for Lancs 1976 after playing as professional for Preston in Northern League. Left county after 1980 season and made debut for Warwickshire in 1981. HS: 31 v Hants (Birmingham) 1981. BB: 7-84 Lancs v Warwickshire (Manchester) 1978. BBC: 4-46 v Northants (Northampton) 1981. BBJPL: 4-23 Lancs v Essex (Ilford) 1979. BBBH: 4-35 Lancs v Hants (Manchester) 1979.

Geoffrey William (Geoff) HUMPAGE (Golden Hillock Comprehensive School, Birmingham) B Birmingham 24/4/1954. RHB, WK, RM. Debut 1974. Cap 1976. 1,000 runs (4) – 1,701 runs (av. 50.02) in 1981 best. Scored two centuries in match (146 and 110) v Glos (Gloucester) 1981. Benson & Hedges Gold Awards: 2. HS: 146 v Glos (Gloucester) 1981. HSGC/NW: 58 v Somerset (Taunton) 1978. HSJPL: 108* v Middlesex (Birmingham) 1980. HSBH: 93 v Yorks (Birmingham) 1981. BBJPL: 4-53 v Glos (Moreton-in-Marsh) 1981.

Alvin Isaac (Kalli) KALLICHARRAN B Port Mourant, Berbice, Guyana 21/3/1949. LHB, OB. 5ft 4ins tall. Debut 1966-67 for Guyana in Shell Shield competition. Debut for county 1971. Cap 1972. Played for Queensland in 1977-78 Sheffield Shield competition. Tests: 66 for West Indies between 1971-72 and 1980-81 scoring 100* and 101 in first two innings in Tests v New Zealand and captaining country in 9 Tests. Tours: West Indies to England 1973, 1976 and 1980. India, Sri Lanka and Pakistan 1974-75, Australia 1975-76, India and Sri Lanka 1978-79 (captain), Australia and New Zealand 1979-80, Pakistan 1980-81. 1,000 runs (6) – 1,343 runs (av. 41.96) in 1977 best. Also scored 1,249 runs (av. 56.77) on 1974-75 tour. Benson & Hedges Gold Awards: 2. HS: 197 Guyana v Jamaica (Kingston) 1973-74. HSUK: 170* v Northants (Northampton) 1979. HSTC: 187 West Indies v India (Bombay) 1978-79. HSGC/NW: 88 v Glamorgan (Birmingham) 1972. HSJPL: 102* v Notts (Birmingham) 1981. HSBH: 109 v Glos (Bristol) 1978. BB: 4-48 v Derbyshire (Birmingham) 1978. Played and coached in Transvaal in 1981-82.

Christopher (Chris) LETHBRIDGE B Castleford (Yorks) 23/6/1961. RHB, RM. Played for Yorks 2nd XI in 1980. Debut 1981 taking wicket of G. Boycott with his first ball in first-class cricket. HS: 69 v Yorks (Birmingham) in debut match. HSJPL: 31* v Somerset (Taunton) 1981.

Peter John LEWINGTON B Finchampstead (Berks) 30/1/1950. RHB, OB. Played for Berkshire from 1967 to 1969. Debut 1970. Left staff after 1976 season and has played subsequently for Berkshire. May re-appear for Warwickshire in 1982. HS: 34 v Essex (Birmingham) 1973. BB: 7-52 v Worcs (Worcester) 1975.

Timothy Andrew (Andy) LLOYD (Oswestry Boys' HS) B Oswestry (Shropshire) 5/11/1956. LHB, RM. Played for both Shropshire and county 2nd XI in 1975. Appeared in one John Player League match in 1976 v Yorks (Leeds). Debut 1977. Played for Orange Free State in 1978-79 and 1979-80 Castle Bowl competitions. Cap 1980. 1,000 runs (2) – 1,445 runs (av. 34.40) in 1981 best. HS: 138 v Somerset (Birmingham) 1981. HSGC/NW: 81 v Devon (Birmingham) 1980. HSJPL: 90 v Kent (Birmingham) 1980. HSBH: 60 v Kent (Oval) 1981.

Gordon John LORD (Warwick School) B Warwick 25/4/1961. LHB, SLA. Toured Australia 1979 and West Indies 1980 with England Young Cricketers. Joined staff in 1980. Has yet to appear in first-class cricket.

Robert Keith MAGUIRE (Smith's Wood School, Chelmsley Wood, Birmingham) B Birmingham 20/3/1961. RHB, RM. Joined staff in 1980. Has yet to appear in first-class cricket.

Dean MARSH (Ash Green School, Exhall, Coventry) B Bedworth (Warwickshire) 3/12/1963. RHB, RM. Played for 2nd XI since 1980. Joined staff 1981. Has yet to appear in first-class cricket.

Christopher (Chris) MAYNARD (Bishop Vesey's GS, Sutton Coldfield) B Haslemere (Surrey) 8/4/1958. RHB, WK. Played for 2nd XI since 1976. Debut 1978. HS: 85 v Kent (Birmingham) 1979. HSJPL: 35 v Essex (Birmingham) 1979. HSBH: 17* v Yorks (Leeds) 1980.

Philip Robert OLIVER B West Bromwich (Staffs) 9/5/1956. RHB, OB. Played for Shropshire 1972-74. Debut 1975. HS: 171* v Northants (Northampton) 1981. HSGC/NW: 32* v Oxfordshire (Birmingham) 1980. HSJPL: 78* v Hants (Southampton) 1978. HSBH: 46 v Essex (Chelmsford) 1979. BBJPL: 3-36 v Middlesex (Lord's) 1977. Has played soccer for Telford in Southern League.

Stephen Peter (Steve) PERRYMAN (Sheldon Heath Comprehensive School) B Yardley, Birmingham 22/10/1955. RHB, RM. Debut 1974. Cap 1977. Benson & Hedges Gold Awards: 1. HS: 43 v Somerset (Birmingham) 1977. HSJPL: 17* v Worcs (Birmingham) 1975. HSBH: 18 v Essex (Chelmsford) 1979. BB: 7-49 v Hants (Bournemouth) 1978. BBGC/NW: 3-35 v Middlesex (Lord's) 1977. BBJPL: 4-19 v Surrey (Oval) 1975. BBBH: 4-17 v Minor Counties (West) (Birmingham) 1978.

Gladstone Cleopthas SMALL (Moseley School, Birmingham) B St. George, Barbados 18/10/1961. RHB, RFM. Played for 2nd XI in 1979. Toured New Zealand with D.H. Robins' XI in 1979-80 and made debut v Northern Districts (Hamilton). Debut for county 1980. HS: 21* v Somerset (Birmingham) 1981. HSJPL: 17 v Notts (Birmingham) 1980. HSBH: 19* v Yorks (Birmingham) 1981. BB: 6-76 v Surrey (Oval) 1981. BBJPL: 5-29 v Surrey (Birmingham) 1980.

David Martin SMITH (Caludon Castle Comprehensive School, Coventry) B Coventry 21/1/1962. No Relation to K.D. Smith. LHB, SLA. Played for 2nd XI since 1979. Debut 1981. One match v Hants (Birmingham). HS: 16* v Hants (Birmingham) 1981.

Kenneth David SMITH (Heaton GS, Newcastle-upon-Tyne) B Jesmond, New-

WARWICKSHIRE

castle-upon-Tyne 9/7/1956. RHB. Son of Kenneth D. Smith, former Northumberland and Leics player. Played for 2nd XI 1972. Debut 1973. Cap 1978. 1,000 runs (3) – 1,582 runs (av. 36.79) in 1980 best. Benson & Hedges Gold Awards: 1. HS: 140 v Worcs (Worcester) 1980. HSGC/NW: 64 v Sussex (Hove) 1980. HSJPL: 60 v Glamorgan (Swansea) 1979. HSBH: 84 v Worcs (Worcester) 1980.

Paul SMITH (Heaton School, Newcastle-upon-Tyne) B Newcastle upon Tyne 15/4/1964. Youngest brother of K.D. Smith. RHB, RM. Played for 2nd XI since 1980 and has been on MCC staff at Lord's. Has yet to appear in first-class cricket.

Simon Paul SUTCLIFFE (King George V GS, Southport and Oxford) B Watford 22/5/1960. Son of Peter W. Sutcliffe, former national coach. RHB, OB. Debut for Oxford U 1980. Blues 1980-81. University Secretary in 1981. Debut for county 1981, having played previously for 2nd XI. HS: 16 Oxford U v Somerset (Oxford) 1980. BB: 6-19 Oxford U v Warwickshire (Oxford) 1980.

Robert George Dylan (Bob) WILLIS (Guildford RGS) B Sunderland 30/5/1949. RHB, RF. Debut for Surrey 1969. Left staff after 1971 season and made debut for Warwickshire in 1972. Cap 1972. *Wisden* 1977. Appointed County Captain in 1980. Benefit in 1981. Awarded MBE In 1982 New Year Honours List. Tests: 63 between 1970-71 and 1981. Tours: Australia and New Zealand 1970-71 (flown out as replacement for A. Ward) and 1974-75, West Indies 1973-74 and 1980-81 (vice-captain) – returned early through injury, India, Sri Lanka and Australia 1976-77, Pakistan and New Zealand 1977-78, Australia 1978-79 (vice-captain), Australia and India 1979-80 (vice-captain), India and Sri Lanka 1981-82 (vice-captain). Hat-tricks (2) v Derbyshire (Birmingham) 1972 and v West Indians (Birmingham) 1976. Also in John Player League v Yorks (Birmingham) 1973. Gillette Man of the Match Awards: 1 (for Surrey). Benson & Hedges Gold Awards: 4 HS: 43 v Middlesex (Birmingham) 1976. HSTC: 24 v India (Manchester) 1974, 24* v Australia (Oval) 1977, 24 v Australia (Adelaide) 1978-79 and 24* v West Indies (Oval) 1980. HSGC/NW: 12* Surrey v Sussex (Oval) 1970. HSJPL: 52* v Derbyshire (Birmingham) 1975. HSBH: 25* v Northants (Northampton) 1977. BB: 8-32 v Glos (Bristol) 1977. BBTC: 8-43 v Australia (Leeds) 1981. BBGC/NW: 6-49 Surrey v Middlesex (Oval) 1970. BBJPL: 4-12 v Middlesex (Lord's) 1973. BBBH: 7-32 v Yorkshire (Birmingham) 1981. Played soccer (goalkeeper) for Guildford City.

Simon Howard WOOTTON (Arthur Terry School, Sutton Coldfield) B Perivale (Middlesex) 24/2/1959. LHB, SLA. Played for 2nd XI since 1978. Debut 1981. HS: 77 v Sri Lankans (Birmingham) 1981. HSJPL: 22 v Essex (Birmingham) 1981. HSBH: 33 v Kent (Oval) 1981.

NB The following players whose particulars appeared in the 1981 Annual have been omitted: N.J. Bulpitt (not re-engaged), D.R. Doshi (not re-engaged), D.C. Hopkins (not re-engaged), S.J. Rouse (not re-engaged), J.A. Snow and G.P. Thomas (not re-engaged).

The career records of Doshi, Hopkins, Rouse and Thomas will be found elsewhere in this Annual.

County Averages

Schweppes County Championship: Played 22, won 2, drawn 9, lost 11.
All first-class matches: Played 23, won 2, drawn 10, lost 11.

BATTING AND FIELDING

Cap		M	I	NO	Runs	HS	Avge	100	50	Ct	St
1972	A.I. Kallicharran	13	23	6	923	135	54.29	3	4	7	—
—	P.R. Oliver	8	14	3	554	171*	50.36	2	1	2	—
1976	G.W. Humpage	21	38	4	1657	146	48.73	6	7	36	10
1965	D.L. Amiss	22	41	0	1722	145	42.00	6	5	13	—
1980	T.A. Lloyd	23	43	1	1445	138	34.40	3	5	10	—
—	A.M. Ferreira	15	24	6	583	67*	32.38	—	3	4	—
1974	S.J. Rouse	3	4	1	88	55*	29.33	—	1	1	—
—	Asif Din	21	37	4	878	73*	26.60	—	4	11	—
1978	K.D. Smith	15	26	2	614	93	25.58	—	5	4	—
—	G.P. Thomas	6	12	1	263	52	23.90	—	1	6	—
—	S.H. Wootton	6	11	2	204	77	22.66	—	1	4	—
1972	R.G.D Willis	7	8	3	106	33*	21.20	—	—	1	—
—	C. Lethbridge	8	10	1	146	69	16.22	—	1	3	—
1980	D.R. Doshi	18	22	12	98	35	9.80	—	—	4	—
—	G.C. Small	19	26	4	198	21*	9.00	—	1	8	—
1977	S.P. Perryman	16	20	9	98	16*	8.90	—	—	5	—
—	W. Hogg	22	27	3	193	31	8.04	—	1	2	—
—	S.P. Sutcliffe	4	4	1	5	4	1.66	—	—	—	—

Played in two matches:
R.I.H.B. Dyer 9, 0, 7, 7 (2 ct); C. Maynard 70, 0, 22, 0 (5 ct 1 st).
Played in one match: D.C. Hopkins 17 (1 ct); D.M. Smith 16*, 5 (1 ct).

BOWLING

	Type	O	M	R	W	Avge	Best	5 wI	10 wM
R.G.D. Willis	RF	138.3	29	371	13	28.53	5-61	—	—
W. Hogg	RFM	521.2	102	1794	50	35.88	4-46	—	—
G.C. Small	RFM	395.3	52	1590	42	37.85	6-76	1	—
D.R. Doshi	SLA	669.3	163	1949	45	43.31	5-73	1	—
S.P. Perryman	RM	305.4	64	1046	24	43.58	5-52	1	—
A.M. Ferreira	RM	436.3	83	1542	32	48.18	4-73	—	—
C. Lethbridge	RM	113	12	501	7	71.57	2-26	—	—
Asif Din	LB	70	8	371	5	74.20	1-11	—	—
S.P. Sutcliffe	OB	124.3	17	485	6	80.83	2-68	—	—

Also bowled: D.C. Hopkins 13-3-35-0; A.I. Kallicharran 35.5-3-133-2; T.A. Lloyd 24-2-106-0; S.J. Rouse 42.3-8-169-2; D.M. Smith 23-3-98-1; S.H. Wootton 1-0-7-0.

County Records

First-class cricket

Highest innings	For	657-6d v Hampshire (Birmingham)	1899
totals:	Agst	887 by Yorkshire (Birmingham)	1896
Lowest innings	For	16 v Kent (Tonbridge)	1913
totals:	Agst	15 by Hampshire (Birmingham)	1922

WARWICKSHIRE

Highest indi-	For	305* F.R. Foster v Worcestershire (Dudley)	1914
vidual innings:	Agst	316 R.H. Moore for Hants (Bournemouth)	1937
Best bowling	For	10-41 J.D. Bannister v Combined Services	
in an innings:		(Birmingham)	1959
	Agst	10-36 H. Verity for Yorkshire (Leeds)	1931
Best bowling	For	15-76 S. Hargreave v Surrey (The Oval)	1903
in a match:	Agst	17-92 A.P. Freeman for Kent (Folkestone)	1932
Most runs in a season:		2,417 (av. 60.42) M.J.K. Smith	1959
runs in a career:		33,862 (av. 36.18) William Quaife	1894-1928
100s in a season:		8 by R.E.S. Wyatt	1937
		and R.B. Kanhai	1972
100s in a career:		71 by William Quaife	1894-1928
wickets in a season:		180 (av. 15.13) W.E. Hollies	1946
wickets in a career:		2,201 (av. 20.45) W.E. Hollies	1932-1957

RECORD WICKET STANDS

1st	377	N.F. Horner & K. Ibadulla v Surrey (The Oval)	1960
2nd	465*	J.A. Jameson & R.B. Kanhai v Gloucestershire (Birmingham)	1974
3rd	327	S. Kinneir & William Quaife v Lancashire (Birmingham)	1901
4th	402	R.B. Kanhai & K. Ibadulla v Notts (Nottingham)	1968
5th	268	Walter Quaife & William Quaife v Essex (Leyton)	1900
6th	220	H.E. Dollery & J. Buckingham v Derbyshire (Derby)	1938
7th	250	H.E. Dollery & J.S. Ord v Kent (Maidstone)	1953
8th	228	A.J.W. Croom & R.E.S. Wyatt v Worcestershire (Dudley)	1925
9th	154	G.W. Stephens & A.J.W. Croom v Derbyshire (Birmingham)	1925
10th	128	F.R. Santall & W. Sanders v Yorkshire (Birmingham)	1930

One-day cricket

Highest innings totals:	Gillette Cup/ NatWest Trophy	314-6 v Oxfordshire (Birmingham)	1980
	John Player League	265-5 v Northamptonshire (Northampton)	1979
	Benson & Hedges Cup	291-5 v Lancashire (Manchester)	1981
Lowest innings totals:	Gillette Cup/ NatWest Trophy	109 v Kent (Canterbury)	1971
	John Player League	65 v Kent (Maidstone)	1979
	Benson & Hedges Cup	96 v Leicestershire (Leicester)	1972
Highest indi- vidual innings:	Gillette Cup/ NatWest Trophy	126 R.B. Kanhai v Lincolnshire (Birmingham)	1971
	John Player League	123* J.A. Jameson v Nottinghamshire (Nottingham)	1973
	Benson & Hedges Cup	119* R.B. Kanhai v Northamptonshire (Northants)	1975
Best bowling figures:	Gillette Cup/ NatWest Trophy	6-32 K. Ibadulla v Hants (Birmingham)	1965
	John Player League	5-13 D.J. Brown v Worcestershire (Worcester)	1970
	Benson & Hedges Cup	7-32 R.G.D. Willis v Yorkshire (Birmingham)	1981

WORCESTERSHIRE

Formation of present club: 1865.
Colours: Dark Green and Black.
Badge: Shield, *Argent*, bearing *Fess* between three *Pears Sable*.
County Champions (3): 1964, 1965 and 1974.
Gillette Cup Finalists (2): 1963 and 1966.
NatWest Trophy Second Round: 1981.
John Player League Champions: 1971.
Benson & Hedges Cup Finalists (2): 1973 and 1976.
Gillette Man of the Match Awards: 18.
NatWest Man of the Match Awards: Nil.
Benson & Hedges Gold Awards: 25.

Secretary: M.D. Vockins, County Ground, New Road, Worcester WR2 4QQ.
Captain: G.M. Turner.
Prospects of Play Telephone No: (0905) 422011.

Hartley Leroy ALLEYNE B Bridgetown, Barbados 27/2/1957. RHB, RF. Debut for Barbados in one Shell Shield match in 1978-79. Played for Lincolnshire and as a professional for Rochdale in Central Lancashire League in 1979. Debut for county 1980. Cap 1981. Hat-trick v Middlesex (Lord's) 1981. HS: 72 v Lancs (Stourport-on-Severn) 1980. HSGC/NW: 19 v Somerset (Taunton) 1980. HSJPL: 32 v Kent (Worcester) 1980. HSBH: 10 v Essex (Worcester) 1980. BB: 8-43 v Middlesex (Lord's) 1981. BBGC/NW: 3-27 v Somerset (Taunton) 1980. BBJPL: 4-24 v Lancs (Worcester) 1980. BBBH: 3-39 v Lancs (Manchester) 1980.

Timothy Stephen CURTIS (Worcester Royal GS) B Chislehurst (Kent) 15/1/1960. RHB, LB. Played for 2nd XI since 1976. Debut 1979. HS: 59* v Warwickshire (Birmingham) 1980. HSNW: 29 v Derbyshire (Derby) 1981. HSJPL: 33* v Middlesex (Lord's) 1981.

Norman GIFFORD B Ulverston (Lancs) 30/3/1940. LHB, SLA. Joined staff 1958 and made debut 1960. Cap 1961. Appointed county captain in 1971 after being vice-captain since 1969. Relinquished captaincy after 1980. Benefit (£11,047) in 1974. *Wisden* 1974. Awarded MBE in 1978 Birthday Honours list. Second benefit in 1981. Tests: 15 between 1964 and 1973. Played in one match for Rest of World v Australia 1971-72. Tours: Rest of World to Australia 1971-72, India, Pakistan and Sri Lanka 1972-73. 100 wkts: (3) – 133 wkts (av. 19.66) in 1961 best. Hat-trick v Derbyshire (Chesterfield) 1965. Took 4 wkts in 6 balls v Cambridge U (Cambridge) 1972. Gillette Man of Match Awards: 1. Benson & Hedges Gold Awards: 2. HS: 89 v Oxford U (Oxford) 1963. HSTC: 25* v New Zealand (Nottingham) 1973. HSGC/NW: 38 v Warwickshire (Lord's) 1966. HSJPL: 29 v Essex (Worcester) 1974. HSBH: 33 v Kent (Lord's) 1973. BB: 8-28 v Yorks (Sheffield) 1968. BBTC: 5-55 v Pakistan (Karachi) 1972-73. BBGC/NW: 4-7 v Surrey (Worcester) 1972. BBJPL: 5-28 v Northants (Worcester) 1979. BBBH: 6–8 v Minor Counties (South) (High Wycombe) 1979.

Edward John Orton (Ted) HEMSLEY (Bridgnorth GS) B Norton, Stoke-on-Trent 1/9/1943. RHB, RM. Debut 1963. Cap 1969. Benefit in 1982. Shared in 6th-wkt partnership record for county, 227 with D.N. Patel v Oxford U (Oxford) 1976. Scored 1,168 runs (av. 38.93) in 1978, Benson & Hedges Gold Awards: 3. HS: 176* v Lancs (Worcester) 1977. HSGC/NW: 73 v Sussex (Hove) 1972. HSJPL: 75* v

WORCESTERSHIRE

Glamorgan (Cardiff) 1979. HSBH: 95* v Warwickshire (Worcester) 1980. BB: 3-5 v Warwickshire (Worcester) 1971. BBJPL: 4-42 v Essex (Worcester) 1971. Soccer for Shrewsbury Town, Sheffield United and Doncaster Rovers.

David John HUMPHRIES B Alveley (Shropshire) 6/8/1953. LHB, WK. Played for Shropshire 1971-73. Debut for Leics 1974. Left county after 1976 season and made debut for Worcs in 1977. Cap 1978. Gillette Man of Match Awards: 1. HS: 111* v Warwickshire (Worcester) 1978. HSGC/NW: 58 v Glamorgan (Worcester) 1977. HSJPL: 62 v Notts (Dudley) 1977. HSBH: 34 v Leics (Leicester) 1981.

John Darling INCHMORE (Ashington GS) B Ashington (Northumberland) 22/2/1949. RHB, RFM. Played for Northumberland in 1970. Played for both Warwickshire and Worcs 2nd XIs in 1972 and for Stourbridge in Birmingham League. Debut 1973. Cap 1976. Played for Northern Transvaal in 1976-77 Currie Cup competition. Benson & Hedges Gold Awards: 2. HS: 113* v Essex (Worcester) 1974. HSGC/NW: 19* v Leics (Leicester) 1979. HSJPL: 45 v Northants (Worcester) 1981 and 45 v Derbyshire (Chesterfield) 1981. HSBH: 49* v Somerset (Taunton) 1976. BB: 8-58 v Yorks (Worcester) 1977. BBGC/NW: 3-11 v Essex (Worcester) 1975. BBJPL: 4-9 v Northants (Dudley) 1975. BBBH: 4-21 v Combined Universities (Cambridge) 1980.

Philip Anthony (Phil) NEALE (Frederick Gough Comprehensive School, Bottesford and John Leggott Sixth Form College, Scunthorpe) B Scunthorpe (Lincs) 5/6/1954. RHB. Played for Lincolnshire 1973-74. Debut 1975. Cap 1978. 1,000 runs: (3) – 1,305 runs (av. 42.09) in 1979 best. HS: 163* v Notts (Worcester) 1979. HSGC/NW: 68 v Glos (Bristol) 1976. HSJPL: 84 v Glos (Bristol) 1980. HSBH: 128 v Lancs (Manchester) 1980. Soccer for Lincoln City. Studied at Leeds University and obtained Degree in Russian.

Joseph Alan ORMROD (Kirkaldy HS) B Ramsbottom (Lancs) 22/12/1942. RHB, OB. Debut 1962. Cap 1966. Benefit (£19,000) in 1977. Tour: Pakistan 1966-67. 1,000 runs: (12) – 1,535 runs (av. 45.14) in 1978 best. Scored two centuries in match (101 and 131*) v Somerset (Worcester) 1980. Shared in 4th wkt partnership record for county, 281 with Younis Ahmed v Notts (Nottingham) 1979. Benson & Hedges Gold Awards: 4. HS: 204* v Kent (Dartford) 1973. HSGC/NW: 59 v Essex (Worcester) 1975. HSJPL: 110* v Kent (Canterbury) 1975. HSBH: 124* v Glos (Worcester) 1976. BB: 5-27 v Glos (Bristol) 1972. BBJPL: 3-51 v Hants (Worcester) 1972.

Dipak Narshibhai PATEL (George Salter Comprehensive School, West Bromwich) B Nairobi, Kenya 25/10/1958. Has lived in UK since 1967. RHB, OB. Debut 1976. Cap 1979. Scored 1,155 runs (av. 32.08) in 1981. Shared in 6th wkt partnership record for county, 227 with E.J.O. Hemsley v Oxford U (Oxford) 1981. HS: 138 v Warwickshire (Worcester) 1981. HSNW: 42 v Derbyshire (Derby) 1981. HSJPL: 82 v Surrey (Oval) 1981. HSBH: 39 v Glamorgan (Cardiff) 1979. BB: 6-47 v Oxford U (Oxford) 1980. BBJPL: 3-22 v Glos (Moreton-in-Marsh) 1978. BBBH: 3-42 v Yorks (Worcester) 1980.

Alan Paul PRIDGEON B Wall Heath (Staffs) 22/2/1954. RHB, RM. 6ft 3ins tall. Joined staff 1971. Debut 1972. Cap 1980. HS: 34 v Glamorgan (Swansea) 1978. HSGC/NW: 13* v Somerset (Taunton) 1980. HSJPL: 16* v Essex (Dudley) 1976. HSBH: 10 v Leics (Leicester) 1976. BB: 7-35 v Oxford U (Oxford) 1976. BBGC/NW: 3-25 v Somerset (Taunton) 1980. BBJPL: 6-26 v Surrey (Worcester)

1978. BBBH: 3-57 v Warwickshire (Birmingham) 1976. Soccer for Ledbury Town in West Midland League.

Mark Stephen SCOTT (Creighton School, Muswell Hill) B Muswell Hill (Middlesex) 10/3/1959. RHB. Played for Middlesex 2nd XI 1977-78, Glamorgan 2nd XI 1979 and for county 2nd XI 1980. Debut 1981, scoring 968 runs (av. 26.88). HS: 109 v Glos (Bristol) 1981. HSJPL: 42 v Glos (Worcester) 1981.

William Richard Keay THOMAS (Dean Close School, Cheltenham) B Redditch (Worcs) 22/7/1960. RHB, RM. Played for 2nd XI in 1980. Debut 1981. One match v Sri Lankans (Worcester). HS: 44 v Sri Lankans (Worcester) 1981.

Glenn Maitland TURNER (Otago Boys' HS) B Dunedin, New Zealand 26/5/1947. RHB, OB. Debut for Otago in Plunket Shield competition 1964-65 whilst still at school. Debut for county 1967. Cap 1968. *Wisden* 1970. Benefit (£21,103) in 1978. Appointed county captain in 1981. Tests: 39 for New Zealand between 1968-69 and 1976-77 captaining country in 10 Tests. Tours: New Zealand to England 1969 and 1973 (vice-captain), India and Pakistan 1969-70, Australia 1969-70 and 1973-74 (vice-captain), West Indies 1971-72, Pakistan and India 1976-77 (captain). 1,000 runs: (14) – 2,416 runs (av. 67.11) in 1973 best, including 1,018 runs (av. 78.30) by 31 May – the first occasion since 1938. Scored 1,284 runs (av. 85.60) in West Indies and Bermuda 1971-72. Scored 1,244 runs av. 77.75) in 1975-76 – record aggregate for New Zealand season. Scored 10 centuries in 1970, a county record. Scored two centuries in match on six occasions (122 and 128*) v Warwickshire (Birmingham) 1972, (101 and 110*) New Zealand v Australia (Christchurch) 1973-74, (135 and 108) Otago v Northern Districts (Gisborne) 1974-75, (105 and 186*) Otago v Central Districts (Dunedin) 1974-75, (161 and 101) v Northants (Stourbridge) 1981, and (147* and 139) v Warwickshire (Worcester) 1981. Scored 141* out of 169 – 83.4% of total – v Glamorgan (Swansea) 1977 – a record for first-class cricket. Gillette Man of Match Awards: 1. Benson & Hedges Gold Awards: 5. HS: 259 twice in successive innings, New Zealanders v Guyana and New Zealand v West Indies (Georgetown) 1971-72. HSUK: 228* v Glos (Worcester) 1980. HSGC/NW: 117* v Lancs (Worcester) 1971. HSJPL: 147 v Sussex (Horsham) 1980. HSBH: 143* v Warwickshire (Birmingham) 1976. BB: 3-18 v Pakistanis (Worcester) 1967. Has played hockey for Worcs and had trial for Midlands.

Andrew John WEBSTER (Forest of Needham HS, Rolleston-on-Dove, Burton-on-Trent) B Burton-on-Trent (Staffs) 5/3/1959. 6ft 4ins tall. LHB, RM. Played for Staffordshire in 1980. Debut 1981. One match v Kent (Canterbury).

Martin John WESTON B Worcester 8/4/1959. RHB, RM. Played for 2nd XI since 1978. Debut 1979. HS: 43 v Sri Lankans (Worcester) 1979. HSJPL: 10* v Surrey (Oval) 1981.

Mohammad YOUNIS AHMED (Moslem HS, Lahore) B Jullundur, Pakistan 20/10/1947. LHB, LM/SLA. Younger brother of Saeed Ahmed, Pakistan Test cricketer. Debut 1961-62 for Pakistan Inter Board Schools XI v South Zone at age of 14 years 4 months. Debut for Surrey 1965. Cap 1969. Played for South Australia in 1972-73 Sheffield Shield competition. Not re-engaged by county after 1978 season. Debut for Worcs and cap 1979. Is regarded as an English player for qualification purposes. Tests: 2 for Pakistan v New Zealand 1969-70. 1,000 runs: (10) – 1,760 runs (av. 47.56) in 1969 best. Shared in 4th wkt partnership record for county, 281 with J.A. Ormrod v Notts (Nottingham) 1979. Benson & Hedges Gold Awards: 3 (1 for Surrey). HS: 221* v Notts (Nottingham) 1979. HSTC: 62 Pakistan v New Zealand (Karachi) 1969-70. HSGC/NW: 87 Surrey v Middlesex (Oval) 1970. HSJPL: 113

163

WORCESTERSHIRE

Surrey v Warwickshire (Birmingham) 1976 and 113 v Yorks (Worcester) 1979.
HSBH: 115 v Yorks (Worcester) 1980. BB: 4-10 Surrey v Cambridge U (Cambridge) 1975. BBC: 3-33 v Oxford U (Oxford) 1979. BBJPL: 3-26 v Surrey (Oval) 1979. BBBH: 4-37 v Northants (Northampton) 1980.

NB. The following players whose particulars appeared in the 1981 Annual have been omitted. J. Birkenshaw (left staff and has become a first-class umpire), P.B. Fisher, S.P. Henderson (not re-engaged). M. Saunders (left staff after 1980 season). In addition J. Cumbes who was not re-engaged has joined Warwickshire and his particulars will be found under that county.

The career records of Birkenshaw, Fisher, Henderson and Cumbes will be found elsewhere in this Annual.

County Averages

Schweppes County Championship: Played 22, won 5, drawn 8, lost 9.
All first-class matches: Played 25, won 5, drawn 10, lost 10.

BATTING AND FIELDING

Cap		M	I	NO	Runs	HS	Avge	100	50	Ct	St
1966	J.A. Ormrod	4	6	3	279	100*	93.00	1	1	1	—
1968	G.M. Turner	24	42	4	2101	168	55.28	9	6	21	—
1979	Younis Ahmed	22	39	8	1637	116	52.80	3	9	12	—
1978	P.A. Neale	23	41	5	1247	145*	34.63	4	3	9	—
1979	D.N. Patel	22	40	4	1155	138	32.08	3	2	10	—
1978	D.J. Humphries	18	28	7	575	64*	25.38	—	4	29	14
—	M.S. Scott	19	37	1	968	109	26.88	1	6	8	—
1976	J.D. Inchmore	18	21	2	428	63*	22.52	—	1	3	—
1969	E.J.O. Hemsley	20	30	5	540	73	21.60	—	1	11	—
1961	N. Gifford	24	23	8	284	37*	18.93	—	—	5	—
—	J. Birkenshaw	10	10	0	165	54	16.50	—	1	10	—
—	P.B. Fisher	7	8	3	74	28*	14.80	—	—	5	—
1980	A.P. Pridgeon	24	22	11	126	34	11.45	—	—	8	—
—	M.J. Weston	4	6	1	53	22	10.60	—	—	3	—
1978	J. Cumbes	10	9	4	50	15*	10.00	—	—	2	—
—	S.P. Henderson	6	9	1	83	37	10.37	—	—	—	—
—	T.S. Curtis	5	7	1	38	11	6.33	—	—	—	—
1981	H.L. Alleyne	13	13	3	43	16	4.30	—	—	2	—

Played in one match W.R.K. Thomas 44, 13*; A.J. Webster 6.

BOWLING

	Type	O	M	R	W	Avge	Best	5 wI	10 wM
H.L. Alleyne	**RF**	324.3	63	1019	39	26.12	8-43	1	1
J. Cumbes	**RM**	306.3	75	848	28	30.28	5-69	1	—
A.P. Pridgeon	**RM**	673.1	119	1978	56	35.32	5-63	1	—
J.D. Inchmore	**RFM**	355	63	1166	30	38.86	5-85	1	—
N. Gifford	**SLA**	961.4	253	2476	63	39.30	6-67	1	—
D.N. Patel	**OB**	597.3	137	1749	43	46.67	5-76	2	—
J. Birkenshaw	**OB**	202.5	40	644	11	58.54	3-131	—	—

Also bowled: T.S. Curtis 4-2-13-1; E.J.O. Hemsley 14-0-77-0; P.A. Neale 19.1-0-102-0; M.S. Scott 10-1-37-0; W.R.K. Thomas 17-4-54-0; A.J. Webster 6-0-18-0; M.J. Weston 15.4-3-68-0; Younis Ahmed 62-9-183-3.

County Records

First-class Cricket

Highest innings	For	633 v Warwickshire (Worcester)	1906
totals:	Agst	701-4d by Leicestershire (Worcester)	1906
Lowest innings	For	24 v Yorkshire (Huddersfield)	1903
totals:	Agst	30 by Hampshire (Worcester)	1903
Highest indi-	For	276 F.L. Bowley v Hampshire (Dudley)	1914
vidual innings	Agst	331* J.D.B. Robertson for Middlesex (Worcester)	1949
Best bowling	For	9-23 C.F. Root v Lancashire (Worcester)	1931
in an innings	Agst	10-51 J. Mercer for Glamorgan (Worcester)	1936
Best bowling	For	15-87 A.J. Conway v Glos (Moreton-in-Marsh)	1914
in a match:	Agst	17-212 J.C. Clay for Glamorgan (Swansea)	1937
Most runs in a season:		2654 (av. 52.03) H.H.I. Gibbons	1934
runs in a career:		34490 (av. 34.04) D. Kenyon	1946-1967
100s in a season:		10 by G.M. Turner	1970
100s in a career:		70 by D. Kenyon	1946-1967
wickets in a season:		207 (av. 17.52) C.F. Root	1925
wickets in a career:		2143 (av. 23.73) R.T.D. Perks	1930-1955

RECORD WICKET STANDS

1st	309	F.L. Bowley & H.K. Foster v Derbyshire (Derby)	1901
2nd	274	H.H.I. Gibbons & Nawab of Pataudi v Kent (Worcester)	1933
		H.H.I. Gibbons & Nawab of Pataudi v Glam (Worcester)	1934
3rd	314	M.J. Horton & T.W. Graveney v Somerset (Worcester)	1962
4th	281	J.A. Ormrod & Younis Ahmed v Notts (Nottingham)	1979
5th	393	E.G. Arnold & W.B. Burns v Warwickshire (Birmingham)	1909
6th	227	E.J.O. Hemsley & D.N. Patel v Oxford U (Oxford)	1976
7th	197	H.H.I. Gibbons & R. Howorth v Surrey (The Oval)	1938
8th	145*	F. Chester & W.H. Taylor v Essex (Worcester)	1914
9th	181	J.A. Cuffe & R.D. Burrows v Gloucestershire (Worcester)	1907
10th	119	W.B. Burns & G.A. Wilson v Somerset (Worcester)	1906

One-day Cricket

Highest innings	GC/NatWest Trophy	265-9 Lancashire (Worcester)	1980
	John Player League	307-4 v Derbys (Worcester)	1975
	Benson & Hedges Cup	314-5 v Lancs (Manchester)	1980
Lowest innings	Gillette Cup/	98 v Durham	
totals:	NatWest Trophy	(Chester-le-Street)	1968
	John Player League	86 v Yorkshire (Leeds)	1969
	Benson & Hedges Cup	92 v Oxford & Cambridge Universities (Cambridge)	1975
Highest indi-	Gillette Cup/	117* G.M. Turner v	
vidual innings:	NatWest Trophy	Lancashire (Worcester)	1971
	John Player League	147 G.M. Turner v Sussex (Horsham)	1980
	Benson & Hedges Cup	143* G.M. Turner v Warwickshire (Birmingham)	1976
Best bowling	Gillette Cup/	6-14 J.A. Flavell v Lancashire	
figures:	NatWest Trophy	(Worcester)	1963
	John Player League	6-26 A.P. Pridgeon v Surrey (Worcester)	1978
	Benson & Hedges Cup	6-8 N. Gifford v Minor Co. (South) (High Wycombe)	1979

YORKSHIRE

Formation of present club: 1863, reorganised 1891.
Colours: Oxford blue, Cambridge blue, and gold.
Badge: White rose.
County Champions (31): 1867, 1870, 1893, 1896, 1898,
1900, 1901, 1902, 1905, 1908, 1912, 1919, 1922, 1923,
1924, 1925, 1931, 1932, 1933, 1935, 1937, 1938, 1939,
1946, 1959, 1960, 1962, 1963, 1966, 1967, and 1968.
Joint Champions (2): 1869 and 1949.
Gillette Cup Winners (2): 1965 and 1969.
NatWest Trophy First Round: 1981.
John Player League runners-up: 1973.
Benson & Hedges Cup Finalists: 1972.
Fenner Trophy Winners: 1972, 1974 and 1981.
Gillette Man of the Match Awards: 14.
NatWest Man of the Match Awards: Nil.
Benson & Hedges Gold Awards: 24.

Secretary: J. Lister, Headingley Cricket Ground, Leeds LS6 3BU.
Cricket Manager: R. Illingworth, CBE.
Captain: C.M. Old.

Charles William Jeffrey (Bill) ATHEY (Acklam Hall School, Middlesbrough) B
Middlesbrough 27/9/1957. RHB, RM. Toured West Indies with England Young
Cricketers 1976. Debut 1976. Cap 1980. Tests: 3 in 1980 and 1980-81. Tour: West
Indies 1980-81 (as replacement for B.C. Rose). Scored 1,123 runs (av. 33.02) in
1980. Gillette Man of Match Awards: 2. Benson & Hedges Gold Awards: 1. HS:
131* v Sussex (Leeds) 1976 and 131 v Somerset (Taunton) 1978. HSTC: 9 v Australia
(Lord's) 1980. HSGC/NW: 115 v Kent (Leeds) 1980. HSJPL: 118 v Leics (Leicester)
1978. HSBH: 74* v Combined Universities (Oxford) 1980. BB: 3-38 v Surrey (Oval)
1978. BBJPL: 5-35 v Derbyshire (Chesterfield) 1981. BBBH: 3-32 v Middlesex
(Lord's) 1979.

David Leslie BAIRSTOW (Hanson GS, Bradford) B Bradford 1/9/1951. RHB,
WK. Can bowl RM. Debut 1970 whilst still at school. Played for MCC Schools at
Lord's in 1970. Cap 1973. Played for Griqualand West in 1976-77 and 1977-78
(captain) Currie Cup and Castle Bowl competitions. Benefit in 1982. Tests: 4
between 1979 and 1980-81. Tours: Australia 1978-79 (flown out as replacement for
R.W. Tolchard), Australia and India 1979-80, West Indies 1980-81. Scored 1,083
runs (av. 40.11) in 1981. Dismissed 70 batsmen (64 ct 6 st) in 1971, including 9 in
match and 6 in innings (all ct) v Lancs (Manchester). Benson & Hedges Gold
Awards: 4. HS: 145 v Middlesex (Scarborough) 1980. HSTC: 59 v India (Oval)
1979. HSNW: 52* v Kent (Canterbury) 1981. HSJPL: 78 v Surrey (Scarborough)
1981. HSBH: 103* v Derbyshire (Derby) 1981. BB: 3-82 Griqualand West v
Transvaal B (Johannesburg) 1976-77. Soccer for Bradford City.

Geoffrey (Geoff) BOYCOTT (Hemsworth GS) B Fitzwilliam (Yorks) 21/10/1940.
RHB, RM. Plays in contact lenses. Debut 1962. Cap 1963. Elected Best Young
Cricketer of the Year in 1963 by the Cricket Writers' Club. *Wisden* 1964. County
captain from 1971 to 1978. Played for Northern Transvaal in 1971-72. Benefit
(£20,639) in 1974. Awarded OBE in 1980 Birthday Honours List. Tests: 104 between
1964 and 1981 captaining England in 4 Tests in 1977-78. Played in 2 matches against
Rest of World in 1970. Tours: South Africa 1964-65, Australia and New Zealand

1965-66 and 1970-71 (returned home early through broken arm injury), West Indies 1967-68, 1973-74 and 1980-81. Pakistan and New Zealand 1977-78 (vice captain), Australia 1978-79, Australia and India 1979-80, India and Sri Lanka 1981-82. 1,000 runs (19) – 2,503 runs (av. 100.12) in 1971 best. Only English batsman ever to have an average of 100 for season and repeated the feat in 1979 with 1,538 runs (av. 102.53). Also scored 1,000 runs in South Africa 1964-65 (1,135 runs, av. 56.75), West Indies 1967-68 (1,154 runs, av. 82.42), Australia 1970-71 (1,535 runs, av. 95.93). Scored two centuries in match (103 and 105) v Notts (Sheffield) 1966 and (160* and 116) England v The Rest (Worcester) 1974. Completed 30,000 runs in 1977 and scored his 100th century in Leeds Test of that year – only player to have done so in a Test match. Scored 155 v India (Birmingham) 1979 to become the second batsman to have scored a century in a Test on all six grounds in this country. Gillette Man of Match Awards: 2. Benson & Hedges Gold Awards: 7. HS: 261* MCC v President's XI (Bridgetown) 1973-74. HSUK: 260* v Essex (Colchester) 1970. HSTC: 246* v India (Leeds) 1967. HSGC/NW: 146 v Surrey (Lord's) 1965. HSJPL: 108* v Northants (Huddersfield) 1974. HSBH: 142 v Worcs (Worcester) 1980. BB: 4-14 v Lancs (Manchester) 1979. BBTC: 3-47 England v South Africa (Cape Town) 1964-65.

Philip (Phil) CARRICK B Armley, Leeds 16/7/1952. RHB, SLA. Debut 1970. Cap 1976. Played for Eastern Province in 1976-77 Currie Cup competition. HS: 131* v Northants (Northampton) 1980. HSGC/NW: 19* v Kent (Leeds) 1980. HSJPL: 29 v Glamorgan (Swansea) 1980. HSBH: 19* v Notts (Bradford) 1979. BB: 8-33 v Cambridge U (Cambridge) 1973. BBJPL: 3-32 v Hants (Bournemouth) 1976 and 3-32 v Notts (Nottingham) 1979.

Simon John DENNIS (Scarborough College) B Scarborough 18/10/1960. Nephew of Sir Leonard Hutton and F. Dennis, former Yorkshire player. RHB, LFM. Played for 2nd XI since 1977. Toured Australia with England Young Cricketers in 1979. Debut 1980. HS: 5 v Surrey (Harrogate) 1981 and 5* v Somerset (Sheffield) 1981. BB: 5-35 v Somerset (Sheffield) 1981. BBJPL: 3-19 v Hants (Middlesbrough) 1981.

Philip Richard HART (Pindar School, Scarborough) B Seamer (Yorks) 12/1/1951. RHB, SLA. Debut 1981, bowling seven consecutive maiden overs before conceding his first run and taking wicket of Intikhab Alam with seventh delivery, v Surrey (Harrogate). HS: 11 v Glamorgan (Cardiff) 1981.

Stuart Neil HARTLEY (Beckfoot GS) B Shipley (Yorks) 18/3/1956. RHB, RM. Played for 2nd XI since 1975. Debut 1978. Acted as captain in a number of matches in 1981. HS: 106 v Notts (Nottingham) 1981. HSGC/NW: 23 v Surrey (Oval) 1980. HSJPL: 54* v Warwickshire (Birmingham) 1979. HSBH: 17 v Warwickshire (Birmingham) 1981. BB: 3-40 v Glos (Sheffield) 1980. BBJPL: 3-31 v Notts (Scarborough) 1980.

Peter Geoffrey INGHAM (Ashville College, Harrogate) B Sheffield 28/9/1956. RHB, RM. Played for 2nd XI since 1974. Debut 1979. HS: 64 v Northants (Leeds) 1980. HSJPL: 87* v Glos (Hull) 1980.

Paul William JARVIS (Bydales School, Marske-by-the-Sea) B Redcar 29/6/1965. RHB, RFM. Debut 1981 aged 16 years 75 days. One match v Sussex (Hove). HS: 5 v Sussex (Hove) 1981.

Mark JOHNSON (Ashleigh School, Sheffield) B Gleadles, Sheffield 23/4/1958. RHB, RM. Played for Derbyshire 2nd XI in 1980. Debut 1981. HSJPL: 15* v Surrey

YORKSHIRE

(Scarborough) 1981. BB: 4-48 v Warwickshire (Scarborough) 1981. BBBH: 4-18 v Scotland (Bradford) 1981.

James Derek (Jim) LOVE B Leeds 22/4/1955. RHB, RM. Debut 1975. Cap 1980. Scored 1,203 runs (av. 33.41) in 1981. Benson & Hedges Gold Awards: 1. HS: 170* v Worcs (Worcester) 1979. HSGC/NW: 61* v Hants (Southampton) 1980. HSJPL: 90* v Derbyshire (Chesterfield) 1979. HSBH: 118* v Scotland (Bradford) 1981.

Richard Graham LUMB (Percy Jackson GS, Doncaster and Mexborough GS) B Doncaster 27/2/1950. 6ft 3ins tall. RHB, RM. Played in MCC Schools matches at Lord's 1968. Debut 1970 after playing in one John Player League match in 1969. Cap 1974. Appointed County vice-captain for 1981, but subsequently resigned post. 1,000 runs (5) – 1,532 runs (av. 41.40) in 1975 best. HS: 159 v Somerset (Harrogate) 1979. HSGC/NW: 56 v Shropshire (Wellington) 1976. HSJPL: 101 v Notts (Scarborough) 1976. HSBH: 90 v Northants (Bradford) 1980.

Martyn Douglas MOXON (Holgate GS, Barnsley) B Barnsley 4/5/1960. RHB, RM. Played in two John Player League matches in 1980, without batting or bowling. Debut 1981 scoring 115 in second innings of debut match. HS: 116 v Essex (Leeds) 1981. HSJPL: 20 v Surrey (Scarborough) 1981. HSBH: 22 v Somerset (Leeds) 1981.

Christopher Middleton (Chris) OLD (Acklam Hall Secondary GS, Middlesbrough) B Middlesbrough 22/12/1948. 6ft 3ins tall. LHB, RFM. Debut 1966. Cap 1969. Elected Best Young Cricketer of the Year in 1970 by the Cricket Writers' Club. *Wisden* 1978. Benefit (£32,916) in 1979. Appointed County Captain in 1981. Played for Northern Transvaal in 1981-82 Currie Cup Competition. Tests: 46 between 1972-73 and 1981. Played in 2 matches against Rest of World 1970. Tours: India, Pakistan and Sri Lanka 1972-73, West Indies 1973-74 and 1980-81, Australia and New Zealand 1974-75, India, Sri Lanka and Australia 1976-77, Pakistan and New Zealand 1977-78, Australia 1978-79. Scored century in 37 minutes v Warwickshire (Birmingham) 1977 – second fastest ever in first-class cricket. Took 4 wickets in 5 balls, England v Pakistan (Birmingham) 1978. Benson & Hedges Gold Awards: 3. HS: 116 v Indians (Bradford) 1974. HSTC: 65 v Pakistan (Oval) 1974. HSGC/NW: 29 v Lancs (Leeds) 1974. HSJPL: 82 v Somerset (Bath) 1974 and 82* v Somerset (Glastonbury) 1976. HSBH: 78* v Scotland (Bradford) 1981. BB: 7-20 v Glos (Middlesbrough) 1969. BBTC: 7-50 v Pakistan (Birmingham) 1978. BBGC/NW: 4-9 v Durham (Middlesbrough) 1978. BBJPL: 5-53 v Sussex (Hove) 1971. BBBH: 4-17 v Derbyshire (Bradford) 1973.

Alan RAMAGE (Warsett School, Brotton) B Guisborough 29/11/1957. LHB, RFM. Played for 2nd XI since 1974 and in six John Player matches and one Benson & Hedges Cup match between 1975 and 1977. Debut 1979. HS: 52 v Glos (Bristol) 1981. HSBH: 17* v Combined Universities (Barnsley) 1976. BB: 5-65 v Surrey (Harrogate) 1981. BBGC/NW: 3-33 v Hants (Southampton) 1980. BBJPL: 3-51 v Kent (Canterbury) 1977. BBBH: 3-63 v Warwickshire (Leeds) 1980. Has played soccer for Middlesbrough.

Steven John RHODES (Carlton-Bolling School, Bradford) B Bradford 17/6/1964. Son of W.E. Rhodes who played for Nottinghamshire from 1961 to 1964. RHB, WK. Played for 2nd XI 1980. Debut 1981 aged 17 years 35 days. One match v Sri Lankans (Sheffield).

Kevin SHARP (Abbey Grange C.E. High School, Leeds) B Leeds 6/4/1959. LHB, OB. Debut 1976. Captained England under-19 v West Indies under-19 in 1978 and scored 260* in match at Worcester. HS: 116 v Sri Lankans (Sheffield) 1981.

HSGC/NW: 25 v Middlesex (Lord's) 1979. HSJPL: 54 v Somerset (Scarborough) 1981. HSBH: 45 v Warwickshire (Leeds) 1980.

Arnold SIDEBOTTOM (Broadway GS, Barnsley) B Barnsley 1/4/1954. RHB, RFM. Played for 2nd XI since 1971 and in Schools matches at Lord's in that year. Debut 1973. Cap 1980. HS: 124 v Glamorgan (Cardiff) 1977. HSGC/NW: 45 v Hants (Bournemouth) 1977. HSJPL: 31 v Sussex (Hove) 1975 and 31 v Northants (Scarborough) 1980. HSBH: 15 v Notts (Bradford) 1979. BB: 7-18 v Oxford U (Oxford) 1980. BBGC/NW: 4-35 v Kent (Leeds) 1980. BBJPL: 4-24 v Surrey (Scarborough) 1975. BBBH: 3-21 Minor Counties (North) (Jesmond) 1978. Soccer for Manchester United, Huddersfield Town and Halifax Town.

Graham Barry STEVENSON (Minsthorpe GS) B Ackworth (Yorks) 16/12/1955. RHB, RM. Played for 2nd XI in 1972. Debut 1973. Cap 1978. Tests: 2 in 1979-80 and 1980-81. Tours: Australia and India 1979-80 (flown out as a replacement for M. Hendrick), West Indies 1980-81. HS: 111 v Derbyshire (Chesterfield) 1980. HSTC: 27* v India (Bombay) 1979-80. HSGC/NW: 27 v Glos (Leeds) 1976. HSJPL: 56 v Somerset (Scarborough) 1981. HSBH: 16 v Middlesex (Lord's) 1977. BB: 8-57 v Northants (Leeds) 1980. BBTC: 3-111 v West Indies (St. John's) 1980-81. BBGC/NW: 4-57 v Lancs (Leeds) 1974. BBJPL: 5-41 v Leics (Leicester) 1976. BBBH: 5-28 v Kent (Canterbury) 1978.

Stephen STUCHBURY (Ecclesfield GS) B Sheffield 22/6/1954. LHB, LFM. Played for 2nd XI since 1975. Debut 1978. One match v New Zealanders (Leeds) and also played in six John Player League Matches. Did not play in 1979 or 1980. Re-appeared in 1981. HS: 4* v Lancs (Leeds) 1981. BB: 3-82 v Lancs (Leeds) 1981.

John Peter WHITELEY (Ashville College, Harrogate) B Otley, Yorks 28/2/1955. RHB, OB. Played for 2nd XI since 1972. Debut 1978. HS: 20 v Northants (Northampton) 1979. HSJPL: 14 v Lancs (Leeds) 1981. BB: 4-14 v Notts (Scarborough) 1978. Studied at Bristol University and obtained degree in Chemistry.

NB. The following player whose particulars appeared in the 1981 annual has been omitted: S.P. Coverdale.
In addition, J.H. Hampshire has joined Derbyshire and his particulars will be found under that county.

County Averages

Schweppes County Championship: Played 22, won 5, drawn 8, lost 9
All first-class matches: Played 24, won 5, drawn 10, lost 9.

BATTING AND FIELDING

Cap		M	I	NO	Runs	HS	Avge	100	50	Ct	St
1963	G. Boycott	10	16	2	617	124	44.07	2	2	4	—
1963	J.H. Hampshire	20	37	4	1425	127	43.18	4	6	17	—
1973	D.L. Bairstow	23	38	11	1083	88*	40.11	—	10	43	6
1980	J.D. Love	22	39	4	1161	161	34.14	2	6	17	—
1974	R.G. Lumb	15	25	1	706	145	29.41	1	3	1	—
—	K. Sharp	8	14	0	395	116	28.21	1	2	6	—
—	M.D. Moxon	11	19	0	518	116	27.26	2	—	8	—
—	S.N. Hartley	18	29	3	654	106	25.15	1	3	-9	—

YORKSHIRE

Cap		M	I	NO	Runs	HS	Avge	100	50	Ct	St
1980	C.W.J. Athey	21	38	2	891	123*	24.75	1	4	22	—
1969	C.M. Old	16	17	5	272	55	22.66	—	1	2	—
1980	A. Sidebottom	15	21	4	376	52*	22.11	—	1	5	—
—	A. Ramage	7	9	2	116	52	16.57	—	1	—	—
—	J.P. Whiteley	19	23	11	164	19*	13.66	—	—	8	—
1978	G.B. Stevenson	20	21	0	355	57	13.14	—	1	8	—
1976	P. Carrick	20	27	3	239	28	9.95	—	—	3	—
—	P.R. Hart	3	5	0	23	11	4.60	—	—	1	—
—	S.J. Dennis	6	7	3	14	5*	3.50	—	—	—	—
—	M. Johnson	4	4	2	2	1	1.00	—	—	1	—

Played in two matches: P.G. Ingham 15, 11, 17, 18; S. Stuchbury 2, 1*, 4*.
Played in one match: P.W. Jarvis 5, 0*; S.J. Rhodes did not bat.

BOWLING

	Type	O	M	R	W	Avge	Best	5 wI	10 wM
A. Sidebottom	RFM	304.5	88	899	47	19.12	6-62	3	—
C.M. Old	RFM	388.3	422	990	43	23.02	5-52	1	—
S.J. Dennis	LFM	162.1	36	490	20	24.50	5-35	1	—
S. Stuchbury	LFM	42	7	176	6	29.33	3-82	—	—
G.B. Stevenson	RM	537.4	122	1857	61	30.44	7-46	3	—
A. Ramage	RFM	148	22	550	18	30.55	5-65	1	—
J.P. Whiteley	OB	392	93	1124	34	33.05	4-50	—	—
P. Carrick	SLA	532.1	169	1412	35	40.34	4-76	—	—
M. Johnson	RM	85.5	17	301	7	43.00	4-48	—	—
S.N. Hartley	RM	124.1	22	479	9	53.22	1-13	—	—

Also bowled: C.W.J. Athey 39.3-7-111-2; D.L. Bairstow 6-1-14-0; G. Boycott 11-5-18-0; J.H. Hampshire 7-2-22-1; P.R. Hart 58-17-140-2; P.W. Jarvis 18-2-74-0; J.D. Love 20-4-71-0; M.D. Moxon 6-0-23-0

County Records

First-class cricket

Highest innings totals:	For	887 v Warwickshire (Birmingham)	1896
	Agst	630 by Somerset (Leeds)	1901
Lowest innings totals:	For	23 v Hampshire (Middlesbrough)	1965
	Agst	13 by Nottinghamshire (Nottingham)	1901
Highest individual innings:	For	341 G.H. Hirst v Leicestershire (Leicester)	1905
	Agst	318* W.G. Grace for Gloucestershire (Cheltenham)	1876
Best bowling in an innings:	For	10-10 H. Verity v Nottinghamshire (Leeds)	1932
	Agst	10-37 C.V. Grimmett for Australians (Sheffield)	1930
Best bowling in a match:	For	17-91 H. Verity v Essex (Leyton)	1933
	Agst	17-91 H. Dean for Lancashire (Liverpool)	1913
Most runs in a career:		38561 (av. 50.21) H. Sutcliffe	1919-1945
100s in a season:		12 by H. Sutcliffe	1932
100s in a career:		112 by H. Sutcliffe	1919-1945
wickets in a season:		240 (av. 12.72) W. Rhodes	1900
wickets in a career:		3608 (av. 16.00) W. Rhodes	1898-1930

RECORD WICKET STANDS

1st	555	P. Holmes & H. Sutcliffe v Essex (Leyton)	1932
2nd	346	W. Barber & M. Leyland v Middlesex (Sheffield)	1932
3rd	323	H. Sutcliffe & M. Leyland v Glamorgan (Huddersfield)	1928
4th	312	G.H. Hirst & D. Denton v Hampshire (Southampton)	1914
5th	340	E. Wainwright & G.H. Hirst v Surrey (The Oval)	1899
6th	276	M. Leyland & E. Robinson v Glamorgan (Swansea)	1926
7th	254	D.C.F. Burton & W. Rhodes v Hampshire (Dewsbury)	1919
8th	292	Lord Hawke & R. Peel v Warwickshire (Birmingham)	1896
9th	192	G.H. Hirst & S. Haigh v Surrey (Bradford)	1898
10th	148	Lord Hawke & D. Hunter v Kent (Sheffield)	1898

One-day cricket

Highest innings totals:	Gillette Cup/ NatWest Trophy	317-4 v Surrey (Lord's)	1965
	John Player League	248-5 v Derbyshire (Chesterfield)	1979
	Benson & Hedges Cup	269-6 v Worcestershire (Worcester)	1980
Lowest innings totals:	Gillette Cup/ NatWest Trophy	76 v Surrey (Harrogate)	1970
	John Player League	74 v Warwickshire (Birmingham)	1972
	Benson & Hedges Cup	114 v Kent (Canterbury)	1978
Highest individual innings:	Gillette Cup/ NatWest Trophy	146 G. Boycott v Surrey (Lord's)	1965
	John Player League	119 J.H. Hampshire v Leicestershire (Hull)	1971
	Benson & Hedges Cup	142 G. Boycott v Worcestershire (Worcester)	1980
Best bowling figures:	Gillette Cup/ NatWest Trophy	6-15 F.S. Trueman v Somerset (Taunton)	1965
	John Player League	7-15 R.A. Hutton v Worcestershire (Leeds)	1969
	Benson & Hedges Cup	6-27 A.G. Nicholson v Minor Counties (North) (Middlesbrough)	1972

CAMBRIDGE UNIVERSITY

Captain: D.R. Pringle
Secretary: S.J.G. Doggart

Robin James BOYD-MOSS (Bedford School and Magdalene College) B Hatton, Ceylon (now Sri Lanka) 16/2/1959. RHB, SLA. Played for Bedfordshire 1977-79. Debut for University and also for Northants 1980, Blue 1980-81. HS: 84 v Lancs (Cambridge) 1981. HSBH: 58 v Northants (Northampton) 1980. Rugby Blue 1980-81, 1981-82. Third year student, reading Land Economy.

Antony Roy CLARK (St Andrew's College, Grahamstown and Downing College) B Grahamstown, South Africa 7/11/1956. RHB. Debut 1981. One match v Notts. HS: 12 v Notts (Cambridge) 1981. Studied History as post-graduate student from Rhodes University, South Africa. No longer in residence.

Richard James COMPTON-BURNETT (Eton College and Pembroke College) B Windsor 1/7/1961. Son of A.C. Burnett, former Cambridge Blue and Glamorgan player. RHB. Played for Middlesex 2nd XI in 1979. Debut 1981. One match v Notts. HS: 18 v Notts (Cambridge) 1981. Second year student, reading Law.

Simon Jonathon Graham DOGGART (Winchester College and Magdalene College) B Winchester 8/2/1961. Son of G.H.G. Doggart and grandson of A.G. Doggart, both former Cambridge Blues, father also played for Sussex and England. LHB, OB. Debut 1980, Blue 1980-81. Secretary for 1982. HS: 69* v Lancs (Cambridge) 1981. BB: 3-54 v Oxford U (Lord's) 1980. Third year student, reading History.

Richard Stuart DUTTON (Wrekin College and Fitzwilliam College) B Liverpool 24/11/1959. RHB, RM. Debut 1981. HS: 7* v Northants (Cambridge) 1981. Third year student, reading History.

Timothy David Warneford EDWARDS (Sherborne School and St. John's College) B Merton (Surrey) 6/12/1958. LHB. Played for Hants 2nd XI since 1978. Debut 1979, Blue 1981. HS: 57 v Notts (Cambridge) 1981. Studied for degree in Law. No longer in residence.

Christopher Frederick Evelyn GOLDIE (St. Paul's School and Pembroke College) B Johannesburg 2/11/1960. RHB, WK. Played for Middlesex 2nd XI in 1979 and 1980 as member of county staff. Debut 1981, Blue 1981. HS: 77 v Oxford U. (Lord's) 1981. Third year student, reading Archaeology and Anthropology.

Kenneth Ian HODGSON (Oundle School and Downing College) B Port Elizabeth, South Africa 24/2/1960. RHB, RM. Played for Warwickshire 2nd XI in 1977 and Buckinghamshire in 1980. Debut 1981, Blue 1981. HS: 30* v Oxford U. (Lord's) 1981. HSBH: 16* v Somerset (Cambridge) 1981. BB: 4-77 v Sussex (Cambridge) 1981. Half-Blue for squash rackets. Third year student, reading Law.

Rupert James Alexander HUXTER (Magdalen College School, Oxford and St. Catharine's College) B Abingdon (Berks) 29/10/1959. RHB, RM. Debut 1981, Blue 1981. HS: 20 v Sussex (Cambridge) 1981. Studied for English Degree. No longer in residence.

John Peter Crispin MILLS (Oundle School and Corpus Christi College) B

Kettering (Northants) 6/12/1958. Son of J.M. Mills, former Cambridge captain. RHB, RM. Debut 1979, Blue 1979-80-81. Secretary for 1981. Debut for Northants 1981. HS: 111 Combined Universities v Sri Lankans (Oxford) 1981. HSBH: 19 v Kent (Canterbury) 1981. Fourth year student, reading Land Economy.

Anthony Johnathan MURLEY (Oundle School and St. Catharine's College) B Radlett (Herts) 7/8/1957. Son of Sir Reginald Murley (past President of The Royal College of Surgeons). RHB, RM. Played for Hertfordshire in 1979 and 1980. Debut 1981. HS: 48 v Northants (Cambridge) 1981. Blue for Golf and Half-Blue for Rugby Fives. Studied for Land Economy Degree. No longer in residence.

André ODENDAAL (Queen's College, Queenstown, Stellenbosch University and St. John's College) B Queenstown, South Africa 4/5/1954. RHB, OB. Debut 1980, Blue 1980. Not in residence in 1981, but has returned and will be available in 1982. Played for Boland in South African Breweries Bowl Competition in 1980-81. HS: 61 v Leics (Cambridge) 1980. HSBH: 74 v Warwickshire (Birmingham) 1980. Third year graduate student, reading for Doctor of Philosophy Degree. Has written books on South African cricket.

Robert William Michael PALMER (Bedford School and St. Catharine's College) B Hong Kong 4/6/1960. RHB, RM. Played for Warwickshire and Worcestershire 2nd XI's in 1979 and Worcs 2nd XI in 1980. Debut 1981. One match v Worcs (Cambridge). Second year student, reading Law.

Derek Raymond PRINGLE (Felsted School and Fitzwilliam College) B Nairobi, Kenya 18/9/1958. 6ft. 4½in. tall. Son of late Donald Pringle who played for East Africa in 1975 Prudential Cup. Debut for Essex 1978. Debut for University 1979, Blue 1979-80-81. Captain for 1982. HS: 127* v Worcs (Cambridge) 1981. HSBH: 58 v Essex (Cambridge) 1979. BB: 6-90 v Warwickshire (Cambridge) 1980. Fourth year student, reading Land Economy.

Harold Fleming TORKINGTON (Stockport GS and Fitzwilliam College) B Poynton (Cheshire) 4/12/1959. RHB. Has played for Cheshire. Debut 1981. One match v Notts (Cambridge). Studied Veterinary Surgery. No longer in residence.

David William VAREY (Birkenhead School and Pembroke College) B Darlington 15/10/1961. RHB. Played for Cheshire in 1977 and Lancashire 2nd XI 1980. Debut 1981. HS: 39 v Leics (Leicester) 1981. Second year student, reading French and German.

N.B. The following players whose particulars appeared in the 1981 annual have been omitted as they are no longer in residence: N.C. Crawford, P.D. Hemsley, D.C. Holliday, M.G. Howat, A.M. Mubarak, I.G. Peck and N. Russom.

CAMBRIDGE UNIVERSITY

UNIVERSITY RECORDS

Highest Innings	For	703-9d v Sussex (Hove)	1890
Totals:	Agst	703-3d by West Indians (Cambridge)	1950
Lowest Innings	For	30 v Yorkshire (Cambridge)	1928
Totals:	Agst	32 by Oxford U (Lord's)	1878
Highest Individual Innings:	For	254* K.S. Duleepsinhji v Middlesex (Cambridge)	1927
	Agst	304* E.D. Weekes for West Indies (Cambridge)	1950
Best Bowling in an Innings:	For	10-69 S.M.J. Woods v C.I. Thornton's XI (Cambridge)	1890
	Agst	10-38 S.E. Butler for Oxford U (Lord's)	1871
Best Bowling in a Match:	For	15-88 S.M.J. Woods v C.I. Thornton's XI (Cambridge)	1890
	Agst	15-95 S.E. Butler for Oxford U (Lord's)	1871
Most runs in a season:		1581 (av. 79.05) D.S. Sheppard	1952
runs in a career:		4310 (av.38.48) J.M. Brearley	1961-1968
100s in a season:		7 by D.S. Sheppard	1952
100s in a career:		14 by D.S. Sheppard	1950-1952
wickets in a season:		80 (av. 17.63) O.S. Wheatley	1958
wickets in a career:		208 (av. 21.82) G. Goonesena	1954-1959

RECORD WICKET STANDS

1st	349	J.G. Dewes & D.S. Sheppard v Sussex (Hove)	1950
2nd	429*	J.G. Dewes & G.H.G. Doggart v Essex (Cambridge)	1949
3rd	284	E.T. Killick & G.C. Grant v Essex (Cambridge)	1929
4th	275	R. de W.K. Winlaw & J.H. Human v Essex (Cambridge)	1934
5th	220	R. Subba Row & F.C.M. Alexander v Nottinghamshire (Nottingham)	1953
6th	245	J.L. Bryan & C.T. Ashton v Surrey (Oval)	1921
7th	289	G. Goonesena & G.W. Cook v Oxford U (Lord's)	1957
8th	145	H. Ashton & A.E.R. Gilligan v Free Foresters (Cambridge)	1920
9th	200	G.W. Cook & C.S. Smith v Lancashire (Liverpool)	1957
10th	177	A.E.R. Gilligan & J.H. Naumann v Sussex (Hove)	1919

OXFORD UNIVERSITY

Captain: R.G.P. Ellis
Secretary: K.A. Hayes

Ralph Stewart COWAN (Lewes Priory School and Magdalen College) B Hamlin, West Germany 30/3/1960, 6ft. 4in. tall. RHB, RM. Has played for Sussex 2nd XI. Debut 1980, Blue 1980-81. HS: 113 v Glos (Oxford) 1981. HSBH: 11 v Somerset (Cambridge) 1981. Soccer Blues 1979-80, 1980-81, 1981-82. Third year student, reading Chemistry.

Ian James CURTIS (Whitgift School and Lincoln College) B Purley (Surrey) 13/5/1959, 6ft. 3¾in. tall. LHB, SLA/SLC. Has played for Surrey 2nd XI. Debut 1980, Blue 1980. HS: 9* v Hants (Oxford) and 9 v Worcs (Oxford) 1980. HSBH: 12* v Northants (Northampton) 1980. BB: 4-58 v Yorks (Oxford) 1981. Half-Blues for Rugby Fives 1978-79 and 1979-80. Studied for Degree in Agricultural and Forest Sciences and is now in fourth year studying for D.Phil Degree.

Richard Gary Peter ELLIS (Haileybury College and St. Edmund Hall) B Paddington, London 20/12/1960. RHB, OB. Played for Middlesex 2nd XI in 1980. Debut 1981, Blue 1981. Captain for 1982. HS: 63 v Middlesex (Oxford) 1981. HSBH: 32 v Essex (Chelmsford) 1981. Half-Blue for Squash Rackets. Second year student, reading History.

Rupert Adam GORDON-WALKER (King Alfred's School, Wantage and Keble College) B Moniaive (Dumfriesshire) 10/8/1961. LHB, WK. Debut 1981. HS: 12 v Leics (Oxford) 1981. Second year student, reading History.

Simon John HALLIDAY (Downside School and St. Benet's Hall) B Haverfordwest (Pembrokeshire) 13/7/1960. RHB, RM. Has played for Dorset. Debut 1980, Blue 1980. Did not play in 1981. HS: 37 v Middlesex (Oxford) 1980. Rugby Blues 1979-80 and 1980-81. Studied for Degree in Classics and Modern Languages. Is now in fourth year studying for Certificate of Education.

Kevin Anthony HAYES (Queen Elizabeth's GS, Blackburn and Merton College) B Mexborough (Yorks) 26/9/1962. RHB, RM. Debut for Lancs 1980, Blue 1981. Secretary for 1982. HS: 59 v Glos (Oxford) 1981. HSBH: 17 v Essex (Chelmsford) 1981. Soccer Blues 1980-81, 1981-82. Second year student, studying Chemistry.

Peter Nigel HUXFORD (Richard Hale School, Hertford and Christ Church College) B Enfield (Middlesex) 17/2/1960. LHB, WK. Debut 1980, Blue 1981. HS: 10 v Kent (Oxford) 1981. Studied for Degree in Modern History and is now in fourth year studying for Certificate of Education.

Robert MARSDEN (Merchant Taylors' School, Northwood and Christ Church College) B Kensington, London 2/4/1959. RHB, OB. Debut 1979. Did not play in 1981. HS: 50 v Worcs (Oxford) 1980. Studied for Degree in History and is now in fourth year studying for Certificate of Education.

Roger Peter MOULDING (Haberdashers Aske's School, Elstree and Christ Church College) B Enfield (Middlesex) 3/1/1958. RHB, LB. Debut for Middlesex 1977. One match v Cambridge U (Cambridge). Debut for University 1978. Blues 1978-79-80-81. Secretary in 1979 and Captain in 1981. HS: 77* v Worcs (Worcester)

OXFORD UNIVERSITY

1978. HSBH: 27 v Somerset (Taunton) 1978. Obtained First-Class Honours Degree in Chemistry and is now in fifth year studying for D.Phil Degree.

Stuart Peter RIDGE (Dr. Challenor's GS, Amersham and Worcester College) B Beaconsfield (Bucks) 23/11/1961. RHB, RM. Played for Buckinghamshire in 1980. Debut 1981. One match v Leics. Soccer Blue (goalkeeper) 1981-82. Second year student, reading Physics.

Timothy John TAYLOR (Stockport GS and Magdalen College) B Romiley (Cheshire) 28/3/1961. RHB, SLA. Played for Cheshire 1980. Debut for University and Lancashire in 1981. Also played for Minor Counties v Sri Lankans (Reading) 1981. Blue 1981. HS: 28* v Kent (Oxford) 1981. BB: 5-81 v Middlesex (Oxford) 1981. Third year student, reading Law.

N.B. The following players whose particulars appeared in the 1981 annual have been omitted as they are no longer in residence: T.E.O. Bury, J.P. Durack, R.A.B. Ezekowitz, D.C.G. Foster, J.M. Knight, M.C.L. MacPherson, N.V.H. Mallett, J.O.D. Orders, J.L. Rawlinson, J.J. Rogers, C.J. Ross, J.F.W. Sanderson, S.P. Sutcliffe and S.M. Wookey.

UNIVERSITY RECORDS

Highest Innings	For	651 v Sussex (Hove)	1895
Totals:	Agst	679-6d by Australians (Oxford)	1938
Lowest Innings	For	12 v MCC (Oxford)	1877
Totals:	Agst	36 by MCC (Oxford)	1867
Highest Indi-	For	281 K.J. Key v Middlesex (Chiswick)	1887
vidual Innings:	Agst	338 W.W. Read for Surrey (Oval)	1888
Best Bowling	For	10-38 S.E. Butler v Cambridge U (Lord's)	1871
in an Innings:	Agst	10-49 W.G. Grace for MCC (Oxford)	1886
Best Bowling	For	15-95 S.E. Butler v Cambridge U (Lord's)	1871
in a Match:	Agst	16-225 J.E. Walsh for Leicestershire (Oxford)	1953
Most runs in a season:		1307 (av. 93.35) Nawab of Pataudi (Snr.)	1931
runs in a career:		3319 (av. 47.41) N.S. Mitchell-Innes	1934-1937
100s in a season:		6 by Nawab of Pataudi (Snr.)	1931
100s in a career:		9 by A.M. Crawley	1927-1930
		Nawab of Pataudi (Snr.)	1928-31
		N.S. Mitchell-Innes	1934-37
		M.P. Donnelly	1946-47
wickets in a season:		70 (av. 18.15) I.A.R. Peebles	1930
wickets in a career:		182 (av. 19.38) R.H.B. Bettington	1920-1923

RECORD WICKET STANDS

1st	338	T. Bowring & H. Teesdale v Gentlemen (Oxford)	1908
2nd	226	W.G. Keighley & H.A. Pawson v Cambridge U (Lord's)	1947
3rd	273	F.C. de Saram & N.S. Mitchell-Innes v Gloucestershire (Oxford)	1934
4th	276	P.G.T. Kingsley & N.M. Ford v Surrey (Oval)	1930
5th	256*	A.A. Baig & C.A. Fry v Free Foresters (Oxford)	1959
6th	270	D.R. Walsh & S.A. Westley v Warwickshire (Oxford)	1969
7th	340	K.J. Key & H. Philipson v Middlesex (Oxford)	1887
8th	133	J.V. Richardson & T.B. Raikes v Free Foresters (Oxford)	1924
9th	160	H. Philipson & A.C.M. Croome v MCC (Lord's)	1889
10th	149	F.H. Hollins & B.A. Collins v MCC (Oxford)	1901

THE FIRST-CLASS UMPIRES FOR 1982

N.B. The abbreviations used below are as for 'The Counties and their Players'.

William Edward (Bill) ALLEY B Sydney, Australia 3/2/1919. LHB, RM. Played for New South Wales 1945-46 to 1947-48. Subsequently came to England to play League cricket and then for Somerset from 1957 to 1968. *Wisden* 1961. Testimonial (£2,700) in 1961. Tours: India and Pakistan 1949-50, Pakistan 1963-64 with Commonwealth team. Scored 3,019 runs (av. 56.96) in 1961 including 2,761 runs and 10 centuries for county, both being records. Gillette Man of Match Awards: 3. HS: 221* v Warwickshire (Nuneaton) 1961. BB: 8-65 v Surrey (Oval) 1962. Career record: 19,612 runs (av. 31.88), 31 centuries, 768 wkts (av. 22.68). Appointed 1969. Umpired in 10 Tests between 1974 and 1981.

Harold Denis BIRD B Barnsley 19/4/1933. RHB, RM. Played for Yorks from 1956 to 1959 and for Leics from 1960 to 1964. Was subsequently professional at Paignton CC. HS: 181* Yorks v Glamorgan (Bradford) 1959. Career record: 3,315 runs (av. 20.71), 2 centuries. Appointed 1970. Umpired in 21 Tests between 1973 and 1981.

Jack BIRKENSHAW B Rothwell (Yorks) 13/11/1940. LHB, OB. Played for Yorks from 1958 to 1960, for Leics from 1961 to 1980 and for Worcs in 1981. Benefit (£13,000) in 1974. Tests: 5 in 1972-73 and 1973-74. Tours: India, Pakistan and Sri Lanka 1972-73, West Indies 1973-74. Gillette Man of Match Awards: 1 (for Leics). HS: 131 Leics v Surrey (Guildford) 1969. BB: 8-94 Leics v Somerset (Taunton) 1972. Career Record: 12,780 runs (av. 23.57), 4 centuries, 1,073 wkts (av. 27.28). Appointed 1982.

William Lloyd BUDD B Hawkley (Hants) 25/10/1913. RHB, RFM. Played for Hampshire from 1934 to 1946. HS: 77* v Surrey (Oval) 1937. BB: 4-22 v Essex (Southend) 1937. Career record: 941 runs (av. 11.47), 64 wkts (av. 39.15). Was on Minor Counties list for some years. Appointed 1969. Umpired in 4 Tests between 1976 and 1978.

David John CONSTANT B Bradford-on-Avon (Wilts) 9/11/1941. LHB, SLA. Played for Kent from 1961 to 1963 and for Leics from 1965 to 1968. HS: 80 v Glos (Bristol) 1966. Career record: 1,517 runs (av. 19.20), 1 wkt (36.00). Appointed 1969. Umpired in 22 Tests between 1971 and 1981.

Cecil (Sam) COOK B Tetbury (Glos) 23/8/1921. RHB, SLA. Played for Gloucestershire from 1946 to 1964. Benefit (£3,067) in 1957. Took wicket with first ball in first-class cricket. Tests: 1 v SA 1947. HS: 35* v Sussex (Hove) 1957. BB: 9-42 v Yorks (Bristol) 1947. Career record: 1,964 runs (av. 5.39), 1,782 wkts (av. 20.52). Appointed 1971, after having withdrawn from appointment in 1966.

Peter James EELE B Taunton 27/1/1935. LHB, WK. Played for Somerset between 1958 and 1966. HS: 103* v Pakistan Eaglets (Taunton) 1963. Career record: 612 runs (av. 12.24), 1 century, 106 dismissals (87 ct, 19 st). Appointed 1981.

David Gwilliam Lloyd EVANS B Lambeth, London 27/7/1933. RHB, WK. Played for Glamorgan from 1956 to 1969. Benefit (£3,500) in 1969. HS: 46* v Oxford U (Oxford) 1961. Career record: 2,875 runs (av. 10.53), 558 dismissals (502 ct, 56 st). Appointed 1971. Umpired in 1 Test in 1981.

Robert Stephen (Bob) HERMAN B Southampton 30/11/1946. Son of O.W. ('Lofty') Herman (former Hants player and first-class umpire). RHB, RFM. Played for Middlesex from 1965 to 1971 and for Hants from 1972 to 1977. Played for Dorset in 1978 and 1979. Benson & Hedges Gold Awards: 2. HS: 56 v Worcs (Portsmouth) 1972. BB: 8-42 v Warwickshire (Portsmouth) 1972. Career record: 1,426 runs (av. 10.25), 506 wkts (av. 26.28). Appointed 1980.

Khalid (Billy) IBADULLA B Lahore 20/12/1935. RHB, RM/OB. Played for Warwickshire from 1954 to 1972, having made first-class debut for Pakistan touring team in India 1952-53. Also played for Otago and Tasmania whilst coaching there. Benefit (£7,797) in 1969. Has coached in this country and New Zealand since retirement. Tests: 4 for Pakistan between 1964-65 and 1967. Gillette Man of Match Awards: 2. HS: 171 v Oxford U (Oxford) 1961. BB: 7-22 v Derbyshire (Chesterfield) 1967. Career record: 17,039 runs (av. 27.30), 22 centuries, 462 wkts (av. 30.87). Appointed 1982.

Arthur JEPSON B Selston (Notts) 12/7/1915. RHB, RFM. Played for Notts from 1938 to 1959. Benefit (£2,000) in 1951. HS: 130 v Worcs (Nottingham) 1950. BB: 8-45 v Leics (Nottingham) 1958. Career record: 6,369 runs (av. 14.31), 1 century, 1,051 wkts (av. 29.08). Soccer (goalkeeper) for Port Vale, Stoke City and Lincoln City. Appointed 1960 and is longest-serving umpire on list. Umpired in 4 Tests between 1966 and 1969.

Raymond (Ray) JULIEN B Cosby (Leics) 23/8/1936. RHB, WK. Played for Leicestershire from 1953 (debut at age of 16) to 1971, but lost regular place in side to R.W. Tolchard in 1966. HS: 51 v Worcs (Worcester) 1962. Career record: 2,581 runs (av. 9.73), 421 dismissals (382 ct, 39 st). Appointed 1972.

Mervyn John KITCHEN B Nailsea (Somerset) 1/8/1940. LHB, RM. Played for Somerset from 1960 to 1979. Testimonial (£6,000) in 1973. Gillette Man of Match Awards: 2. Benson & Hedges Gold Awards: 1. HS: 189 v Pakistanis (Taunton) 1967. Career record: 15,230 runs (av. 26.25), 17 centuries, 2 wkts (av. 54.50). Appointed 1982.

Barrie LEADBEATER B Harehills, Leeds 14/8/1943. RHB, RM. Played for Yorkshire from 1966 to 1979. Joint benefit in 1980 with G.A. Cope. Gillette Man of Match Awards: 1 (in 1969 Cup Final). HS: 140* v Hants (Portsmouth) 1976. Career record: 5,373 runs (av. 25.34), 1 century, 1 wkt (av. 5.00). Appointed 1981.

Barrie John MEYER B Bournemouth 21/8/1932. RHB, WK. Played for Gloucestershire from 1957 to 1971. Benefit 1971. HS: 63 v Indians (Cheltenham) 1959, v Oxford U (Bristol) 1962 and v Sussex (Bristol) 1964. Career record: 5,367 runs (av. 14.19), 826 dismissals (707 ct, 119 st). Soccer for Bristol Rovers, Plymouth Argyle, Newport County and Bristol City. Appointed 1973. Umpired in 8 Tests between 1978 and 1981.

Donald (Don) Osmund OSLEAR B Cleethorpes (Lincs) 3/3/1929. Has not played first-class cricket. Played soccer for Grimsby Town, Hull City and Oldham Athletic. Also played ice hockey. Has umpired in county second XI matches since 1972. Appointed in 1975. Umpired in 4 Tests in 1980 and 1981.

Kenneth Ernest (Ken) PALMER B Winchester 22/4/1937. RHB, RFM. Played for Somerset from 1955 to 1969. Testimonial (£4,000) in 1968. Tour: Pakistan with Commonwealth team 1963-64. Coached in Johannesburg 1964-65 and was called upon by MCC to play in final Test v South Africa owing to injuries to other bowlers. Tests: 1 v South Africa 1964-65. HS: 125* v Northants (Northampton) 1961. BB: 9-

57 v Notts (Nottingham) 1963. Career record: 7,771 runs (av. 20.66), 2 centuries, 866 wkts (av. 21.34). Appointed 1972. Umpired in 8 Tests between 1978 and 1981.

Roy PALMER B Devizes (Wilts) 12/7/1942. RHB, RFM. Younger brother of K.E. Palmer. Played for Somerset from 1965 to 1970. Gillette Man of Match Awards: 2. HS: 84 v Leics (Taunton) 1967. BB: 6-45 v Middlesex (Lord's) 1967. Career record: 1,037 runs (av. 13.29). 172 wkts (av. 31.62). Appointed 1980.

Nigel Trevor PLEWIS B Nottingham 5/9/1934. Former policeman. Has not played first-class cricket. Umpired in 2nd XI games since 1968. On Minor Counties reserve list 1980, and on list 1981. Appointed 1982.

David Robert SHEPHERD B Bideford (Devon) 27/12/1940. RHB, RM. Played for Gloucestershire from 1965 to 1979, scoring 108 in debut match v Oxford U. Joint benefit in 1978 with J. Davey. Gillette Man of Match Awards: 1. Benson & Hedges Gold Awards: 1. HS: 153 v Middlesex (Bristol) 1968. Career record: 10,672 runs (av. 24.47), 12 centuries, 2 wkts (av. 53.00). Appointed 1981.

Charles Terry SPENCER B Leicester 18/8/1931. RHB, RFM. Played for Leicestershire from 1952 to 1974. Benefit (£3,500) in 1964. HS: 90 v Essex (Leicester) 1964. BB: 9-63 v Yorks (Huddersfield) 1954. Career record: 5,871 runs (av. 10.77), 1,367 wkts (av. 26.69). Appointed 1979.

Jack VAN GELOVEN B Leeds 4/1/1934. RHB, RM. Played for Yorkshire in 1955 and for Leicestershire from 1956 to 1965. Subsequently played for Northumberland in Minor Counties competition from 1966 to 1973. HS: 157* v Somerset (Leicester) 1960. BB: 7-56 v Hants (Leicester) 1959. Career record: 7,522 runs (av. 19.43), 5 centuries, 486 wkts (av. 28.62). Appointed 1977.

Alan Geoffrey Thomas WHITEHEAD B Butleigh (Somerset) 28/10/1940. LHB, SLA. Played for Somerset from 1957 to 1961. HS: 15 v Hants (Southampton) 1959 and 15 v Leics (Leicester) 1960. BB: 6-74 v Sussex (Eastbourne) 1959. Career record: 137 runs (av. 5.70), 67 wkts (av. 34.41). Served on Minor Counties list in 1969. Appointed 1970.

Peter Bernard WIGHT B Georgetown, British Guiana 25/6/1930. RHB, OB. Played for British Guiana in 1950-51 and for Somerset from 1953 to 1965. Benefit (£5,000) in 1963. HS: 222* v Kent (Taunton) 1959. BB: 6-29 v Derbyshire (Chesterfield) 1957. Career record: 17,773 runs (av. 33.09), 28 centuries, 68 wkts (av. 32.26). Appointed 1966.

NB. The Test match panel for 1982 is H.D. Bird, D.J. Constant, D.G.L. Evans, B.J. Meyer, K.E. Palmer and A.G.T. Whitehead.

FIRST CLASS AVERAGES 1981

Compiled by Barry McCaully

The following averages include everyone who appeared in first-class cricket during the season.

†*Indicates left-handed batsman*

Batting and fielding

	Cap	M	I	NO	Runs	HS	Avge	100	50	Ct	St
†Abrahams, J. (La)	—	14	22	4	438	74	24.33	—	2	8	—
Acfield, D.L. (Ex)	1970	22	18	11	40	8*	5.71	—	—	5	—
Agnew, J.P. (Le)	—	12	16	6	143	26	14.30	—	—	9	—
Alderman, T.M. (Aus)	—	12	11	6	34	12*	6.80	—	—	11	—
Alleyne, H.L. (Wo)	1981	13	13	3	43	16	4.30	—	—	2	—
Allott, P.J.W. (E/La/TCC)	1981	22	28	8	243	52*	12.15	—	1	6	—
Amiss, D.L. (Wa)	1965	22	41	0	1722	145	42.00	6	5	13	—
Anderson, I.J. (Ire)	—	1	1	0	99	99	99.00	—	1	—	—
Anderson, I.S. (D)	—	11	15	4	96	44	8.72	—	—	8	—
Arnold, G.G. (Sx)	1979	18	17	7	180	46*	18.00	—	—	7	—
Asif Din (Wa)	—	21	37	4	878	73*	26.60	—	4	11	—
Asif Iqbal (K)	1968	19	31	3	1252	112	44.71	2	9	5	—
Aslett, D.G. (K)	—	2	4	2	188	146*	94.00	1	—	1	—
Athey, C.W.J. (Y/MCC)	1980	22	40	2	930	123*	24.47	1	4	22	—
Bailey, D. (MCo)	—	1	2	1	53	33	53.00	—	—	—	—
†Bailey, M.J. (H)	—	10	13	3	67	14	6.70	—	—	6	—
Bainbridge, P. (Gs)	1981	22	36	11	1019	105*	40.76	2	8	8	—
Bairstow, D.L. (Y)	1973	23	38	11	1083	88*	40.11	—	10	43	6
Balderstone, J.C. (Le)	1973	23	39	3	1266	150*	35.16	3	5	16	—
Baptiste, E.A. (K)	—	15	22	4	359	37*	19.94	—	—	8	—
Barclay, J.R.T. (Sx/TCC)	1976	23	38	5	874	107*	26.48	2	3	30	—
†Barlow, G.D. (M)	1976	22	38	5	1313	177	39.78	4	3	9	—
Barnett, K.J. (D)	—	17	23	4	443	67*	23.31	—	3	11	—
Barwick, S.R. (Gm)	—	5	4	3	20	11*	20.00	—	—	1	—
Beard, G. R. (Aus)	—	9	9	2	131	36	18.71	—	—	—	—
Bell, D.L. (Sc)	—	1	2	1	90	60	90.00	—	1	—	—
†Benson, M.R. (K)	1981	21	36	3	1063	114	32.21	2	6	9	—
Birch, J.D. (Nt)	1981	20	27	6	757	111	36.04	1	5	18	—
†Birkenshaw, J. (Wo)	—	10	10	0	165	54	16.50	—	1	10	—
Booden, C.D. (No)	—	2	2	1	4	4*	4.00	—	—	1	—
Boon, T.J. (Le)	—	15	26	2	542	83	22.58	—	2	7	—
Booth, P. (Le)	1976	5	7	1	116	35*	19.33	—	—	4	—
Booth Jones, T.D. (Sx)	—	16	27	0	541	95	20.03	—	3	6	—
†Border, A.R. (Aus)	—	13	21	5	807	123*	50.43	3	4	16	—
Bore, M.K. (Nt)	1980	15	14	5	60	11*	6.66	—	—	4	—
Botham, I.T. (E/So)	1976	16	24	2	925	149*	42.04	3	4	19	—
Boycott, G. (E/Y)	1963	16	28	2	1009	137	38.80	3	3	6	—
Boyd-Moss, R.J. (No/CU/OCU)	—	17	32	3	522	84	18.00	—	3	6	—

	Cap	M	I	NO	Runs	HS	Avge	100	50	Ct	St
Brain, B.M. (Gs)	1977	9	6	2	59	42	14.75	—	—	3	—
Brassington, A.J. (Gs)	1978	4	3	1	10	9	5.00	—	—	3	1
†Breakwell, D. (So)	1976	12	13	2	284	58	25.81	—	3	2	—
Brearley, J.M. (E/M)	1964	19	33	1	1445	145	45.15	6	5	14	—
Briers, N.E. (Le)	1981	23	36	3	1194	116	36.18	3	5	7	—
Bright, R.J. (Aus)	—	15	18	1	280	42	16.47	—	—	12	—
†Broad, B.C. (Gs)	1981	22	40	4	1117	115	31.02	1	6	15	—
Brown, A. (Sc)	—	1	0	16	16	16.00	—	—	2	—
†Butcher, A.R. (Sy)	1975	19	38	6	1444	154*	45.12	4	5	14	—
Butcher, I.P. (Le)	—	1	2	0	56	42	28.00	—	—	—	—
Butcher, R.O. (M)	1979	20	33	3	695	106*	23.16	1	5	32	—
Capel, D.J. (No)	—	1	2	1	37	37	37.00	—	—	1	—
Carrick, P. (Y)	1976	20	27	3	239	28	9.95	—	—	3	—
Carter, R.M. (No)	—	15	17	3	132	42*	9.42	—	—	9	—
Chappell, T.M. (Aus)	—	12	18	2	409	91	25.56	—	2	3	—
†Cheatle, R.G.L. (Sy)	—	1	1	1	5	5*	—	—	—	1	—
†Childs, J.H. (Gs)	1977	22	18	10	120	20	15.00	—	—	13	—
Clark, A.R. (CU)	—	1	2	0	13	12	6.50	—	—	—	—
Clark, J. (Sc)	—	1	1	0	22	22	22.00	—	—	—	—
Clarke, S.T. (Sy)	1980	10	14	1	342	100*	26.30	1	1	8	—
Clift, P.B. (Le)	1976	11	17	2	430	73	28.66	—	2	8	—
†Clinton, G.S. (Sy)	1980	22	44	2	1191	123	28.35	3	6	7	—
Cobb, R.A. (Le)	—	8	12	0	275	54	22.91	—	1	5	—
Cockbain, I. (La)	—	6	10	1	262	85	29.11	—	2	4	—
Compton-Burnett, R.J. (CU)	—	1	2	0	23	18	11.50	—	—	—	—
Cook, C.R. (M)	—	6	12	2	249	79	24.90	—	1	5	—
Cook, G. (No)	1975	24	43	3	1759	146*	43.97	5	11	23	—
Cook, N.G.B. (Le/MCC)	—	25	25	8	184	62	10.82	—	1	18	—
†Cooper, K.E. (Nt)	1980	19	20	2	132	27	7.33	—	—	8	—
Corlett, S.C. (Ire)	—	1	1	0	1	1	1.00	—	—	—	—
Cowan, R.S. (OU)	—	8	15	0	406	113	27.06	1	2	10	1
Cowans, N.G. (M)	—	3	1	0	10	10	10.00	—	—	2	—
Cowdrey, C.S. (K)	1979	17	27	4	757	97	32.91	—	6	15	—
Cowley, N.G. (H)	1978	23	29	1	451	67	16.10	—	2	4	—
Cumbes, J. (Wo)	1978	10	9	4	50	15*	10.00	—	—	2	—
†Curtis, I.J. (OU)	—	3	4	0	7	7	1.75	—	—	2	—
Curtis, T.S. (Wo)	—	5	7	1	38	11	6.33	—	—	—	—
Curzon, C.C. (H)	—	1	2	1	53	31*	53.00	—	—	1	—
Daniel, W.W. (M)	1977	21	22	11	195	53*	17.72	—	1	2	—
Daniels, S.A.B. (Gm)	—	5	8	4	30	10*	7.50	—	—	4	—
Davies, T. (Gm)	—	1	2	0	15	11	7.50	—	—	5	1
Davison, B.F. (Le)	1971	22	35	5	1198	123*	39.93	1	9	21	—
Deakin, M.J. (D)	—	4	6	0	45	15	7.50	—	—	9	—
De Mel, A.L.F. (SL)	—	10	13	1	229	94	19.08	—	2	3	—
†Denning, P.W. (So)	1973	24	36	6	1087	102*	36.23	1	8	14	—
Dennis, S.J. (Y)	—	6	7	3	14	5*	3.50	—	—	—	—
De Silva, D.S. (SL)	—	6	6	1	186	97	37.20	—	1	2	—
†De Silva, G.R.A. (SL)	—	8	9	2	35	11	5.00	—	—	4	—
Devapriya, H.H. (SL)	—	5	10	0	247	68	24.70	—	2	9	3
Dexter, R.E. (Nt)	—	8	14	3	209	57	19.00	—	1	13	—
Dias, R.L. (SL)	—	11	17	2	607	127	40.46	1	2	6	—

181

	Cap	M	I	NO	Runs	HS	Avge	100	50	Ct	St
†Dilley, G.R. (E/K)	1980	14	14	6	189	56	23.62	—	1	5	—
Dixon, J.H. (Gs)	—	1	—	—	—	—	—	—	—	—	—
†Doggart, S.J.G. (CU)	—	7	8	3	139	69*	27.80	—	1	1	—
Donald, W.A. (Sc)	—	1	2	0	35	18	17.50	—	—	1	—
†Doshi, D.R. (Wa)	1980	18	22	12	98	35	9.80	—	—	4	—
Doughty, R.J. (Gs)	—	1	2	0	17	10	8.50	—	—	—	—
Downton, P.R. (E/M/TCC)	1981	23	29	6	382	44	16.60	—	—	45	8
†Dredge, C.H. (So)	1978	19	16	10	51	14	8.50	—	—	9	—
Dudleston, B. (Gs)	—	1	1	0	99	99	99.00	—	1	2	—
Dutton, R.S. (CU)	—	4	3	3	7	7*	—	—	—	2	—
Dyer, R.I.H.B. (Wa)	—	2	4	0	23	9	5.75	—	—	2	—
Dyson, J. (Aus)	—	13	20	1	582	102	30.63	1	3	2	—
Ealham, A.G.E. (K)	1970	3	5	0	141	48	28.20	—	—	2	—
East, D.E. (Ex)	—	13	17	3	144	28	10.28	—	—	21	5
East, R.E. (Ex)	1967	20	25	4	333	47	15.85	—	—	9	—
Edmonds, P.H. (M)	1974	23	31	6	391	93	15.64	—	1	24	—
†Edwards, T.D.W. (CU)	—	10	18	1	366	57	21.52	—	1	4	—
Ellis, R.G.P. (OU/OCU)	—	9	17	0	462	63	27.17	—	3	7	—
†Ellison, R.M. (K)	—	7	11	6	237	61*	47.40	—	3	3	—
Emburey, J.E. (E/M/TCC)	1977	18	21	4	330	57	19.41	—	1	21	—
Ezekowitz, R.A.B. (OU)	—	8	15	0	295	93	19.66	—	1	6	—
Featherstone, N.G. (Gm)	1980	23	39	5	1105	113*	32.50	2	9	27	—
Fernando, L.J. (SL)	—	4	1	1	7	7*	—	—	—	4	—
Ferreira, A.M. (Wa)	—	15	24	6	583	67*	32.38	—	3	4	—
Fisher, P.B. (Wo)	—	7	8	3	74	28*	14.80	—	—	5	—
Fletcher, K.W.R. (Ex)	1963	18	29	4	1180	165*	47.20	4	5	18	—
Foster, N.A. (Ex)	—	1	1	1	8	8*	—	—	—	—	—
†Fowler, G. (La)	1981	24	42	3	1560	143	40.00	3	9	24	3
Francis, D.A. (Gm)	—	3	5	0	67	28	13.40	—	—	2	—
French, B.N. (Nt)	1980	20	23	0	261	31	11.34	—	—	51	2
Garner, J. (So)	1979	18	18	2	324	90	20.25	—	2	10	—
Garnham, M.A. (Le)	—	18	27	4	513	74	22.30	—	1	45	7
Gatting, M.W. (E/M/TCC)	1977	19	33	6	1492	186*	55.25	4	7	22	—
†Gifford, N. (Wo)	1961	24	23	8	284	37*	18.93	—	—	5	—
†Gladwin, C. (Ex)	—	1	1	0	53	53	53.00	—	1	—	—
Goldie, C.F.E. (CU/OCU)	—	11	13	2	181	77	16.45	—	1	11	2
Gooch, G.A. (E/Ex/MCC)	1975	16	31	0	1345	164	43.38	5	5	11	—
†Gordon-Walker, R.A. (OU)	—	3	5	1	19	12	4.75	—	—	3	2
†Gould, I.J. (Sx)	1981	21	26	3	594	52	25.82	—	2	59	6
†Gower, D.I. (E/Le/MCC)	1977	19	33	4	1418	156*	48.89	5	7	20	—
Graveney, D.A. (Gs)	1976	20	22	7	427	105*	28.46	1	—	10	—
Green, A.M. (Sx)	—	3	5	0	107	38	21.40	—	—	1	—
Greenidge, C.G. (H)	1972	19	30	1	1442	140	49.72	4	9	24	—
Greensword, S. (MCo)	—	1	1	0	10	10	10.00	—	—	—	—
Greig, I.A. (Sx)	1981	23	34	4	911	118*	30.36	1	4	14	—
Griffiths, A. (MCo)	—	1	1	0	26	26	26.00	—	—	—	—
Griffiths, B.J. (No)	1978	23	16	5	30	8	2.72	—	—	4	—
†Gunasekera, Y. (SL)	—	6	7	1	216	63	36.00	—	2	3	—

182

	Cap	M	I	NO	Runs	HS	Avge	100	50	Ct	St
Gunatilleke, H.M. (SL)	—	9	10	4	78	24	13.00	—	—	11	8
Hacker, P.J. (Nt)	1980	7	5	4	18	8*	18.00	—	—	2	—
†Hadlee, R.J. (Nt)	1978	21	26	3	745	142*	32.39	1	3	14	—
Halliday, M. (Ire)	—	1	1	1	4	4*	—	—	—	—	—
Hampshire, J.H. (Y)	1963	20	37	4	1425	127	43.18	4	6	17	—
Hardie, B.R. (Ex)	1974	23	39	4	1339	129	38.25	3	7	17	—
Harpur, T. (Ire)	—	1	1	0	6	6	6.00	—	—	1	—
Harris, M.J. (Nt)	1970	8	10	4	162	44*	27.00	—	—	8	—
Hart, P.R. (Y)	—	3	5	0	23	11	4.60	—	—	1	—
Harte, C.C.J. (Ire)	—	1	1	0	39	39	39.00	—	—	—	—
Hartley, S.N. (Y)	—	18	29	3	654	106	25.15	1	3	9	—
Hassan, S.B. (Nt)	1970	13	20	5	641	97*	42.73	—	6	15	—
Hayes, F.C. (La)	1972	12	20	3	470	126	27.64	1	2	3	—
Hayes, K.A. (La/OU)	—	7	12	0	273	59	22.75	—	2	1	—
†Hayward, R.E. (H)	—	7	13	3	285	101*	28.50	1	1	3	—
Head, T.J. (Sx)	—	2	4	1	73	52*	24.33	—	1	6	—
†Heath, J.R.P. (Sx)	—	4	7	2	215	101*	43.00	1	1	2	—
Hemmings, E.E. (Nt)	1980	22	23	4	257	44	13.52	—	—	6	—
Hemsley, E.J.O. (Wo)	1969	20	30	5	540	73	21.60	—	1	11	—
Hemsley, P.D. (CU)	—	2	4	1	14	10	4.66	—	—	1	—
†Henderson, S.P. (Wo)	—	6	9	1	83	37	10.37	—	—	—	—
Hendrick, M. (E/D)	1972	13	12	6	87	21	14.50	—	—	8	—
Hettiaratchy, N.D.P. (SL)	—	10	13	1	400	80	33.33	—	3	11	—
Hignell, A.J. (Gs)	1977	22	33	5	979	102*	34.96	1	5	20	—
Hill, A. (D)	1976	22	32	8	940	107	39.16	2	5	6	—
Hobbs, R.N.S. (Gm)	1979	15	15	10	101	49*	20.20	—	—	7	—
Hodgson, K.I. (CU)	—	9	9	3	148	30*	24.66	—	—	2	—
Hogg, R.M. (Aus)	—	11	8	2	15	6	2.50	—	—	2	—
Hogg, W. (Wa/MCC)	—	23	27	3	193	31	8.04	—	—	3	—
Holding, M.A. (La)	—	7	8	2	66	32	11.00	—	—	2	—
Holliday, D.C. (CU)	—	10	11	2	204	57	22.66	—	1	6	—
Holmes, G.C. (Gm)	—	14	23	8	394	70*	26.26	—	2	6	—
Hopkins, D.C. (Wa)	—	1	1	0	17	17	17.00	—	—	1	—
Hopkins, J.A. (Gm)	1977	23	41	1	1217	135	30.42	4	3	15	—
Howarth, G.P. (Sy)	1974	8	16	1	480	110*	32.00	1	3	3	—
Hughes, D.P. (La)	1970	24	39	5	1002	126	29.47	1	5	19	—
Hughes, K.J. (Aus)	—	15	24	1	679	89	29.52	—	5	8	—
Hughes, S.P. (M/TCC)	1981	13	14	5	57	18	6.33	—	—	3	—
Humpage, G.W. (Wa/MCC)	1976	22	39	5	1701	146	50.02	6	7	37	10
†Humphries, D.J. (Wo)	1978	18	28	7	575	64*	27.38	—	4	29	14
†Huxford, P.N. (OU)	—	5	8	4	23	10	5.75	—	—	3	2
Huxter, R.J.A. (CU)	—	4	5	0	34	20	6.80	—	—	—	—
Illingworth, N.J.B. (Nt)	—	1								1	—
Imran Khan (Sx)	1978	18	27	6	857	107*	40.80	2	3	6	—
Inchmore, J.D. (Wo)	1976	18	21	2	428	63*	22.52	—	1	3	—
Ingham, P.G. (Y)	—	2	4	0	61	18	15.25	—	—	—	—
Intikhab Alam (Sy)	1969	17	31	3	469	79	16.75	—	2	2	—
Jackman, R.D. (Sy/MCC)	1970	20	26	10	331	31	20.08	—	1	7	—
Jackson, P.B. (Ire)	—	1	1	1	42	42*	—	—	—	—	—
James, K.D. (M)	—	1	1	1	5	5*	—	—	—	1	—
Jarvis, K.B.S. (K)	1977	23	17	4	26	12	2.00	—	—	7	—

183

	Cap	M	I	NO	Runs	HS	Avge	100	50	Ct	St
Jarvis, P.W. (Y)	—	1	2	1	5	5	5.00	—	—	—	—
Javed Miandad (Gm)	1980	22	37	7	2083	200*	69.43	8	7	11	—
Jennings, K.F. (So)	—	2	1	0	4	4	4.00	—	—	2	—
Jesty, T.E. (H)	1971	23	35	6	891	99	30.72	—	5	13	—
Johnson, G.W. (K)	1970	24	38	8	698	107	23.26	1	1	15	—
Johnson, M. (Y)	—	4	4	2	2	2	1.00	—	—	1	—
Johnson, P.D. (MCo)	—	1	2	0	66	66	33.00	—	1	—	—
Johnston, H.G.F. (Sc)	—	1	1	0	0	0	0.00	—	—	—	—
†Jones, A. (Gm)	1962	23	41	2	1192	109	30.56	1	5	5	—
Jones, A.A. (Gm)	—	3	3	2	14	9	14.00	—	—	1	—
†Jones, A.L. (Gm)	—	6	12	1	204	81	18.54	—	1	3	—
†Jones, A.N. (Sx)	—	5	5	2	17	8	5.66	—	—	1	—
Jones, E.W. (Gm)	1967	23	31	2	232	33	8.00	—	—	46	10
†Kallicharran, A.I. (Wa)	1972	13	23	6	923	135	54.29	3	4	7	—
Kaluperuma, L.W. (SL)	—	11	14	4	189	40	18.90	—	—	6	—
Kapil Dev (No)	—	3	5	0	175	79	35.00	—	1	1	—
Kemp, N.J. (K)	—	1	1	1	5	5*	—	—	—	—	—
†Kennedy, A. (La)	1975	24	42	0	1044	180	24.85	1	3	5	—
Kent, M.F. (Aus)	—	10	15	0	347	92	23.13	—	3	11	—
Ker, A.B.M. (Sc)	—	1	2	0	65	65	32.50	—	1	—	—
Ker, J.E. (Sc)	—	1	1	1	24	24*	—	—	—	—	—
Kirsten, P.N. (D)	1978	21	35	6	1605	228	55.34	3	7	11	—
Knight, J.M. (OU)	—	5	9	2	136	41*	19.42	—	—	1	—
†Knight, R.D.V. (Sy/MCC)	1978	22	42	1	1045	96	25.48	—	6	16	—
Knott, A.P.E. (E/K)	1965	21	32	5	795	70*	29.44	—	6	45	8
Lamb, A.J. (No)	1978	24	43	9	2049	162	60.26	5	14	20	—
Lamb, T.M. (No)	1978	24	21	8	126	31	9.69	—	—	8	—
Larkins, W. (E/No/TCC)	1976	22	39	1	1545	157	40.65	4	8	3	—
Lawlor, P.J. (Gm)	—	1	2	0	8	8	4.00	—	—	1	—
Lawrence, D.V. (Gs)	—	1	—	—	—	—	—	—	—	—	—
Lawson, G.F. (Aus)	—	10	9	3	140	38*	23.33	—	—	4	—
Lee, P.G. (La)	1972	13	14	4	64	12*	6.40	—	—	—	—
†Leiper, R.J. (Ex)	—	1	2	0	50	49	25.00	—	—	—	—
Le Roux, G.S. (Sx)	1981	19	20	7	340	65*	26.15	—	1	6	—
Lethbridge, C. (Wa)	—	8	10	1	146	69	16.22	—	1	3	—
Lever, J.K. (Ex)	1970	22	20	4	147	21	9.18	—	—	6	—
Lewis, R.V. (MCo)	—	1	2	1	100	53*	100.00	—	1	—	—
Lillee, D.K. (Aus)	—	8	11	4	158	40*	22.57	—	—	3	—
Lilley, A.W. (Ex)	—	12	21	0	616	90	29.33	—	5	8	—
†Llewellyn, M.J. (Gm)	1977	7	9	1	43	15	5.37	—	—	8	—
Lloyd, B.J. (Gm)	—	22	28	2	242	31	9.30	—	—	19	—
†Lloyd, C.H. (La)	1969	18	31	2	1324	145	45.65	1	10	13	—
†Lloyd, D. (La)	1968	21	35	3	1122	146*	35.06	3	3	13	—
†Lloyd, T.A. (Wa)	1980	23	43	1	1445	138	34.40	3	5	10	—
†Lloyds, J.W. (So)	—	21	35	2	837	127	25.36	1	5	11	—
Love, J.D. (Y/TCC)	1980	23	40	4	1203	161	33.41	2	6	18	—
Lumb, R.G. (Y)	1974	15	25	1	706	145	29.41	1	3	1	—
Lynch, M.A. (Sy)	—	19	37	6	958	120*	30.90	2	3	8	—
McEvoy, M.S.A. (Ex)	—	11	19	0	367	56	19.31	—	3	10	—
McEwan, K.S. (Ex)	1974	22	37	1	1420	141	39.44	6	6	17	—
McIntyre, E.J. (Sc)	—	1	1	0	6	6	6.00	—	—	1	—

184

	Cap	M	I	NO	Runs	HS	Avge	100	50	Ct	St
Mackintosh, K.S. (Sy)	—	1									
Madugalle, R.S. (SL)	—	11	13	0	247	47	19.00	—	—	8	—
Maher, B.J.M. (D)	—	2	3	1	6	4*	3.00	—	—	6	2
Mallender, N.A. (No)	—	17	20	6	123	18	8.78	—	—	9	—
Mallett, N.V.H. (OU)	—	7	12	2	139	52	13.90	—	1	2	—
Malone, S.J. (H)	—	8	6	1	44	23	8.80	—	—	3	—
Marks, V.J. (So)	1979	23	31	7	591	81*	24.62	—	3	9	—
†Marsh, R.W. (Aus)	—	10	16	1	368	72*	24.53	—	2	26	2
Marshall, M.D. (H)	1981	17	23	3	425	75*	21.25	—	1	6	—
Maynard, C. (Wa)	—	2	4	0	92	70	23.00	—	1	5	1
Mendis, G.D. (Sx/TCC)	1980	22	40	3	1522	137	41.13	2	10	6	—
Mendis, L.R.D. (SL)	—	11	14	2	545	99	45.41	—	5	7	—
Merry, W.G. (M)	—	7	5	4	24	14*	24.00	—	—	1	—
Metson, C.P. (M)	—	1	1	1	38	38*	—	—	—	1	—
Miller, G. (D)	1976	21	31	3	552	81	19.71	—	5	19	—
Mills, J.P.C. (No/CU/OCU)	—	13	24	1	648	111	28.17	1	4	4	—
Moir, D.G. (D)	—	3	4	1	26	16	8.66	—	—	1	—
Monkhouse, G. (Sy)	—	4	6	4	37	28*	18.50	—	—	2	—
Monteith, J.D. (M)	—	8	11	2	61	16*	6.77	—	—	8	—
†Morris, H. (Gm)	—	1	2	0	21	16	10.50	—	—	1	—
Moseley, E.A. (Gm)	1981	15	19	3	306	57	19.12	—	2	5	—
Moseley, H.R. (So)	1972	20	21	8	162	36*	12.46	—	—	9	—
Moulding, R.P. (OU/OCU)	—	9	16	0	159	24	9.93	—	—	3	—
Moxon, M.D. (Y)	—	11	19	0	518	116	27.26	2	—	8	—
Murley, A.J. (CU)	—	6	11	0	152	48	13.81	—	—	2	—
†Nash, M.A. (Gm)	1969	23	31	5	282	36*	10.84	—	—	12	—
Neale, P.A. (Wo)	1978	23	41	5	1247	145*	34.63	4	3	9	—
Needham, A. (Sy)	—	1	2	1	7	6*	7.00	—	—	—	—
Newman, P.G. (D/TCC)	—	16	15	4	93	27	8.45	—	—	5	—
Nicholas, M.C.J. (H)	—	19	32	5	721	101*	26.70	1	3	9	—
O'Brien, B.A. (Ire)	—	1	1	0	39	39	39.00	—	—	1	—
O'Brien, N.T. (MCo)	—	1	1	0	14	14	14.00	—	—	1	—
†Old, C.M. (E/Y)	1969	18	21	6	335	55	22.33	—	1	2	—
Oldham, S. (D)	1980	15	14	5	92	33	10.22	—	—	3	—
Olive, M. (So)	—	3	6	0	72	19	12.00	—	—	1	—
Oliver, P.R. (Wa)	—	8	14	3	554	171*	50.36	2	1	2	—
†Ollis, R.L. (So)	—	2	4	0	60	22	15.00	—	—	1	—
Ontong, R.C. (Gm)	1979	23	40	5	968	151*	27.65	2	2	7	—
†Orders, J.O.D. (OU/OCU)	—	9	17	1	241	38	15.06	—	—	3	—
Ormrod, J.A. (Wo)	1966	4	6	3	279	100*	93.00	1	1	1	—
O'Shaughnessy, S.J. (La)	—	14	18	2	223	38	13.93	—	1	3	—
Palmer, R.W.M. (CU)	—	1					—				
Parker, P.W.G. (E/Sx/TCC)	1979	23	41	10	1412	136	45.54	4	6	21	—
Parks, R.J. (H)	—	23	29	8	330	37*	15.71	—	—	49	3
Parsons, D. (MCo)	—	1	1	0	1	1	1.00	—	—	—	—
†Parsons, G.J. (Le)	—	19	23	7	252	50	15.75	—	1	5	—
Patel, D.N. (Wo)	1979	22	40	4	1155	138	32.08	3	2	10	—

185

	Cap	M	I	NO	Runs	HS	Avge	100	50	Ct	St
Pauline, D.B. (Sy)	—	2	4	0	17	12	4.25	—	—	—	—
Payne, I.R. (Sy)	—	5	8	0	45	18	5.62	—	—	5	—
Peck, I.G. (No/CU/OCU)	—	9	15	2	233	45	17.92	—	—	5	1
Perry, N.J. (Gm)	—	1	1	0	0	0	0.00	—	—	1	—
Perryman, S.P. (Wa)	1977	16	20	9	98	16*	8.90	—	—	5	—
Philip, N. (Ex)	1978	22	37	4	720	80*	21.81	—	3	10	—
Phillipson, C.P. (Sx)	1980	21	30	10	485	56*	24.25	—	1	28	—
Pigott, A.C.S. (Sx)	—	2	2	0	46	39	23.00	—	—	1	—
Plumb, S.G. (MCo)	—	1	2	0	29	19	14.50	—	—	1	—
Pocock, N.E.J. (H)	1980	15	15	1	393	63	28.07	—	2	10	—
Pocock, P.I. (Sy)	1967	18	21	10	154	46	14.00	—	—	9	—
Pont, K.R. (Ex)	1976	16	27	3	692	89	28.83	—	5	5	—
Popplewell, N.F.M. (So)	—	17	25	2	513	51*	22.30	—	1	20	—
Potter, L. (K)	—	3	6	1	99	42*	19.80	—	—	3	—
Pridgeon, A.P. (Wo)	1980	24	22	11	126	34	11.45	—	—	8	—
†Priestley, N. (No)	—	1	1	1	20	20*	—	—	—	1	2
Pringle, D.R. (Ex/CU/OCU)	—	18	28	7	596	127*	28.38	1	3	3	—
Prior, J.A. (Ire)	—	1	1	0	20	20	20.00	—	—	—	—
Procter, M.J. (Gs)	1968	7	11	0	225	46	20.45	—	—	6	—
Radford, N.V. (La)	—	15	19	7	330	76*	27.50	—	2	8	—
Radley, C.T. (M)	1967	23	40	7	1177	101*	35.66	1	7	19	—
†Ramage, A. (Y)	—	7	9	2	116	52	16.57	—	1	—	—
Ranasinghe, A.N. (SL)	—	10	14	1	340	54*	26.15	—	2	4	—
Randall, D.W. (Nt)	1973	18	29	5	1093	162*	45.54	3	6	21	—
†Ratnayeke, J.R. (SL)	—	6	7	4	28	10	9.33	—	—	1	—
†Reidy, B.W. (La)	1980	15	23	2	624	96	29.71	—	5	16	—
Rhodes, S.J. (Y)	—	1	—	—	—	—	—	—	—	—	—
Rice, C.E.B. (Nt)	1975	21	30	4	1462	172	56.23	6	6	25	—
Rice, J.M. (H)	1975	11	19	3	639	161*	39.93	2	2	7	—
Richards, C.J. (Sy)	1978	19	31	4	680	63	25.18	—	4	30	7
Richards, I.V.A. (So)	1974	20	33	3	1718	196	57.26	7	5	18	—
Ridge, S.P. (OU)	—	1	2	1	7	7*	7.00	—	—	—	—
Rixon, S.J. (Aus)	—	8	9	2	146	40	20.85	—	—	20	2
Roberts, A.M.E. (Le)	—	11	17	2	347	57	23.13	—	2	2	—
Robertson, F. (Sc)	—	1	1	0	12	12	12.00	—	—	—	—
Robinson, R.T. (Nt)	—	19	33	7	687	91	26.42	—	3	12	—
Roebuck, P.M. (So)	1978	22	34	8	1057	91	40.65	—	9	13	—
Rogers, J.J. (OU)	—	8	14	0	253	54	18.07	—	1	1	—
Roope, G.R.J. (Sy)	1969	20	37	4	829	96*	25.12	—	5	44	1
†Rose B.C. (So)	1975	23	39	4	1005	107	28.71	1	5	21	—
†Rouse, S.J. (Wa)	1974	3	4	1	88	55*	29.33	—	1	1	—
Rowe, C.J.C. (K)	1977	5	10	0	142	54	14.20	—	1	2	—
†Russell, R.C. (Gs)	—	1	1	1	1	1*	—	—	—	7	1
Russom, N. (So/CU/OCU)	—	10	17	5	366	65	30.50	—	3	3	—
†Sadiq Mohammad (Gs)	1973	18	32	1	917	203	29.58	2	2	16	—
Sarfraz Nawaz (No)	1975	11	16	3	366	90	28.15	—	1	9	—
Saxelby, K. (Nt)	—	4	4	2	23	10*	11.50	—	—	3	—
†Scott, C.J. (La)	—	14	16	5	99	27*	9.00	—	—	25	4
Scott, C.W. (Nt)	—	2	2	0	14	8	7.00	—	—	2	1
Scott, M.S. (Wo)	—	19	37	1	968	109	26.88	1	6	8	—
Selvey, M.W.W. (M)	1973	17	18	1	242	57	14.23	—	2	7	—

186

	Cap	M	I	NO	Runs	HS	Avge	100	50	Ct	St
Sharp, G. (No)	1973	21	29	5	544	69*	22.66	—	2	45	2
†Sharp, K. (Y)	—	8	14	0	395	116	28.21	1	2	6	—
Shepherd, J.N. (K)	1967	15	20	6	310	59*	22.14	—	2	4	—
Sidebottom, A. (Y)	1980	15	21	4	376	52*	22.11	—	1	5	—
Simmons, J. (La)	1971	16	22	6	340	65*	21.25	—	1	14	—
†Slack, W.N. (M)	1981	18	32	3	1372	248*	47.31	3	9	6	—
Slocombe, P.A. (So)	1978	4	6	2	173	62*	43.25	—	2	1	—
Small, G.C. (Wa)	—	19	26	4	198	21*	9.00	—	—	8	—
Smith, C.L. (H)	1981	8	15	2	428	81*	32.92	—	3	5	—
†Smith, D.J. (Sx)	—	1	2	0	3	2	1.50	—	—	—	—
†Smith, D.M. (Sy)	1980	17	32	4	684	84*	24.42	—	3	16	—
†Smith, D.M. (Wa)	—	1	2	1	21	16*	21.00	—	—	1	—
Smith, K.D. (Wa/MCC)	1978	16	28	3	630	93	25.20	—	5	4	—
Smith, N. (Ex)	1975	10	12	4	191	41	23.87	—	—	23	4
Southern, J.W. (H)	1978	13	13	6	230	46	32.85	—	—	5	—
Speak, G.J. (La)	—	2	2	2	0	0*	—	—	—	—	—
Steele, D.S. (D)	1979	21	32	3	902	137	31.10	1	5	15	—
Steele, J.F. (Le)	1971	19	32	2	819	116	27.30	1	6	11	—
Stevenson, G.B. (Y)	1978	20	27	0	355	57	13.14	—	1	8	—
Stevenson, K. (H)	1979	24	23	9	232	31	16.57	—	—	7	—
Stewart, A.J. (Sy)	—	1	2	0	10	8	5.00	—	—	3	—
Stovold, A.W. (Gs)	1976	21	35	5	927	104	30.90	1	6	27	18
†Stovold, M.W. (Gs)	—	8	10	3	142	39	20.28	—	—	4	—
†Stuchbury, S. (Y)	—	2	3	2	7	4*	7.00	—	—	—	—
Surridge, D. (Gs)	—	6	3	3	2	2*	—	—	—	1	—
Sutcliffe, S.P. (Wa/OU/OCU)	—	12	17	4	32	6	2.46	—	—	2	—
Swan, R.G. (Sc)	—	1	2	1	63	38	63.00	—	—	—	—
Tavaré, C.J. (E/K)	1978	22	40	7	1770	156	53.63	4	12	18	—
Taylor, C.R.V. (M)	—	2	3	0	25	19	8.33	—	—	6	—
Taylor, D.J.S. (So)	1971	24	28	7	370	48*	17.61	—	—	56	6
Taylor, L.B. (Le)	1981	21	16	9	74	22	10.57	—	—	7	—
Taylor, N.R. (K)	—	11	19	2	385	99	22.64	—	3	12	—
Taylor, R.W. (E/D)	1962	19	22	4	259	100	14.38	1	—	46	12
Taylor, T.J. (La/MCo/OU/OCU)	—	9	14	6	78	28*	9.75	—	—	2	—
Terry, V.P. (H)	—	5	7	2	139	94*	27.80	—	1	2	—
†Thomas, D.J. (Sy)	—	14	24	5	323	47	17.00	—	—	7	—
Thomas, G.P. (Wa)	—	6	12	1	263	52	23.90	—	1	6	—
Thomas, J.G. (Gm)	—	5	8	3	53	13*	10.60	—	—	3	—
Thomas, W.R.K. (Wo)	—	1	2	1	57	44	57.00	—	—	—	—
Thomson, J.R. (M)	—	6	8	1	63	35	12.60	—	—	4	—
†Tindall, R.M. (No)	—	6	8	1	126	29*	18.00	—	—	3	—
Todd, P.A. (Nt)	1977	21	37	4	899	112	27.24	1	4	8	—
Tolchard, J.G. (MCo)	—	1	1	1	2	2*	—	—	—	—	—
Tolchard, R.W. (Le)	1966	17	24	8	535	104*	33.43	1	2	15	1
Tomlins, K.P. (M)	—	10	16	3	403	79*	31.00	—	3	7	—
Torkington, H.F. (CU)	—	1	2	0	9	9	4.50	—	—	1	—
Torrens, R. (Ire)	—	1	1	0	0	0	0.00	—	—	—	—
Tremlett, T.M. (H)	—	16	25	1	636	80	26.50	—	4	3	—
Tunnicliffe, C.J. (D)	1977	21	25	1	246	39	10.25	—	—	9	—
†Turner, D.R. (H)	1970	22	30	6	704	106	29.33	1	4	4	—
Turner, G.M. (Wo)	1968	24	42	4	2101	168	55.28	9	6	21	—
Turner, S. (Ex)	1970	20	30	10	782	73*	39.10	—	4	13	—

	Cap	M	I	NO	Runs	HS	Avge	100	50	Ct	St
Underwood, D.L. (K)	1964	23	21	10	162	50	14.72	—	1	10	—
Van Der Bijl, V.A.P. (M)	1980	1	—	—	—	—	—	—	—	—	—
Varey, D.W. (CU)	—	3	5	1	81	39	20.25	—	—	2	—
Waller, C.E. (Sx)	1976	22	15	6	148	51*	16.44	—	1	11	—
Warke, S.J.S. (Ire)	—	1	1	0	4	4	4.00	—	—	1	—
Warnapura, B. (SL)	—	10	16	1	408	75*	27.20	—	2	—	—
†Warner, C.J. (Sc)	—	1	1	0	1	1	1.00	—	—	—	—
Waterton, S.N.V. (K)	—	5	5	1	50	28	12.50	—	—	10	3
†Webster, A.J. (Wo)	—	1	1	0	6	6	6.00	—	—	—	—
†Weightman, N.I. (Nt)	—	3	5	0	139	105	27.80	1	—	3	—
Wellham, D.M. (Aus)	—	9	13	4	497	135*	55.22	2	1	3	—
Wells, A.P. (Sx)	—	1	1	0	63	63	63.00	—	1	1	—
Wells, C.M. (Sx/MCC)	—	14	22	4	517	111	28.72	1	2	4	—
Wenlock, D.A. (Le)	—	2	3	0	91	62	30.33	—	1	1	—
Weston, M.J. (Wo)	—	4	6	1	53	22	10.60	—	—	3	—
Wettimuny, S. (SL)	—	10	14	2	527	95*	43.91	—	5	3	—
Whiteley, J.P. (Y)	—	19	23	11	164	19*	13.66	—	—	8	—
Whitney, M.R. (Aus/Gs)	—	6	7	0	5	4	0.71	—	—	3	—
Wijesuriya, R.G.C.E. (SL)	—	5	3	1	14	6*	7.00	—	—	3	—
Wild, D.J. (No)	—	6	10	3	106	30	15.14	—	—	1	—
Wilkins, A.H. (Gs)	—	21	23	3	117	31	5.85	—	—	7	—
Willey, P. (E/No)	1971	13	21	1	495	82	24.75	—	2	2	—
Williams, R.G. (No)	1979	23	38	2	1197	142*	33.25	3	6	15	—
Willis, R.G.D. (E/Wa)	1972	13	18	5	149	33*	11.46	—	—	3	—
Wills, R. (Ire)	—	1	1	0	48	48	48.00	—	—	—	—
Wilson, P.H.L. (Sy)	—	4	4	2	3	2*	1.50	—	—	2	—
Windaybank, S.J. (Gs)	—	11	12	3	203	46*	22.55	—	—	2	—
Wood, B. (D)	1980	22	37	6	1439	153	46.41	3	8	13	—
†Wood, G.M. (Aus)	—	15	24	2	690	81	31.36	—	5	8	—
†Wood, L.J. (K)	—	1	2	0	5	5	2.50	—	—	—	—
Woolmer, R.A. (E/K)	1970	21	38	1	934	119*	25.24	1	4	15	—
†Wootton, S.J. (Wa)	—	6	11	2	204	77	22.66	—	1	4	—
†Wright, J.G. (D)	1977	20	32	1	1257	150	40.54	4	6	9	—
†Yallop, G.N. (Aus)	—	14	22	3	624	114	32.84	1	3	8	—
†Yardley, T.J. (No)	1978	23	35	8	803	96*	29.74	—	4	23	—
†Yeabsley, D.I. (MCo)	—	1	1	0	3	3	3.00	—	—	—	—
†Younis Ahmed (Wo)	1979	22	39	8	1637	116	52.80	3	9	12	—
Zaheer Abbas (Gs)	1975	21	36	10	2306	215*	88.69	10	10	9	—

Bowling

	Type	O	M	R	W	Avge	Best	5 wI	10 wM
Abrahams, J. (La)	OB	203.5	52	567	14	40.50	3-27	—	—
Acfield, D.L. (Ex)	OB	769.5	232	1719	76	22.61	2-55	4	1
Agnew, J.P. (Le)	RF	221	45	775	24	32.29	5-72	1	—
Alderman, T.M. (Aus)	RFM	402.5	100	1064	51	20.86	6-135	4	—
Alleyne, H.L. (Wo)	RF	324.3	63	1019	39	26.12	8-43	1	1
Allott, P.J.W. (E/La/TCC)	RFM	673.5	174	1963	85	23.09	8-48	3	—
Anderson, I.J. (Ire)	OB	12	1	32	1	32.00	1-16	—	—
Anderson, I.S. (D)	OB	73	16	257	7	36.71	4-35	—	—
Arnold, G.G. (Sx)	RFM	458.1	122	1121	40	28.02	6-39	1	—
Asif Din (Wa)	LB	70	8	371	5	74.20	1-11	—	—
Asif Iqbal (K)	RM	9.4	2	61	1	61.00	1-17	—	—
Athey, C.W.J. (Y/MCC)	RM	39.3	7	111	2	55.50	1-0	—	—
Bailey, D. (MCo)	OB	17	0	67	3	22.33	3-67	—	—
Bailey, M.J. (H)	OB	140	24	489	8	61.12	4-138	—	—
Bainbridge, P. (Gs)	RM	355.1	85	1009	33	30.57	5-68	1	—
Bairstow, D.L. (Y)	RM	6	1	14	0	—	—	—	—
Balderstone, J.C. (Le)	SLA	159.3	43	444	14	31.71	4-17	—	—
Baptiste, E.A. (K)	RFM	280.2	64	844	29	29.10	5-37	1	—
Barclay, J.R.T. (Sx/TCC)	OB	387.5	96	969	37	26.18	4-47	—	—
Barlow, G.D. (M)	RM	0.3	0	7	0	—	—	—	—
Barnett, K.J. (D)	LB	117.3	21	435	4	108.75	2-58	—	—
Barwick, S.R. (Gm)	RM	71	33	133	7	19.00	2-10	—	—
Beard, G.R. (Aus)	RM/OB	209.1	58	559	16	34.93	4-92	—	—
Benson, M.R. (K)	OB	4	0	28	0	—	—	—	—
Birkenshaw, J. (Wo)	OB	202.5	40	644	11	58.54	3-131	—	—
Booden, C.D. (No)	RM	51	11	147	3	49.00	2-30	—	—
Boon, T.J. (Le)	RM	3	0	7	0	—	—	—	—
Booth, P. (Le)	RFM	76	21	207	6	34.50	3-52	—	—
Border, A.R. (Aus)	SLA	24	6	65	2	32.50	1-12	—	—
Bore, M.K. (Nt)	LM	474.5	158	1075	36	29.86	4-46	—	—
Botham, I.T. (E/So)	RFM	574.2	156	1712	67	25.55	6-90	4	1
Boycott, G. (E/Y)	RM	14	7	20	0	—	—	—	—
Boyd-Moss, R.J. (No/CU/OCU)	SLA	136	35	465	11	42.27	2-24	—	—
Brain, B.M. (Gs)	RFM	205	49	609	16	38.06	3-34	—	—
Breakwell, D. (So)	SLA	241	44	719	19	37.84	6-38	1	—
Briers, N.E. (Le)	RM	64.2	15	171	5	34.20	2-32	—	—
Bright, R.J. (Aus)	SLA	473.4	178	1056	40	26.40	5-57	2	—
Broad, B.C. (Gs)	RM	120	31	443	6	73.83	2-70	—	—
Butcher, A.R. (Sy)	SLA	64.3	15	247	10	24.70	2-15	—	—
Capel, D.J. (No)	RM	3	0	6	0	—	—	—	—
Carrick, P. (Y)	SLA	532.1	169	1412	35	40.34	4-76	—	—
Carter, R.M. (No)	RM	184.4	32	676	18	37.55	4-52	—	—
Chappell, T.M. (Aus)	RM	4	1	18	0	—	—	—	—
Cheatle, R.G.L. (Sy)	SLA	18	4	52	1	52.00	1-33	—	—
Childs, J.H. (Gs)	SLA	768.4	208	1962	75	26.16	9-56	7	—
Clark, J. (Sc)	RM	23	8	69	2	34.50	2-69	—	—
Clarke, S.T. (Sy)	RF	339.4	98	734	49	14.97	6-66	5	—

189

	Type	O	M	R	W	Avge	Best	5 wI	10 wM
Clift, P.B. (Le)	RM	308.2	82	799	29	27.55	6-47	2	1
Cockbain, I. (La)	SLA	6	1	14	0	—	—	—	—
Cook, G. (No)	SLA	36.4	10	145	2	72.50	1-7	—	—
Cook, N.G.B. (Le/MCC)	SLA	829	277	2030	65	31.23	7-81	2	—
Cooper, K.E. (Nt)	RM	423.3	125	1081	43	25.13	4-13	—	—
Corlett, S.C. (Ire)	RM	43	9	112	2	56.00	1-29	—	—
Cowan, R.S. (OU)	RM	41	12	94	1	94.00	1-9	—	—
Cowans, N.G. (M)	RFM	54	9	155	8	19.37	5-58	1	—
Cowdrey, C.S. (K)	RM	75.1	14	271	6	45.16	2-14	—	—
Cowley, N.G. (H)	OB	368.5	92	1134	27	42.00	4-134	—	—
Cumbes, J. (Wo)	RM	306.3	75	848	28	30.28	5-69	1	—
Curtis, I.J. (OU)	SLA /								
	SLC	76	30	132	5	26.40	4-58	—	—
Curtis, T.S. (Wo)	LB	4	2	13	1	13.00	1-13	—	—
Daniel, W.W. (M)	RF	514.2	103	1494	67	22.29	6-64	2	—
Daniels, S.A.B. (Gm)	RFM	89	18	326	8	40.75	3-33	—	—
De Mel, A.L.F. (SL)	RM	245	42	816	15	54.40	3-37	—	—
Denning, P.W. (So)	OB	3	0	18	0	—	—	—	—
Dennis, S.J. (Y)	LFM	162.1	36	490	20	24.50	5-35	1	—
De Silva, D.S. (SL)	LBG	262	73	681	25	27.24	7-55	2	—
De Silva, G.R.A. (SL)	SLA	301	106	646	26	24.84	4-41	—	—
Dias, R.L. (SL)	RM	1	0	3	0	—	—	—	—
Dilley, G.R. (E/K)	RF	281.5	57	936	28	33.42	4-24	—	—
Dixon, J.H. (Gs)	RM	24	5	79	1	79.00	1-52	—	—
Doggart, S.J.G. (CU)	OB	162.1	51	364	6	60.66	3-66	—	—
Donald, W.A. (Sc)	RM	5	2	5	0	—	—	—	—
Doshi, D.R. (Wa)	SLA	669.3	163	1949	45	43.31	5-73	1	—
Doughty, R.J. (Gs)	RM	27	10	55	2	27.50	2-28	—	—
Dredge, C.H. (So)	RM	498.2	129	1286	54	23.81	6-37	2	—
Dudleston, B. (Gs)	SLA	7	0	30	0	—	—	—	—
Dutton, R.S. (CU)	RM	26	2	131	1	131.00	1-45	—	—
Dyson, J. (Aus)	RM	1	0	2	0	—	—	—	—
East, R.E. (Ex)	SLA	680.2	190	1513	53	28.54	7-49	3	1
Edmonds, P.H. (M)	SLA	899	280	1814	73	24.84	6-93	3	—
Edwards, T.D.W. (CU)	RM	20	7	58	1	58.00	1-17	—	—
Ellison, R.M. (K)	RM	70.2	18	144	4	36.00	1-11	—	—
Emburey, J.E. (E/M/TCC)	OB	803.4	236	1782	73	24.41	7-88	8	3
Featherstone, N.G. (Gm)	OB	16	7	38	1	38.00	1-26	—	—
Fernando, L.J. (SL)	RM	71	11	234	1	234.00	1-37	—	—
Ferreira, A.M. (Wa)	RM	436.3	83	1542	32	48.18	4-73	—	—
Foster, N.A. (Ex)	RM	25	5	90	1	90.00	1-37	—	—
Fowler, G. (La)		1	0	12	0	—	—	—	—
Garner, J. (So)	RF	605.4	182	1349	88	15.32	7-25	7	4
Gatting, M.W. (E/M/TCC)	RM	39	13	101	3	33.66	3-40	—	—
Gifford, N. (Wo)	SLA	961.4	253	2476	63	39.30	6-67	1	—
Gooch, G.A. (E/Ex/MCC)	RM	78	23	243	6	40.50	3-47	—	—
Gould, I.J. (Sx)	RM	3	1	2	0	—	—	—	—
Graveney, D.A. (Gs)	SLA	486.3	148	1078	48	22.45	6-54	3	1

190

	Type	O	M	R	W	Avge	Best	5 wI	10 wM
Greenidge, C.G. (H)	RM	0.4	0	1	0	—	—	—	—
Greensword, S. (MCo)	RM	13	6	25	1	25.00	1-25	—	—
Greig, I.A. (Sx)	RM	477	100	1469	76	19.32	7-43	4	2
Griffiths, B.J. (No)	RFM	681.5	196	1841	70	26.30	8-50	2	—
Gunasekara, Y. (SL)	LM/SLA	1	0	5	0	—	—	—	—
Hacker, P.J. (Nt)	LFM	175.5	53	446	23	19.39	4-34	—	—
Hadlee, R.J. (Nt)	RF	708.4	231	1564	105	14.89	7-25	4	—
Halliday, M. (Ire)	OB	41	17	80	2	40.00	2-41	—	—
Hampshire, J.H. (Y)	LB	7	2	22	1	22.00	1-22	—	—
Harpur, T. (Ire)		3	1	5	0	—	—	—	—
Harris, M.J. (Nt)	LBG	8	1	39	0	—	—	—	—
Hart, P.R. (Y)	SLA	58	17	140	2	70.00	1-22	—	—
Hartley, S.N. (Y)	RM	124.1	22	479	9	53.22	1-13	—	—
Hayes, K.A. (La/OU)	RM	6.2	1	33	0	—	—	—	—
Hayward, R.E. (H)		2	0	5	0	—	—	—	—
Hemmings, E.E. (Nt)	OB	804.2	262	1857	90	20.63	7-59	6	2
Hemsley, E.J.O. (Wo)	RM	14	0	77	0	—	—	—	—
Hemsley, P.D. (CU)	RM	33.5	6	90	0	—	—	—	—
Hendrick, M. (E/D)	RFM	425.4	119	1013	36	28.13	5-41	1	—
Hignell, A.J. (Gs)	LB	4.1	0	23	2	11.50	2-13	—	—
Hill, A. (D)	OB	1.1	0	5	0	—	—	—	—
Hobbs, R.N.S. (Gm)	LBG	390.3	99	1151	35	32.88	5-67	2	—
Hodgson, K.I. (CU)	RM	175.1	29	597	20	29.85	4-77	—	—
Hogg, R.M. (Aus)	RF	217.2	51	657	27	24.33	6-87	1	—
Hogg, W. (Wa/MCC)	RFM	547.2	109	1853	51	36.33	4-46	—	—
Holding, M.A. (La)	RF	271.1	75	715	40	17.87	6-74	4	1
Holliday, D.C. (CU)	LB	30	4	96	1	96.00	1-71	—	—
Holmes, G.C. (Gm)	RM	49	9	193	7	27.57	2-22	—	—
Hopkins, D.C. (Wa)	RM	13	3	35	0	—	—	—	—
Howarth, G.P. (Sy)	OB	7	2	24	0	—	—	—	—
Hughes, D.P. (La)	SLA	292.5	83	780	21	37.14	4-40	—	—
Hughes, K.J. (Aus)	RM	5.5	2	14	0	—	—	—	—
Hughes, S.P. (M/TCC)	RFM	355.1	67	1132	44	25.72	6-75	3	—
Huxter, R.J.A. (CU)	RM	88.3	21	224	5	44.80	2-49	—	—
Illingworth, N.J.B. (Nt)	RM	7	3	16	1	16.00	1-4	—	—
Imran Khan (Sx)	RF	565.1	137	1464	66	22.18	6-52	2	1
Inchmore, J.D. (Wo)	RFM	355	63	1166	30	38.86	5-85	1	—
Intikhab Alam (Sy)	LBG	555.4	153	1585	65	24.38	5-44	3	—
Jackman, R.D. (Sy/MCC)	RFM	608.3	142	1606	66	24.33	6-70	4	—
James, K.D. (M)	LM	14	3	34	0	—	—	—	—
Jarvis, K.B.S. (K)	RFM	586.3	137	1885	81	23.27	7-65	5	2
Jarvis, P.W. (Y)	RFM	18	2	74	0	—	—	—	—
Javed Miandad (Gm)	LBG	37	7	108	3	36.00	2-12	—	—
Jennings, K.F. (Sc)	RM	29	4	74	4	18.50	3-52	—	—
Jesty, T.E. (H)	RM	437.4	136	1033	52	19.86	6-25	3	—
Johnson, G.W. (K)	OB	625.3	177	1577	57	27.57	6-33	2	—
Johnson, M. (Y)	RM	85.5	17	301	7	43.00	4-48	—	—
Johnston, H.G.F. (Sc)	SLA	30	10	60	2	30.00	2-60	—	—
Jones, A. (Gm)	OB	1.1	1	4	0	—	—	—	—
Jones, A.A. (Gm)	RFM	69	14	237	8	29.62	3-23	—	—
Jones, A.N. (Sx)	RFM	83	11	283	17	16.64	4-33	—	—

191

	Type	O	M	R	W	Avge	Best	5 wI	10 wM
Kallicharran, A.I. (Wa)	OB	35.5	3	133	2	66.50	1-14	—	—
Kalyperuma, L.W. (SL)	OB	393.3	88	1045	31	33.70	5-34	1	—
Kapil Dev (No)	RFM	96	25	316	6	52.66	2-24	—	—
Kemp, N.J. (K)	RM	7	1	32	0	—	—	—	—
Kennedy, A. (La)	RM	33	7	102	2	51.00	1-20	—	—
Ker, J.E. (Sc)	RM	19	5	36	1	36.00	1-36	—	—
Kirsten, P.N. (D)	OB	32	6	98	2	49.00	1-7	—	—
Knight, J.M. (OU)	RM	98	25	291	5	58.20	2-44	—	—
Knight, R.D.V. (Sy/MCC)	RM	285	82	741	18	41.16	2-18	—	—
Knott, A.P.E. (E/K)	OB	2	2	0	0	—	—	—	—
Lamb, A.J. (No)	RM	8	1	35	0	—	—	—	—
Lamb, T.M. (No)	RM	674.1	183	1701	59	28.83	4-31	—	—
Larkins, W. (E/No/TCC)	RM	21.2	5	91	4	22.75	2-22	—	—
Lawlor, P.J. (Gm)	OB	13	2	50	1	50.00	1-36	—	—
Lawrence, D.V. (Gs)	RFM	19	4	86	0	—	—	—	—
Lawson, G.F. (Aus)	RFM	218.1	53	652	25	26.08	7-81	2	—
Lee, P.G. (La)	RFM	285.1	81	816	25	32.64	6-44	2	1
Le Roux, G.S. (Sx)	RF	559.1	133	1582	81	19.53	8-107	3	1
Lethbridge, C. (Wa)	RM	113	12	501	7	71.57	2-26	—	—
Lever, J.K. (Ex)	LFM	680.5	149	2049	80	25.61	8-49	4	1
Lillee, D.K. (Aus)	RF	377.4	102	1028	47	21.87	7-89	3	1
Lloyd, B.J. (Gm)	OB	619.3	142	1717	53	32.39	8-70	1	—
Lloyd, D. (La)	SLA	205.2	49	586	12	48.83	2-18	—	—
Lloyd, T.A. (Wa)	RM	24	2	106	0	—	—	—	—
Lloyds, J.W. (So)	OB	144.2	29	482	10	48.20	3-12	—	—
Love, J.D. (Y/TCC)	RM	20	4	71	0	—	—	—	—
Lynch, M.A. (Sy)	RM/OB	28.4	7	97	3	32.33	3-6	—	—
McEvoy, M.S.A. (Ex)	RM	27	7	99	3	33.00	3-20	—	—
McEwan, K.S. (Ex)	OB	9.5	1	66	0	—	—	—	—
McIntyre, E.J. (Sc)	OB	8	2	15	0	—	—	—	—
Mackintosh, K.S. (Sy)	RM	19	5	65	2	32.50	2-19	—	—
Mallender, N.A. (No)	RFM	396.5	94	1170	49	23.87	6-37	1	—
Mallett, N.V.H. (OU)	RM	152.5	34	455	11	41.36	5-52	1	—
Malone, S.J. (H)	RM	147	27	518	14	37.00	3-88	—	—
Marks, V.J. (So)	OB	699.5	195	1571	49	32.06	5-34	2	—
Marsh, R.W. (Aus)	RM	0.2	0	0	1	0.00	1-0	—	—
Marshall, M.D. (H)	RF	531.3	166	1321	68	19.42	6-57	5	—
Mendis, G.D. (Sx/TCC)	RM	0.3	0	2	0	—	—	—	—
Merry, W.G. (M)	RM	125	27	378	13	29.07	2-17	—	—
Miller, G. (D)	OB	466.2	137	1281	33	38.81	4-27	—	—
Moir, D.G. (D)	SLA	62.2	14	203	2	101.50	1-20	—	—
Monkhouse, G. (Sy)	RM	83	17	224	7	32.00	3-45	—	—
Monteith, J.D. (M)	SLA	222.3	58	596	24	24.83	5-60	2	—
Moseley, E.A. (Gm)	RFM	355.4	87	942	52	18.11	6-23	3	—
Moseley, H.R. (So)	RFM	436	100	1291	49	26.34	4-16	—	—
Moxon, M.D. (Y)	RM	6	0	23	0	—	—	—	—
Murley, A.J. (CU)	RM	2	1	1	0	—	—	—	—
Nash, M.A. (Gm)	LM	565.4	153	1728	71	24.33	7-62	2	—
Neale, P.A. (Wo)	RM	19.1	0	102	0	—	—	—	—

192

	Type	O	M	R	W	Avge	Best	5 wI	10 wM
Needham, A. (Sy)	OB	16	5	57	1	57.00	1-27	—	—
Newman, P.G. (D/TCC)	RFM	359.5	65	1204	50	24.08	5-51	1	—
Nicholas, M.C.J. (H)	RM	1.5	0	4	1	4.00	1-4	—	—
O'Brien, N.T. (MCo)	RM	10	3	23	1	23.00	1-23	—	—
Old, C.M. (E/Y)	RFM	472.3	149	1165	48	24.27	5-52	1	—
Oldham, S. (D)	RFM	314.2	55	1025	23	44.56	3-35	—	—
Ontong, R.C. (Gm)	RFM	457.5	97	1369	49	27.93	6-62	1	1
Orders, J.O.D. (OU/OCU)	LM	77	12	228	4	57.00	2-44	—	—
O'Shaughnessy, S.J. (La)	RM	103.2	20	345	11	31.36	3-17	—	—
Palmer, R.W.M. (CU)	LM	7	1	30	1	30.00	1-30	—	—
Parker, P.W.G. (E/Sx/TCC)	RM	5	3	19	0	—	—	—	—
Parks, R.J. (H)	RM	0.3	0	0	0	—	—	—	—
Parsons, D. (MCo)	LM	13.1	2	53	1	53.00	1-53	—	—
Parsons, G.J. (Le)	RM	462.3	94	1452	45	32.26	4-44	—	—
Patel, D.N. (Wo)	OB	597.3	137	1749	43	40.67	5-76	2	—
Pauline, D.B. (Sy)	RM	2	0	14	0	—	—	—	—
Payne, I.R. (Sy)	RM	86	25	250	8	31.25	2-28	—	—
Perry, N.J. (Gm)	SLA	19	1	89	2	44.50	1-31	—	—
Perryman, S.P. (Wa)	RM	305.4	64	1046	24	43.58	5-52	1	—
Phillip, N. (Ex)	RFM	521.1	87	1725	51	33.82	6-40	1	—
Phillipson, C.P. (Sx)	RM	2	0	15	0	—	—	—	—
Pigott, A.C.S. (Sx)	RFM	41	4	135	4	33.75	2-49	—	—
Plumb, S.G. (MCo)	RM	5	0	13	0	—	—	—	—
Pocock, N.E.J. (H)	LM	7.3	3	36	1	36.00	1-10	—	—
Pocock, P.I. (Sy)	OB	603.1	180	1511	46	32.84	4-54	—	—
Pont, K.R. (Ex)	RM	45	10	137	1	137.00	1-32	—	—
Popplewell, N.F.M. (So)	RM	194.2	42	598	18	33.22	5-33	1	—
Pridgeon, A.P. (Wo)	RM	673.1	119	1978	56	35.32	5-63	1	—
Pringle, D.R. (Ex/CU/OCU)	RM	383	85	1138	30	37.93	4-39	—	—
Prior, J.A. (Ire)	RM	19	8	37	0	—	—	—	—
Procter, M.J. (Gs)	RF/OB	172.5	45	513	19	27.00	5-80	1	—
Radford, N.V. (La)	RFM	303.2	58	1140	21	54.28	5-107	1	—
Radley, C.T. (M)	LB	5	0	21	0	—	—	—	—
Ramage, A. (Y)	RFM	148	22	550	18	30.55	5-65	1	—
Ranasinghe, A.N. (SL)	LM/SLA	228	58	624	17	36.70	5-65	1	—
Ratnayeke, J.R. (SL)	RFM	111	22	388	9	43.11	3-38	—	—
Reidy, B.W. (La)	LM	129	25	436	8	54.50	3-67	—	—
Rice, C.E.B. (Nt)	RFM	494.5	142	1248	65	19.20	6-44	1	—
Rice, J.M. (H)	RM	64.5	13	258	5	51.60	2-25	—	—
Richards, I.V.A. (So)	OB	185.5	38	585	13	45.00	4-55	—	—
Ridge, S.P. (OU)	RM	23	6	65	1	65.00	1-50	—	—
Rixon, S.J. (Aus)	RM	2	0	19	0	—	—	—	—
Roberts, A.M.E. (Le)	RF	310.1	80	923	37	24.94	5-49	2	1
Robertson, F. (Sc)	RM	34	4	117	3	39.00	3-117	—	—
Robinson, R.T. (Nt)	RM	1	0	5	0	—	—	—	—
Roope, G.R.J. (Sy)	RM	39	9	105	4	26.25	2-30	—	—
Rose, B.C. (So)	LM	2.5	0	9	0	—	—	—	—
Rouse, S.J. (Wa)	LFM	42.3	8	169	2	84.50	2-46	—	—

193

	Type	O	M	R	W	Avge	Best	5 wI	10 wM
Rowe, C.J.C. (K)	OB	21	3	89	0	—	—	—	—
Russom, N. (So/CU/OCU)	RM	246.3	56	710	19	37.36	2-18	—	—
Sadiq Mohammad (Gs)	LBG	102.4	15	412	11	37.45	3-34	—	—
Sarfraz Nawaz (No)	RFM	251.4	46	815	33	24.69	6-84	1	—
Saxelby, K. (Nt)	RM	99.4	24	293	12	24.41	4-64	—	—
Scott, M.S. (Wo)	OB	10	1	37	0	—	—	—	—
Selvey, M.W.W. (M)	RFM	388.3	114	1054	35	30.11	5-79	2	—
Shepherd, J.N. (K)	RM	424.3	111	1136	28	40.57	5-61	1	—
Sidebottom, A. (Y)	RFM	305.5	88	899	47	19.12	6-62	3	—
Simmons, J. (La)	OB	332.5	111	740	29	25.51	5-39	1	—
Slack, W.N. (M)	RM	10	1	33	0	—	—	—	—
Small, G.C. (Wa)	RFM	395.3	52	1590	42	37.85	6-76	1	—
Smith, C.L. (H)	OB	41	7	149	2	74.50	1-21	—	—
Smith, D.M. (Sy)	RM	18	8	38	1	38.00	1-23	—	—
Smith, D.M. (Wa)	SLA	23	3	98	1	98.00	1-55	—	—
Southern, J.W. (H)	SLA	362.1	98	952	20	47.60	5-108	1	—
Speak, G.J. (La)	RFM	15	1	54	0	—	—	—	—
Steele, D.S. (D)	SLA	403	141	1019	46	22.15	7-53	4	—
Steele, J.F. (Le)	SLA	323.3	86	787	27	29.14	4-31	—	—
Stevenson, G.B. (Y)	RM	537.4	122	1857	61	30.44	7-46	3	—
Stevenson, K. (H)	RFM	595.5	119	1966	57	34.49	5-32	3	—
Stovold, M.W. (Gs)	RM	2	0	6	0	—	—	—	—
Stuchbury, S. (Y)	LFM	42	7	176	6	29.33	3-82	—	—
Surridge, D. (Gs)	RFM	139.5	23	476	9	52.88	2-47	—	—
Sutcliffe, S.P. (Wa/OU/OCU)	OB	434.2	85	1281	32	40.03	4-54	—	—
Tavaré, C.J. (E/K)	RM	11	2	96	0	—	—	—	—
Taylor, L.B. (Le)	RFM	547.1	131	1628	75	21.70	7-28	2	—
Taylor, N.R. (K)	OB	4	0	23	0	—	—	—	—
Taylor, T.J. (La/MCo/OU/OCU)	SLA	331.1	99	731	27	27.07	5-81	1	—
Terry, V.P. (H)	RM	13.5	4	39	0	—	—	—	—
Thomas, D.J. (Sy)	LM	323.5	77	933	34	27.44	5-31	—	—
Thomas, J.G. (Gm)	RM	80.3	10	355	10	35.50	4-65	—	—
Thomas, W.R.K. (Wo)	RM	17	4	54	0	—	—	—	—
Thomson, J.R. (M)	RF	162.3	30	522	23	22.69	4-66	—	—
Tindall, R.M. (No)	SLA	44	10	169	2	84.50	2-1	—	—
Tolchard, R.W. (Le)	RM	2	0	14	0	—	—	—	—
Tomlins, K.P. (M)	RM	30	7	84	2	42.00	2-54	—	—
Torrens, R. (Ire)	RFM	29.1	14	68	6	11.33	6-42	1	—
Tremlett, T.M. (H)	RM	196	68	383	14	27.35	4-11	—	—
Tunnicliffe, C.J. (D)	LFM	499.2	111	1563	42	37.21	5-34	3	—
Turner, D.R. (H)	RM	23.1	7	88	4	22.00	2-7	—	—
Turner, S. (Ex)	RFM	483	132	1203	44	27.34	5-55	1	—
Underwood, D.L. (K)	LM	774.3	282	1788	78	22.92	7-93	5	1
Van Der Bijl, V.A.P. (M)	RFM	29	12	38	1	38.00	1-32	—	—
Waller, C.E. (Sx)	SLA	513	152	1264	44	28.72	5-36	2	—
Warnapura, B. (SL)	RM	63.2	17	215	5	43.00	2-33	—	—

	Type	O	M	R	W	Avge	Best	5 wI	10 wM
Webster, A.J. (Wo)	RM	6	0	18	0	—	—	—	—
Wellham, D.M. (Aus)	RM	2	0	11	1	11.00	1-11	—	—
Wells, C.M. (Sx/MCC)	RM	89	19	299	10	29.90	4-48	—	—
Wenlock, D.A. (Le)	RM	15	3	47	1	47.00	1-10	—	—
Weston, M.J. (Wo)	RM	15.4	3	68	0	—	—	—	—
Wettimuny, S. (SL)	RM	10	5	18	1	18.00	1-7	—	—
Whiteley, J.P. (Y)	OB	392	93	1124	34	33.05	4-50	—	—
Whitney, M.R. (Aus/Gs)	LFM	223	49	726	24	30.25	5-60	1	—
Wijesuriya, R,G.C.E. (SL)	SLA	194	57	467	15	31.13	5-35	1	—
Wild, D.J. (No)	RM	80	15	306	3	102.00	2-52	—	—
Wilkins, A.H. (Gs)	LM	630	146	1892	52	36.38	8-57	1	—
Willey, P. (E/No)	OB	297	98	589	23	25.60	5-46	2	1
Williams, R.G. (No)	OB	612.2	163	1686	48	35.12	5-88	2	—
Willis, R.G.D. (E/Wa)	RF	391.1	85	1037	42	24.69	8-43	2	—
Wilson, P.H.L. (Sy)	RFM	48	9	141	2	70.50	2-61	—	—
Wood, B. (D)	RM	254.3	58	815	17	47.94	2-12	—	—
Wood, L.J. (K)	SLA	43	11	124	4	31.00	4-124	—	—
Woolmer, R.A. (E/K)	RM	47	11	141	4	35.25	2-11	—	—
Wootton, S.H. (Wa)	SLA	1	0	7	0	—	—	—	—
Wright, J.G. (D)	RM	2	1	4	0	—	—	—	—
Yallop, G.N. (Aus)	LM/SLA	69	14	241	6	40.16	4-63	—	—
Yardley, T.J. (No)	RM	1	0	3	0	—	—	—	—
Yeabsley, D.I. (MCo)	LM	25	8	63	1	63.00	1-63	—	—
Younis Ahmed (Wo)	LM	62	9	183	3	61.00	1-12	—	—
Zaheer Abbas (Gs)	OB	12	2	42	3	14.00	3-32	—	—

WITH
A DINERS CARD
YOU'RE NEVER
CAUGHT OUT.

DINERS CLUB INTERNATIONAL.
IT DOES YOU CREDIT.

Diners Club House, Kingsmead, Farnborough, Hants. GU14 7SR.
Telephone: (0252) 516261.

CAREER FIGURES FOR THE LEADING PLAYERS

The following are the abbreviated figures of the leading batsmen and bowlers based on their career averages, and fielders and wicket-keepers based on the number of their catches and dismissals. The figures are complete to the end of the 1981 season and the full career records will be found in the main tables overleaf. The qualification for inclusion for batsmen and bowlers is 100 innings and 100 wickets respectively.

Only those players likely to play first-class county cricket in 1982 have been included.

BATTING AND BOWLING

BATSMEN	Runs	Avge	100's	BOWLERS	Wkts	Avge
G. Boycott	39,451	56.03	124	J. Garner	418	17.42
A.J. Lamb	9,684	52.06	21	M.D. Marshall	340	18.88
Zaheer Abbas	27,999	51.94	88	D.L. Underwood	2,004	19.61
Javed Miandad	14,919	50.57	42	W.W. Daniel	432	20.09
C.H.Lloyd	25,767	49.36	69	G. S. Le Roux	299	20.27
I.V.A. Richards	18,906	49.10	57	S.T. Clarke	309	20.77
G.M. Turner	33,042	49.09	98	R.J. Hadlee	623	20.87
P.N. Kirsten	10,345	43.64	25	M. Hendrick	666	20.96
D.L. Amiss	33,446	43.38	81	A.M.E. Roberts	662	21.12
A.L. Kallicharran	20,177	42.83	47	C.E.B. Rice	646	21.50
C.G. Greenidge	20,068	42.69	44	G.G. Arnold	1,124	21.95
C.E.B. Rice	13,730	40.62	24	C.M. Old	869	22.09
C.J. Tavaré	8,256	39.88	17	E.A. Moseley	103	22.15
B.F. Davison	20,994	39.09	38	N. Gifford	1,689	22.59
K.W.R. Fletcher	31,050	38.71	53	R.D. Jackman	1,326	22.59

FIELDING AND WICKET-KEEPING

FIELDERS	Ct	WICKET-KEEPERS	Total	Ct	St
G.R.J. Roope	586	R.W. Taylor	1,446	1,284	162
K.W.R. Fletcher	528	A.P.E. Knott	1,143	1,027	116
D.S. Steele	469	R.W. Tolchard	932	824	108
C.T. Radley	422	E.W. Jones	867	779	88
J.H. Hampshire	406	D.L. Bairstow	724	628	96
J.M. Brearley	400	D.J.S. Taylor	661	581	80
G.M. Turner	397	G. Sharp	518	445	73
J.A. Ormrod	366	N. Smith	446	395	51
D.L. Amiss	323	G.W. Humpage	300	268	32
D. Lloyd	316	I.J. Gould	265	232	33
C.G. Greenidge	312	R.R. Downton	227	200	27
J.F. Steele	302	D.J. Humphries	226	187	39
C.H. Lloyd	300	A.W. Stovold	223	180	43
Asif Iqbal	297	C.J. Richards	221	189	32
Sadiq Mohammad	289	B.N. French	216	192	24

CAREER RECORDS
Compiled by Michael Fordham

The following career records are for all players appearing in first-class cricket in the 1981 season.

A few cricketers who did not re-appear for their counties in 1981, but who may do so in 1982, as well as others who appeared only in John Player League and other one-day matches are also included.

Aggregates of 1,000 runs overseas are preceded by a + sign, e.g. D.L. Amiss 17+1.

BATTING AND FIELDING

	M	I	NO	Runs	HS	Avge	100s	1000 runs in season	Ct	St
Abrahams, J.	121	184	22	3803	126	23.47	2	—	73	—
Acfield, D.L.	309	315	155	1407	42	8.79	—	—	101	—
Agnew, J.P.	37	37	6	267	31	8.61	—	—	15	—
Alderman, T.M.	59	59	28	200	26*	6.45	—	—	41	—
Alleyne, H.L.	35	37	6	326	72	10.51	—	—	7	—
Allott, P.J.W.	49	47	15	335	52*	10.46	—	—	11	—
Amiss, D.L.	504	866	95	33446	262*	43.38	81	17+1	323	—
Anderson. I.J.	18	31	8	935	147	40.65	3	—	9	—
Anderson, I.S.	35	49	12	521	75	14.08	—	—	20	—
Arnold, G.G.	362	374	86	3941	73	13.68	—	—	122	—
Asif Din	21	37	4	878	73*	26.60	—	—	11	—
Asif Iqbal	430	686	~74	22817	196	37.28	44	7+2	297	—
Aslett, D.G.	2	4	2	188	146*	94.00	1	—	1	—
Athey, C.W.J.	121	198	13	4706	131*	25.43	7	1	114	2
Bailey, D.	32	46	2	1265	136	28.75	1	—	13	—
Bailey, M.J.	19	28	9	225	24	11.84	—	—	8	—
Bainbridge, P.	58	95	17	2034	105*	26.07	2	1	28	—
Bairstow, D.L.	288	417	77	7793	145	22.92	3	1	628	96
Balderstone, J.C.	283	438	46	13133	178*	33.50	19	7	150	—
Baptiste, E.A.	15	22	4	359	37*	19.94	—	—	8	—
Barclay, J.R.T.	181	309	26	7119	119	25.15	9	4	142	—
Barlow, G.D.	177	279	42	8203	177	34.61	15	5	91	—
Barnett, K.J.	58	82	10	1606	96	22.30	—	—	34	—
Barwick, S.R.	5	4	3	20	11*	20.00	—	—	1	—
Beard, G.R.	44	58	8	1063	71	21.26	—	—	18	—
Bell, D.L.	7	13	3	234	60	23.40	—	—	3	—
Benson, M.R.	30	49	5	1311	114	29.79	2	1	11	—
Birch, J.D.	100	146	25	2854	111	23.58	2	—	78	—
Birkenshaw, J.	490	665	123	12780	131	23.57	4	—	318	—
Booden, C.D.	4	3	2	10	6*	10.00	—	—	2	—
Boon, T.J.	25	42	5	922	83	24.91	—	—	7	—
Booth, P.	90	80	21	767	58*	13.00	—	—	27	—
Booth Jones, T.D.	26	44	1	1034	95	24.04	—	—	8	—
Border, A.R.	84	146	21	6059	200	48.47	16	0+2	77	—
Bore, M.K.	127	125	41	649	37*	7.72	—	—	38	—

	M	I	NO	Runs	HS	Avge	100s	1000 runs in season	Ct	St
Borrington, A.J.	122	203	24	4230	137	23.63	3	—	57	—
Botham, I.T.	175	268	23	7414	228	30.26	15	2	173	—
Boycott, G.	499	827	123	39451	261*	56.03	124	19+3	206	—
Boyd-Moss, R.J.	33	55	4	948	84	18.58	—	—	13	—
Brain, B.M.	259	271	68	1704	57	8.39	—	—	50	—
Brassington, A.J.	102	130	38	715	28	7.77	—	—	170	39
Breakwell, D.	229	303	63	4720	100*	19.66	1	—	81	—
Brearley, J.M.	434	735	93	24085	312*	37.51	42	10	400	12
Briers, N.E.	95	152	13	3592	119	25.84	7	1	32	—
Bright, R.J.	100	136	28	2171	108	20.10	1	—	69	—
Broad, B.C.	51	91	7	2590	129	30.83	5	1	25	—
Brooks, K.G.	1	2	0	11	8	5.50	—	—	2	—
Brown, A.	4	6	0	63	25	10.50	—	—	3	—
Butcher, A.R.	175	290	28	8413	216*	32.11	15	3	74	—
Butcher, I.P.	2	2	0	56	42	28.00	—	—	—	—
Butcher, R.O.	101	165	10	4246	179	27.39	5	—	114	—
Capel, D.J.	1	2	1	37	37	37.00	—	—	1	—
Carrick, P.	191	241	47	4203	131*	21.66	3	—	99	—
Carter, R.M.	40	48	9	447	42*	11.46	—	—	17	—
Chappell, T.M.	57	96	8	2668	150	30.31	4	—	29	—
Cheatle, R.G.L.	55	42	16	310	49	11.92	—	—	52	—
Childs, J.H.	117	106	63	309	20	7.18	—	—	49	—
Clark, A.R.	1	2	0	13	12	6.50	—	—	—	—
Clark, J.	12	15	3	101	29	8.41	—	—	12	—
Clarke, S.T.	77	86	17	1072	100*	15.53	1	—	38	—
Clift, P.B.	194	278	63	4951	88*	23.02	—	—	103	—
Clinton, G.S.	104	179	16	4793	134	29.40	6	3	35	—
Cobb, R.A.	11	16	0	324	54	20.25	—	—	8	—
Cockbain, I.	24	38	7	673	85	21.70	—	—	14	—
Compton-Burnett, R.J.	1	2	0	23	18	11.50	—	—	—	—
Cook, C.R.	6	12	2	249	79	24.90	—	—	5	—
Cook, G.	258	455	32	12484	172	29.51	18	6	265	—
Cook, N.G.B.	71	69	24	508	75	11.28	—	—	40	—
Cooper, K.E.	90	85	18	495	35	7.38	—	—	30	—
Corlett, S.C.	27	38	6	463	60	14.46	—	—	23	—
Cowan, R.S.	15	26	1	719	113	28.76	1	—	11	1
Cowans, N.G.	5	3	0	12	10	4.00	—	—	2	—
Cowdrey, C.S.	94	128	20	2966	101*	27.46	1	—	70	—
Cowley, N.G.	136	209	28	3790	109*	20.93	1	—	56	—
Croft, C.E.H.	96	106	42	637	46*	9.95	—	—	17	—
Cumbes, J.	147	119	60	466	43	7.89	—	—	30	—
Curtis, I.J.	12	16	7	34	9*	3.77	—	—	3	—
Curtis, T.S.	9	14	2	165	59*	13.75	—	—	1	—
Curzon, C.C.	18	23	5	307	45	17.05	—	—	32	3
Daniel, W.W.	129	112	49	760	53*	12.06	—	—	22	—
Daniels, S.A.B.	5	8	4	30	10*	7.50	—	—	4	—
Davies, T.	2	2	0	15	11	7.50	—	—	8	1
Davison, B.F.	360	590	53	20994	189	39.09	38	11	274	—
Deakin, M.J.	4	6	0	45	15	7.50	—	—	9	—
De Mel, A.L.F.	12	16	2	312	94	22.28	—	—	5	—

199

	M	I	NO	Runs	HS	Avge	100s	1000 runs in season	Ct	St
Denning, P.W.	229	381	37	9922	184	28.84	8	6	117	—
Dennis, S.J.	10	9	4	15	5*	3.00	—	—	3	—
De Silva, D.S.	42	61	10	1037	97	20.33	—	—	24	—
De Silva, G.R.A.	43	50	21	217	75	7.48	—	—	20	—
Devapriya, H.	6	12	0	376	95	31.33	—	—	12	5
Dexter, R.E.	22	36	6	464	57	15.46	—	—	23	—
Dias, R.L.	40	67	10	1791	127	31.42	1	—	15	—
Dilley, G.R.	65	68	30	641	81	16.86	—	—	31	—
Dixon, J.H.	16	20	8	77	13*	6.41	—	—	6	—
Doggart, S.J.G.	16	19	5	313	69*	22.35	—	—	7	—
Donald, W.A.	3	4	0	35	18	8.75	—	—	1	—
Doshi, D.R.	190	203	59	1147	44	7.96	—	—	52	—
Doughty, R.J.	1	2	0	17	10	8.50	—	—	—	—
Downton, P.R.	92	105	19	1446	90*	16.81	—	—	200	27
Dredge, C.H.	97	106	37	922	56*	13.36	—	—	39	—
Dudleston, B.	287	486	45	14316	202	32.46	31	8	228	7
Dutton, R.S.	4	3	3	7	7*	—	—	—	2	—
Dyer, R.I.H.B.	2	4	0	23	9	5.75	—	—	2	—
Dyson, J.	70	125	12	4143	197	36.66	8	0+1	29	—
Ealham, A.G.E.	304	464	67	10949	153	27.57	7	3	175	—
East, D.E.	13	17	3	144	28	10.28	—	—	21	5
East, R.E.	364	465	105	6384	113	17.73	1	—	223	—
Edmonds, P.H.	242	326	56	5253	141*	19.45	2	—	244	—
Edwards, T.D.W.	12	21	2	393	57	20.68	—	—	5	—
Ellis, R.G.P.	9	17	0	462	63	27.17	—	—	7	—
Ellison, R.M.	7	11	6	237	61*	47.40	—	—	3	—
Emburey, J.E.	143	171	48	2269	91*	18.44	—	—	143	—
Ezekowitz, R.A.B.	18	32	1	635	93	20.48	—	—	13	—
Featherstone, N.G.	322	515	54	13698	147	29.71	12	4	269	—
Fernando, L.J.	5	2	1	7	7*	7.00	—	—	2	—
Ferreira, A.M.	78	115	20	2670	106	28.10	1	—	39	—
Fisher, P.B.	57	85	14	654	42	9.21	—	—	92	11
Fletcher, K.W.R.	564	935	133	31050	228*	38.71	53	17	528	—
Forster, G.	2	1	1	17	17*	—	—	—	1	—
Foster, N.A.	2	2	2	16	8*	—	—	—	—	—
Fowler, G.	36	58	4	1846	143	34.18	4	1	31	5
Francis, D.A.	94	162	26	2932	110	21.55	1	—	45	—
French, B.N.	97	117	28	1255	70*	14.10	—	—	192	24
Gard, T.	12	11	5	124	51*	20.66	—	—	17	5
Garner, J.	93	97	20	1457	104	18.92	1	—	62	—
Garnham, M.A.	23	32	6	577	74	22.19	—	—	49	9
Gatting, M.W.	139	215	32	6565	186*	35.87	8	3	123	—
Gifford, N.	556	655	203	6147	89	13.59	—	—	273	—
Gladwin, C.	1	1	0	53	53	53.00	—	—	—	—
Goldie, C.F.E.	11	13	2	181	77	16.45	—	—	11	2
Gooch, G.A.	184	313	27	10716	205	37.46	25	5	154	—
Gordon-Walker, R.A.	3	5	1	19	12	4.75	—	—	3	2
Gould, I.J.	115	152	21	2827	128	21.58	1	—	232	33
Gower, D.I.	147	230	21	7527	200*	36.01	15	3	81	—

200

	M	I	NO	Runs	HS	Avge	100s	1000 runs in season	Ct	St
Graveney, D.A.	194	267	63	3741	119	18.33	2	—	87	—
Green, A.M.	4	6	0	107	38	17.83	—	—	1	—
Greenidge, C.G.	291	499	29	20068	273*	42.69	44	10	312	—
Greensword, S.	41	71	8	1025	84*	16.26	—	—	29	—
Greig, I.A.	67	93	12	2095	118*	25.86	1	—	38	—
Griffiths, A.	1	1	0	26	26	26.00	—	—	—	—
Griffiths, B.J.	95	78	29	141	11	2.87	—	—	20	—
Gunasekera, Y.	7	9	2	340	79*	48.57	—	—	4	—
Gunatilleke, H.M.	16	19	4	129	25	8.60	—	—	22	13
Hacker, P.J.	63	73	28	427	35	9.48	—	—	13	—
Hadlee, R.J.	152	208	37	4154	142*	24.29	4	—	71	—
Halliday, M.	8	6	3	39	13*	13.00	—	—	3	—
Halliday, S.J.	5	7	1	135	37	22.50	—	—	3	—
Hampshire, J.H.	519	835	100	25410	183*	34.57	41	14	406	—
Hardie, B.R.	185	307	37	9028	162	33.43	12	6	169	—
Harpur, T.	2	2	0	10	6	5.00	—	—	2	—
Harris, M.J.	342	578	56	19081	201*	36.55	41	11	287	14
Hart, P.R.	3	5	0	23	11	4.60	—	—	1	—
Harte, C.C.J.	2	3	0	82	40	27.33	—	—	—	—
Hartley, S.N.	36	58	6	1163	106	22.36	1	—	17	—
Hassan, S.B.	272	449	44	11926	182*	29.44	13	5	246	1
Hayes, F.C.	246	384	56	11995	187	36.57	20	6	161	—
Hayes, K.A.	8	13	0	300	59	23.07	—	—	2	—
Hayward, R.E.	8	14	3	285	101*	25.90	1	—	4	—
Head, T.J.	22	26	6	335	52*	16.75	—	—	54	6
Heath, J.R.P.	5	8	2	215	101*	35.83	1	—	2	—
Hemmings, E.E.	246	339	73	5512	86	20.72	—	—	113	—
Hemsley, E.J.O.	227	365	56	9347	176*	30.24	8	1	172	—
Hemsley, P.D.	3	5	2	26	12*	8.66	—	—	1	—
Henderson, S.P.	24	36	4	467	64	14.59	—	—	12	—
Hendrick, M.	231	229	91	1419	46	10.28	—	—	149	—
Hettiaratchy, N.D.P.	15	22	1	599	80	28.52	—	—	14	—
Higgs, K.	508	528	206	3622	98	11.29	—	—	311	—
Hignell, A.J.	135	224	24	5751	149*	28.75	9	2	135	—
Hill, A.	168	295	27	7703	160*	28.74	9	2	64	—
Hobbs, R.N.S.	440	546	138	4940	100	12.10	2	—	294	—
Hodgson, K.I.	9	9	3	148	30	24.66	—	—	2	—
Hogg, R.M.	61	88	9	736	42	9.31	—	—	15	—
Hogg, W.	68	68	16	313	31	6.01	—	—	12	—
Holding, M.A.	75	98	18	1005	62	12.56	—	—	28	—
Holliday, D.C.	29	37	8	522	76*	18.00	—	—	15	—
Holmes, G.C.	44	69	19	1070	100*	21.40	1	—	16	—
Hopkins, D.C.	36	44	12	332	34*	10.37	—	—	8	—
Hopkins, J.A.	160	283	15	7585	230	28.30	11	5	120	1
Howarth, G.P.	229	404	31	12307	183	32.99	23	3	150	—
Hughes, D.P.	283	351	70	5670	126	20.17	2	1	188	—
Hughes, K.J.	113	195	9	6423	213	34.53	11	0+2	86	—
Hughes, S.P.	22	24	10	74	18	5.28	—	—	8	—
Humpage, G.W.	142	227	25	7252	146	35.90	12	4	268	32
Humphries, D.J.	107	152	27	2998	111*	23.98	2	—	187	39
Huxford, P.N.	7	9	4	27	10	5.40	—	—	3	2

	M	I	NO	Runs	HS	Avge	100s	1000 runs in season	Ct	St
Huxter, R.J.A.	4	5	0	34	20	6.80	—	—	—	—
Illingworth, N.G.B.	1	—	—	—	—	—	—	—	1	—
Imran Khan	241	384	54	10663	170	32.31	19	3	78	—
Inchmore, J.D.	134	160	34	2016	113	16.00	1	—	45	—
Ingham, P.G.	8	14	0	290	64	20.71	—	—	—	—
Intikhab Alam	488	723	78	14327	182	22.21	9	—	228	—
Jackman, R.D.	375	451	147	5163	92*	16.98	—	—	171	—
Jackson, P.B.	1	1	1	42	42*	—	—	—	—	—
James, K.D.	2	2	1	21	16	21.00	—	—	1	—
Jarvis, K.B.S.	138	96	42	156	12*	2.88	—	—	36	—
Jarvis, P.W.	1	2	1	5	5	5.00	—	—	—	—
Javed Miandad	213	352	57	14919	311	50.57	42	3+5	202	3
Jennings, K.F.	68	73	24	521	49	10.63	—	—	48	—
Jesty, T.E.	298	473	58	11598	159*	27.94	13	4	170	1
Johnson, G.W.	301	478	48	10819	168	25.16	11	3	230	—
Johnson, M.	4	4	2	2	2	1.00	—	—	1	—
Johnson, P.D.	89	149	14	3363	106*	24.91	2	1	33	—
Johnston, H.G.F.	2	3	0	24	12	8.00	—	—	—	—
Jones, A.	598	1084	65	33499	204*	32.87	51	21	277	—
Jones, A.A.	214	216	68	799	33	5.9	—	—	50	—
Jones, A.L.	56	101	7	1736	83	18.46	—	—	28	—
Jones, A.N.	5	5	2	17	8	5.66	—	—	1	—
Jones, E.W.	375	552	111	7817	146*	17.72	3	—	779	88
Kallicharran, A.I.	323	526	55	20177	197	42.83	47	7+1	222	—
Kaluperuma, L.W.	49	65	18	846	96	18.00	—	—	40	—
Kapil Dev	82	116	9	2626	193	24.54	3	—	45	—
Kemp, N.J.	13	13	2	89	23	8.09	—	—	3	—
Kennedy, A.	141	231	19	6056	180	28.56	6	3	78	—
Kent, M.F.	61	106	10	3400	171	35.41	7	—	60	—
Ker, A.B.M.	1	2	0	65	65	32.50	—	—	—	—
Ker, J.E.	6	9	3	113	50	18.83	—	—	2	—
Kirsten, P.N.	151	263	26	10345	228	43.64	25	4+1	94	—
Knight, J.M.	23	35	3	318	41*	9.93	—	—	3	—
Knight, R.D.V.	315	555	46	15915	165*	31.26	25	10	237	—
Knott, A.P.E.	430	631	113	15578	156	30.07	16	2	1027	116
Lamb, A.J.	137	234	48	9684	178	52.06	21	3	96	—
Lamb, T.M.	138	140	52	1067	77	12.12	—	—	39	—
Larkins, W.	171	290	21	8464	170*	31.46	19	4	80	—
Lawlor, P.J.	1	2	0	8	8	4.00	—	—	1	—
Lawrence, D.V.	1	—	—	—	—	—	—	—	—	—
Lawson, G.F.	47	56	14	521	39	12.40	—	—	26	—
Lee, P.G.	199	163	68	779	26	8.20	—	—	29	—
Leiper, R.J.	1	2	0	50	49	25.00	—	—	—	—
Le Roux, G.S.	74	93	37	1400	70*	25.00	—	—	30	—
Lethbridge, C.	8	10	1	146	69	16.22	—	—	3	—
Lever, J.K.	362	373	153	2441	91	11.09	—	—	144	—
Lewington, P.J.	68	68	17	348	34	6.82	—	—	31	—
Lewis, R.V.	105	190	14	3471	136	19.72	2	—	65	—
Lillee, D.K.	149	185	54	1892	73*	14.44	—	—	47	—

	M	I	NO	Runs	HS	Avge	100s	1000 runs in season	Ct	St
Lilley, A.W.	18	30	1	829	100*	28.58	1	—	9	—
Llewellyn, M.J.	134	211	29	4200	129*	23.07	3	—	86	—
Lloyd, B.J.	108	140	37	1178	45*	11.43	—	—	69	—
Lloyd, C.H.	398	604	82	25767	242*	49.36	69	9+4	300	—
Lloyd, D.	374	601	69	17391	214*	32.68	32	10	316	—
Lloyd, T.A.	90	158	19	4670	138	33.59	6	2	59	—
Lloyds, J.W.	36	58	5	1342	127	25.32	1	—	20	—
Love, J.D.	102	169	23	4508	170*	30.87	8	1	63	—
Lumb, R.G.	205	341	26	10017	159	31.80	20	5	114	—
Lynch, M.A.	53	94	11	2023	120*	24.37	3	—	26	—
McEvoy, M.S.A.	43	74	1	1371	67*	18.78	—	—	42	—
McEwan, K.S.	252	429	35	15035	218	38.15	37	8	236	7
McIntyre, E.J.	1	1	0	6	6	6.00	—	—	1	—
Mackintosh, K.S.	20	21	8	186	23*	14.30	—	—	9	—
Madugalle, R.S.	20	24	0	530	88	22.08	—	—	17	—
Maher, B.J.M.	2	3	1	6	4*	3.00	—	—	6	2
Mallender, N.A.	22	26	9	127	18	7.47	—	—	10	—
Mallett, N.V.H.	11	20	2	237	52	13.16	—	—	3	—
Malone, S.J.	17	17	6	114	23	10.36	—	—	4	—
Marks, V.J.	135	209	30	5064	105	28.29	1	—	58	—
Marsden, R.	8	13	0	243	50	18.69	—	—	5	—
Marsh, R.W.	213	334	36	9585	236	32.16	10	0+1	640	58
Marshall, M.D.	91	118	16	1792	75*	17.56	—	—	39	—
Maru, R.J.	12	12	2	102	25	10.20	—	—	12	—
Maynard, C.	25	29	6	567	85	24.65	—	—	39	5
Mendis, G.D.	107	189	16	5576	204	32.23	7	2	59	1
Mendis, L.R.D.	60	101	9	3226	194	35.06	5	—	25	1
Merry, W.G.	23	17	11	42	14*	7.00	—	—	3	—
Metson, C.P.	1	1	1	38	38*	—	—	—	1	—
Miller, G.	203	297	43	6560	98*	25.82	1	—	135	—
Mills, J.P.C.	32	51	2	1196	111	24.40	1	—	11	—
Moir, D.G.	4	6	1	96	44	19.20	—	—	1	—
Monkhouse, G.	4	6	4	37	28*	18.50	—	—	2	—
Monteith, J.D.	24	33	5	338	78	12.07	—	—	19	—
Morris, H.	1	2	0	21	16	10.50	—	—	—	—
Moseley, E.A.	29	35	9	600	70*	23.07	—	—	7	—
Moseley, H.R.	195	198	81	1420	67	12.13	—	—	72	—
Moulding, R.P.	29	46	4	654	77*	15.57	—	—	13	—
Moxon, M.D.	11	19	0	518	116	27.26	2	—	8	—
Murley, A.J.	6	11	0	152	48	13.81	—	—	2	—
Nash, M.A.	315	447	65	6884	130	18.02	2	—	135	—
Neale, P.A.	123	214	23	6281	163*	32.88	12	3	52	—
Needham, A.	14	15	2	90	21	6.92	—	—	5	—
Newman, P.G.	19	19	7	153	29*	12.75	—	—	6	—
Nicholas, M.C.J.	44	75	9	1714	112	25.96	3	—	21	—
O'Brien, B.A.	11	17	1	319	45*	19.93	—	—	6	—
O'Brien, N.T.	2	2	0	27	14	13.50	—	—	1	—
Odendaal, A.	12	19	0	426	61	22.42	—	—	8	—
Old, C.M.	302	369	76	6478	116	22.10	6	—	181	—

203

	M	I	NO	Runs	HS	Avge	100s	1000 runs in season	Ct	St
Oldham, S.	83	55	23	222	50	6.93	—	—	25	—
Olive, M.	17	32	2	467	50	15.56	—	—	9	—
Oliver, P.R.	82	119	20	2536	171*	25.61	2	—	42	—
Ollis, R.L.	2	4	0	60	22	15.00	—	—	1	—
Ontong, R.C.	145	244	22	5476	151*	24.66	8	1	60	—
Orders, J.O.D.	27	49	3	1072	79	23.30	—	—	9	—
Ormrod, J.A.	428	720	87	20004	204*	31.60	30	12	366	—
O'Shaughnessy, S.J.	18	23	4	314	50*	16.52	—	—	5	—
Palmer, R.W.M.	1	—	—	—	—	—	—	—	1	—
Parker, P.W.G.	136	233	33	7151	215	35.75	17	5	83	—
Parks, R.J.	30	42	11	563	64*	18.16	—	—	61	8
Parsons, D.	1	0	1	1	1	1.00	—	—	—	—
Parsons, G.J.	40	46	12	420	50	12.35	—	—	13	—
Patel, D.N.	112	168	15	3796	138	24.81	8	1	67	—
Pauline, D.B.	11	15	1	179	46	12.78	—	—	2	—
Payne, I.R.	17	23	1	141	29	6.40	—	—	15	—
Peck, I.G.	25	36	4	410	45	12.81	—	—	12	1
Perry, N.J.	13	12	4	19	6	2.37	—	—	9	—
Perryman, S.P.	131	129	52	745	43	9.67	—	—	49	—
Phillip, N.	150	224	31	4703	134	24.36	1	—	48	—
Phillipson, C.P.	149	200	58	2703	87	19.03	—	—	110	—
Pigott, A.C.S.	29	37	5	468	55	14.62	—	—	9	—
Pilling, H.	333	542	68	15279	149*	32.23	25	8	89	—
Plumb, S.G.	3	5	1	97	37*	24.25	—	—	1	—
Pocock, N.E.J.	66	103	10	2105	143*	22.63	1	—	61	—
Pocock, P.I.	451	490	123	4289	75*	11.68	—	—	158	—
Pont, K.R.	142	223	29	4572	113	23.56	5	—	72	—
Popplewell, N.F.M.	63	85	15	1553	135*	22.18	1	—	44	—
Potter, L.	3	6	1	99	42*	19.80	—	—	3	—
Pridgeon, A.P.	121	114	54	521	34	8.68	—	—	36	—
Priestley, N.	1	1	1	20	20*	—	—	—	1	2
Pringle, D.R.	49	70	15	1773	127*	32.23	4	—	25	—
Prior, J.A.	1	1	0	20	20	20.00	—	—	—	—
Procter, M.J.	381	637	55	21307	254	36.60	47	9	312	—
Radford, N.V.	37	49	12	855	76*	23.10	—	—	19	—
Radley, C.T.	428	692	97	21113	171	35.48	36	14	422	—
Ramage, A.	16	17	7	169	52	16.90	—	—	1	—
Ranasinghe, A.N.	27	46	6	891	70	22.27	—	—	20	—
Randall, D.W.	244	418	36	13418	209	35.12	21	7	151	—
Ratnayeke, J.R.	7	8	5	43	15*	14.33	—	—	1	—
Reidy, B.W.	98	149	24	3442	131*	27.53	2	—	58	—
Rhodes, S.J.	1	—	—	—	—	—	—	—	—	—
Rice, C.E.B.	246	400	62	13730	246	40.62	24	7	185	—
Rice, J.M.	145	227	18	4314	161*	20.64	2	—	127	—
Richards, C.J.	104	117	25	1588	63	17.26	—	—	190	32
Richards, I.V.A.	249	413	28	18906	291	49.10	57	8+3	239	1
Ridge, S.P.	1	2	1	7	7*	7.00	—	—	—	—
Rixon, S.J.	86	128	21	2192	128	20.48	3	—	230	33
Roberts, A.M.E.	172	215	52	2396	63	14.69	—	—	39	—
Robertson, F.	12	17	1	163	51	10.18	—	—	3	—

205

	M	I	NO	Runs	HS	Avge	100s	1000 runs in season	Ct	St
Taylor, L.B.	72	50	26	162	22	6.75	—	—	22	—
Taylor, N.R.	22	38	6	902	110	28.18	1	—	21	—
Taylor, R.W.	551	760	140	10549	100	17.01	1	—	1284	162
Taylor, T.J.	9	14	6	78	28*	9.75	—	—	2	—
Terry, V.P.	15	23	2	328	94*	15.61	—	—	6	—
Thomas, D.J.	47	67	16	601	47	11.78	—	—	16	—
Thomas, G.P.	8	15	1	277	52	19.78	—	—	6	—
Thomas, J.G.	6	9	3	87	34	14.50	—	—	3	—
Thomas, W.R.K.	1	2	1	57	44	57.00	—	—	—	—
Thomson, J.R.	115	138	32	1420	61	13.39	—	—	45	—
Tindall, R.M.	14	22	4	330	60*	18.33	—	—	6	—
Todd, P.A.	144	255	14	6707	178	27.82	6	3	93	—
Tolchard, J.G.	78	109	17	1865	78	20.27	—	—	24	—
Tolchard, R.W.	434	607	174	13670	126*	31.57	12	—	824	108
Tomlins, K.P.	32	46	6	889	94	22.22	—	—	19	—
Torkington, H.F.	1	2	0	9	9	4.50	—	—	1	—
Torrens, R.	5	6	1	25	16	5.00	—	—	1	—
Tremlett, T.M.	47	79	10	1606	88	23.27	—	—	14	—
Tunnicliffe, C.J.	117	132	28	1358	82*	13.05	—	—	54	—
Turner, D.R.	305	506	45	13013	181*	28.22	20	6	156	—
Turner, G.M.	443	771	98	33042	259	49.09	98	14+3	397	—
Turner, S.	304	442	89	8208	121	23.25	4	—	198	—
Underwood, D.L.	520	551	146	3773	80	9.31	—	—	227	—
Van der Bijl, V.A.P.	134	165	40	2013	87	16.10	—	—	49	—
Varey, D.W.	3	5	1	81	39	20.25	—	—	2	—
Waller, C.E.	184	186	71	1107	51*	9.62	—	—	95	—
Warke, S.J.S.	1	1	0	4	4	4.00	—	—	1	—
Warnapura, B.	48	81	8	2040	154	27.94	2	—	21	—
Warner, C.J.	5	8	1	132	48	18.85	—	—	3	—
Waterton, S.N.V.	12	14	2	160	40*	13.33	—	—	21	4
Webster, A.J.	1	1	0	6	6	6.00	—	—	—	—
Weightman, N.I.	3	5	0	139	105	27.80	1	—	3	—
Wellham, D.M.	14	21	6	905	135*	60.33	4	—	8	—
Wells, A.P.	1	1	0	63	63	63.00	—	—	1	—
Wells, C.M.	41	60	10	1621	135	32.42	2	1	14	—
Wenlock, D.A.	7	10	4	133	62	22.16	—	—	2	—
Weston, M.J.	7	10	1	137	43	15.22	—	—	5	—
Wettimuny, S.	15	23	2	626	95*	29.80	—	—	6	—
White, R.A.	413	642	105	12452	116*	23.18	5	1	189	—
Whiteley, J.P.	41	36	16	225	20	11.25	—	—	18	—
Whitney, M.R.	10	9	0	9	4	1.00	—	—	9	—
Wijesuriya, R.G.C.E.	11	8	3	65	25	13.00	—	—	10	—
Wild, D.J.	7	12	3	128	30	14.22	—	—	2	—
Wilkins, A.H.	92	107	26	713	70	8.80	—	—	31	—
Willey, P.	308	502	76	11412	227	26.78	15	2	120	—
Williams, R.G.	112	180	18	4526	175*	27.93	9	3	50	—
Willis, R.G.D.	241	256	111	1981	43	13.66	—	—	103	—
Willows, A.	3	1	0	1	1	1.00	—	—	—	—
Wills, R.	1	1	0	48	48	48.00	—	—	—	—

	M	I	NO	Runs	HS	Avge	100s	1000 runs in season	Ct	St
Wilson, P.H.L.	42	33	16	181	29	10.64	—	—	7	—
Windybank, S.J.	14	17	3	367	53	26.21	—	—	3	—
Wood, B.	333	551	71	16580	198	34.54	29	8	263	—
Wood, G.M.	79	142	9	4545	126*	34.17	10	0+1	63	—
Wood, L.J.	1	2	0	5	5	2.50	—	—	—	—
Woolmer, R.A.	311	480	67	13373	171	32.38	26	5	214	1
Wootton, S.H.	6	11	2	204	77	22.66	—	—	4	—
Wright, J.G.	153	273	19	9518	166*	37.47	19	4	90	—
Yallop, G.N.	111	193	22	6951	172	40.64	17	0+2	82	1
Yardley, T.J.	256	383	68	8176	135	25.95	5	1	228	2
Yeabsley, D.I.	4	6	3	27	14*	9.00	—	—	1	—
Younis Ahmed	372	627	92	20461	221*	38.24	32	10	208	—
Zaheer Abbas	359	613	74	27999	274	51.94	88	10+5	234	—

BOWLING

	Runs	Wkts	Avge	BB	5 wI	10 wM	100 wkts in season
Abrahams, J.	646	14	46.14	3-27	—	—	—
Acfield, D.L.	20292	742	27.34	8-55	28	3	—
Agnew, J.P.	2287	83	27.55	6-70	2	—	—
Alderman, T.M.	5267	222	23.72	6-63	9	—	—
Alleyne, H.L.	3022	117	25.82	8-43	5	2	—
Allott, P.J.W.	3501	135	25.93	8-48	5	—	—
Amiss, D.L.	700	18	38.88	3-21	—	—	—
Anderson, I.J.	249	17	14.64	5-21	1	—	—
Anderson, I.S.	514	9	57.11	4-35	—	—	—
Arnold, G.G.	24672	1124	21.95	8-41	46	3	1
Asif Din	371	5	74.20	1-11	—	—	—
Asif Iqbal	8776	291	30.15	6-45	5	—	—
Aslett, D.G.	—	—	—	—	—	—	—
Athey, C.W.J.	852	18	47.33	3-38	—	—	—
Bailey, D.	139	3	46.33	3-67	—	—	—
Bailey, M.J.	920	16	57.50	5-89	1	—	—
Bainbridge, P.	1812	55	32.94	5-68	1	—	—
Bairstow, D.L.	181	5	36.20	3-82	—	—	—
Balderstone, J.C.	7522	291	25.84	6-25	5	—	—
Baptiste, E.A.	844	29	29.10	5-37	1	—	—
Barclay, J.R.T.	6459	229	28.20	6-61	7	1	—
Barlow, G.D.	52	3	17.33	1-6	—	—	—
Barnett, K.J.	1191	18	66.16	4-76	—	—	—
Barwick, S.R.	130	7	10.00	3-10	—	—	—
Beard, G.R.	2777	103	26.96	5-33	6	1	—
Bell, D.L.	—	—	—	—	—	—	—
Benson, M.R.	28	0	—	—	—	—	—
Birch, J.D.	1816	37	49.08	6-64	1	—	—

207

	Runs	Wkts	Avge	BB	5 wI	10 wM	100 wkts in season
Birkenshaw, J.	29276	1073	27.28	8-94	44	4	2
Booden, C.D.	258	3	86.00	2-30	—	—	—
Boon, T.J.	57	0	—	—	—	—	—
Booth, P.	4549	162	28.08	6-93	1	—	—
Booth Jones, T.D.	—	—	—	—	—	—	—
Border, A.R.	1371	38	36.07	4-61	—	—	—
Bore, M.K.	8796	291	30.22	8-89	7	—	—
Borrington, A.J.	19	0	—	—	—	—	—
Botham, I.T.	15224	635	23.97	8-34	38	7	1
Boycott, G.	1240	36	34.44	4-14	—	—	—
Boyd-Moss, R.J.	740	14	52.85	2-24	—	—	—
Brain, B.M.	20194	824	24.50	8-55	33	6	—
Brassington, A.J.	10	0	—	—	—	—	—
Breakwell, D.	12887	418	30.83	8-39	12	1	—
Brearley, J.M.	189	3	63.00	1-6	—	—	—
Briers, N.E.	248	6	41.33	2-32	—	—	—
Bright, R.J.	7431	267	27.83	7-87	14	2	—
Broad, B.C.	552	9	61.33	2-14	—	—	—
Brooks, K.G.	—	—	—	—	—	—	—
Brown, A.	—	—	—	—	—	—	—
Butcher, A.R.	3299	89	37.06	6-48	1	—	—
Butcher, I.P.	—	—	—	—	—	—	—
Butcher, R.O.	34	0	—	—	—	—	—
Capel, D.J.	6	0	—	—	—	—	—
Carrick, P.	14123	496	28.47	8-33	23	2	—
Carter, R.M.	1347	36	37.41	4-27	—	—	—
Chappell, T.M.	426	15	28.40	3-22	—	—	—
Cheatle, R.G.L.	3120	101	30.89	6-32	6	—	—
Childs, J.H.	9286	320	29.01	9-56	18	2	—
Clark, A.R.	—	—	—	—	—	—	—
Clark, J.	721	35	20.60	4-10	—	—	—
Clarke, S.T.	6421	309	20.77	6-39	16	1	—
Clift, P.B.	12984	522	24.87	8-17	18	1	—
Clinton, G.S.	86	4	21.50	2-8	—	—	—
Cobb, R.A.	—	—	—	—	—	—	—
Cockbain, I.	14	0	—	—	—	—	—
Compton-Burnett, R.J.	—	—	—	—	—	—	—
Cook, C.R.	—	—	—	—	—	—	—
Cook, G.	292	3	97.25	1-7	—	—	—
Cook, N.G.B.	5255	191	27.51	7-81	8	—	—
Cooper, K.E.	5608	195	28.75	6-32	4	—	—
Corlett, S.C.	1834	52	35.26	5-32	2	—	—
Cowan, R.S.	178	3	59.33	1-9	—	—	—
Cowans, N.G.	241	10	24.10	5-58	1	—	—
Cowdrey, C.S.	677	19	35.63	3-17	—	—	—
Cowley, N.G.	7365	206	35.75	5-44	3	—	—
Croft, C.E.H.	8307	356	23.33	8-29	16	1	—
Cumbes, J.	10454	358	29.20	6-24	13	—	—
Curtis, I.J.	724	18	40.22	4-58	—	—	—
Curtis, T.S.	15	1	15.00	1-13	—	—	—
Curzon, C.C.	—	—	—	—	—	—	—

	Runs	Wkts	Avge	BB	5 wI	10 wM	100 wkts in season
Daniel, W.W.	8680	432	20.09	7-95	18	4	—
Daniels, S.A.B.	326	8	40.75	3-33	—	—	—
Davies, T.	—	—	—	—	—	—	—
Davison, B.F.	2617	82	31.91	5-52	1	—	—
Deakin, M.J.	—	—	—	—	—	—	—
De Mel, A.L.F.	910	15	60.66	3-37	—	—	—
Denning, P.W.	96	1	96.00	1-4	—	—	—
Dennis, S.J.	727	26	27.96	5-35	1	—	—
De Silva, D.S.	4297	176	24.41	8-46	13	5	—
De Silva, G.R.A.	3751	152	24.67	6-30	4	—	—
Devapriya, H.	—	—	—	—	—	—	—
Dexter, R.E.	—	—	—	—	—	—	—
Dias, R.L.	6	0	—	—	—	—	—
Dilley, G.R.	4144	149	27.81	6-66	4	—	—
Dixon, J.H.	1136	21	54.09	5-44	2	—	—
Doggart, S.J.G.	756	15	50.40	3-54	—	—	—
Donald, W.A.	5	0	—	—	—	—	—
Doshi, D.R.	18298	715	25.59	7-29	30	4	1
Doughty, R.J.	55	2	27.50	2-28	—	—	—
Downton, P.R.	—	—	—	—	—	—	—
Dredge, C.H.	6962	244	28.53	6-37	9	—	—
Dudleston, B.	1093	40	27.32	4-6	—	—	—
Dutton, R.S.	131	1	131.00	1-45	—	—	—
Dyer, R.I.H.B.	—	—	—	—	—	—	—
Dyson, J.	2	0	—	—	—	—	—
Ealham, A.G.E.	189	3	63.00	1-1	—	—	—
East, D.E.	—	—	—	—	—	—	—
East, R.E.	23766	938	25.33	8-30	46	10	—
Edmonds, P.H.	19410	772	25.14	8-132	31	4	—
Edwards, T.D.W.	58	1	58.00	1-17	—	—	—
Ellis, R.G.P.	—	—	—	—	—	—	—
Ellison, R.M.	144	4	36.00	1-11	—	—	—
Emburey, J.E.	11356	481	23.60	7-36	32	8	—
Ezekowitz, R.A.B.	—	—	—	—	—	—	—
Featherstone, N.G.	4959	181	27.39	5-32	4	—	—
Fernando, L.J.	241	1	241.00	1-37	—	—	—
Ferreira, A.M.	6200	197	31.47	8-38	8	1	—
Fisher, P.B.	—	—	—	—	—	—	—
Fletcher, K.W.R.	1890	46	41.08	5-41	1	—	—
Forster, G.	150	3	50.00	2-30	—	—	—
Foster, N.A.	170	4	42.50	3-51	—	—	—
Fowler, G.	12	0	—	—	—	—	—
Francis, D.A.	6	0	—	—	—	—	—
French, B.N.	—	—	—	—	—	—	—
Gard, T.	—	—	—	—	—	—	—
Garner, J.	7283	418	17.42	8-31	22	4	—
Garnham, M.A.	—	—	—	—	—	—	—
Gatting, M.W.	1742	65	26.80	5-59	1	—	—
Gifford, N.	38164	1689	22.59	8-28	78	12	3

209

	Runs	Wkts	Avge	BB	5 wI	10 wM	100 wkts in season
Gladwin, C.	—	—	—	—	—	—	—
Goldie, C.F.E.	—	—	—	—	—	—	—
Gooch, G.A.	2147	55	39.03	5-40	1	—	—
Gordon-Walker, R.A.	—	—	—	—	—	—	—
Gould, I.J.	3	0	—	—	—	—	—
Gower, D.I.	62	3	20.66	3-47	—	—	—
Graveney, D.A.	13122	459	28.58	8-85	22	4	—
Green, A.M.	—	—	—	—	—	—	—
Greenidge, C.G.	438	16	27.37	5-49	1	—	—
Greensword, S.	917	28	32.75	3-22	—	—	—
Greig, I.A.	3495	129	27.09	7-43	5	2	—
Griffiths, A.	—	—	—	—	—	—	—
Griffiths, B.J.	7284	252	28.90	8-50	7	—	—
Gunasekera, Y.	5	0	—	—	—	—	—
Gunatilleke, H.M.	—	—	—	—	—	—	—
Hacker, P.J.	4115	128	32.14	6-35	2	—	—
Hadlee, R.J.	1300	623	20.87	7-23	32	5	1
Halliday, M.	449	20	22.45	5-39	1	—	—
Halliday, S.J.	—	—	—	—	—	—	—
Hampshire, J.H.	1607	30	53.56	7-52	2	—	—
Hardie, B.R.	60	2	30.00	2-39	—	—	—
Harpur, T.	5	0	—	—	—	—	—
Harris, M.J.	3459	79	43.78	4-16	—	—	—
Hart, P.R.	140	2	70.00	1-22	—	—	—
Harte, C.C.J.	—	—	—	—	—	—	—
Hartley, S.N.	635	14	45.35	3-40	—	—	—
Hassan, S.B.	407	6	67.83	3-33	—	—	—
Hayes, F.C.	15	0	—	—	—	—	—
Hayes, K.A.	33	0	—	—	—	—	—
Hayward, R.E.	5	0	—	—	—	—	—
Head, T.J.	—	—	—	—	—	—	—
Heath, J.R.P.	—	—	—	—	—	—	—
Hemmings, E.E.	19524	674	28.96	7-33	31	8	—
Hemsley, E.J.O.	2417	69	35.02	3-5	—	—	—
Hemsley, P.D.	143	1	143.00	1-4	—	—	—
Henderson, S.P.	46	0	—	—	—	—	—
Hendrick, M.	13960	666	20.96	8-45	24	3	—
Hettiaratchy, N.D.P.	—	—	—	—	—	—	—
Higgs, K.	36132	1530	23.61	7-19	49	5	5
Hignell, A.J.	184	3	61.33	2-13	—	—	—
Hill, A.	133	5	26.60	3-5	—	—	—
Hobbs, R.N.S.	29776	1099	27.09	8-63	50	8	2
Hodgson, K.I.	597	20	29.85	4-77	—	—	—
Hogg, R.M.	5012	219	22.88	6-74	12	3	—
Hogg, W.	4900	175	28.00	7-84	5	1	—
Holding, M.A.	6379	268	23.80	8-92	13	2	—
Holliday, D.C.	400	6	66.66	2-23	—	—	—
Holmes, G.C.	957	26	36.80	5-86	1	—	—
Hopkins, D.C.	2021	53	38.13	6-67	1	—	—
Hopkins, J.A.	27	0	—	—	—	—	—
Howarth, G.P.	3113	102	30.51	5-32	1	—	—

210

	Runs	Wkts	Avge	BB	5 wI	10 wM	100 wkts in season
Hughes, D.P.	16948	572	29.62	7-24	20	2	—
Hughes, K.J.	44	1	44.00	1-0	—	—	—
Hughes, S.P.	1897	74	25.63	6-75	4	—	—
Humpage, G.W.	130	3	43.33	2-13	—	—	—
Humphries, D.J.	—	—	—	—	—	—	—
Huxford, P.N.	—	—	—	—	—	—	—
Huxter, R.J.A.	224	5	44.80	2-49	—	—	—
Illingworth, N.G.B.	16	1	16.00	1-4	—	—	—
Imran Khan	19303	824	23.42	7-52	46	8	—
Inchmore, J.D.	9797	338	28.98	8-58	13	1	—
Ingham, P.G.	—	—	—	—	—	—	—
Intikhab Alam	43455	1570	27.67	8-54	85	13	1
Jackman, R.D.	29955	1326	22.59	8-40	65	8	1
Jackson, P.B.	—	—	—	—	—	—	—
James, K.D.	63	4	15.75	3-14	—	—	—
Jarvis, K.B.S.	10228	387	26.42	8-97	13	3	—
Jarvis, P.W.	74	0	—	—	—	—	—
Javed Miandad	5428	172	31.55	7-39	6	—	—
Jennings, K.F.	3403	96	35.44	5-18	1	—	—
Jesty, T.E.	12824	480	26.71	7-75	17	—	—
Johnson, G.W.	13224	439	30.12	6-32	15	2	—
Johnson, M.	301	7	43.00	4-48	—	—	—
Johnson, P.D.	972	11	88.36	3-34	—	—	—
Johnston, H.G.F.	86	3	28.66	2-60	—	—	—
Jones, A.	333	3	111.00	1-24	—	—	—
Jones, A.A.	15414	549	28.07	9-51	23	3	—
Jones, A.L.	17	0	—	—	—	—	—
Jones, A.N.	283	17	16.64	4-33	—	—	—
Jones, E.W.	5	0	—	—	—	—	—
Kallicharran, A.I.	1841	37	49.75	4-48	—	—	—
Kaluperuma, L.W.	3411	122	27.95	8-43	6	1	—
Kapil Dev	7175	277	25.90	8-38	15	2	—
Kemp, N.J.	621	12	51.75	6-119	1	—	—
Kennedy, A.	370	9	41.11	3-58	—	—	—
Kent, M.F.	3	0	—	—	—	—	—
Ker, A.B.M.	—	—	—	—	—	—	—
Ker, J.E.	181	5	36.20	1-2	—	—	—
Kirsten, P.N.	1933	51	37.90	4-44	—	—	—
Knight, J.M.	1413	33	43.36	4-69	—	—	—
Knight, R.D.V.	10888	312	34.89	6-44	4	—	—
Knott, A.P.E.	82	2	41.00	1-5	—	—	—
Lamb, A.J.	91	4	22.75	1-1	—	—	—
Lamb, T.M.	9193	320	28.72	7-56	9	—	—
Larkins, W.	958	25	38.32	3-34	—	—	—
Lamon, P.J.	50	1	50.00	1-30	—	—	—
Lawrence, D.V.	86	0	—	—	—	—	—
Lawson, G.F.	3728	152	24.52	7-81	5	—	—
Lee, P.G.	15238	597	25.52	8-34	29	7	2
Leiper, R.J.	—	—	—	—	—	—	—

211

	Runs	Wkts	Avge	BB	5 wI	10 wM	100 wkts in season
Le Roux, G.S.	6063	299	20.27	8-107	14	2	—
Lethbridge, C.	501	7	71.57	2-26	—	—	—
Lever, J.K.	26501	1110	23.87	8-49	49	5	2
Lewington, P.J.	5411	188	28.78	7-52	6	—	—
Lewis, R.V.	104	1	104.00	1-59	—	—	—
Lillee, D.K.	15716	703	22.35	8-29	43	12	—
Lilley, A.W.	—	—	—	—	—	—	—
Llewellyn, M.J.	615	23	26.73	4-35	—	—	—
Lloyd, B.J.	7056	171	41.26	8-70	1	—	—
Lloyd, C.H.	4104	114	36.00	4-48	—	—	—
Lloyd, D.	5971	199	30.00	7-38	4	1	—
Lloyd, T.A.	303	3	101.00	1-14	—	—	—
Lloyds, J.W.	1395	38	36.71	6-61	2	1	—
Love, J.D.	144	0	—	—	—	—	—
Lumb, R.G.	—	—	—	—	—	—	—
Lynch, M.A.	175	5	35.00	3-6	—	—	—
McEvoy, M.S.A.	103	3	34.33	3-20	—	—	—
McEwan, K.S.	161	2	80.50	1-0	—	—	—
McIntyre, E.J.	15	0	—	—	—	—	—
Mackintosh, K.S.	1022	25	40.88	4-49	—	—	—
Madugalle, R.S.	32	0	—	—	—	—	—
Maher, B.J.M.	—	—	—	—	—	—	—
Mallender, N.A.	1563	56	27.91	6-37	1	—	—
Mallett, N.V.H.	841	19	44.26	5-52	1	—	—
Malone, S.J.	1076	29	37.10	3-56	—	—	—
Marks, V.J.	9381	271	34.61	6-33	10	—	—
Marsden, R.	—	—	—	—	—	—	—
Marsh, R.W.	74	1	74.00	1-0	—	—	—
Marshall, M.D.	6422	340	18.88	7-56	19	1	—
Maru, R.J.	678	16	42.37	3-29	—	—	—
Maynard, C.	—	—	—	—	—	—	—
Mendis, G.D.	11	0	—	—	—	—	—
Mendis, L.R.D.	30	1	30.00	1-4	—	—	—
Merry, W.G.	1353	46	29.41	4-24	—	—	—
Metson, C.P.	—	—	—	—	—	—	—
Miller, G.	12439	507	24.53	7-54	24	5	—
Mills, J.P.C.	5	0	—	—	—	—	—
Moir, D.G.	281	6	46.83	4-43	—	—	—
Monkhouse, G.	224	7	32.00	3-45	—	—	—
Monteith, J.D.	1644	89	18.47	7-38	7	1	—
Morris, H.	—	—	—	—	—	—	—
Moseley, E.A.	2282	103	22.15	6-23	5	—	—
Moseley, H.R.	12683	522	24.29	6-34	14	1	—
Moulding, R.P.	—	—	—	—	—	—	—
Moxon, M.D.	23	0	—	—	—	—	—
Murley, A.J.	1	0	—	—	—	—	—
Nash, M.A.	24172	951	25.41	9-56	44	5	—
Neale, P.A.	174	1	174.00	1-15	—	—	—
Needham, A.	498	10	49.80	3-25	—	—	—
Newman, P.G.	1347	54	24.94	5-51	1	—	—

	Runs	Wkts	Avge	BB	5 wI	10 wM	100 wkts in season
Nicholas, M.C.J.	72	1	72.00	1-4	—	—	—
O'Brien, B.A.	—	—	—	—	—	—	—
O'Brien, N.T.	101	1	101.00	1-23	—	—	—
Odendaal, A.	—	—	—	—	—	—	—
Old, C.M.	19203	869	22.09	7-20	32	1	—
Oldham, S.	5450	172	31.68	5-40	2	—	—
Olive, M.	—	—	—	—	—	—	—
Oliver, P.R.	2115	27	78.33	2-28	—	—	—
Ollis, R.L.	—	—	—	—	—	—	—
Ontong, R.C.	8516	283	30.09	7-60	9	1	—
Orders, J.O.D.	656	11	59.63	2-16	—	—	—
Ormrod, J.A.	1089	25	43.56	5-27	1	—	—
O'Shaughnessy, S.J.	415	12	34.58	3-17	—	—	—
Palmer, R.W.M.	30	1	30.00	1-30	—	—	—
Parker, P.W.G.	455	8	56.87	2-23	—	—	—
Parks, R.J.	0	0	—	—	—	—	—
Parsons, D.	53	1	53.00	1-53	—	—	—
Parsons, G.J.	2586	85	30.42	4-38	—	—	—
Patel, D.N.	5374	140	38.38	6-47	6	—	—
Pauline, D.B.	19	0	—	—	—	—	—
Payne, I.R.	575	11	52.27	2-28	—	—	—
Peck, I.G.	—	—	—	—	—	—	—
Perry, N.J.	920	21	43.80	3-51	—	—	—
Perryman, S.P.	9371	309	30.32	7-49	16	3	—
Phillip, N.	10987	427	25.73	6-33	14	1	—
Phillipson, C.P.	5156	152	33.92	6-56	4	—	—
Pigott, A.C.S.	1710	50	34.20	4-40	—	—	—
Pilling, H.	195	1	195.00	1-42	—	—	—
Plumb, S.G.	60	2	30.00	2-47	—	—	—
Pocock, N.E.J.	142	3	47.33	1-4	—	—	—
Pocock, P.I.	34962	1354	25.82	9-57	51	6	1
Pont, K.R.	2320	68	34.11	5-33	1	—	—
Popplewell, N.F.M.	2808	66	42.54	5-33	1	—	—
Potter, L.	—	—	—	—	—	—	—
Pridgeon, A.P.	9115	247	36.90	7-35	4	1	—
Priestley, N.	—	—	—	—	—	—	—
Pringle, D.R.	2774	87	31.88	6-90	1	1	—
Prior, J.A.	37	0	—	—	—	—	—
Procter, M.J.	26277	1370	19.18	9-71	68	14	2
Radford, N.V.	2845	86	33.08	6-41	4	1	—
Radley, C.T.	84	6	14.00	1-0	—	—	—
Ramage, A.	1123	37	30.35	5-65	1	—	—
Ranasinghe, A.N.	1194	31	38.51	5-65	1	—	—
Randall, D.W.	123	0	—	—	—	—	—
Ratnayeke, J.R.	436	12	36.33	3-38	—	—	—
Reidy, B.W.	2051	50	41.02	5-61	1	—	—
Rhodes, S.J.	—	—	—	—	—	—	—
Rice, C.E.B.	13891	646	21.50	7-62	19	1	—
Rice, J.M.	7467	227	32.89	7-48	3	—	—

	Runs	Wkts	Avge	BB	5 wI	10 wM	100 wkts in season
Richards, C.J.	—	—	—	—	—	—	—
Richards, I.V.A.	4101	100	41.01	4-55	—	—	—
Ridge, S.P.	65	1	65.00	1-50	—	—	—
Rixon, S.J.	20	0	—	—	—	—	—
Roberts, A.M.E.	13987	662	21.12	8-47	31	4	1
Robertson, F.	743	36	20.63	6-58	2	—	—
Robinson, R.T.	52	1	52.00	1-47	—	—	—
Roebuck, P.M.	1870	41	45.60	6-50	1	—	—
Rogers, J.J.	39	1	39.00	1-24	—	—	—
Romaines, P.W.	—	—	—	—	—	—	—
Roope, G.R.J.	8314	222	37.45	5-14	4	—	—
Rose, B.C.	213	6	35.50	3-9	—	—	—
Rouse, S.J.	8312	270	30.78	6-34	5	—	—
Rowe, C.W.C.	2301	59	39.00	6-46	3	1	—
Russell, P.E.	10108	535	30.17	7-46	5	—	—
Russell, R.C.	—	—	—	—	—	—	—
Russom, N.	1662	39	42.61	4-84	—	—	—
Sadiq Mohammad	6767	214	31.62	7-34	7	—	—
Sainsbury, G.E.	268	8	33.50	4-85	—	—	—
Sarfraz Nawaz	21061	890	23.66	9-86	45	4	1
Saxelby, K.	495	14	35.35	4-64	—	—	—
Scott, C.J.	—	—	—	—	—	—	—
Scott, C.W.	—	—	—	—	—	—	—
Scott, M.S.	37	0	—	—	—	—	—
Selvey, M.W.W.	16940	663	25.55	7-20	34	4	1
Sharp, G.	49	1	49.00	1-47	—	—	—
Sharp, K.	41	0	—	—	—	—	—
Shepherd, J.N.	25637	953	26.90	8-40	47	2	—
Sidebottom, A.	4131	165	25.03	7-18	6	2	—
Simmons, J.	17747	642	27.64	7-59	19	2	—
Slack, W.N.	36	0	—	—	—	—	—
Slocombe, P.A.	43	2	21.50	1-5	—	—	—
Small, G.C.	2504	66	37.93	6-76	1	—	—
Smith, C.L.	210	2	105.00	1-21	—	—	—
Smith, D.J.	—	—	—	—	—	—	—
Smith, D.M. (Sy)	1443	27	53.44	3-40	—	—	—
Smith, D.M. (Wa)	98	1	98.00	1-55	—	—	—
Smith, K.D.	3	0	—	—	—	—	—
Smith, N.	—	—	—	—	—	—	—
Southern, J.W.	10003	330	30.31	6-46	13	—	—
Speak, G.J.	54	0	—	—	—	—	—
Spelman, G.D.	291	7	41.57	2-27	—	—	—
Steele, D.S.	10105	424	23.83	8-29	16	2	—
Steele, J.F.	10407	404	25.75	7-29	9	—	—
Stevenson, G.B.	9915	358	27.69	8-57	15	2	—
Stevenson, K.	9824	333	29.50	7-22	15	—	—
Stewart, A.J.	—	—	—	—	—	—	—
Stovold, A.W.	86	2	43.00	1-0	—	—	—
Stovold, M.W.	6	0	—	—	—	—	—
Stuchbury, S.	236	8	29.50	3-82	—	—	—
Surridge, D.	1092	40	27.30	4-22	—	—	—

214

	Runs	Wkts	Avge	BB	5 wI	10 wM	100 wkts in season
Sutcliffe, S.P.	2030	56	36.25	6-19	1	—	—
Swan, R.G.	—	—	—	—	—	—	—
Tavaré, C.J.	254	2	127.00	1-20	—	—	—
Taylor, C.R.V.	—	—	—	—	—	—	—
Taylor, D.J.S.	15	0	—	—	—	—	—
Taylor, L.B.	5052	197	25.64	7-28	4	—	—
Taylor, N.R.	43	0	—	—	—	—	—
Taylor, R.W.	46	0	—	—	—	—	—
Taylor, T.J.	731	27	27.07	5-81	1	—	—
Terry, V.P.	39	0	—	—	—	—	—
Thomas, D.J.	3321	92	36.09	6-84	2	—	—
Thomas, G.P.	—	—	—	—	—	—	—
Thomas, J.G.	487	11	44.27	4-65	—	—	—
Thomas, W.R.K.	54	0	—	—	—	—	—
Thomson, J.R.	10851	452	24.00	7-33	20	3	—
Tindall, R.M.	331	4	82.75	2-1	—	—	—
Todd, P.A.	3	0	—	—	—	—	—
Tolchard, J.G.	5	0	—	—	—	—	—
Tolchard, R.W.	34	1	34.00	1-4	—	—	—
Tomlins, K.P.	216	2	108.00	2-54	—	—	—
Torkington, H.F.	—	—	—	—	—	—	—
Torrens, R.	300	24	12.50	7-40	2	—	—
Tremlett, T.M.	1475	48	30.72	5-30	1	—	—
Tunnicliffe, C.J.	7680	243	31.60	7-36	5	—	—
Turner, D.R.	322	9	35.77	2-7	—	—	—
Turner, G.M.	189	5	37.80	3-18	—	—	—
Turner, S.	18571	730	25.43	6-26	26	1	—
Underwood, D.L.	39307	2004	19.61	9-28	131	40	9
Van der Bijl, V.A.P.	10597	640	16.55	8-35	35	8	—
Varey, D.W.	—	—	—	—	—	—	—
Waller, C.E.	12581	449	28.02	7-64	17	1	—
Warke, S.J.S.	—	—	—	—	—	—	—
Warnapura, B.	472	11	42.90	2-33	—	—	—
Warner, C.J.	—	—	—	—	—	—	—
Waterton, S.N.V.	—	—	—	—	—	—	—
Webster, A.J.	18	0	—	—	—	—	—
Weightman, N.I.	—	—	—	—	—	—	—
Wellham, D.M.	11	1	11.00	1-11	—	—	—
Wells, A.P.	—	—	—	—	—	—	—
Wells, C.M.	1254	30	41.80	4-23	—	—	—
Wenlock, D.A.	164	3	54.66	2-23	—	—	—
Weston, M.J.	68	0	—	—	—	—	—
Wettimuny, S.	18	1	18.00	1-7	—	—	—
White, R.A.	21138	693	30.50	7-41	28	4	—
Whiteley, J.P.	2187	66	33.13	4-14	—	—	—
Whitney, M.R.	1073	35	30.65	5-60	1	—	—
Wijesuriya, R.G.C.E.	960	29	33.10	5-35	1	—	—
Wild, D.J.	306	3	102.00	2-52	—	—	—

	Runs	Wkts	Avge	BB	5 wI	10 wM	100 wkts in season
Wilkins, A.H.	6618	230	28.77	8-57	9	—	—
Willey, P.	12846	440	29.19	7-37	19	3	—
Williams, R.G.	5094	146	34.89	7-73	6	—	—
Willis, R.G.D.	17381	721	24.10	8-32	30	2	—
Willows, A.	203	8	25.37	4-33	—	—	—
Wills, R.	—	—	—	—	—	—	—
Wilson, P.H.L.	2098	74	28.35	5-36	1	—	—
Windaybank, S.J.	—	—	—	—	—	—	—
Wood, B.	8396	288	29.15	7-52	8	—	—
Wood, G.M.	127	5	25.40	3-18	—	—	—
Wood, L.J.	124	4	31.00	4-124	—	1	—
Woolmer, R.A.	10507	399	26.33	7-47	12	1	—
Wootton, S.H.	7	0	—	—	—	—	—
Wright, J.G.	23	1	23.00	1-4	—	—	—
Yallop, G.N.	555	7	79.28	4-63	—	—	—
Yardley, T.J.	38	0	—	—	—	—	—
Yeabsley, D.I.	389	13	29.92	3-45	—	—	—
Younis Ahmed	1591	39	40.79	4-10	—	—	—
Zaheer Abbas	813	25	32.52	5-15	1	—	—

SERVICETILL
...the bank that works when you don't.

National Westminster Bank
SERVICECARD

JOHN ENGLAND

609000 1246631 2

National Westminster Bank

FIRST-CLASS CRICKET RECORDS

COMPLETE TO END OF 1981 SEASON

Highest Innings Totals

1107	Victoria v New South Wales (Melbourne)	1926-27
1059	Victoria v Tasmania (Melbourne)	1922-23
951-7d	Sind v Baluchistan (Karachi)	1973-74
918	New South Wales v South Australia (Sydney)	1900-01
912-8d	Holkar v Mysore (Indore)	1945-46
910-6d	Railways v Dera Ismail Khan (Lahore)	1964-65
903-7d	England v Australia (Oval)	1938
887	Yorkshire v Warwickshire (Birmingham)	1896
849	England v West Indies (Kingston)	1929-30

NB. There are 22 instances of a side making 800 runs or more in an innings, the last occasion being 951-7 declared by Sind as above.

Lowest Innings Totals

12*	Oxford University v MCC and Ground (Oxford)	1877
12	Northamptonshire v Gloucestershire (Gloucester)	1907
13	Auckland v Canterbury (Auckland)	1877-78
13	Nottinghamshire v Yorkshire (Nottingham)	1901
15	MCC v Surrey (Lord's)	1839
15*	Victoria v MCC (Melbourne)	1903-04
15*	Northamptonshire v Yorkshire (Northampton)	1908
15	Hampshire v Warwickshire (Birmingham)	1922
16	MCC and Ground v Surrey (Lord's)	1872
16	Derbyshire v Nottinghamshire (Nottingham)	1879
16	Surrey v Nottinghamshire (Oval)	1880
16	Warwickshire v Kent (Tonbridge)	1913
16	Trinidad v Barbados (Bridgetown)	1941-42
16	Border v Natal (East London)	1959-60

*Batted one man short

NB. There are 26 instances of a side making less than 20 in an innings, the last occasion being 16 and 18 by Border v Natal at East London in 1959-60. The total of 34 is the lowest by one side in a match.

Highest Aggregates in a Match

2376	(38)	Bombay v Maharashtra (Poona)	1948-49
2078	(40)	Bombay v Holkar (Bombay)	1944-45
1981	(35)	England v South Africa (Durban)	1938-39
1929	(39)	New South Wales v South Australia (Sydney)	1925-26
1911	(34)	New South Wales v Victoria (Sydney)	1908-09
1905	(40)	Otago v Wellington (Dunedin)	1923-24

In England the highest are:

1723	(34)	England v Australia (Leeds) 5 day match	1948
1601	(29)	England v Australia (Lord's) 4 day match	1930
1507	(28)	England v West Indies (Oval) 5 day match	1976
1502	(28)	MCC v New Zealanders (Lord's)	1927
1499	(31)	T.N. Pearce's XI v Australians (Scarborough)	1961
1496	(24)	England v Australia (Nottingham) 4 day match	1938
1494	(37)	England v Australia (Oval) 4 day match	1934
1492	(33)	Worcestershire v Oxford U (Worcester)	1904
1477	(32)	Hampshire v Oxford U (Southampton)	1913
1477	(33)	England v South Africa (Oval) 4 day match	1947
1475	(27)	Northamptonshire v Surrey (Northampton)	1920

Lowest Aggregate in a Match

105	(31)	MCC v Australia (Lord's)	1878
134	(30)	England v The B's (Lord's)	1831
147	(40)	Kent v Sussex (Sevenoaks)	1828
149	(30)	England v Kent (Lord's)	1858
151	(30)	Canterbury v Otago (Christchurch)	1866-67
153	(37)	MCC v Sussex (Lord's)	1843
153	(31)	Otago v Canterbury (Dunedin)	1896-97
156	(30)	Nelson v Wellington (Nelson)	1885-86
158	(22)	Surrey v Worcestershire (Oval)	1954

Wickets that fell are given in parentheses.

Tie Matches

Due to the change of law made in 1948 for tie matches, a tie is now a rarity. The law states that only if the match is played out and the scores are equal is the result a tie.

The most recent tied matches are as follows:

Yorkshire (351-4d & 113) v Leicestershire (328 & 136) at Huddersfield	1954
Sussex (172 & 120) v Hampshire (153 & 139) at Eastbourne	1955
Victoria (244 & 197) v New South Wales (281 & 160) at Melbourne (St. Kilda)	1956-57
(The first tie in Sheffield Shield cricket)	
T.N. Pearce's XI (313-7d & 258) v New Zealanders (268 & 303-8d) at Scarborough	1958
Essex (364-6d & 176-8d) v Gloucestershire (329 & 211) at Leyton	1959
Australia (505 & 232) v West Indies (453 & 284) at Brisbane	1960-61
(The first tie in Test cricket)	
Bahawalpur (123 & 282) v Lahore B (127 & 278) at Bahawalpur	1961-62
Middlesex (327-5d & 123-9d) v Hampshire (277 & 173) at Portsmouth	1967
England XI (312-8d & 190-3d) v England Under-25 XI (320-9d & 182) at Scarborough	1968
Yorkshire (106-9d & 207) v Middlesex (102 & 211) at Bradford	1973
Sussex (245 & 173-5d) v Essex (200-8d & 218) at Hove	1974
South Australia (431 & 171-7d) v Queensland (340-8d & 262) at Adelaide	1976-77
England XI (296-6d & 104) v Central Districts (198 & 202) at New Plymouth	1977-78
Peshawar (139 & 188) v Allied Bank (240 & 87) at Peshawar	1979-80

Highest Individual Scores

499	Hanif Mohammad, Karachi v Bahawalpur (Karachi)	1958-59
452*	D.G. Bradman, New South Wales v Queensland (Sydney)	1929-30
443*	B.B. Nimbalkar, Maharashtra v Kathiawar (Poona)	1948-49
437	W.H. Ponsford, Victoria v Queensland (Melbourne)	1927-28
429	W.H. Ponsford, Victoria v Tasmania (Melbourne)	1922-23
428	Aftab Baloch, Sind v Baluchistan (Karachi)	1973-74
424	A.C. MacLaren, Lancashire v Somerset (Taunton)	1895
385	B. Sutcliffe, Otago v Canterbury (Christchurch)	1952-53
383	C.W. Gregory, New South Wales v Queensland (Brisbane)	1906-07
369	D.G. Bradman, South Australia v Tasmania (Adelaide)	1935-36
365*	C. Hill, South Australia v New South Wales (Adelaide)	1900-01
365*	G.S. Sobers, West Indies v Pakistan (Kingston)	1957-58
364	L. Hutton, England v Australia (Oval)	1938
359*	V.M. Merchant, Bombay v Maharashtra (Bombay)	1943-44
359	R.B. Simpson, New South Wales v Queensland (Brisbane)	1963-64
357*	R. Abel, Surrey v Somerset (Oval)	1899
357	D.G. Bradman, South Australia v Victoria (Melbourne)	1935-36
356	B.A. Richards, South Australia v Western Australia (Perth)	1970-71
355	B. Sutcliffe, Otago v Auckland (Dunedin)	1949-50
352	W.H. Ponsford, Victoria v New South Wales (Melbourne)	1926-27
350	Rashid Israr, National Bank v Habib Bank (Lahore)	1976-77

NB. There are 91 instances of a batsman scoring 300 or more in an innings, the last occasion being 350 by Rashid Israr as above.

Most Centuries in a Season

18	D.C.S. Compton	1947
16	J.B. Hobbs	1925
15	W.R. Hammond	1938
14	H. Sutcliffe	1932

Most Centuries in an Innings

6	for Holkar v Mysore (Indore)	1945-46
5	for New South Wales v South Australia (Sydney)	1900-01
5	for Australia v West Indies (Kingston)	1954-55

Most Centuries in Successive Innings

6	C.B. Fry	1901
6	D.G. Bradman	1938-39
6	M.J. Procter	1970-71
5	E.D. Weekes	1955-56

NB. The feat of scoring 4 centuries in successive innings has been achieved on 31 occasions.

Most Centuries in Succession in Test Matches

5	E.D. Weekes, West Indies	1947-48 and 1948-49
4	J.H.W. Fingleton, Australia	1935-36 and 1936-37
4	A. Melville, South Africa	1938-39 and 1947

Two Double Centuries in a Match

A.E. Fagg, 244 and 202* for Kent v Essex (Colchester)   1938

A Double Century and a Century in a Match

C.B. Fry, 125 and 229, Sussex v Surrey (Hove)	1900
W.W. Armstrong, 157* and 245, Victoria v South Australia (Melbourne)	1920-21
H.T.W. Hardinge, 207 and 102* for Kent v Surrey (Blackheath)	1921
C.P. Mead, 113 and 224, Hampshire v Sussex (Horsham)	1921
K.S. Duleepsinhji, 115 and 246, Sussex v Kent (Hastings)	1929
D.G. Bradman, 124 and 225, Woodfull's XI v Ryder's XI (Sydney)	1929-30
B. Sutcliffe, 243 and 100*, New Zealanders v Essex (Southend)	1949
M.R. Hallam, 210* and 157, Leicestershire v Glamorgan (Leicester)	1959
M.R. Hallam, 203* and 143* Leicestershire v Sussex (Worthing)	1961
Hanumant Singh, 109 and 213*, Rajasthan v Bombay (Bombay)	1966-67
Salahuddin, 256 and 102*, Karachi v East Pakistan (Karachi)	1968-69
K.D. Walters, 242 and 103, Australia v West Indies (Sydney)	1968-69
S.M. Gavaskar, 124 and 220, India v West Indies (Port of Spain)	1970-71
L.G. Rowe, 214 and 100*, West Indies v New Zealand (Kingston)	1971-72
G.S. Chappell, 247* and 133, Australia v New Zealand (Wellington)	1973-74
L. Baichan, 216* and 102, Berbice v Demerara (Georgetown)	1973-74
Zaheer Abbas, 216* and 156*, Gloucestershire v Surrey (Oval)	1976
Zaheer Abbas, 230* and 104*, Gloucestershire v Kent (Canterbury)	1976
Zaheer Abbas, 205* and 108*, Gloucestershire v Sussex (Cheltenham)	1977
Saadat Ali, 141 and 222, Income Tax v Multan (Multan)	1977-78
Talat Ali, 214* and 104, Pakistan International Airways v Punjab (Lahore)	1978-79
Shafiq Ahmed, 129 and 217*, National Bank v Muslim Commercial Bank (Karachi)	1978-79
D.W. Randall, 209 and 146, Nottinghamshire v Middlesex (Nottingham)	1979
Zaheer Abbas, 215* and 150*, Gloucestershire v Somerset (Bath)	1981

Two Centuries in a Match on Most Occasions

7 W.R. Hammond   6 J.B. Hobbs, G.M. Turner, Zaheer Abbas   5 C.B. Fry

NB. 11 Batsmen have achieved the feat on four occasions, 22 batsmen on three occasions and 41 batsmen on two occasions.

Most Centuries

J.B. Hobbs, 197 (175 in England); E.H. Hendren, 170 (151); W.R. Hammond, 167 (134); C.P. Mead, 153 (145); H. Sutcliffe, 149 (135); F.E. Woolley, 145 (135); L. Hutton, 129 (105); G. Boycott, 124 (99); W.G. Grace, 124 (123); D.C.S. Compton, 123 (92); T.W. Graveney, 122 (91); D.G. Bradman, 117 (41); M.C. Cowdrey, 107 (80); A. Sandham, 107 (87); T.W. Hayward, 104 (100); J.H. Edrich, 103 (90); L.E.G. Ames, 102 (89); G.E. Tyldesley, 102 (94).

Highest Individual Batting Aggregate in a Season

Runs		Season	M	Innings	NO	HS	Avge	100s
3,816	D.C.S. Compton	1947	30	50	8	246	90.85	18
3,539	W.J. Edrich	1947	30	52	8	267*	80.43	12

NB. The feat of scoring 3,000 runs in a season has been achieved on 28 occasions, the last instance being by W.E. Alley (3,019 runs, av. 59.96) in 1961.
Since the reduction of the matches in the County Championship in 1969, the highest aggregate in a season is 2,554 runs (av. 75.11) by Zaheer Abbas in 1976.

Partnerships for First Wicket

561	Waheed Mirza and Mansoor Akhtar, Karachi Whites v Quetta (Karachi)	1976-77
555	H. Sutcliffe and P. Holmes, Yorkshire v Essex (Leyton)	1932
554	J.T. Brown and J. Tunnicliffe, Yorkshire v Derbyshire (Chesterfield)	1898
490	E.H. Bowley and J.G. Langridge, Sussex v Middlesex (Hove)	1933
456	W.H. Ponsford and E.R. Mayne, Victoria v Queensland (Melbourne)	1923-24
451*	S. Desai and R.M.H. Binny, Karnataka v Kerala (Chikmagalur)	1977-78
428	J.B. Hobbs and A. Sandham, Surrey v Oxford U (Oval)	1926
424	J.F.W. Nicholson and I.J. Siedle, Natal v Orange Free State (Bloemfontein)	1926-27
418	Kamal Najamuddin and Khalid Alvi, Karachi v Railways (Karachi)	1980-81
413	V.M.H. Mankad and P. Roy, India v New Zealand (Madras)	1955-56
405	C.P.S. Chauhan and M. Gupte, Maharashtra v Vidarbha (Poona)	1972-73

Partnerships for Second Wicket

465*	J.A. Jameson and R.B. Kanhai, Warwickshire v Gloucestershire (Birmingham)	1974
455	K.V. Bhandarkar and B.B. Nimbalkar, Maharashtra v Kathiawar (Poonah)	1948-49
451	D.G. Bradman and W.H. Ponsford, Australia v England (Oval)	1934
446	C.C. Hunte and G.S. Sobers, West Indies v Pakistan (Kingston)	1957-58
429*	J.G. Dewes and G.H.G. Doggart, Cambridge U v Essex (Cambridge)	1949
426	Arshad Pervez and Mohsin Khan, Habib Bank v Income Tax Department (Lahore)	1977-78
398	W. Gunn and A. Shrewsbury, Nottinghamshire v Sussex (Nottingham)	1890

Partnerships for Third Wicket

456	Aslam Ali and Khalid Irtiza, United Bank v Multan (Karachi)	1975-76
445	P.E. Whitelaw and W.N. Carson, Auckland v Otago (Dunedin)	1936-37
434	J.B. Stollmeyer and G.E. Gomez, Trinidad v British Guiana (Port of Spain)	1946-47
424*	W.J. Edrich and D.C.S. Compton, Middlesex v Somerset (Lord's)	1948
410	R.S. Modi and L. Armanath, India v Rest (Calcutta)	1946-47
399	R.T. Simpson and D.C.S. Compton, MCC v NE Transvaal (Benoni)	1948-49

Partnerships for Fourth Wicket

577	Gul Mahomed and V.S. Hazare, Baroda v Holkar (Baroda)	1946-47
574*	C.L. Walcott and F.M.M. Worrell, Barbados v Trinidad (Port of Spain)	1945-46
502*	F.M.M. Worrell and J.D.C. Goddard, Barbados v Trinidad (Bridgetown)	1943-44
448	R. Abel and T.W. Hayward, Surrey v Yorkshire (Oval)	1899
424	I.S. Lee and S.O. Quin, Victoria v Tasmania (Melbourne)	1933-34
411	P.B.H. May and M.C. Cowdrey, England v West Indies (Birmingham)	1957
410	G. Abraham and B. Pandit, Kerala v Andhra (Pulghat)	1959-60
402	W. Watson and T.W. Graveney, MCC v British Guiana (Georgetown)	1953-54
402	R.B. Kanhai and K. Ibadulla, Warwickshire v Nottinghamshire (Nottingham)	1968

Partnerships for Fifth Wicket

405	D.G. Bradman and S.G. Barnes, Australia v England (Sydney)	1946-47
397	W. Bardsley and C. Kellaway, New South Wales v South Australia (Sydney)	1920-21
393	E.G. Arnold and W.B. Burns, Worcestershire v Warwickshire (Birmingham)	1909
360	V.M. Merchant and M.N. Raiji, Bombay v Hyderabad (Bombay)	1947-48
347	D. Brookes and D.W. Barrick, Northamptonshire v Essex (Northampton)	1952

Partnerships for Sixth Wicket

487*	G.A. Headley and C.C. Passailaigue, Jamaica v Lord Tennyson's XI (Kingston)	1931-32
428	W.W. Armstrong and M.A. Noble, Australians v Sussex (Hove)	1902
411	R.M. Poore and E.G. Wynyard, Hampshire v Somerset (Taunton)	1899
376	R. Subba Row and A. Lightfoot, Northamptonshire v Surrey (Oval)	1958
371	V.M. Merchant and R.S. Modi, Bombay v Maharashtra (Bombay)	1943-44

Partnerships for Seventh Wicket

347	D.S. Atkinson and C.C. Depeiza, West Indies v Australia (Bridgetown)	1954-55
344	K.S. Ranjitsinhji and W. Newham, Sussex v Essex (Leyton)	1902
340	K.J. Key and H. Philipson, Oxford U v Middlesex (Chiswick Park)	1887
336	F.C.W. Newman and C.R. Maxwell, Cahn's XI v Leicestershire (Nottingham)	1935
335	C.W. Andrews and E.C. Bensted, Queensland v New South Wales (Sydney)	1934-35

Partnerships for Eighth Wicket

433	V.T. Trumper and A. Sims, Australians v Canterbury (Christchurch)	1913-14
292	R. Peel and Lord Hawke, Yorkshire v Warwickshire (Birmingham)	1896
270	V.T. Trumper and E.P. Barbour, New South Wales v Victoria (Sydney)	1912-13
263	D.R. Wilcox and R.M. Taylor, Essex v Warwickshire (Southend)	1946
255	E.A.V. Williams and E.A. Martindale, Barbados v Trinidad (Bridgetown)	1935-36

Partnerships for Ninth Wicket

283	A.R. Warren and J. Chapman, Derbyshire v Warwickshire (Blackwell)	1910
251	J.W.H.T. Douglas and S.N. Hare, Essex v Derbyshire (Leyton)	1921
245	V.S. Hazare and N.D. Nagarwalla, Maharashtra v Baroda (Poona)	1939-40
239	H.B. Cave and I.B. Leggat, Central Districts v Otago (Dunedin)	1952-53
232	C. Hill and E. Walkley, South Australia v New South Wales (Adelaide)	1900-01

223

Partnerships for Tenth Wicket

307	A.F. Kippax and J.E.H. Hooker, New South Wales v Victoria (Melbourne)	1928-29
249	C.T. Sarwate and S.N. Bannerjee, Indians v Surrey (Oval)	1946
235	F.E. Woolley and A. Fielder, Kent v Worcestershire (Stourbridge)	1909
230	R.W. Nicholls and W. Roche, Middlesex v Kent (Lord's)	1899
228	R. Illingworth and K. Higgs, Leicestershire v Northamptonshire (Leicester)	1977
218	F.H. Vigar and T.P.B. Smith, Essex v Derbyshire (Chesterfield)	1947

BOWLING

Most Wickets in a Season

W		Season	M	O	M	R	Avge
304	A.P. Freeman	1928	37	1976.1	432	5489	18.05
298	A.P. Freeman	1933	33	2039	651	4549	15.26

NB. The feat of taking 250 wickets in a season has been achieved on 12 occasions, the last instance being by A.P. Freeman in 1933 as above. 200 or more wickets in a season have been taken on 59 occasions, the last instance being by G.A.R. Lock (212 wkts, avge 12.02) in 1957.

The most wickets taken in a season since the reduction of County Championship matches in 1969 are as follows.

W		Season	M	O	M	R	Avge
131	L.R. Gibbs	1971	23	1024.1	295	2475	18.89
121	R.D. Jackman	1980	23	746.2	220	1864	15.40
119	A.M.E. Roberts	1974	21	727.4	198	1621	13.62

NB. 100 wickets in a season have been taken on 31 occasions since 1969.

All Ten Wickets in an Innings

The feat has been achieved on 69 occasions.
On three occasions: A.P. Freeman, 1929, 1930 and 1931.
On two occasions: J.C. Laker, 1956, H. Verity, 1931 and 1932, V.E. Walker, 1859 and 1865.
Instances since the war:
W.E. Hollies, Warwickshire v Nottinghamshire (Birmingham) 1946; J.M. Sims of Middlesex playing for East v West (Kingston) 1948; J.K.R. Graveney, Gloucestershire v Derbyshire (Chesterfield) 1949; T.E. Bailey, Essex v Lancashire (Clacton) 1949; R. Berry, Lancashire v Worcestershire (Blackpool) 1953; S.P. Gupte, Bombay v Pakistan Services (Bombay), 1954-55; J.C. Laker, Surrey v Australians (Oval) 1956; J.C. Laker, England v Australia (Manchester) 1956; G.A.R. Lock, Surrey v Kent (Blackheath) 1956; K. Smales, Nottinghamshire v Gloucestershire (Stroud) 1956; P. Chatterjee, Bengal v Assam (Jorhat) 1956-57; J.D. Bannister, Warwickshire v Combined Services (Birmingham) 1959; A.J.G. Pearson, Cambridge U v Leicestershire (Loughborough) 1961; N.I. Thomson, Sussex v Warwickshire (Worthing) 1964; P.J. Allan, Queensland v Victoria (Melbourne) 1965-66; I. Brayshaw, Western Australia v Victoria (Perth) 1967-68; Shahid Mahmood, Karachi Whites v Khairpur (Karachi) 1969-70.

Nineteen Wickets in a Match

J.C. Laker 19-90 (9-37 and 10-53), England v Australia (Manchester) 1956.

Eighteen Wickets in a Match

H.A. Arkwright 18-96 (9-43 and 9-53), MCC v Gentlemen of Kent (Canterbury) 1861 (twelve-a-side match).

Seventeen Wickets in a Match

The feat has been achieved on 18 occasions.

Instances between the two wars were: A.P. Freeman (for 67 runs), Kent v Sussex (Hove) 1922; F.C.L. Matthews (89 runs), Nottinghamshire v Northamptonshire (Nottingham) 1923; C.W.L. Parker (56 runs), Gloucestershire v Essex (Gloucester 1925; G.R. Cox (106 runs), Sussex v Warwickshire (Horsham) 1926; A.P. Freeman (92 runs), Kent v Warwickshire (Folkestone)1932; H. Verity (91 runs), Yorkshire v Essex (Leyton) 1933; J.C. Clay (212 runs), Glamorgan v Worcestershire (Swansea) 1937; T.W.J. Goddard (106 runs), Gloucestershire v Kent (Bristol) 1939. There has been no instance since the last war.

Most Hat-tricks in a Career

7 D.V.P. Wright.

6 T.W.J. Goddard, C.W.L. Parker.

5 S. Haigh, V.W.C. Jupp, A.E.G. Rhodes, F.A. Tarrant.

NB. Ten bowlers have achieved the feat on four occasions and 24 bowlers on three occasions.

The 'Double' Event

3,000 runs and 100 wickets: J.H. Parks, 1937.

2,000 runs and 200 wickets: G.H. Hirst, 1906.

2,000 runs and 200 wickets: F.E. Woolley (4), J.W. Hearne (3), G.H. Hirst (2), W. Rhodes (2), T.E. Bailey, D.E. Davies, W.G. Grace, G.L. Jessop, V.W.C. Jupp, James Langridge, F.A. Tarrant, C.L. Townsend, L.F. Townsend.

1,000 runs and 200 wickets: M.W. Tate (3), A.E. Trott (2), A.S. Kennedy.

Most 'Doubles': W. Rhodes (16), G.H. Hirst (14), V.W.C. Jupp (10).

'Double' in first season: D.B. Close, 1949. At the age of 18, Close is the youngest player ever to perform this feat.

The feat of scoring 1,000 runs and taking 100 wickets has been achieved on 302 occasions, the last instance being F.J. Titmus in 1967.

FIELDING

Most catches in a season:	78 W.R. Hammond	1928
	77 M.J. Stewart	1957
Most catches in a match:	10 W.R. Hammond, Gloucestershire v Surrey (Cheltenham)	1928
Most catches in an innings:	7 M.J. Stewart, Surrey v Northamptonshire (Northampton)	1957
	7 A.S. Brown, Gloucestershire v Nottinghamshire (Nottingham)	1966

WICKET-KEEPING

Most dismissals in a season:	127 (79ct, 48st), L.E.G. Ames	1929

NB. The feat of making 100 dismissals in a season has been achieved on 12 occasions, the last instance being by R. Booth (100 dismissals—91ct, 9st) in 1964.

Most dismissals in a match:	12 E. Pooley (8 ct, 4 st) Surrey v Sussex (Oval)	1868
	12 D. Tallon (9 ct, 3 st), Queensland v New South Wales (Sydney)	1938-39
	12 H.B. Taber (9 ct, 3 st), New South Wales v South Australia (Adelaide)	1968-69
Most catches in a match:	11 A. Long, Surrey v Sussex (Hove)	1964
	11 R.W. Marsh, Western Australia v Victoria (Perth)	1975-76
Most dismissals in an innings:	8 A.T.W. Grout (8 ct), Queensland v W. Australia (Brisbane)	1959-60

TEST CRICKET RECORDS

COMPLETE TO END OF VARIOUS SERIES
IN AUSTRALIA AND INDIA

Matches between England and Rest of the World 1970 and between Australia and Rest of the World 1971-72 are excluded.

HIGHEST INNINGS TOTALS

903-7d	England v Australia (Oval)	1938
849	England v West Indies (Kingston)	1929-30
790-3d	West Indies v Pakistan (Kingston)	1957-58
758-8d	Australia v West Indies (Kingston)	1954-55
729-6d	Australia v England (Lord's)	1930
701	Australia v England (Oval)	1934
695	Australia v England (Oval)	1930
687-8d	West Indies v England (Oval)	1976
681-8d	West Indies v England (Port of Spain)	1953-54
674	Australia v India (Adelaide)	1947-48
668	Australia v West Indies (Bridgetown)	1954-55
659-8d	Australia v England (Sydney)	1946-47
658-8d	England v Australia (Nottingham)	1938
657-8d	Pakistan v West Indies (Bridgetown)	1957-58
656-8d	Australia v England (Manchester)	1964
654-5	England v South Africa (Durban)	1938-39
652-8d	West Indies v England (Lord's)	1973
650-6d	Australia v West Indies (Bridgetown)	1964-65

The highest innings for the countries not mentioned above are:

644-7d	India v West Indies (Kanpur)	1978-79
622-9d	South Africa v Australia (Durban)	1969-70
551-9d	New Zealand v England (Lord's)	1973

NB. There are 44 instances of a side making 600 or more in an innings in a Test Match.

LOWEST INNINGS TOTALS

26	New Zealand v England (Auckland)	1954-55
30	South Africa v England (Port Elizabeth)	1895-96
30	South Africa v England (Birmingham)	1924
35	South Africa v England (Cape Town)	1898-99
36	Australia v England (Birmingham)	1902
36	South Africa v Australia (Melbourne)	1931-32
42	Australia v England (Sydney)	1887-88
42	New Zealand v Australia (Wellington)	1945-46
42†	India v England (Lord's)	1974
43	South Africa v England (Cape Town)	1888-89
44	Australia v England (Oval)	1896
45	England v Australia (Sydney)	1886-87
45	South Africa v Australia (Melbourne)	1931-32
47	South Africa v England (Cape Town)	1888-89
47	New Zealand v England (Lord's)	1958

†Batted one man short

The lowest innings for the countries not mentioned above are:

76	West Indies v Pakistan (Dacca)	1958-59
62	Pakistan v Australia (Perth)	1981-82

HIGHEST INDIVIDUAL INNINGS

365*	G.S. Sobers, West Indies v Pakistan (Kingston)	1957-58
364	L. Hutton, England v Australia (Oval)	1938
337	Hanif Mohammad, Pakistan v West Indies (Bridgetown)	1957-58
336*	W.R. Hammond, England v New Zealand (Auckland)	1932-33
334	D.G. Bradman, Australia v England (Leeds)	1930
325	A. Sandham, England v West Indies (Kingston)	1929-30
311	R.B. Simpson, Australia v England (Manchester)	1964
310*	J.H. Edrich, England v New Zealand (Leeds)	1965
307	R.M. Cowper, Australia v England (Melbourne)	1965-66
304	D.G. Bradman, Australia v England (Leeds)	1934
302	L.G. Rowe, West Indies v England (Bridgetown)	1973-74
299*	D.G. Bradman, Australia v South Africa (Adelaide)	1931-32
291	I.V.A. Richards, West Indies v England (Oval)	1976
287	R.E. Foster, England v Australia (Sydney)	1903-04
285*	P.B.H. May, England v West Indies (Birmingham)	1957
278	D.C.S. Compton, England v Pakistan (Nottingham)	1954
274	R.G. Pollock, South Africa v Australia (Durban)	1969-70
274	Zaheer Abbas, Pakistan v England (Birmingham)	1971
270*	G.A. Headley, West Indies v England (Kingston)	1934-35
270	D.G. Bradman, Australia v England (Melbourne)	1936-37
266	W.H. Ponsford, Australia v England (Oval)	1934
262*	D.L. Amiss, England v West Indies (Kingston)	1973-74
261	F.M.M. Worrell, West Indies v England (Nottingham)	1950
260	C.C. Hunte, West Indies v Pakistan (Kingston)	1957-58
259	G.M. Turner, New Zealand v West Indies (Georgetown)	1971-72
258	T.W. Graveney, England v West Indies (Nottingham)	1957
258	S.M. Nurse, West Indies v New Zealand (Christchurch)	1968-69
256	R.B. Kanhai, West Indies v India (Calcutta)	1958-59
256	K.F. Barrington, England v Australia (Manchester)	1964
255*	D.J. McGlew, South Africa v New Zealand (Wellington)	1952-53
254	D.G. Bradman, Australia v England (Leeds)	1930
251	W.R. Hammond, England v Australia (Sydney)	1928-29
250	K.D. Walters, Australia v New Zealand (Christchurch)	1976-77
250	S.F.A.F. Bacchus, West Indies v India (Kanpur)	1978-79

The highest individual innings for India is:

231	V.M.H. Mankad, India v New Zealand (Madras)	1955-56

NB. There are 122 instances of a double-century being scored in a Test Match.

HIGHEST RUN AGGREGATES IN A TEST RUBBER

R		Season	T	I	NO	HS	Avge	100s	50s
974	D.G. Bradman (A v E)	1930	5	7	0	334	139.14	4	—
905	W.R. Hammond (E v A)	1928-29	5	9	1	251	113.12	4	—
834	R.N. Harvey (A v SA)	1952-53	5	9	0	205	92.66	4	3
829	I.V.A. Richards (WI v E)	1976	4	7	0	291	118.42	3	2
827	C.L. Walcott (WI v A)	1954-55	5	10	0	155	82.70	5	2
824	G.S. Sobers (WI v P)	1957-58	5	8	2	365*	137.33	3	3
810	D.G. Bradman (A v E)	1936-37	5	9	0	270	90.00	3	1
806	D.G. Bradman (A v SA)	1931-32	5	5	1	299*	201.50	4	—
779	E.D. Weekes (WI v I)	1948-49	5	7	0	194	111.28	4	2
774	S.M. Gavaskar (I v WI)	1970-71	4	8	3	220	154.80	4	3
758	D.G. Bradman (A v E)	1934	5	8	0	304	94.75	2	1
753	D.C.S. Compton (E v SA)	1947	5	8	0	208	94.12	4	2

RECORD WICKET PARTNERSHIPS – ALL TEST CRICKET

1st	413	V.M.H. Mankad & P. Roy, I v NZ (Madras)		1955-56
2nd	451	W.H. Ponsford & D.G. Bradman, A v E (Oval)		1934
3rd	370	W.J. Edrich & D.C.S. Compton, E v SA (Lord's)		1947
4th	411	P.B.H. May & M.C. Cowdrey, E v WI (Birmingham)		1957
5th	405	S.G. Barnes & D.G. Bradman, A v E (Sydney)		1946-47
6th	346	J.H.W. Fingleton & D.G. Bradman, A v E (Melbourne)		1936-37
7th	347	D.S. Atkinson & C.C. Depeiza, WI v A (Bridgetown)		1954-55
8th	246	L.E.G. Ames & G.O.B. Allen, E v NZ (Lord's)		1931
9th	190	Asif Iqbal & Intikhab Alam, P v E (Oval)		1967
10th	151	B.F. Hastings & R.O. Collinge, NZ v P (Auckland)		1972-73

WICKET PARTNERSHIPS OF OVER 300

451	2nd W.H. Ponsford & D.G. Bradman, A v E (Oval)	1934
446	2nd C.C. Hunte & G.S. Sobers, WI v P (Kingston)	1957-58
413	1st V.M.H. Mankad & P. Roy, I v NZ (Madras)	1955-56
411	4th P.B.H. May & M.C. Cowdrey, E v WI (Birmingham)	1957
405	5th S.G. Barnes & D.B. Bradman, A v E (Sydney)	1946-47
399	4th G.S. Sobers & F.M.M. Worrell, WI v E (Bridgetown)	1959-60
388	4th W.H. Ponsford & D.G. Bradman, A v E (Leeds)	1934
387	1st G.M. Turner & T.W. Jarvis, NZ v WI (Georgetown)	1971-72
382	2nd L. Hutton & M. Leyland, E v A (Oval)	1938
382	1st W.M. Lawry & R.B. Simpson, A v WI (Bridgetown)	1964-65
370	3rd W.J. Edrich & D.C.S. Compton, E v SA (Lord's)	1947
369	2nd J.H. Edrich & K.F. Barrington, E v NZ (Leeds)	1965
359	1st L. Hutton & C. Washbrook, E v SA (Johannesburg)	1948-49
350	4th Mushtaq Mohammad & Asif Iqbal, P v NZ (Dunedin)	1972-73
347	7th D.S. Atkinson & C.C. Depeiza, WI v A (Bridgetown)	1954-55
346	6th J.H.W. Fingleton & D.G. Bradman, A v E (Melbourne)	1936-37
344*	2nd S.M. Gavaskar & D.B. Vengsarkar, I v WI (Calcutta)	1978-79
341	3rd E.J. Barlow & R.G. Pollock, SA v A (Adelaide)	1963-64
338	3rd E.D. Weekes & F.M.M. Worrell, WI v E (Port of Spain)	1953-54
336	4th W.M. Lawry & K.D. Walters, A v WI (Sydney)	1968-69
323	1st J.B. Hobbs & W. Rhodes, E v A (Melbourne)	1911-12
319	3rd A. Melville & A.D. Nourse, SA v E (Nottingham)	1947
316†	G.R. Viswanath & Yashpal Sharma, I v E (Madras)	1981-82
308	7th Waqar Hasan & Imtiaz Ahmed, P v NZ (Lahore)	1955-56
303	3rd I.V.A. Richards & A.I. Kallicharran, WI v E (Nottingham)	1976
301	2nd A.R. Morris & D.G. Bradman, A v E (Leeds)	1948

† 415 runs were added for this wicket in two separate partnerships. D.B. Vengsarkar retired hurt and was replaced by Yashpal Sharma after 99 runs had been added.

HAT-TRICKS

F.R. Spofforth	Australia v England (Melbourne)	1878-79
W. Bates	England v Australia (Melbourne)	1882-83
J. Briggs	England v Australia (Sydney)	1891-92
G.A. Lohmann	England v South Africa (Port Elizabeth)	1895-96
J.T. Hearne	England v Australia (Leeds)	1899
H. Trumble	Australia v England (Melbourne)	1901-02
H. Trumble	Australia v England (Melbourne)	1903-04
T.J. Matthews (2)*	Australia v South Africa (Manchester)	1912
M.J.C. Allon†	England v New Zealand (Christchurch)	1929-30
T.W.J. Goddard	England v South Africa (Johannesburg)	1938-39
P.J. Loader	England v West Indies (Leeds)	1957
L.F. Kline	Australia v South Africa (Cape Town)	1957-58
W.W. Hall	West Indies v Pakistan (Lahore)	1958-59
G.M. Griffin	South Africa v England (Lord's)	1960
L.R. Gibbs	West Indies v Australia (Adelaide)	1960-61
P.J. Petherick	New Zealand v Pakistan (Lahore)	1976-77

*In each innings. †Four wickets in five balls.

NINE OR TEN WICKETS IN AN INNINGS

10-53	J.C. Laker, England v Australia (Manchester)	1956
9-28	G.A. Lohmann, England v South Africa (Johannesburg)	1895-96
9-37	J.C. Laker, England v Australia (Manchester)	1956
9-69	J.M. Patel, India v Australia (Kanpur)	1959-60
9-86	Sarfraz Nawaz, Pakistan v Australia (Melbourne)	1978-79
9-95	J.M. Noreiga, West Indies v India (Port of Spain)	1970-71
9-102	S.P. Gupte, India v West Indies (Kanpur)	1958-59
9-103	S.F. Barnes, England v South Africa (Johannesburg)	1913-14
9-113	H.J. Tayfield, South Africa v England (Johannesburg)	1956-57
9-121	A.A. Mailey, Australia v England (Melbourne)	1920-21

NB. There are 39 instances of a bowler taking 8 wickets in an innings in a Test Match.

FIFTEEN OR MORE WICKETS IN A MATCH

19-90	J.C. Laker, England v Australia (Manchester)	1956
17-159	S.F. Barnes, England v South Africa (Johannesburg)	1913-14
16-137	R.A.L. Massie, Australia v England (Lord's)	1972
15-28	J. Briggs, England v South Africa (Cape Town)	1888-89
15-45	G.A. Lohmann, England v South Africa (Port Elizabeth)	1895-96
15-99	C. Blythe, England v South Africa (Leeds)	1907
15-104	H. Verity, England v Australia (Lord's)	1934
15-124	W. Rhodes, England v Australia (Melbourne)	1903-04

NB. There are 7 instances of a bowler taking 14 wickets in a Test Match.

HIGHEST WICKET AGGREGATES IN A TEST RUBBER

Wkts		Season	Tests	Balls	Mdns	Runs	Avge	5 wl	10 M
49	S.F. Barnes (E v SA)	1913–14	4	1356	56	536	10.93	7	3
46	J.C. Laker (A v E)	1956	5	1703	127	442	9.60	4	2
44	C.V. Grimmett (A v SA)	1935-36	5	2077	140	642	14.59	5	3
42	T.M. Alderman (A v E)	1981	6	1950	76	893	21.26	4	—
41	R.M. Hogg (A v E)	1978-79	6	1740	60	527	12.85	5	2
39	D.K. Lillee (A v E)	1981	6	1870	81	870	22.30	2	1
39	A.V. Bedser (E v A)	1953	5	1591	58	682	17.48	5	1
38	M.W. Tate (E v A)	1924-25	5	2528	62	881	23.18	5	1
37	W.J. Whitty (A v SA)	1910-11	5	1395	55	632	17.08	2	—
37	H.J. Tayfield (SA v E)	1956-57	5	2280	105	636	17.18	4	1
36	A.E.E. Vogler (SA v E)	1909-10	5	1349	33	783	21.75	4	1
36	A.A. Mailey (A v E)	1920-21	5	1465	27	946	26.27	4	2
35	G.A. Lohmann (E v SA)	1895-96	3	520	38	203	5.80	4	2
35	B.S. Chandrasekhar (I v E)	1972-73	5	1747	83	662	18.91	4	—

MOST WICKET-KEEPING DISMISSALS IN AN INNINGS

7 (7 ct)	Wasim Bari, Pakistan v New Zealand (Auckland)	1978-79
7 (7 ct)	R.W. Taylor, England v India (Bombay)	1979-80
6 (6 ct)	A.T.W. Grout, Australia v South Africa (Johannesburg)	1957-58
6 (6 ct)	D.T. Lindsay, South Africa v Australia (Johannesburg)	1966-67
6 (6 ct)	J.T. Murray, England v India (Lord's)	1967
6 (5 ct, 1 st)	S.M.H. Kirmani, India v New Zealand (Christchurch)	1975-76

MOST WICKET-KEEPING DISMISSALS IN A MATCH

10 (10 ct)	R.W. Taylor, England v India (Bombay)	1979-80

MOST WICKET-KEEPING DISMISSALS IN A SERIES

26 (23 ct, 3 st)	J.H.B. Waite, South Africa v New Zealand	1961-62
26 (26 ct)	R.W. Marsh, Australia v West Indies	1975-76

HIGHEST WICKET-KEEPING DISMISSAL AGGREGATES

Total			Tests	Ct	St
297	R.W. Marsh	(A)	80	286	11
269	A.P.E. Knott	(E)	95	250	19
219	T.G. Evans	(E)	91	173	46
189	D.L. Murray	(WI)	62	181	8
187	A.T.W. Grout	(A)	51	163	24
165	Wasim Bari	(P)	61	145	20
141	J.H.B. Waite	(SA)	50	124	17
130	W.A.S. Oldfield	(A)	54	78	52
129	S.M.H. Kirmani	(I)	54	102	27
114	J.M. Parks	(E)	46	103	11
114	R.W. Taylor	(E)	35	107	7

NB. Parks's figures include 2 catches as a fielder.

HIGHEST RUN AGGREGATES

Runs			Tests	Inns	NO	HS	Avge	100s	50s
8114	G. Boycott	(E)	108	193	23	246*	47.72	22	42
8032	G.S. Sobers	(WI)	93	160	21	365*	57.78	26	30
7624	M.C. Cowdrey	(E)	114	188	15	182	44.06	22	38
7249	W.R. Hammond	(E)	85	140	16	336*	58.45	22	24
6996	D.G. Bradman	(A)	52	80	10	334	99.94	29	13
6971	L. Hutton	(E)	79	138	15	364	56.67	19	33
6806	K.F. Barrington	(E)	82	131	15	256	58.67	20	35
6718	S.M. Gavaskar	(I)	75	134	9	221	53.74	24	30
6227	R.B. Kanhai	(WI)	79	137	6	256	47.53	15	28
6149	R.N. Harvey	(A)	79	137	10	205	48.41	21	24
6056	G.S. Chappell	(A)	73	130	15	247*	52.66	19	29
5831	C.H. Lloyd	(WI)	85	143	10	242*	43.84	14	30
5807	D.C.S. Compton	(E)	78	131	15	278	50.06	17	28
5746	G.R. Viswanath	(I)	81	140	9	222	43.86	14	31
5410	J.B. Hobbs	(E)	61	102	7	211	56.94	15	28
5357	K.D. Walters	(A)	74	125	14	250	48.26	15	33
5345	I.M. Chappell	(A)	75	136	10	196	42.42	14	26
5234	W.M. Lawry	(A)	67	123	12	210	47.15	13	27
5138	J.H. Edrich	(E)	77	127	9	310*	43.54	12	24
4882	T.W. Graveney	(E)	79	123	13	258	44.38	11	20
4869	R.B. Simpson	(A)	62	111	7	311	46.81	10	27
4737	I.R. Redpath	(A)	66	120	11	171	43.45	8	31
4555	H. Sutcliffe	(E)	54	84	9	194	60.73	16	23
4537	P.B.H. May	(E)	66	106	9	285*	46.77	13	22
4502	E.R. Dexter	(E)	62	102	8	205	47.89	9	27
4455	E.D. Weekes	(WI)	48	81	5	207	58.61	15	19
4399	A.I. Kallicharran	(WI)	66	109	10	187	44.43	12	21
4389	A.P.E. Knott	(E)	95	149	15	135	32.75	5	30
4334	R.C. Fredericks	(WI)	59	109	7	169	42.49	8	26
4129	I.V.A. Richards	(WI)	47	74	4	291	58.98	13	17
3915	Hanif Mohammad	(P)	55	97	8	337	43.98	12	15
3860	F.M.M. Worrell	(WI)	51	87	9	261	49.48	9	22
3837	Majid Khan	(P)	60	102	5	167	39.55	8	18
3798	C.L. Walcott	(WI)	44	74	7	220	56.68	15	14
3643	Mushtaq Mohammad	(P)	57	100	7	201	39.17	10	19
3631	P.R. Umrigar	(I)	59	94	8	223	42.22	12	14
3612	D.L. Amiss	(E)	50	88	10	262*	46.30	11	11
3599	A.W. Greig	(E)	58	93	4	148	40.43	8	20

Runs			Tests	Inns	NO	HS	Avge	100s	50s
3575	Asif Iqbal	(P)	58	99	7	175	38.85	11	12
3533	A.R. Morris	(A)	46	79	3	206	46.48	12	12
3525	E.H. Hendren	(E)	51	83	9	205*	47.63	7	21
3471	B. Mitchell	(SA)	42	80	9	189*	48.88	8	21
3448	B.E. Congdon	(NZ)	61	114	7	176	32.22	7	19
3428	J.R. Reid	(NZ)	58	108	5	142	33.28	6	22
3412	C. Hill	(A)	49	89	2	191	39.21	7	19
3303	R.W. Marsh	(A)	80	128	11	132	28.23	3	15
3283	F.E. Woolley	(E)	64	98	7	154	36.07	5	23
3245	C.C. Hunte	(WI)	44	78	6	260	45.06	8	13
3234	K.W.R. Fletcher	(E)	58	94	13	216	39.92	7	19
3208	V.L. Manjrekar	(I)	55	92	10	189*	39.12	7	15
3163	V.T. Trumper	(A)	48	89	8	214*	39.04	8	13
3107	C.C. McDonald	(A)	47	83	4	170	39.32	5	17
3104	B.F. Butcher	(WI)	44	78	6	209*	43.11	7	16
3092	K.J. Hughes	(A) ·	45	83	5	213	39.64	7	15
3073	A.L. Hassett	(A)	43	69	3	198*	46.56	10	11
3061	C.G. Borde	(I)	55	97	11	177*	35.59	5	18
3013	A.R. Border	(A)	39	72	12	162	50.21	9	17

HIGHEST WICKET AGGREGATES

Wkts			Tests	Balls	Mdns	Runs	Avge	5 wI	10 wM
321	D.K. Lillee	(A)	60	16004	547	7385	23.00	22	7
309	L.R. Gibbs	(WI)	79	27115	1313	8989	29.09	18	2
307	F.S. Trueman	(E)	67	15178	522	6625	21.57	17	3
289	D.L. Underwood	(E)	85	21527	1218	7579	26.22	16	6
266	B.S. Bedi	(I)	67	21364	1096	7637	28.71	14	1
252	J.B. Statham	(E)	70	16056	595	6261	24.84	9	1
248	R. Benaud	(A)	63	19108	805	6704	27.03	16	1
246	G.D. McKenzie	(A)	60	17681	547	7328	29.78	16	3
242	B.S. Chandrasekhar	(I)	58	15963	584	7199	29.74	16	2
239	R.G.D. Willis	(E)	68	13162	348	6090	25.48	13	—
236	A.V. Bedser	(E)	51	15918	572	5876	24.89	15	5
235	G.S. Sobers	(WI)	93	21599	995	7999	34.03	6	—
228	R.R. Lindwall	(A)	61	13650	418	5251	23.03	12	—
219	I.T. Botham	(E)	47	11146	452	4944	22.57	18	4
216	C.V. Grimmett	(A)	37	14513	735	5231	24.21	21	7
202	J.A. Snow	(E)	49	12021	415	5387	26.66	8	1
193	J.C. Laker	(E)	46	12027	673	4101	21.24	9	3
192	W.W. Hall	(WI)	48	10421	312	5066	26.38	9	1
189	S.F. Barnes	(E)	27	7873	356	3106	16.43	24	7
189	E.A.S. Prasanna	(I)	49	14353	602	5742	30.38	10	2
186	A.K. Davidson	(A)	44	11587	432	3819	20.53	14	2
174	G.A.R. Lock	(E)	49	13147	819	4451	25.58	9	3
173	A.M.E. Roberts	(WI)	40	9674	332	4481	25.90	10	2
170	K.R. Miller	(A)	55	10461	338	3906	22.97	7	1
170	H.J. Tayfield	(SA)	37	13568	602	4405	25.91	14	2
166	J.R. Thomson	(A)	39	8425	231	4428	26.67	6	—
162	V.M.H. Mankad	(I)	44	14686	777	5236	32.32	8	2
160	W.A. Johnston	(A)	40	11048	370	3826	23.91	7	—
158	S. Ramadhin	(WI)	43	13939	813	4579	28.98	10	1
155	R.J. Hadlee	(NZ)	35	8941	246	4238	27.34	11	3
155	M.W. Tate	(E)	39	12523	581	4055	26.16	7	1
153	F.J. Titmus	(E)	53	15118	777	4931	32.22	7	—

MOST TEST APPEARANCES FOR EACH COUNTRY

NB. The abandoned match at Melbourne in 1970-71 is excluded from these figures.

England		Australia	
M.C. Cowdrey	114	R.W. Marsh	80
G. Boycott	108	R.N. Harvey	79
A.P.E. Knott	95	I.M. Chappell	75
T.G. Evans	91	K.D. Walters	74
W.R. Hammond	85	G.S. Chappell	73
D.L. Underwood	85	W.M. Lawry	67
K.F. Barrington	82	I.R. Redpath	66
T.W. Graveney	79	R. Benaud	63
L. Hutton	79	R.B. Simpson	62
D.C.S. Compton	78	R.R. Lindwall	61
J.H. Edrich	77	D.K. Lillee	60
J.B. Statham	70	G.D. McKenzie	60
R.G.D. Willis	68	S.E. Gregory	58
F.S. Trueman	67	K.R. Miller	55
P.B.H. May	66	W.A.S. Oldfield	54
F.E. Woolley	64	D.G. Bradman	52
E.R. Dexter	62	A.T.W. Grout	51
T.E. Bailey	61	W.W. Armstrong	50
J.B. Hobbs	61		
R. Illingworth	61		

South Africa		West Indies	
J.H.B. Waite	50	G.S. Sobers	93
A.W. Nourse	45	C.H. Lloyd	85
B. Mitchell	42	L.R. Gibbs	79
H.W. Taylor	42	R.B. Kanhai	79
T.L. Goddard	41	A.I. Kallicharran	66
R.A. McLean	40	D.L. Murray	62
H.J. Tayfield	37	R.C. Fredericks	59
D.J. McGlew	34	F.M.M. Worrell	51
A.D. Nourse	34	W.W. Hall	48
E.J. Barlow	30	E.D. Weekes	48
W.R. Endean	28	I.V.A. Richards	47
P.M. Pollock	28	B.F. Butcher	44
K.G. Viljoen	27	C.C. Hunte	44
H.B. Cameron	26	C.L. Walcott	44
E.A.B. Rowan	26	S. Ramadhin	43
S.J. Snooke	26	V.A. Holder	40
		A.M.E. Roberts	40

New Zealand

B.E. Congdon	61
J.R. Reid	58
M.G. Burgess	50
B. Sutcliffe	42
G.T. Dowling	39
G.M. Turner	39
J.M. Parker	36
R.O. Collinge	35
R.J. Hadlee	35
K.J. Wadsworth	33
R.C. Motz	32
V. Pollard	32
B.F. Hastings	31
H.J. Howarth	30
B.R. Taylor	30

India

G.R. Viswanath	81
S.M. Gavaskar	75
B.S. Bedi	67
P.R. Umrigar	59
B.S. Chandrasekhar	58
C.G. Borde	55
V.L. Manjrekar	55
S.M.H. Kirmani	54
S. Venkataraghavan	50
E.A.S. Prasanna	49
D.B. Vengsarkar	48
F.M. Engineer	46
M.A.K. Pataudi	46
V.M.H. Mankad	44
P. Roy	43
R.G. Nadkarni	41
C.P.S. Chauhan	40

Pakistan

Wasim Bari	61
Majid Khan	60
Asif Iqbal	58
Mushtaq Mohammad	57
Hanif Mohammad	55
Intikhab Alam	47
Zaheer Abbas	45
Sarfraz Nawaz	42
Imtiaz Ahmed	41
Sadiq Mohammad	41
Saeed Ahmed	41
Wasim Raja	40
Javed Miandad	37
Imran Khan	36
Fazal Mahmood	34

TEST CAREER RECORDS

(to the conclusion of series in India and Australia 1981-82, but not Sri Lanka)

compiled by Brian Heald

ENGLAND

BATTING AND FIELDING

	M	I	NO	Runs	HS	Avge	100	50	Ct	St
P.J.W. Allott	2	3	1	72	52*	36.00	—	1	—	—
C.W.J. Athey	3	6	0	17	9	2.83	—	—	2	—
D.L. Amiss	50	88	10	3612	262*	46.30	11	11	24	—
D.L. Bairstow	4	7	1	125	59*	20.83	—	1	12	1
G.D. Barlow	3	5	1	17	7*	4.25	—	—	—	—
I.T. Botham	47	72	3	2417	149*	35.02	9	9	58	—
G. Boycott	108	193	23	8114	246*	47.72	22	42	33	—
J.M. Brearley	39	66	3	1442	91	22.88	—	9	52	—
A.R. Butcher	1	2	0	34	20	17.00	—	—	—	—
R.O. Butcher	3	5	0	71	32	14.20	—	—	3	—
G.R. Dilley	16	25	7	313	56	17.38	—	2	4	—
P.R. Downton	4	7	1	59	26*	9.83	—	—	8	—
P.H. Edmonds	18	21	5	277	50	17.31	—	1	21	—
J.E. Emburey	21	32	6	326	57	12.53	—	1	14	—
K.W.R. Fletcher	58	94	13	3234	216	39.92	7	19	51	—
M.W. Gatting	19	32	2	686	59	22.86	—	6	14	—
G.A. Gooch	41	73	4	2487	153	36.04	4	15	35	—
D.I. Gower	37	62	5	2417	200*	42.40	4	12	16	—
F.C. Hayes	9	17	1	244	106*	15.25	1	—	7	—
M. Hendrick	30	35	15	128	15	6.40	—	—	25	—
R.D. Jackman	2	3	0	14	7	4.66	—	—	—	—
A.P.E. Knott	95	149	15	4389	135	32.75	5	30	250	19
W. Larkins	6	11	0	176	34	16.00	—	—	3	—
J.K. Lever	20	29	4	306	53	12.24	—	1	11	—
G. Miller	25	34	3	828	98	26.70	—	5	11	—
C.M. Old	46	66	9	845	65	14.82	—	2	22	—
P.W.G. Parker	1	2	0	13	13	6.50	—	—	—	—
P.I. Pocock	17	27	2	165	33	6.60	—	—	13	—
D.W. Randall	27	45	4	1125	174	27.43	2	6	18	—
G.R.J. Roope	21	32	4	860	77	30.71	—	7	35	—
B.C. Rose	9	16	2	358	70	25.57	—	2	4	—
M.W.W. Selvey	3	5	3	15	5*	7.50	—	—	1	—
G.B. Stevenson	2	2	1	28	27*	28.00	—	—	—	—
C.J. Tavaré	10	17	0	593	149	34.88	1	3	8	—
R.W. Taylor	35	46	4	700	97	16.66	—	2	107	7
D.L. Underwood	85	115	35	937	45*	11.71	—	—	44	—
P. Willey	20	38	5	923	102*	27.96	2	4	3	—
R.G.D. Willis	68	94	42	581	24*	11.17	—	—	24	—
R.A. Woolmer	19	34	2	1059	149	33.09	3	2	10	—

BOWLING

	Balls	Runs	Wkts	Avge	Best	5 wI	10 wM
P.J.W. Allott	336	223	4	55.75	2-17	—	—
I.T. Botham	11146	4944	219	22.57	8-34	18	4
G. Boycott	944	382	7	54.57	3-47	—	—
A. R. Butcher	12	9	0	—	—	—	—
G.R. Dilley	2758	1401	45	31.13	4-24	—	—
P.H. Edmonds	4083	1251	49	25.53	7-66	2	—
J.E. Emburey	4717	1608	50	32.16	5-124	1	—
K.W.R. Fletcher	285	193	2	96.50	1-6	—	—
M.W. Gatting	32	18	0	—	—	—	—
G.A. Gooch	937	348	8	43.50	2-12	—	—
D.I. Gower	12	2	1	2.00	1-1	—	—
M. Hendrick	6208	2248	87	25.83	4-28	—	—
R.D. Jackman	440	198	6	33.00	3-65	—	—
J.K. Lever	4115	1785	67	26.64	7-46	3	1
G. Miller	3801	1242	43	28.88	5-44	1	—
C.M. Old	8858	4020	143	28.11	7-50	4	—
P.I. Pocock	4482	2023	47	43.04	6-79	3	—
D.W. Randall	16	3	0	—	—	—	—
G.R.J. Roope	172	76	0	—	—	—	—
M.W.W. Selvey	492	343	6	57.16	4-41	—	—
G.B. Stevenson	312	183	5	36.60	3-111	—	—
C.J. Tavaré	12	11	0	—	—	—	—
R.W. Taylor	12	6	0	—	—	—	—
D.L. Underwood	21527	7579	289	26.22	8-51	16	6
P. Willey	1067	441	6	73.50	2-73	—	—
R.G.D. Willis	13162	6090	239	25.48	8-43	13	—
R.A. Woolmer	546	299	4	74.75	1-8	—	—

AUSTRALIA

BATTING AND FIELDING

	M	I	NO	Runs	HS	Avge	100	50	Ct	St
T.M. Alderman	11	16	8	43	12*	5.37	—	—	14	—
G.R. Beard	3	5	0	114	49	22.80	—	—	—	—
A.R. Border	39	72	12	3013	162	50.21	9	17	49	—
R.J. Bright	14	23	4	269	33	14.15	—	—	7	—
G.S. Chappell	73	130	15	6056	247*	52.66	19	29	102	—
T.M. Chappell	3	6	1	79	27	15.80	—	—	2	—
W.M. Darling	14	27	1	697	91	26.80	—	6	5	—
G. Dymock	21	32	7	236	31*	9.44	—	—	1	—
J. Dyson	16	31	3	686	127*	24.50	2	1	5	—
J.D. Higgs	22	36	16	111	16	5.55	—	—	3	—
A.M.J. Hilditch	9	18	0	452	85	25.11	—	4	9	—
R.M. Hogg	22	36	4	246	36	7.68	—	—	5	—
D.W. Hookes	8	15	0	436	85	29.06	—	3	2	—
K.J. Hughes	45	83	5	3092	213	39.64	7	15	36	—

235

	M	I	NO	Runs	HS	Avge	100	50	Ct	St
A.G. Hurst	12	20	3	102	26	6.00	—	—	3	—
M.F. Kent	3	6	0	171	54	28.50	—	2	6	—
B.M. Laird	15	29	1	1057	92	37.75	—	9	11	—
G.F. Lawson	5	8	2	56	16	9.33	—	—	1	—
D.K. Lillee	60	82	21	851	73*	13.95	—	1	17	—
R.B. McCosker	25	46	5	1622	127	39.56	4	9	21	—
R.W. Marsh	80	128	11	3303	132	28.23	3	15	286	11
L.S. Pascoe	14	19	9	106	30*	10.60	—	—	2	—
S.J. Rixon	10	19	3	341	54	21.31	—	2	31	4
P.R. Sleep	3	6	0	95	64	15.83	—	1	—	—
J.R. Thomson	39	54	13	508	49	12.39	—	—	18	—
P.M. Toohey	15	29	1	893	122	31.89	1	7	9	—
K.D. Walters	74	125	14	5357	250	48.26	15	33	43	—
D.F. Whatmore	7	13	0	293	77	22.53	—	2	13	—
D.M. Wellham	4	7	0	221	103	31.57	1	—	1	—
M.R. Whitney	2	4	0	4	4	1.00	—	—	—	—
J.M. Wiener	6	11	0	281	93	25.54	—	2	4	—
G.M. Wood	34	67	5	2089	126	33.69	6	9	28	—
K.J. Wright	10	18	5	219	55*	16.84	—	1	31	4
G.N. Yallop	32	61	3	2101	172	36.22	6	7	16	—
B. Yardley	22	40	4	743	74	20.91	—	3	20	—

BOWLING

	Balls	Runs	Wkts	Avge	Best	5 wI	10 wM
T.M. Alderman	2925	1341	55	24.38	6-135	4	—
G.R. Beard	259	109	1	109.00	1-26	—	—
A.R. Border	1004	334	8	41.75	2-35	—	—
R.J. Bright	3106	1126	34	33.11	7-87	3	1
G.S. Chappell	4664	1661	45	36.91	5-61	1	—
G. Dymock	5545	2116	78	27.12	7-67	5	1
J.D. Higgs	4752	2057	66	31.16	7-143	2	—
R.M. Hogg	4652	1937	82	23.62	6-74	5	2
D.W. Hookes	30	15	0	—	—	—	—
K.J. Hughes	84	22	0	—	—	—	—
A.G. Hurst	3054	1200	43	27.90	5-28	2	—
B.M. Laird	18	12	0	—	—	—	—
G.F. Lawson	913	414	16	25.87	7-81	1	—
D.K. Lillee	16004	7385	321	23.00	7-83	22	7
R.W. Marsh	60	51	0	—	—	—	—
L.S. Pascoe	3403	1668	64	26.06	5-59	1	—
P.R. Sleep	373	223	2	111.50	1-16	—	—
J.R. Thomson	8425	4428	166	26.67	6-46	6	—
P.M. Toohey	2	4	0	—	—	—	—
K.D. Walters	3295	1425	49	29.08	5-66	1	—
D.F. Whatmore	30	11	0	—	—	—	—
M.R. Whitney	468	246	5	49.20	2-50	—	—
J.M. Wiener	78	41	0	—	—	—	—
G.N. Yallop	192	116	1	116.00	1-21	—	—
B. Yardley	5849	2507	82	30.57	7-98	4	1

WEST INDIES

BATTING AND FIELDING

	M	I	NO	Runs	HS	Avge	100	50	Ct	St
S.F.A.F. Bacchus	19	30	0	782	250	26.06	1	3	17	—
S.T. Clarke	11	16	5	172	35*	15.63	—	—	2	—
C.E.H. Croft	27	37	22	158	33	10.53	—	—	8	—
W.W. Daniel	5	5	2	29	11	9.66	—	—	2	—
P.J. Dujon	3	6	1	227	51	45.40	—	1	9	—
J. Garner	28	36	2	400	60	11.76	—	1	22	—
H.A. Gomes	22	35	2	1418	126	42.96	4	8	4	—
C.G. Greenidge	36	63	3	2569	134	42.81	5	19	39	—
D.L. Haynes	24	38	1	1431	184	38.67	3	8	13	—
M.A. Holding	31	44	8	434	58*	12.05	—	2	9	—
A.I. Kallicharran	66	109	10	4399	187	44.43	12	21	51	—
C.L. King	9	16	3	418	100*	32.15	1	2	5	—
C.H. Lloyd	85	143	10	5831	242*	43.84	14	30	63	—
M.D. Marshall	12	16	1	126	45	8.40	—	—	5	—
E.H. Mattis	4	5	0	145	71	29.00	—	1	3	—
D.A. Murray	19	31	3	601	84	21.46	—	3	57	5
R. Nanan	1	2	0	16	8	8.00	—	—	2	—
D.R. Parry	12	20	3	381	65	22.41	—	3	4	—
I.V.A. Richards	47	74	4	4129	291	58.98	13	17	48	—
A.M.E. Roberts	40	54	9	610	54	13.55	—	1	8	—
L.G. Rowe	30	49	2	2047	302	43.55	7	7	17	—

BOWLING

	Balls	Runs	Wkts	Avge	Best	5 wI	10 wM
S.F.A.F. Bacchus	6	3	0	—	—	—	—
S.T. Clarke	2477	1171	42	27.88	5-126	1	—
C.E.H. Croft	6165	2913	125	23.30	8-29	3	—
W.W. Daniel	788	381	15	25.44	4-53	—	—
J. Garner	6648	2560	124	20.64	6-56	2	—
H.A. Gomes	744	266	5	53.20	2-20	—	—
C.G. Greenidge	26	4	0	—	—	—	—
D.L. Haynes	18	8	1	8.00	1-2	—	—
M.A. Holding	7162	3194	139	22.97	8-92	10	2
A.I. Kallicharran	406	158	4	39.50	2-16	—	—
C.L. King	582	282	3	94.00	1-30	—	—
C.H. Lloyd	1716	622	10	62.90	2-13	—	—
M.D. Marshall	2220	1083	34	31.85	4-25	—	—
E.H. Mattis	36	14	0	—	—	—	—
R. Nanan	216	91	4	22.75	2-57	—	—
D.R. Parry	1909	936	23	40.69	5-15	1	—
I.V.A. Richards	1924	703	13	54.07	2-19	—	—
A.M.E. Roberts	9674	4481	173	25.90	7-54	10	2
L.G. Rowe	86	44	0	—	—	—	—

NEW ZEALAND

BATTING AND FIELDING

	M	I	NO	Runs	HS	Avge	100	50	Ct	St
R.W. Anderson	9	18	0	423	92	23.50	—	3	1	—
S.L. Boock	12	19	6	37	8	2.84	—	—	8	—
B.P. Bracewell	5	10	2	17	8	2.12	—	—	1	—
J.G. Bracewell	4	6	1	29	16	5.80	—	—	2	—
M.G. Burgess	50	92	6	2684	119*	31.20	5	14	34	—
B.L. Cairns	23	37	5	489	52*	15.28	—	1	17	—
J.V. Coney	15	26	4	726	82	33.00	—	6	16	—
B.A. Edgar	15	27	1	771	129	29.65	2	3	9	—
G.N. Edwards	8	15	0	377	55	25.13	—	3	7	—
R.J. Hadlee	35	61	7	1149	103	21.27	1	5	18	—
G.P. Howarth	25	46	4	1605	147	38.21	6	5	13	—
W.K. Lees	17	31	3	642	152	22.92	1	—	35	7
P.E. McEwan	3	6	0	56	21	9.33	—	—	3	—
J.M. Parker	36	63	2	1498	121	24.53	3	5	30	—
J.F. Reid	4	7	1	269	123*	44.83	1	1	2	—
I.D.S. Smith	4	6	2	70	20	17.50	—	—	13	—
M.C. Snedden	3	3	1	2	2	1.00	—	—	1	—
G.B. Troup	10	12	4	31	13*	3.87	—	—	2	—
P.N. Webb	2	3	0	11	5	3.66	—	—	2	—
J.G. Wright	17	31	1	776	110	25.86	1	3	8	—

BOWLING

	Balls	Runs	Wkts	Avge	Best	5 wI	10 wM
S.L. Boock	2107	706	19	37.15	5-67	1	—
B.P. Bracewell	838	456	10	45.60	3-110	—	—
J.G. Bracewell	837	290	11	26.36	5-75	1	—
M.G. Burgess	498	212	6	35.33	3-23	—	—
B.L. Cairns	5917	2233	67	33.32	6-85	4	—
J.V. Coney	1029	337	9	37.44	3-28	—	—
R.J. Hadlee	8941	4238	155	27.34	7-23	11	3
G.P. Howarth	470	223	3	74.33	1-13	—	—
W.K. Lees	5	4	0	—	—	—	—
J.M. Parker	40	24	1	24.00	1-24	—	—
M.C. Snedden	570	251	7	35.85	2-40	—	—
G.B. Troup	2334	948	29	32.68	6-95	1	1

INDIA

BATTING AND FIELDING

	M	I	NO	Runs	HS	Avge	100	50	Ct	St
R.M.H. Binny	9	15	2	198	46	15.23	—	—	7	—
C.P.S. Chauhan	40	68	2	2084	97	31.57	—	16	38	—
D.R. Doshi	24	27	7	99	20	4.95	—	—	10	—
S.M. Gavaskar	75	134	9	6718	221	53.74	24	30	67	—
K.D. Ghavri	39	57	14	913	86	21.23	—	2	16	—
Kapil Dev	38	55	6	1468	126*	29.95	2	7	15	—
S.M.H. Kirmani	54	79	13	1774	101*	26.87	1	8	102	27
Kirti Azad	4	6	0	107	24	17.83	—	—	2	—
S. Madan Lal	22	35	8	497	55*	18.40	—	1	11	—
A. Malhotra	2	2	0	31	31	15.50	—	—	—	—
S.M. Patil	13	22	2	730	174	36.50	1	4	6	—
B. Reddy	4	5	1	38	21	9.50	—	—	9	2
P. Roy	2	3	1	71	60*	35.50	—	1	1	—
R.J. Shastri	9	11	3	188	93	23.50	—	1	5	—
K. Srikkanth	4	6	0	119	65	19.83	—	1	1	—
T.E. Srinivasan	1	2	0	48	29	24.00	—	—	—	—
D.B. Vengsarkar	48	78	8	2676	157*	38.22	5	14	40	—
G.R. Viswanath	81	140	9	5746	222	43.86	14	31	56	—
N.S. Yadav	15	19	6	207	43	15.92	—	—	4	—
Yashpal Sharma	22	33	5	1071	140	38.25	2	6	3	—
Yograj Singh	1	2	0	10	6	5.00	—	—	—	—

BOWLING

	Balls	Runs	Wkts	Avge	Best	5 wI	10 wM
R.M.H. Binny	1133	632	15	42.13	3-53	—	—
C.P.S. Chauhan	174	106	2	53.00	1-4	—	—
D.R. Doshi	7036	2275	84	27.08	6-103	3	—
S.M. Gavaskar	304	163	1	163.00	1-34	—	—
K.D. Ghavri	7042	3656	109	33.54	5-33	4	—
Kapil Dev	8341	4181	147	28.44	7-56	10	1
Kirti Azad	294	158	1	158.00	1-35	—	—
S. Madan Lal	3411	1409	43	32.76	5-23	4	—
S.M. Patil	537	177	8	22.12	2-28	—	—
R.J. Shastri	2280	739	27	27.37	5-125	1	—
K. Srikkanth	36	10	0			—	—
D.B. Vengsarkar	23	13	0			—	—
G.R. Viswanath	70	46	1	46.00	1-11	—	—
N.S. Yadav	3139	1449	41	35.34	4-35	—	—
Yograj Singh	90	63	1	63.00	1-63	—	—

PAKISTAN

BATTING AND FIELDING

	M	I	NO	Runs	HS	Avge	100	50	Ct	St
Abdul Qadir	8	12	2	131	29*	13.10	—	—	5	—
Azhar Khan	1	1	0	14	14	14.00	—	—	—	—
Azmat Rana	1	1	0	49	49	49.00	—	—	—	—
Ehteshamuddin	4	1	0	2	2	2.00	—	—	2	—
Ejaz Faqih	2	4	0	63	34	15.75	—	—	—	—
Haroon Rashid	16	28	1	890	122	32.96	2	3	7	—
Imran Khan	36	59	7	1291	123	24.82	1	3	10	—
Iqbal Qasim	29	36	11	205	32	8.20	—	—	25	—
Javed Miandad	37	63	12	2868	206	56.32	7	17	35	1
Majid Khan	60	102	5	3837	167	39.55	8	18	67	—
Mansoor Akhtar	3	6	0	78	56	13.00	—	—	3	—
Mohammad Nazir	8	11	7	89	29*	22.55	—	—	2	—
Mohsin Khan	8	13	0	353	46	27.15	—	—	8	—
Mudassar Nazar	22	35	1	1057	126	31.08	2	5	15	—
Rizwan-uz-Zaman	1	2	0	8	4	4.00	—	—	—	—
Sadiq Mohammad	41	74	2	2579	166	35.81	5	10	28	—
Sarfraz Nawaz	42	57	8	760	55	15.51	—	3	23	—
Shafiq Ahmed	6	10	1	99	27*	11.00	—	—	—	—
Sikander Bakht	23	30	11	121	22*	6.36	—	—	6	—
Taslim Arif	6	10	2	501	210*	62.62	1	2	6	3
Tausif Ahmed	3	1	0	0	0	0.00	—	—	—	—
Wasim Bari	61	91	22	1109	85	16.07	—	5	145	20
Wasim Raja	40	66	11	2203	117*	40.05	2	16	11	—
Zaheer Abbas	45	79	6	2889	274	39.57	6	11	27	—

BOWLING

	Balls	Runs	Wkts	Avge	Best	5 wI	10 wM
Abdul Qadir	1855	703	22	31.95	6-44	1	—
Azhar Khan	18	2	1	2.00	1-1	—	—
Ehteshamuddin	856	329	15	21.93	5-47	1	—
Ejaz Faqih	156	85	1	85.00	1-76	—	—
Haroon Rashid	8	3	0	—	—	—	—
Imran Khan	9215	4081	144	28.34	6-63	8	1
Iqbal Qasim	7362	2744	89	30.83	7-49	3	2
Javed Miandad	1344	620	17	36.47	3-74	—	—
Majid Khan	3572	1452	27	53.77	4-45	—	—
Mohammad Nazir	1798	635	26	24.42	7-99	2	—
Mohsin Khan	8	3	0	—	—	—	—
Mudassar Nazar	1109	476	11	43.27	3-48	—	—
Sadiq Mohammad	90	98	0	—	—	—	—
Sarfraz Nawaz	10359	4309	133	32.39	9-86	4	1
Shafiq Ahmed	8	1	0	—	—	—	—
Sikander Bakht	4288	2126	63	33.74	8-69	3	1
Taslim Arif	30	28	1	28.00	1-28	—	—
Tausif Ahmed	866	356	12	29.66	4-64	—	—
Wasim Bari	8	2	0	—	—	—	—
Wasim Raja	2770	1295	35	37.00	4-68	—	—
Zaheer Abbas	20	2	0	—	—	—	—

AT LEAST THIS YEAR YOUR MONEY NEEDN'T GET LOST.

You can go on your holiday in an easier state of mind if you go to NatWest first.

They'll provide you with Travel Cheques which can be exchanged nearly anywhere in the world. If you lose them, you need not lose a penny.

NatWest can also arrange foreign currency. Pop into any branch. Even if you haven't got a bank account.

And you may purchase your travel facilities with your NatWest Access card.

♻ National Westminster Bank

MINOR COUNTIES
FINAL TABLE

	P	W	L	D	NR	Pts	Avge
Durham	10	7	0	2	1	78	7.80
Norfolk	10	4	2	4	0	55	5.50
Cambridgeshire	10	4	2	4	0	46	4.60
Somerset II	8	2	1	3	2	36	4.50
Bedfordshire	10	3	3	4	0	44	4.40
Cheshire	10	4	4	1	1	43	4.30
Shropshire	10	3	4	3	0	42	4.20
Wiltshire	10	3	2	4	1	42	4.20
Cumberland	8	2	3	3	0	33	4.12
Suffolk	10	2	3	5	0	40	4.00
Buckinghamshire	12	4	6	2	0	47	3.91
Staffordshire	10	3	4	3	0	33	3.80
Northumberland	12	3	5	4	0	45	3.75
Berkshire	10	2	2	6	0	37	3.70
Lincolnshire	10	2	3	5	0	37	3.70
Oxfordshire	10	2	2	6	0	37	3.70
Hertfordshire	10	3	2	5	0	35	3.50
Lancashire II	8	2	3	3	0	25	3.12
Cornwall	10	2	3	4	1	29	2.90
Dorset	10	2	5	2	1	27	2.70
Devonshire	10	1	1	7	1	26	2.60

MINOR COUNTIES FIXTURES 1982

MAY

Wed	26	Cheshire v Durham: Cheadle Hulme
Sun	30	Lincolnshire v Cambridgeshire: Sleaford

JUNE

Wed	2	Cumberland v Cheshire: Millom
Mon	7	Lancashire II v Cheshire: Lytham
		Shropshire v Staffordshire: Shrewsbury (London Road)
Tues	8	Hertfordshire v Norfolk: Watford
Sun	13	Northumberland v Lincolnshire: Jesmond
		Cheshire v Staffordshire: Macclesfield
Mon	14	Lancashire II v Cumberland: Fleetwood
		Durham v Shropshire: Chester-le-Street
Wed	16	Cambridgeshire v Norfolk: Wisbech
Sun	20	Cumberland v Northumberland: Penrith
Mon	21	Cheshire v Lancashire II: Wallasey
Wed	23	Hertfordshire v Cambridgeshire: Letchworth
		Staffordshire v Shropshire: Smethwick
Sun	27	Oxfordshire v Buckinghamshire: Morris Motors
Mon	28	Lancashire II v Northumberland: Preston
Wed	30	Cambridgeshire v Lincolnshire: Papworth
		Hertfordshire v Bedfordshire: St. Albans (Clarence Park)

JULY

Sun	4	Lincolnshire v Cumberland: Grimsby (Ross ground)
		Cornwall v Somerset II: Truro
		Buckinghamshire v Oxfordshire: Slough
Wed	7	Shropshire v Cheshire: Wellington
Sun	11	Northumberland v Cumberland: Jesmond
		Staffordshire v Cheshire: Knypersley
		Berkshire v Buckinghamshire: Finchampstead (Nr Wokingham)
Sun	18	Bedfordshire v Cambridgeshire: Bedford School
		Northumberland v Durham: Jesmond
		Lincolnshire v Staffordshire: Lincoln
		Cornwall v Devon: Falmouth
		Berkshire v Oxfordshire: Maidenhead (Boyne Hill)
Mon	19	Hertfordshire v Buckinghamshire: Hertford (Balls Park)
		Wiltshire v Somerset II: Chippenham
Tues	20	Bedfordshire v Shropshire: Dunstable
Wed	21	Wiltshire v Oxfordshire: Trowbridge
		Cambridgeshire v Suffolk: Fenners
Sun	25	Oxfordshire v Berkshire: Oxford (St Edward's)
		Durham v Cumberland: Darlington
		Bedfordshire v Buckinghamshire: Bedford (Goldington Bury)
		Cheshire v Shropshire: Nantwich
		Cornwall v Dorset: St Austell
Mon	26	Norfolk v Cambridgeshire: Lakenham
		Staffordshire v Northumberland: Brewood
Tues	27	Devon v Dorset: Exeter
		Wiltshire v Berkshire: Bemerton, Salisbury
Wed	28	Cambridgeshire v Bedfordshire: March
		Cheshire v Northumberland: Bowdon
		Norfolk v Buckinghamshire: Lakenham
Thurs	29	Oxfordshire v Wiltshire: Banbury (XX Club)
Fri	30	Suffolk v Buckinghamshire: Ipswich (G.R.E.)
Sat	31	Dorset v Berkshire: Sherborne School

AUG

Sun	1	Oxfordshire v Cornwall: Oxfordshire (Christ Church)
		Cumberland v Lancashire II: Kendal
		Durham v Northumberland: Durham City
		Shropshire v Bedfordshire: St Georges (Telford)
Mon	2	Norfolk v Lincolnshire: Lakenham
		Devon v Berkshire: Torquay
		Suffolk v Hertfordshire: Mildenhall
Tues	3	Wiltshire v Cornwall: Swindon
Wed	4	Norfolk v Hertfordshire: Lakenham
Thurs	5	Devon v Somerset II: Exmouth
		Dorset v Cornwall: Weymouth
		Berkshire v Wiltshire: Bradfield College
Fri	6	Norfolk v Suffolk: Lakenham
Sun	8	Bedfordshire v Hertfordshire: Henlow
		Northumberland v Cheshire: Jesmond
		Buckinghamshire v Suffolk: Chesham
Mon	9	Oxfordshire v Devon: Abingdon
		Staffordshire v Lincolnshire: Stone
		Dorset v Wiltshire: Weymouth
		Shropshire v Lancashire II: Bridgnorth

Tues	10	Bedfordshire v Suffolk: Luton (Wardown Park)
		Durham v Cheshire: Hartlepool
Wed	11	Berkshire v Devon: Reading
		Somerset II v Cornwall: Taunton
Fri	13	Dorset v Devon: Bournemouth
Sat	14	Buckinghamshire v Bedfordshire: Stowe School
Sun	15	Cumberland v Durham: Carlisle
		Berkshire v Dorset: Kidmore End, Reading
		Cornwall v Wiltshire: Penzance
		Hertfordshire v Suffolk: Old Merchant Taylors
Mon	16	Northumberland v Staffordshire: Jesmond
		Lancashire II v Shropshire: East Lancs (Blackburn)
Tues	17	Somerset II v Wiltshire: Weston-Super-Mare
		Suffolk v Norfolk: Felixstowe
Wed	18	Durham v Staffordshire: Stockton-on-Tees
		Devon v Cornwall: Bovey Tracey
		Buckinghamshire v Berkshire: Monks Risborough (Molins S.C.)
Thurs	19	Suffolk v Cambridgeshire: Bury St Edmunds
		Dorset v Somerset II: Canford School
Sun	22	Cheshire v Cumberland: Oxton
		Lincolnshire v Norfolk: Spalding
		Buckinghamshire v Hertfordshire: High Wycombe
Mon	23	Northumberland v Lancashire II: Jesmond
		Cornwall v Oxfordshire: Troon
		Shropshire v Durham: Newport
Tues	24	Wiltshire v Dorset: Devizes
Wed	25	Cambridgeshire v Hertfordshire: Fenners
		Devon v Oxfordshire: Sidmouth
		Staffordshire v Durham: Longton
Thurs	26	Somerset II v Dorset: Taunton
Sun	29	Somerset II v Devon: Taunton
		Suffolk v Bedfordshire: Ipswich (Ransomes)
		Buckinghamshire v Norfolk: Amersham

OTHER MATCHES

| Sun | 16 May | Minor Counties South XI v Lavinia, Duchess of Norfolk's XI: Arundel Park (1 day) |
| Thurs | 5 Aug | Minor Counties v Pakistan: Slough (2 days) |

BENSON & HEDGES CUP 1982

Sat	15 May	Derbyshire v Minor Counties
Sat	22 May	Minor Counties v Worcestershire: Wellington
Tues	25 May	Yorkshire v Minor Counties: Bradford
Thurs	27 May	Minor Counties v Leicestershire: Wellington

YOUNG CRICKETER OF THE YEAR

At the end of each season the members of the Cricket Writers' Club select by ballot the player they consider the best young cricketer of the season.

M.W. Gatting (Middlesex) was elected last year.

The selections to date are:

1950 R. Tattersall (Lancashire)	1966 D.L. Underwood (Kent)
1951 P.B.H. May (Surrey)	1967 A.W. Greig (Sussex)
1952 F.S. Trueman (Yorkshire)	1968 R.H.M. Cottam (Hampshire)
1953 M.C. Cowdrey (Kent)	1969 A. Ward (Derbyshire)
1954 P.J. Loader (Surrey)	1970 C.M. Old (Yorkshire)
1955 K.F. Barrington (Surrey)	1971 J. Whitehouse (Warwickshire)
1956 B. Taylor (Essex)	1972 D.R. Owen-Thomas (Surrey)
1957 M.J. Stewart (Surrey)	1973 M. Hendrick (Derbyshire)
1958 A.C.D. Ingleby-Mackenzie	1974 P.H. Edmonds (Middlesex)
(Hampshire)	1975 A. Kennedy (Lancashire)
1959 G. Pullar (Lancashire)	1976 G. Miller (Derbyshire)
1960 D.A. Allen (Gloucestershire)	1977 I.T. Botham (Somerset)
1961 P.H. Parfitt (Middlesex)	1978 D.I. Gower (Leicestershire)
1962 P.J. Sharpe (Yorkshire)	1979 P.W.G. Parker (Sussex)
1963 G. Boycott (Yorkshire)	1980 G.R. Dilley (Kent)
1964 J.M. Brearley (Middlesex)	1981 M.W. Gatting (Middlesex)
1965 A.P.E. Knott (Kent)	

NB. An additional award was made in 1980 to C.W.J. Athey (Yorkshire) as the best young batsman of the year.

SCORING OF POINTS IN THE SCHWEPPES CHAMPIONSHIP

The scheme is as follows:

(a) For a win, 16 points, plus any points scored in the first innings.

(b) In a tie, each side to score 8 points, plus any points scored in the first innings.

(c) If the scores are equal in a drawn match, the side batting in the fourth innings to score 8 points, plus any points scored in the first innings.

(d) First innings points (awarded only for performances in the first 100 overs of each innings and retained whatever the result of the match).

   (i) A maximum of 4 batting points to be available as follows: 150 to 199 runs—1 point; 200 to 249 runs—2 points; 250 to 299 runs—3 points; 300 runs or over—4 points.

   (ii) A maximum of 4 bowling points to be available as follows: 3-4 wickets taken—1 point; 5-6 wickets taken—2 points; 7-8 wickets taken—3 points; 9-10 wickets taken—4 points.

(e) If play starts when less than eight hours playing time remains and a one innings match is played, no first innings points shall be scored. The side winning on the one innings to score 12 points.

(f) The side which has the highest aggregate of points gained at the end of the season shall be the Champion County. Should any sides in the Schweppes Championship Table be equal on points, the side with most wins will have priority.

PRINCIPAL FIXTURES 1982

Including play on Sunday

Wednesday 21 April

Cambridge: Cambridge U v Glam

Saturday 24 April

Cambridge: Cambridge U v Notts
Oxford: Oxford U v Northants

Saturday 24/Sunday 25 April

Brighton Centre: Indoor Cricket
Competition

Wednesday 28 April

Cambridge: Cambridge U v Middx
Oxford: Oxford U v Worcs

Saturday 1 May

Lords: MCC v Notts
Cambridge: Cambridge U v Warwicks
Oxford: Oxford U v Kent

Wednesday 5 May

Schweppes Championship
Southampton: Hants v Leics
Old Trafford: Lancs v Notts
Lord's: Middx v Essex
Northampton: Northants v Yorks
Taunton: Somerset v Sussex
The Oval: Surrey v Kent
Edgbaston: Warwicks v Glam
Worcester: Worcs v Derbys
Other Match
Oxford: Oxford U v Glos

Thursday 6 May

Arundel: Lavinia Duchess of Norfolk's
XI v India

Saturday 8 May

Benson & Hedges Cup
Bristol: Glos v Glam
Canterbury: Kent v Hants
Old Trafford: Lancs v Scotland
Leicester: Leics v Derbys
Northampton: Northants v Notts
Taunton: Somerset v Combined U
The Oval: Surrey v Essex
Headingley: Yorks v Worcs

Other Match
Edgbaston: *Warwicks v India

Sunday 9 May

John Player League
Bristol: Glos v Middx
Old Trafford: Lancs v Glam
Leicester: Leics v Derbys
Northampton: Northants v Somerset
Trent Bridge: Notts v Hants
The Oval: Surrey v Kent
Hove: Sussex v Essex
Huddersfield: Yorks v Worcs

Wednesday 12 May

Schweppes Championship
Derby: Derbys v Somerset
Bristol: Glos v Worcs
Dartford: Kent v Warwicks
Leicester: Leics v Surrey
Lord's: Middx v Northants
Hove: Sussex v Essex
Headingley: Yorks v Glam
Other Matches
Trent Bridge: Notts v India
Cambridge: Cambridge U v Lancs
Oxford: Oxford U v Hants

Saturday 15 May

Benson & Hedges Cup
Derby: Derbys v Minor Counties
Chelmsford: Essex v Kent
Bournemouth: Hants v Sussex
Lord's: Middx v Somerset
Trent Bridge: Notts v Warwicks
Worcester: Worcs v Leics
Glasgow (Titwood): Scotland v
Northants
Oxford: Combined U v Glos
Other Matches
Bradford: Yorks v India
Old Trafford: Lancs v Surrey (one
day)

Sunday 16 May

John Player League
Derby: Derbys v Essex
Bournemouth: Hants v Middx
Canterbury: Kent v Glam
Old Trafford: Lancs v Glos

Leicester: Leics v Yorks
Trent Bridge: Notts v Worcs
Hove: Sussex v Somerset
Edgbaston: Warwicks v Surrey

Wednesday 19 May

Schweppes Championship
Cardiff: Glam v Leics
Old Trafford: Lancs v Derbys
Northampton: Northants v Surrey
Trent Bridge: Notts v Hants
Hastings: Sussex v Glos
Edgbaston: Warwicks v Yorks
Worcester: Worcs v Somerset
Other Matches
Lord's: MCC v India
Cambridge: Cambridge U v Essex
Oxford: Oxford U v Middx

Saturday 22 May

Benson & Hedges Cup
Chelmsford: Essex v Hants
Cardiff: Glam v Combined U
Bristol: Glos v Middx
Leicester: Leics v Yorks
Northampton: Northants v Lancs
The Oval: Surrey v Sussex
Edgbaston: Warwicks v Scotland
Wellington (Shropshire): Minor
  Counties v Worcs
Other Match
Canterbury: *Kent v India

Sunday 23 May

John Player League
Chelmsford: Essex v Hants
Cardiff: Glam v Leics
Moreton-in-Marsh: Glos v Worcs
Lord's: Middx v Notts
Bedford (School): Northants v Lancs
Taunton: Somerset v Derbys
Bradford: Yorks v Warwicks

Tuesday 25 May

Benson & Hedges Cup
Swansea: Glam v Somerset
Canterbury: Kent v Surrey
Old Trafford: Lancs v Warwicks
Hove: Sussex v Essex
Worcester: Worcs v Derbys
Bradford: Yorks v Minor Counties
Glasgow (Titwood): Scotland v Notts
Cambridge: Combined U v Middx

Wednesday 26 May

To be arranged: Ireland v India (two
  days)

Thursday 27 May

Benson & Hedges Cup
Chesterfield: Derbys v Yorks
Southampton: Hants v Surrey
Lord's: Middx v Glam
Trent Bridge: Notts v Lancs
Taunton: Somerset v Glos
Hove: Sussex v Kent
Edgbaston: Warwicks v Northants
Wellington (Shropshire): Minor
  Counties v Leics

Saturday 29 May

Schweppes Championship
Chesterfield: Derbys v Notts
Chelmsford: Essex v Surrey
Swansea: Glam v Glos
Leicester: Leics v Northants
Lord's: Middx v Sussex
Taunton: Somerset v Kent
Worcester: Worcs v Warwicks
Headingley: *Yorks v Lancs
Other Match
Southampton: *Hants v India

Sunday 30 May

John Player League
Chesterfield: Derbys v Warwicks
Swansea: Glam v Somerset
Gloucester: Glos v Sussex
Lord's: Middx v Essex
Trent Bridge: Notts v Northants
The Oval: Surrey v Leics
Worcester: Worcs v Kent

Wednesday 2 June

**PRUDENTIAL TROPHY
HEADINGLEY:
ENGLAND v INDIA
(first one-day international match)**

Schweppes Championship
Swansea: Glam v Somerset
Gloucester: Glos v Lancs
Bournemouth: Hants v Kent
Hinckley: Leics v Yorks
Lord's: Middx v Derbys
Northampton: Northants v Notts

WISDEN CRICKETERS' ALMANACK 1982

EDITED BY JOHN WOODCOCK

The 119th edition features Mike Brearley on
SOME THOUGHTS ON MODERN
CAPTAINCY, Robin Marlar on KEN
BARRINGTON – AN APPRECIATION,
Michael Melford on INDIA – 1932 TO 1982,
Alan Gibson on MIKE PROCTER – A GREAT
ALL-ROUNDER and W A Hadlee on THE
ESCALATING EFFECTS OF POLITICS
IN CRICKET.

1154pp
12pp b/w illustrations
£8.95 (hc)   £7.95 (pb)

WISDEN
ANTHOLOGY
1940-1963

EDITED BY BENNY GREEN

The third volume in this collected WISDEN
ANTHOLOGY covers cricket from the
outbreak of war to the summer of 1962.

1024pp
£22.50
Available from June

From good bookshops everywhere but in case of
difficulty direct from Queen Anne Press Sales,
9 Partridge Drive, Orpington, Kent.
Cash with order + 12p in the £ p&p. Allow 28 days
for delivery.

QUEEN ANNE PRESS
Macdonald & Company

Other Matches
Worcester: Worcs v Zimbabwe
Oxford: Oxford U v Warwicks

Friday 4 June

**PRUDENTIAL TROPHY
THE OVAL:
ENGLAND v INDIA
(second one-day international match)**

Saturday 5 June

Schweppes Championship
Chelmsford: Essex v Somerset
Gloucester: Glos v Derbys
Tunbridge Wells: Kent v Middx
Old Trafford: Lancs v Glam
Trent Bridge: Notts v Worcs
The Oval: Surrey v Hants
Edgbaston: Warwicks v Sussex
Other Matches
Leicester: Leics v Zimbabwe
Northampton: *Northants v India

Sunday 6 June

John Player League
Chelmsford: Essex v Somerset
Old Trafford: Lancs v Sussex
Leicester: Leics v Hants
Edgbaston: Warwicks v Kent
Worcester: Worcs v Derbys
Bradford: Yorks v Glam

Wednesday 9 June

Schweppes Championship
Chesterfield: Derbys v Essex
Swansea: Glam v Middx
Southampton: Hants v Lancs
Tunbridge Wells: Kent v Sussex
Leicester: Leics v Warwicks
Worcester: Worcs v Glos
Other Matches
Trent Bridge: Notts v Zimbabwe (one-
day)
Cambridge: Cambridge U v Northants
Oxford: Oxford U v Surrey

Thursday 10 June

**LORD'S:
ENGLAND v INDIA
(First Cornhill Insurance Test match)**

Other Match
Sheffield: Yorks v Zimbabwe (one-
day)

Saturday 12 June

Schweppes Championship
Cardiff: Glam v Warwicks
Liverpool: Lancs v Essex
Northampton: Northants v Somerset
Trent Bridge: Notts v Kent
The Oval: Surrey v Glos
Hove: Sussex v Worcs
Sheffield: Yorks v Middx

Sunday 13 June

John Player League
Portsmouth: Hants v Derbys
Old Trafford: Lancs v Essex
Leicester: Leics v Middx
Northampton: Northants v Kent
The Oval: Surrey v Glos
Horsham: Sussex v Worcs
Edgbaston: Warwicks v Somerset
Hull: Yorks v Notts

Wednesday 16 June

Benson & Hedges Cup Quarter-Finals

Thursday 17 June

Cambridge: Combined U v India (two
days)

Saturday 19 June

Schweppes Championship
Ilford: Essex v Worcs
Canterbury: Kent v Derbys
Lord's: Middx v Lancs
Trent Bridge: Notts v Warwicks
Bath: Somerset v Hants
Hove: Sussex v Surrey
Middlesbrough: Yorks v Northants
Other Matches
Bristol: *Glos v India
Cambridge: Cambridge U v Leics
Swansea: Glam v Oxford U
To be arranged: *Ireland v MCC

Sunday 20 June

John Player League
Ilford: Essex v Worcs
Canterbury: Kent v Derbys
Lord's: Middx v Lancs

Trent Bridge: Notts v Warwicks
Bath: Somerset v Surrey
Hastings: Sussex v Glam
Middlesbrough: Yorks v Northants

Wednesday 23 June

Schweppes Championship
Ilford: Essex v Yorks
Cardiff: Glam v Worcs
Basingstoke: Hants v Sussex
Leicester: Leics v Kent
Northampton: Northants v Warwicks
Bath: Somerset v Glos
The Oval: Surrey v Lancs
Other Match
Lord's: Middx v Pakistan

Thursday 24 June

**OLD TRAFFORD:
*ENGLAND v INDIA
(Second Cornhill Insurance Test
match)**

Saturday 26 June

Schweppes Championship
Derby: Derbys v Leics
Bristol: Glos v Hants
The Oval: Surrey v Middx
Edgbaston: Warwicks v Somerset
Worcester: Worcs v Lancs
Harrogate: Yorks v Notts
Other Matches
Hove: *Sussex v Pakistan
Lord's: Oxford v Cambridge

Sunday 27 June

John Player League
Derby: Derbys v Yorks
Harlow: Essex v Leics
Ebbw Vale: Glam v Glos
Basingstoke: Hants v Kent
Lord's: Middx v Surrey
Bath: Somerset v Notts
Edgbaston: Warwicks v Northants
Worcester: Worcs v Lancs

Wednesday 30 June

Benson & Hedges Semi-Finals
Other Matches
Harrogate: Tilcon Trophy (Three
days)

Saturday 3 July

Schweppes Championship
Derby: Derbys v Yorks
Maidstone: Kent v Hants
Other Matches
Chelmsford: *Essex v India
Swansea: *Glam v Pakistan
NatWest Bank Trophy (First Round)
Bedford (Goldington Bury): Beds v
Somerset
Leicester: Leics v Norfolk
Enfield: Middx v Cheshire
Northampton: Northants v Ireland
The Oval: Surrey v Durham
Hove: Sussex v Notts
Edgbaston: Warwicks v Cambs
Other Matches
Broughty Ferry: *Scotland v Worcs
(three days)
Old Trafford: Lancs v Glos (one day)

Sunday 4 July

John Player League
Derby: Derbys v Lancs
Maidstone: Kent v Sussex
Leicester: Leics v Warwicks
Tring: Northants v Surrey
Headingley: Yorks v Glos

Wednesday 7 July

Schweppes Championship
Derby: Derbys v Northants
Bristol: Glos v Sussex
Maidstone: Kent v Surrey
Uxbridge: Middx v Leics
Trent Bridge: Notts v Essex
Edgbaston: Warwicks v Lancs
Sheffield: Yorks v Worcs
Other Match
Taunton: Somerset v Pakistan

Thursday 8 July

**THE OVAL:
ENGLAND v INDIA
(Third Cornhill Insurance Test match)**

Saturday 10 July

Schweppes Championship
Cardiff: Glam v Hants
Old Trafford: Lancs v Surrey
Leicester: Leics v Derbys
Northampton: Northants v Essex

Trent Bridge: Notts v Middx
Hove: Sussex v Somerset
Bradford: Yorks v Glos
Other Match
Worcester: *Worcs v Pakistan

Sunday 11 July

John Player League
Cardiff: Glam v Hants
Maidstone: Kent v Somerset
Old Trafford: Lancs v Surrey
Lord's: Middx v Northants
Trent Bridge: Notts v Leics
Edgbaston: Warwicks v Glos
Scarborough: Yorks v Essex

Wednesday 14 July

NatWest Bank Trophy Second round
Luton (Wardown Pk) or Taunton:
  Beds or Somerset v Leics or Norfolk
Chelmsford: Essex v Kent
Cardiff: Glam v Warwicks or Cambs
Southampton: Hants v Derbys
Lord's or Cheadle Hulme: Middx or
  Cheshire v Lancs
The Oval or Chester-le-Street: Surrey
  or Durham v Northants or Ireland
Hove or Trent Bridge: Sussex or Notts
  v Glos
Headingley: Yorks v Worcs
Other Match
Glasgow (Titwood): Scotland v
  Pakistan (two days)

Saturday 17 July

PRUDENTIAL TROPHY
TRENT BRIDGE:
ENGLAND v PAKISTAN
(first one-day international)

Schweppes Championship
Southend: Essex v Derbys
Bristol: Glos v Northants
Portsmouth: Hants v Surrey
Lord's: Middx v Notts
Taunton: Somerset v Glam
Hove: Sussex v Leics
Headingley: Yorks v Warwicks

Sunday 18 July

John Player League
Southend: Essex v Surrey
Bristol: Glos v Northants

Southampton: Hants v Lancs
Lord's: Middx v Derbys
Taunton: Somerset v Yorks
Hove: Sussex v Leics
Worcester: Worcs v Glam

Monday 19 July

PRUDENTIAL TROPHY
OLD TRAFFORD:
ENGLAND v PAKISTAN
(Second one-day international)

Wednesday 21 July

Schweppes Championship
Southend: Essex v Middx
Portsmouth: Hants v Glam
Old Trafford: Lancs v Northants
Worksop: Notts v Yorks
The Oval: Surrey v Somerset
Nuneaton (Griff & Coton): Warwicks
  v Glos
Hereford: Worcs v Kent
Other Match
Leicester: Leics v Pakistan

Saturday 24 July

LORDS: BENSON & HEDGES CUP
FINAL

Schweppes Championship
Leicester: Leics v Essex (will be
  played on 28, 29, 30 July if either
  County in B&H Final)
Taunton: Somerset v Worcs (will be
  played on 8, 9, 10 September if
  either County in B&H Final)
Chesterfield: *Derbys v Pakistan

Sunday 25 July

John Player League
Swansea: Glam v Middx
Bristol: Glos v Hants
Canterbury: Kent v Yorks
Old Trafford: Lancs v Warwicks
Northampton: Northants v Sussex
Taunton: Somerset v Worcs
Croydon (Whitgift School): Surrey v
  Notts

Tuesday 27 July

To be arranged: Ireland v Wales (three
days)

Wednesday 28 July

Schweppes Championship
Southport: Lancs v Warwicks
Leicester: Leics v Essex (if not played on 24, 26, 27 July)
Northampton: Northants v Glos
The Oval: Surrey v Notts
Hove: Sussex v Kent
Worcester: Worcs v Glam

Thursday 29 July

EDGBASTON:
*ENGLAND v PAKISTAN
(First Cornhill Insurance Test match)
Saturday 31 July
Schweppes Championship
Derby: Derbys v Surrey
Cardiff: Glam v Essex
Bournemouth: Hants v Somerset
Leicester: Leics v Glos
Lord's: Middx v Kent
Northampton: Northants v Worcs
Trent Bridge: Notts v Lancs
Scarborough: Yorks v Sussex

Sunday 1 August

John Player League
Derby: Derbys v Surrey
Cardiff: Glam v Essex
Portsmouth: Hants v Somerset
Leicester: Leics v Glos
Lord's: Middx v Kent
Luton: Northants v Worcs
Trent Bridge: Notts v Lancs
Scarborough: Yorks v Sussex

Wednesday 4 August

NatWest Trophy Quarter-Finals

Thursday 5 August

Slough: MCCA v Pakistan (two days)

Saturday 7 August

Schweppes Championship
Swansea: Glam v Northants
Cheltenham: Glos v Notts
Canterbury: Kent v Essex
Old Trafford: Lancs v Yorks
Weston-super-mare: Somerset v Middx
Eastbourne: Sussex v Hants
Edgbaston: Warwicks v Derbys

Stourbridge or Worcester: Worcs v Leics
Other Matches
The Oval: *Surrey v Pakistan
Northampton: *England YCs v West Indies YCs (First 'Test Match' (four days))
Edinburgh (Myreside): *Scotland v Ireland

Sunday 8 August

John Player League
Cheltenham: Glos v Notts
Canterbury: Kent v Essex
Old Trafford: Lancs v Yorks
Weston-super-mare: Somerset v Middx
Eastbourne: Sussex v Hants
Edgbaston: Warwicks v Glam
Worcester: Worcs v Leics
Other Matches
Warwick Under-25 Semi-finals (one-day) (or Sunday 15 August)

Wednesday 11 August

Schweppes Championship
Derby: Derbys v Lancs
Chelmsford: Essex v Hants
Cheltenham: Glos v Middx
Canterbury: Kent v Glam
Leicester: Leics v Yorks
Weston-super-Mare: Somerset v Yorks
Eastbourne: Sussex v Northants
Edgbaston: Warwicks v Surrey

Thursday 12 August

LORD'S: *ENGLAND v PAKISTAN
(Second Cornhill Insurance Test match)

Saturday 14 August

Schweppes Championship
Cheltenham: Glos v Essex
Southampton: Hants v Worcs
Leicester: Leics v Lancs
Northampton: Northants v Derbys
Trent Bridge: Notts v Somerset
Guildford: Surrey v Glam
Coventry (Courtaulds): Warwicks v Middx
Headingley: Yorks v Kent

Sunday 15 August

John Player League
Cheltenham: Glos v Essex
Southampton: Hants v Worcs
Leicester: Leics v Lancs
Milton Keynes: Northants v Derbys
Trent Bridge: Notts v Kent
Guildford: Surrey v Sussex
Edgbaston: Warwicks v Middx
Other Matches
Warwick Under-25 Competition Semi-
finals (one day) (if not played on
Sunday 8 August)

Wednesday 18 August

NatWest Bank Trophy Semi-Finals

Friday 20 August

Scarborough: *England YCs v West
Indies YCs (Second 'Test Match'
(four days))

Saturday 21 August

Schweppes Championship
Chesterfield: Derbys v Sussex
Colchester: Essex v Warwicks
Swansea: Glam v Notts
Folkestone: Kent v Glos
Lord's: Middx v Yorks
Northampton: Northants v Hants
Taunton: Somerset v Leics
Worcester: Worcs v Surrey
Other Match
Old Trafford: *Lancs v Pakistan

Sunday 22 August

John Player League
Chesterfield: Derbys v Sussex
Colchester: Essex v Warwicks
Swansea: Glam v Notts
Folkestone: Kent v Glos
Lord's: Middx v Yorks
Northampton: Northants v Hants
Taunton: Somerset v Leics
Worcester: Worcs v Surrey
Other Match
Edgbaston: Warwick Under-25
Competition Final (one day)

Wednesday 25 August

Schweppes Championship
Colchester: Essex v Leics
Cardiff: Glam v Sussex
Bournemouth: Hants v Glos
Folkestone: Kent v Northants
Blackpool: Lancs v Worcs
Lord's: Middx v Surrey

Thursday 26 August

**HEADINGLEY:
ENGLAND v PAKISTAN
(Third Cornhill Insurance Test match)**

Saturday 28 August

Schweppes Championship
Bristol: Glos v Somerset
Bournemouth: Hants v Yorks
Old Trafford: Lancs v Kent
Northampton: Northants v Leics
Trent Bridge: Notts v Derbys
The Oval: Surrey v Essex
Hove: Sussex v Middx
Edgbaston: Warwicks v Worcs

Sunday 29 August

John Player League
Bristol: Glos v Somerset
Southampton: Hants v Yorks
Old Trafford: Lancs v Kent
Leicester: Leics v Northants
Trent Bridge: Notts v Derbys
The Oval: Surrey v Glam
Hove: Sussex v Middx
Worcester: Worcs v Warwicks

Monday 30 August

Southampton: England YCs v West
Indies YCs (first 'one-day
international')

Tuesday 31 August

Eastbourne: England YCs v West
Indies YCs (second 'one-day
international')

Wednesday 1 September

Schweppes Championship
Derby: Derbys v Hants
Chelmsford: Essex v Kent
Leicester: Leics v Glam

Taunton: Somerset v Warwicks
The Oval: Surrey v Sussex
Worcester: Worcs v Notts
Other Matches
Canterbury: England YCs v West
Indies YCs (Third 'Test Match'
(four days))
Scarborough: Cricket Festival (three
days)

Saturday 4 September

**LORDS: NATWEST BANK TROPHY
FINAL**

Sunday 5 September

John Player League
Derby: Derbys v Glos
Chelmsford: Essex v Notts
Abergavenny: Glam v Northants
The Oval: Surrey v Hants
Edgbaston: Warwicks v Sussex
Other Match
Scarborough: Cricket Festival (three
days)

Wednesday 8 September

Schweppes Championship
Bristol: Glos v Glam
Old Trafford: Lancs v Sussex
Uxbridge: Middx v Hants

Trent Bridge: Notts v Leics
Taunton: Somerset v Worcs (if not
played on 24, 26, 27 July)
Edgbaston: Warwicks v Northants
Scarborough: Yorks v Derbys

Saturday 11 September

Schweppes Championship
Derby: Derbys v Glam
Chelmsford: Essex v Northants
Southampton: Hants v Warwicks
Canterbury: Kent v Leics
Taunton: Somerset v Lancs
The Oval: Surrey v Yorks
Hove: Sussex v Notts
Worcester: Worcs v Middx

Sunday 12 September

John Player League
Derby: Derbys v Glam
Chelmsford: Essex v Northants
Bournemouth: Hants v Warwicks
Canterbury: Kent v Leics
Taunton: Somerset v Lancs
The Oval: Surrey v Yorks
Hove: Sussex v Notts
Worcester: Worcs v Middx

Saturday 18/Sunday 19 September

Possible Double-Wicket Competition

PROPOSED FUTURE CRICKET TOURS

TO ENGLAND
1983 World Cup and New Zealand
1984 West Indies

ENGLAND TOURS OVERSEAS
1982-83 Australia
1983-84 Pakistan and New Zealand

OTHER TOURS

1982-83	Australia to Pakistan	1983-84	West Indies to India
	India to Pakistan		Australia to West Indies
	Pakistan to New Zealand	1984-85	West Indies to Pakistan
	and West Indies		India to West Indies

MICHAEL FORDHAM

The day that Michael Fordham posted his last copy for this annual – the up-dated records after the India v England series – he was due to leave with his wife, Daphne, for a three-week holiday in Miami, by Laker Airways. That very morning the airline went into liquidation, but the Fordhams were re-booked on another airline, and left one day late.

In the previous weeks Michael had been suffering from angina, and was only passed fit to travel forty-eight hours beforehand, but he collapsed when entering a taxi in Miami and died immediately.

First, we offer our most heartfelt condolences to his wife, who thus suffered an irreparable double tragedy of the greatest magnitude. She had previously been married to Roy Webber, who collapsed and died outside Dickens Press in London, the former owners of *Playfair Cricket Annual*, in 1962.

Michael Fordham's contribution to this annual was the biggest single factor in its great success. He undertook the major statistical item – The Counties and Their Players – beginning in 1963, as well as other subjects. All that he did in the world of cricket – and he did a great deal – scoring for BBC Sound and Television, principal contributions to *Wisden* and *The Cricketer Quarterly* (for whom he headed a team of statisticians) – was performed with an unerring accuracy which was almost uncanny, and certainly unique.

His countless friends in cricket will miss him immensely. Michael was a cheerful, happy man, and anyone who knew him as well as I did for over twenty years will be much the poorer for his passing.

G.R.

ISBN 0 356 08592 9

© 1982 Queen Anne Press

Published in 1982 by
Queen Anne Press
Macdonald & Co (Publishers) Ltd
Maxwell House
Worship Street
London EC2

Filmset, printed and bound in
Great Britain by
Hazell Watson & Viney Ltd
Aylesbury, Bucks